THE CONTRACT OF CARRIAGE

CONTEMPORARY COMMERCIAL LAW

Causation in Insurance Contract Law
Meixian Song

Insurance Law in China
Edited by Johanna Hjalmarsson and Dingjing Huang

Maritime Law in China
Emerging Issues and Future Developments
Edited by Johanna Hjalmarsson and Jenny Jingbo Zhang

Illegality in Marine Insurance Law
Feng Wang

Insurance Law Implications of Delay in Maritime Transport
Ayşegül Buğra

Online Arbitration
Faye Fangfei Wang

Double Insurance and Contribution
Nisha Mohamed

The Law and Autonomous Vehicles
Matthew Channon, Lucy McCormick and Kyriaki Noussia

FIDIC Yellow Book
A Commentary
Ben Beaumont

The Contract of Carriage
Multimodal Transport and Unimodal Regulation
Paula Bäckdén

For more information about this series, please visit: www.routledge.com/Contemporary-Commercial-Law/book-series/CCL

THE CONTRACT OF CARRIAGE

MULTIMODAL TRANSPORT AND UNIMODAL REGULATION

PAULA BÄCKDÉN

informa law
from Routledge

First published 2019
by Informa Law from Routledge
2 Park Square, Milton Park, Abingdon, Oxon OX14 4RN

and by Informa Law from Routledge
605 Third Avenue, New York, NY 10017

First issued in paperback 2020

Informa Law from Routledge is an imprint of the Taylor & Francis Group, an informa business

British Library Cataloguing-in-Publication Data
A catalogue record for this book is available from the British Library

Library of Congress Cataloging-in-Publication Data
Names: Bäckdén, Paula, author.
Title: The contract of carriage : multimodal transport and unimodal regulation / By Paula Bäckdén.
Description: New York, NY : Informa Law from Routledge, 2019. | Series: Contemporary commercial law
Identifiers: LCCN 2018045283 | ISBN 9781138393936 (hbk) | ISBN 9780429401442 (ebk)
Subjects: LCSH: Transportation—Law and legislation. | Carriers—Law and legislation. | Delivery of goods (Law) | Transportation engineering.
Classification: LCC K4025 .B33 2019 | DDC 343.09/32—dc23
LC record available at https://lccn.loc.gov/2018045283

ISBN 13: 978-0-367-73183-0 (pbk)
ISBN 13: 978-1-138-39393-6 (hbk)

Typeset in Times New Roman
by Apex CoVantage, LLC

CONTENTS

DETAILED CONTENTS

FOREWORD

This book is the result of my doctoral research carried out at the universities of Göteborg and Oslo. The thesis was defended in Oslo in 2017.
My voyage was assisted by two tug-masters; Professor Svante O. Johansson, who pulled me out from my port of departure, and Professor Erik Røsæg, who pulled (or perhaps pushed) me into this port of destination. In a common effort they threw me a lifebuoy when it turned out I had to swim to reach the shore. Equally important: thank you!

The thesis was initially a work on the multimodal aspects of the Rotterdam Rules. My interest in the new convention sprung out of the fantastic opportunity that Chester D. Hooper, esq. offered me, to join the US delegation at the UNCITRAL negotiations in New York in the spring of 2006. I want to thank Chet for thus planting the seed to this work, as well as the other members of the delegation for being welcoming and inclusive.

Along the journey, there are several persons who have played an important role. They include the following. The former prefects at the Department of Law at the University of Göteborg, Mats Glavå, who offered me a research assistant position in order for me to write my project plan before I was formally admitted to the research program, and Thomas Erhag, who made my transition from Göteborg to the University of Oslo possible in 2014. The former Dean at the Faculty of Law in Oslo, Hans-Petter Graver, who took a chance on me, and the former Institute leader at the Scandinavian Institute of Maritime Law, Trine-Lise Wilhelmsson, who pleaded my cause and convinced the Dean to allow me to work mainly from my home in Göteborg. Thank you.

Friends and colleagues at the Scandinavian Institute of Maritime Law, who welcomed me and included me from the very start, friends and former colleagues at the Department of Law in Göteborg as well as friends and colleagues in the Swedish Maritime Law Association – no one named; no one forgotten; thank you.

Most important of all, my wonderful family who provide perspective on life and work. My husband, Niklas; my life partner and supporter of more than 20 years. Our fantastic children, Vincent and Lovisa; "without you, life would have been less contentful and this thesis completed a long time ago".[1] Thank you!

1 Jonas Malmberg, *Anställningsavtalet. Om anställningsförhållandets individuella reglering* (1997) p. 5.

TABLE OF CASES

TABLE OF LEGISLATION

PART I

INTRODUCTION AND METHOD

CHAPTER 1

Introduction

1.1 The theme

International transport of goods forms the veins of the world's production structure. Every year, several hundred million TEUs[1] are transported all over the world.[2] The value of commercial goods transported accounts for one-quarter of the world's total GDP.[3]

Today's transport of goods is multimodal. Goods are carried from the door of the sender to the door of the consignee ("door-to-door") by a combination of transportation modes. The focus of the transportation customer is that goods are sent to the right place at the right time, without very much attention being paid to the question of by what mode the goods are transported.

However, at the time when states first consolidated their efforts to subject carriers to mandatory liability rules, transport contracts were primarily agreed on a unimodal basis. Even where goods were to be carried by two (or more) different modes, the sender contracted for the separate legs of the transport separately and the goods were received from one carrier and handed over to the next carrier by a local agent. Although the transport as such is multimodal, the contract of carriage is not. From a legal perspective, a transport is only multimodal when the contract of carriage covers more than one mode of transport.[4] Thus, at the time, the world of transport, which is now quite complex, was easily divided into unimodality. Despite efforts made, there is to this day no international regulation that regulates multimodal transport contracts.[5]

The unimodal conventions in force today may, from an outsider's perspective, seem quite homogenous. However, besides the obvious dissimilarities such as varying monetary liability limits and the far-reaching liability exemptions available to the maritime carrier, they all approach issues of central importance such

1 Twenty-foot equivalent unit, a unit of cargo capacity often used to describe the capacity of container ships and container terminals, based on the volume of a 20-foot-long (6.1 m) intermodal container.

2 www.worldshipping.org.

3 According to UNCTAD statistics (available at http://unctadstat.unctad.org), the world's total trade amounted to approximately 19 trillion (10^{12}) USD in 2014 and the world's total GDP, according to the World Bank, amounted in the same year to approximately 78 trillion (10^{12}) USD (http://databank.worldbank.org).

4 The definition of the multimodal contract of carriage is often drawn from the UN Convention on International Multimodal Transport of Goods (Geneva, 24 May 1980) (the "Multimodal Convention"). In this work however, the multimodal contract of carriage will be defined as a contract of carriage that provides (or allows) for carriage of goods by more than one mode of transport.

5 O. Bokareva, *Multimodal Transportation under the Rotterdam Rules* (2015) p. 22.

as applicability and basis of liability in different ways.[6] Whilst the liability of the maritime carrier under the Hague–Visby Rules[7] is fault-based with generous exemptions, the liability of the road and rail carrier under the CMR and the COTIF–CIM regulations[8] is presumed with detailed exceptions and the air carrier's liability under the Montreal Convention[9] is close to strict.[10] And whilst the liability rules regulating air carriage apply to actual air carriage, the maritime liability rules apply to transports carried out under contracts of carriage providing for the issuance of bills of lading and the European land carriage conventions apply to contracts of carriage. This latter approach, which with some modifications has been adopted by the recently drafted Rotterdam Rules,[11] applicable to international maritime carriage and additional transports by other modes, has been the cause of legal uncertainly in relation to multimodal transport contracts.[12]

The multimodal contract of carriage has, from a legal perspective, traditionally and without much ado, been regarded as a collection of agreements, one for each separate mode of transport used to fulfil the multimodal transport contract.[13] However, its nature has come to be challenged in jurisprudence as well as in practice.[14] It has been asserted that the multimodal contract should not be regarded as a collection of agreements, but as a contract *sui generis* and, as such it cannot be considered that the unimodal conventions applicable to contracts for carriage, e.g. by road apply, to a "unimodal leg" of such a multimodal contract.[15] Therefore, as long as there is no consensus in this respect, the multimodal

6 De Wit even holds the differences between the liability systems to be "vast" (R. de Wit, *Multimodal Transport* (1995) p. 7.

7 The International Convention for the Unification of Certain Rules of Law relating to Bills of Lading, Brussels 1924 (the "Hague Rules") and the Protocol to Amend the International Convention for the Unification of Certain Rules of Law Relating to Bills of Lading, 1968 (the "Hague–Visby Rules").

8 The Convention on the Contract for the International Carriage of Goods by Road, Geneva 1956 (the CMR convention); the Convention concerning International Carriage by Rail (the "COTIF–CIM convention"), Berne 1980 as amended by the Vilnius protocol 1999, appendix B (CIM). "CMR" and "COTIF" are abbreviations of the French titles of the conventions, Convention relative au contrat de transport international de marchandises par route and Convention relative aux transports internationaux ferroviaires.

9 The Convention for the Unification of Certain Rules for International Carriage by Air, Montreal 1999 (the "Montreal Convention").

10 Cf. sections 2.3.1, 2.5, 2.6 and 2.7 below.

11 The UN Convention on Contracts for the International Carriage of Goods Wholly or Partly by Sea, New York 2008; (the "Rotterdam Rules").

12 Cf. section 3.4 below.

13 Cf. section 1.2.1 below.

14 Cf. section 3.4 below.

15 S. Mankabady, "Some Legal Aspects of the Carriage of Goods by Container" (1974) 23 Int'l & Comp LQ 317 at p. 324, S. Mankabady, "The Multimodal Transport of Goods Convention: A Challenge to Unimodal Transport Conventions" [1983] 32 Int'l & Comp LQ 120–140, at p. 140), E. Selvig, "Multimodal transport: the 1980 U.N. Convention: papers of a one day seminar: Southampton University, Faculty of Law, 12th September 1980", at p. A3, para. 2. See also J. Ramberg, "Is Multimodal Transport a Contract *sui generis* also within the Field of EU Competition?" in H-J Bull and H. Stemshaug (eds), *EC Shipping Policy* (1997) pp. 163–168, however with some hesitation.

transport contract faces the legal uncertainty of either being subject to mandatory unimodal regulations or to complete freedom of contract with no fallback rules.[16]

These two extremes pose diverse difficulties for the parties to a transport contract. First of all, where the "network system"[17] is applied, and thus each leg of a multimodal transport of goods is deemed to be governed by the unimodal regulation governing that particular mode of transport, there are legal implications relating to overlap between two conventions where two conventions may be applicable at the same time as well as gaps between two regimes where no regime is applicable at all.[18] Secondly, as far as conventions applicable to certain contracts of carriage are concerned, the assertion that such conventions are not applicable to transports carried out under multimodal transport contracts undermines the entire network system and leaves parts of transport carried out under such a contract without regulation. Such complete freedom of contract places the multimodal transport contract in a vacuum that may be hard to justify considering that unimodal transport is subject to mandatory regulations.

Thus, in the absence of a uniform system governing multimodal carriage of goods, application of the network system may seem like a pragmatic solution. However, in a multimodal transport from the warehouse of the sender to the consignee's place of business a number of undesirable effects of the network system may emerge. On the other hand, should the network system not be applied, the absence of a uniform system entails that the transport is not subject to any international regulation. Although that is a situation that may perfectly solve itself through market regulation, objections may be made.

The issue of multimodal transport contracts and the applicability of unimodal conventions to parts of such contracts have been renewed with a twist due to adoption by the UN General Assembly of the Rotterdam Rules.[19] The convention is applicable to contracts for the international carriage of goods by sea, but also to ancillary carriage by other modes carried out under the same contract. Thus, should the convention enter into force, a large number of multimodal contracts will be subject to mandatory regulation. However, existing unimodal regulations may prevent the full applicability of the Rotterdam Rules.

There is a considerable legal discussion regarding regulation of transports carried out under multimodal contracts of carriage, a discussion that has not led to any unanimous view on the problem, which accordingly entails legal uncertainty.[20]

---

16 Cf. section 3.2.4 below.

17 The so-called "network system" is discussed in section 3.2.2 below. The definition thereof used in the current work is a system for asserting a carrier's liability under a multimodal contract of carriage, where each "leg", i.e. unimodal part, of the carriage is considered subject to the rules that govern the mode of transport in question, where such carriage is subject to a unimodal contract of carriage. Although the network system can be applied by way of contract or, as is discussed in section 3.2.3, by way of national legislation, the research question concerns whether the network system *is* applicable, i.e. *ex proprio vigore*, in relation to multimodal contracts of carriage.

18 Cf. section 3.2.2 below.

19 The convention was adopted by the UN General Assembly in 2008 and opened for signatures in 2009.

20 Cf. section 3.4.2 below.

The discussion is carried out against a setting where several European states have seemingly clear precedents, although there is no uniformity on the international level. Thus, legal uncertainty is enhanced by heterogenous interpretation of the uniform rules.[21] Accordingly, a carrier offering international transports in Europe must currently adapt its general terms and conditions to a legal setting where the carriage may be subject to mandatory unimodal rules, which however must be supplemented by fallback rules for non-localized damage. The contract of carriage must also be adapted to a scenario where no mandatory rules, uniform or national, apply and the contract of carriage is therefore subject to freedom of contract. It follows that such general terms and conditions will certainly not appear entirely clear to the future transport customer.

In addition to this legal uncertainty, the contract of carriage seems to be in constant evolution. Multimodal transport has given rise to a number of new appearances of the transport contract due to shippers' increasing unconcern about how goods are carried from the place of loading to their final destination. The carrier is regarded as a service provider whose professional judgment is better suited to determine what modes of transport, routes, and so on will optimize the transport. The spectra of contracts include, on the one hand, explicit multimodal contracts in which the modes of transport are clearly stated and, on the other hand, generic contracts that span contracts where the mode(s) of transport is defined but which gives the carrier an option to change that mode for another,[22] to contracts where the mode(s) of transport is left entirely up to the carrier. Hence, a transport contract may or may not state by what mode or modes of transport the goods are to be transported and may in addition give the carrier the right to choose and/or substitute mode(s) of transport.[23]

These types of contract entail new challenges in relation to the transport conventions that apply to certain contracts, which can be illustrated by the following examples:

(1) Is a contract that explicitly provides for carriage by e.g. sea and road, a contract for carriage by road according to the CMR convention in relation to the road carriage?
(2) Is a contract that explicitly provides for e.g. carriage by air, a contract for carriage by rail according to the COTIF–CIM convention if the carrier utilized his contractual right to substitute the mode of transport?
(3) Does a generic transport contract, which does not specify the mode of transport to be used, provide for carriage by sea[24] if the goods are so carried?

21 Cf. section 3.4.1 below.

22 In this category of contracts, the contract may explicitly provide for one mode of transport only, but – due to the carrier's contractual substitution – carriage is in fact carried out by two modes of transport and thus the carriage becomes multimodal.

23 L. Andersen Roost, *Multimodale Transporter* (2012) p. 66.

24 As the prerequisite is formulated in the Rotterdam Rules, article 1.1.

1.1.1 The contractual approach to applicability

As indicated above, the Gordian knot in relation to regulation of multimodal transport is the applicability of the uniform rules that apply to contracts of carriage. It is the fact that some conventions apply to contracts for the carriage of goods by a certain mode of transport (contracts of carriage by [road])[25] that may prevent their applicability to multimodal contracts of carriage. Under this "contractual approach", the applicability of a convention is connected to the actual contract of carriage. Such a contract must be for carriage of goods by the mode in question, be it by road or by sea or by rail. The contractual approach is used in the CMR convention and the COTIF–CIM convention as well as in the Rotterdam Rules, although it was first introduced into maritime transport through the Hamburg Rules.[26] It may seem a quite straightforward approach, but it has led to practical problems as regards what is to be considered a contract for the carriage of goods by a certain mode.

Along with this approach to applicability, there are, as regards conventions providing rules on the liability of a carrier of goods for lost and damaged goods, two other approaches to defining the scope of applicability that are generally recognized: the modal approach and the documentary approach.[27]

The documentary approach was the solution chosen by the drafters of the Hague Rules in the 1920s. At that time, there was a need to distinguish transport of goods, which were not carried out under a charter party, from those that were.[28] Since carriage of goods as general cargo was usually carried out under bills of lading, the documentary approach suited the purpose and hence the Hague Rules, as well as its successor the Hague–Visby Rules, applies to carriage of goods under bills of lading.[29] The documentary approach thus relates to a particular type of document being used, which triggers the application of certain rules.[30]

---

25 In the following, "[road]" will be used as an example of a mode of transport, indicating that the mode could by any other mode of transport, rail, sea or air, and that "contract of carriage by [road]" could be any contract of carriage as required by the relevant unimodal convention.

26 Although the Hague–Visby Rules applies to contracts of carriage (cf. section 4.5 below), it is generally considered to adhere to the "documentary approach" (M. Sturley *et al.*, *The Rotterdam Rules* (2010) p. 25 and M. Sturley, "Scope of Application" in A. von Zielger et al (eds), *The Rotterdam Rules 2008* (2010) pp. 39–50, at p. 40).

27 M. Sturley *et al.*, *The Rotterdam Rules* (2010) p. 27*ff.*

28 M. Sturley (ed.), *The Legislative History of the Carriage by Sea Act and the Travaux Preparatoires of the Hague Rules*, vol. I (1990) p. 349 (Documents and Proces-Verbaux of the sessions held from 17 to 26 October 1922 in Brussels) and H. Honka, "UNCITRALs konventionsutkast om transport av gods. Tillämpningsregler" (2005) 4–5 JFT 530–540 at 534. Today the distinction between contract of carriage of goods and contracts of affreightment is fundamental and appears to have been so already in 1921. However, in 1886, to Hammarskjöld the distinction was negligible, and he thus included both types of contract in the category of "contracts of carriage" (H. Hammarskjöld, *Om fraktavtalet och dess viktigaste rättsföljder* (1886) p. 11).

29 Hague–Visby Rules articles II and I (b). For a thorough discussion on the prerequisites for applicability of the Hague–Visby Rules, cf. section 4.5 below.

30 H. Honka, "UNCITRALs konventionsutkast om transport av gods. Tillämpningsregler" (2005) 4–5 JFT 530–540, at p. 533.

The carriage of goods by air convention, the Montreal Convention, applies to actual carriage of goods by aircraft, i.e. a modal approach.[31] Clearly, the convention presupposes some form of agreement, but it may be that such an agreement does not have to specify the mode of transport, which facilitates application of the air carriage liability rules to multimodal transports. As will be discussed in Chapter 4 below, the Montreal Convention applies to carriage of goods by air independently of what type of contract of carriage is entered into between the carrier and the contracting consignor. Accordingly, the modal approach applied in the Montreal Convention does not cause any legal problems in relation to multimodal contracts of carriage.

Although it has become apparent that the modal approach conveniently adapts to new types of contract, it may limit the applicability of the convention in another respect. A convention, or other set of rules that applies to actual carriage cannot be applicable until carriage is initiated, i.e. when the period of the carrier's liability begins, which is often when the carrier takes over the goods. However, rules that apply to the actual contract of carriage are effectuated as soon as a contract that complies with the prerequisites set out in the rules has been entered into. Although the two occasions may coincide, it is likely that the contract is entered into some time before the goods are handed over to the carrier, which may entail that the contractual relationship is subject to the rules at a previous point in time compared to the situation where the rules are applicable to the actual transport.[32]

Whichever the approach chosen for the scope of application of a certain set of rules, the aim is to define the sort of transaction to which the rules are to apply. Thus, the drafters have certain transactions in mind that are sought to be captured by the rule formulated. The rationale behind the approach to applicability chosen in a certain set of rules is not easily traceable. Most likely it is the particularities of the trade in question that motivate the approach chosen. Within the maritime trade, the distinction between carriage of particular goods and charter parties entails that the contractual approach alone would risk including contracts of affreightment, which are not sought to be included. This is the obvious reason for the documentary approach in the Hague–Visby Rules.[33]

With other trades such as air transport, road transport and rail transport, the same distinction need not be drawn. However, other particularities of the trade

---

31 Cf. section 4.4 below.

32 Although an interesting issue, the legal consequences of non-performance will not be discussed in the current thesis. In relation to air transport (mainly of passengers) so-called "bumping" has been the subject of several cases, mainly from the USA (*Weiss v El Al Israel Airlines*, 433 F Supp 2d 361 (Southern District of New York (Federal), 2006), *Wolgel v Mexicana Airlines*, 821 F2d 442 (United States Court of Appeal, 7th Cir 1987)). A general observation is that where an air transport has not been initiated, the Montreal Convention does not yet apply (cf. section 4.4 below), whilst in relation to e.g. a road transport, the CMR convention applies *per se* once the contract of carriage has been entered into (cf. section 4.3 below). See also P. Dempsey and S. Johansson, "Montreal v. Brussels: The Conflict of Laws on the Issue of Delay in International Air Carriage" (2010) 35 Air & Space L 207.

33 M. Sturley (ed.), *The Legislative History of the Carriage by Sea Act and the Travaux Preparatoires of the Hague Rules*, vol. I (1990) pp. 93–94.

may necessitate a particular approach. Before 1999, the COTIF–CIM convention provided for applicability of the rules of the conventions to "consignments of goods under a through consignment note",[34] which appears to be a mix between the modal approach and the documentary approach. The convention imposed on the railways, which were generally state owned, an obligation to carry and rested on the presumption that the contract would not be individually negotiated but made up of the general conditions provided by the railway (individual agreements were only permitted to the extent the same conditions would be provided to other consignors in comparable circumstances).[35] In fact, according to the previous COTIF–CIM convention, a contract of carriage was not considered entered into until the goods were handed over to the railway.[36] As regards the modal approach applied already in the predecessor to the Montreal Convention, the Warsaw Convention, in 1929, it can only be assumed that the particular risks of air transport, together with the fact that the rules of the convention also apply to carriage of passengers, prompted the drafters to subsume all transport actually carried out by air under the convention's mandatory ambit.

However, as will be discussed further in section 3.2 below, unauthorized substitution of mode of transport (i.e. substitution that is not contractually permitted) is generally regarded as having no bearing in relation to the applicable liability regime. Thus, if carriage by air is substituted for carriage by road without the consent of the contracting consignor, the carriage by air regime will remain applicable to any damage that may occur during carriage.[37] This seems to entail that in relation to unimodal contracts of carriage, the difference between the contractual and the modal approach to applicability is more theoretical than real.

The CMR convention was the first convention in which the contractual approach to applicability was used, although it must be acknowledged that the documentary approach is in fact the contractual approach "with a twist".[38] There is little to reveal the intention and considerations of the drafters in this respect[39] and although the rules of the convention apply to the contract of carriage, which may be concluded well in advance of the actual carriage, there are no actual liabilities or responsibilities that necessitate such subsumption of the transport

34 Article 1.1 of the COTIF-CIM 1980 states:

> the Uniform Rules shall apply to all consignments of goods for carriage under a through consignment note made out for a route over the territories of at least two States and exclusively over lines and services included in the list provided for in Articles 3 and 10 of the Convention.

35 Articles 3 §1 and 6 §4 of the COTIF–CIM convention 1980.

36 Article 11.1 of the COTIF–CIM convention 1980 states: "The contract of carriage shall come into existence as soon as the forwarding railway has accepted the goods for carriage together with the consignment note".

37 In the case of carriage by air being the contractually agreed mode of transport, this conclusion is even explicit in the Montreal Convention: see article 18.4.

38 Cf. section 4.5 below.

39 Neither Haak (K. Haak, *The Liability of the Carrier under the CMR* (1986)), nor Loewe (*Commentary on the convention of 19 May 1956 on the contract for the international carriage of goods by road (CMR) (GE.75-30686)*, prepared by R. Loewe and published by the UN in 1975) discussed the rationale behind the approach chosen.

under the ambit of the convention at the earlier point in time at which the contract is concluded.

As will be thoroughly discussed in Chapter 4, the nature of the transactions covered by the liability rules of the conventions in question is contractual. The rules regulate the carrier's liability towards the consignee (or consignor) and vice versa. Thus, the rules must be based on a presumption of the existence of a contract of carriage regardless of which approach to applicability is chosen.[40] Although later developments have shown that the contractual approach and the modal approach may be considered heterogenous in respect of their applicability to multimodal contracts of carriage, at the time when the conventions in question were first drafted the consequences of the different approaches must have been negligible.

1.1.2 The aim and perspective of this study

As mentioned above, legal uncertainty exists in relation to the rules applicable to multimodal transport.[41] There is a divergence in opinions both on a theoretical level within legal theory, as well as on a practical level, where the question of the applicability of the unimodal conventions governing the carrier's liability has been answered heterogeneously by the national courts.[42] In addition, newer forms of contracts of carriage do not easily fit into definitions of unimodal or multimodal contracts of carriage. The aim of the current work is to analyse the applicability of existing transport of goods conventions as well as the applicability thereof to transport carried out under multimodal transport contracts. To the extent that the applicability of the liability rules is dependent on the existence of a contract of carriage by a particular mode of transport, the analysis will assume the proposition that contracts of carriage are to be interpreted and defined by applying law of contracts. The question of whether a multimodal contract is subject to certain rules is thus to be settled through interpretation of the contract rather than through the interpretation of the rules of the conventions. Hopefully, this analysis will entail a conclusion as regards the relationship between the multimodal contract of carriage and the unimodal conventions regulating the carrier's liability for goods carried. Although a conclusion to some extent is the "goal", or perhaps destination, of the text, it is the discussion and analysis – the road to the destination – which is the actual purpose.[43]

40 Eftestøl-Wilhelmsson perceives the difference between the contractual approach and the documentary approach as non-existent and asserts that "Most of the transport conventions have a contractual scope", and includes the Hague–Visby Rules in that category (E. Eftestøl-Wilhelmsson, *European Sustainable Carriage of Goods* (2016) p. 69).

41 Multimodal Transport: the feasibility of an international legal instrument, Report by the UNCTAD secretariat, 13 January 2003, UNCTAD/SDTE/TLB/2003/1, at p. 7. For a detailed account of the current legal status, cf. section 3.4 below.

42 Cf. sections 3.4.1 and 3.4.2 below.

43 C. Sandgren, "Är rättsdogmatiken dogmatisk?" in (2005) 118 (4–5) TfR 648–656, at pp. 651–652.

Thus, rather than providing an absolute conclusion regarding the law as it is perceived to stand, this work presents argumentation and proposals for a new approach to interpreting the unimodal conventions, as well as a critique of some existing argumentation. However, no proposals will be made to the "legislator". It appears therefore that three types of reader may be interested in the analyses and discussions thus provided. One is the practising lawyer, seeking arguments to plead a client's case. Another is the judge, imaginable in an appeal or supreme court, who seeks to map the law and legal discussion in order to reach a balanced and informed decision. However, it would also appear that the work contributes to an ongoing debate within academia. Partly, it seems to contribute to the extent that it adds Nordic precedence and doctrine, unavailable to non-speakers of any Nordic language, to the picture. Furthermore, it offers another perspective on much-debated questions and thus hopefully it will be of interest to those taking part in that debate.

1.1.2.1 Research questions

The aim is thus to analyse the applicability of existing transport of goods conventions to multimodal transport contracts. For the reasons that appear in section 1.1.1 above, the focus will be on carriage of goods conventions that apply to contracts for a certain mode of transport. However, my primary research question covers all conventions that are subject to discussion in the current thesis and will hence be: *to what extent can unimodal transport of goods conventions be applied to transport carried out under a multimodal transport contract?*

In order to answer this question, the general applicability of the unimodal international regimes applicable in a European perspective to carriage by sea, road, railway and air, i.e. the Hague–Visby Rules, the CMR convention, the COTIF–CIM convention, the Montreal Convention and the Rotterdam Rules, must be established. As mentioned, the Montreal Convention is applicable to all transport that is in fact carried out by air, the Hague–Visby Rules apply to contracts that provide for the issuance of a bill of lading. The Rotterdam Rules, the CMR convention and the COTIF–CIM convention on the other hand define their prima facie applicability through the contractual approach, that is, their applicability is dependent on there being a contract for carriage. Clearly, a number of prerequisites in each convention must be met in order for the convention to apply, and several arguments may be put forward against the applicability of unimodal conventions that do not relate to the transport contract. However, as stated above, I believe that the core of the issue whether any of the unimodal conventions can be applied to transport carried out under multimodal transport contracts lies in the definition of a contract for the carriage of goods by sea, road or rail. Therefore, a subordinate research question will be: *to what extent can contracts that provide for more than one mode of transport or are in fact carried out by more than one mode of transport be considered a contract for the carriage of goods by a particular mode of transport?*

1.2 Method

1.2.1 The relevance of this study

Multimodal transport is not an entirely new phenomenon and it is the emergence of containers in the 1960s that usually gets the credit for its rapid expansion.[44] It seems, however, that the proposition that unimodal conventions do not apply to carriage under a multimodal contract, which is a condition for the network system, is relatively recent.[45] In Europe the case law was seemingly unanimous up until a judgment of the German Supreme Court in 2008.[46]

In doctrine, it seems that Germany has raised a strong voice in the debate to the effect that the CMR convention cannot be applied to a road transport leg of a multimodal contract.[47] In the UK and the Netherlands the predominating

---

44 R. de Wit, *Multimodal Transport* (1995) p. 5.

45 In 1968, Grönfors discusses various approaches to the carrier's liability for multimodal transports. Although Grönfors (K. Grönfors, *Successiva Transporter* (1968)) settles for the uniform system (and preferably a uniform system for all modes of transport, not only multimodal contracts of carriage) (p. 299*ff*.), it is noticeable that the network system is one of the approaches discussed whilst there is no suggestion that this would meet any legal obstacles (p. 243*ff*.). In two articles in 1974 and 1983 Mankabady seems to take the network system for granted (S. Mankabady, "Some Legal Aspects of the Carriage of Goods by Container" (1974) 23 Int'l & Comp LQ 317, at p. 324 and S. Mankabady, "The Multimodal Transport of Goods Convention: A Challenge to Unimodal Transport Conventions" [1983] 32 Int'l & Comp LQ 120–140, at p. 140). In relation to the adoption of the convention in 1980, Selvig (who was the chairman at the UNCTAD negotiations) proposes the theory of the multimodal contract of carriage as a contract *sui generis* (E. Selvig, "Multimodal transport: the 1980 U.N. Convention: papers of a one day seminar: Southampton University, Faculty of Law, 12th September 1980", at p. A3, para. 2). However, this approach does not seem to have been embraced by other delegates: W. Driscoll and P. Larsen, "The Convention on International Multimodal Transport of Goods" (1982–1983) 57 Tul L Rev 193 at p. 198. From the records it also appears that the United Kingdom did not consider the question of the applicability or non-applicability of the unimodal conventions to multimodal contracts satisfactorily settled through the *sui generis* theory (UNCTAD, *United Nations Conference on a Convention on International Multimodal Transport*, vol. II, Draft Convention and Reports of the Conference, TD/MT/CONF/17/add.1 (1981) p. 16*ff*.) In 1989 Herber holds the network system to be the applicable system according to German precedence (R. Herber, "The European Legal Experience with Multimodalism" (1989–1990) 64 Tul L Rev 611 at p. 629). Ramberg holds the "confusing 'network' of unimodal rules" to be the traditional approach (J. Ramberg, "Is Multimodal Transport a Contract *sui generis* also within the Field of EU Competition?" in H-J. Bull and H. Stemshaug (eds), *EC Shipping Policy* (1997) pp. 163–168, at p. 167. In an UNCTAD report from 2003 it was held the "the present legal framework consists of a complex array of international conventions designed to regulate unimodal carriage, diverse regional/subregional agreements, national laws and standard term contracts" thus suggesting the application of the network system (Multimodal Transport: the feasibility of an international legal instrument, Report by the UNCTAD secretariat, 13 January 2003, UNCTAD/SDTE/TLB/2003/1, at p. 7). See also A. Messent and D. Glass, *CMR: Contracts for the International Carriage of Goods by Road* (2000) p. 16. In 1995, de Wit held that "a uniform liability system would inevitably enter into conflict with the existing unimodal transport conventions", thus indicating that these are applicable to transports under multimodal contracts of carriage (R. de Wit, *Multimodal Transport* (1995) p. 146.

46 German Federal Supreme Court BGH 17 July 2008 (I ZR 181/05). A summary of European case law up until the time the judgment was given can be found in *Quantum Corporation Inc v Plane Trucking Ltd* [2002] 2 Lloyd's Rep 25. See further section 3.4.1 below.

47 I. Koller; "Quantum Corporation Inc. v. Plane Trucking Limited und die Anwendbarkeit der CMR auf die Beförderung mit verschiedenartigen Transportmitteln" (2003) 2 TransportR 45–50. For a summary of German writings, M. Hoeks, *Multimodal Transport Law* (2010) pp. 68–70.

views seems to be the opposite.[48] The arguments put forward concern primarily how certain provisions in the CMR convention do not fit multimodal transport, such as that the road carrier may never *take over* the goods from the shipper as stipulated in article 1, but rather from another carrier.[49] Undoubtedly, the CMR convention was written with unimodal transportation in mind. However, had the drafters of that convention been able to predict the future developments, they might have drafted the convention differently to fit multimodal transport better. In my perception, these may be arguments that show that conventions such as the CMR convention do not particularly fit multimodal transport. That, however, is a different question from whether the convention is applicable to such transport.[50]

The key to applicability is the transport contract. As will be elaborated further in section 3.4 below, the arguments against applicability of unimodal conventions to transports under multimodal contracts is, in essence, that where the rules of a convention, such as the CMR convention, apply to contracts for the carriage of goods by [road], multimodal contracts do not fall within that ambit. In general, the argument is that a multimodal contract is not a contract for the carriage of goods by e.g. road, although in respect of the CMR convention it is proposed that this follows from the convention itself and not just from the classification of the multimodal contract as a contract *sui generis*. However, it is suggested here that the perspective must be turned around. It is the individual transport contract that must be examined to determine whether that particular contract is a contract for the carriage of goods by, in this case, road and that task must be done through contract construction and interpretation. This view has not been assumed previously, at least not in a survey of the extent of this work.

Several authors have thoroughly analysed the multimodal contract of carriage: Hoeks in 2010, Andersen Roost in 2012, Glass in 2012 and Bugden/Lamont-Black in 2013.[51] Somewhat earlier, in 1995 de Wit published a book on multimodal contracts of carriage and as early as 1968 Grönfors published a book on successive transports.[52] In addition, a number of books on the subject have been published that discuss the issue in relation to e.g. carriage by road, as well as a multitude of articles.[53] Because the issue is of international concern, it is

48 K. Haak and M. Hoeks, "Intermodal transport under unimodal arrangements" (2005) 3 TransportR 89–102; M. Clarke, "The line in law between land and sea" (2003) JBL 522–524.

49 The European legal writing will be more thoroughly discussed in section 3.4.2 below.

50 "Applicability" refers to mandatory applicability of the convention according to its own scope of applicability, i.e. applicability *ex proprio vigore*.

51 M. Hoeks, *Multimodal Transport Law* (2010); L. Andersen Roost, *Multimodale Transporter* (2012); D. Glass, *Freight forwarding and multimodal transport contracts* (2012); and P. Bugden and S. Lamont-Black, *Goods in Transit* (2013) 3rd edn). See also O. Bokareva, *Multimodal Transportation under the Rotterdam Rules* (2015) (Diss. defended at the University of Lund, Sweden, although not yet publicly available).

52 R. de Wit; *Multimodal Transport; carrier liability and documentation* (1995) and K. Grönfors; *Successiva Transporter* (1968).

53 See e.g. M. Clarke, "A Multimodal Mix-up" (2002) JBL 210–217; D. Glass, "Meddling in the Multimodal Muddle?" (2006) LMCLQ 307–334; K. Haak and M. Hoeks, "Intermodal transport under unimodal arrangements" (2003) 5 TransportR 89–102; I. Koller, "Quantum Corporation Inc v. Plane Trucking Limited und die Anwendbarkeit der CMR auf die Beföredrung nit verschiedenartigen

desirable that the discussion is not limited to a national arena. Thus, one contribution of the current thesis is that books and articles written in Nordic languages are brought into the international discussion.[54]

The subject of multimodal contracts of carriage and their regulation can be approached in different ways, and has been so as all the above-mentioned works provide different viewpoints. The current work focuses on the contract of carriage, its formation and interpretation, as the key in interpreting the scope of application of the carriage of goods conventions. It is my belief that this viewpoint has not been applied previously, at least not in recent times.[55]

The research questions posed above concern the relation, or tension, between existing regulation of the carriers' liability for goods carried and the forms of contract of carriage that provide for carriage by more than one mode of transport: multimodal contracts of carriage. It is asserted that the question of applicability of unimodal conventions to multimodal contracts has been discussed based on the wording of the articles defining the scope of application of the conventions without proper regard to the rules of treaty interpretation under international law. It is proposed that if the rules of treaty interpretation, customary or as recorded in the Vienna Convention on the Law of Treaties,[56] are properly applied, most of the arguments relating to the non-applicability of conventions, such as the CMR to carriage under multimodal contracts, can be dismissed. It is further proposed that when the rules of treaty interpretation are properly applied, it is the understanding of the contract of carriage in general and the contract of carriage by [road] in particular that will be found to be essential. In particular, the question of what constitutes a contract of carriage, i.e. the ordinary meaning of the term in its legal context, as well as actual interpretation of the contract of carriage in order

Transportmitteln" (2003) TranspR 45–50; S. Mankabady, "Some Legal Aspects of the Carriage of Goods by Container" (1974) 23 Int'l & Comp LQ 317–338; E. Røsæg, "Conflicts of Conventions in the Rotterdam Rules" (2009) 15 JIML 238–248; J. Schelin, "Methods of Interpreting the CMR convention" in (2002) TranspR 382–385; V. Ulfbeck and S. Taiger Ivø, "Optioner og ansvar i transportaftaler" (2008) Erhvervsjuridisk tidskrift 4; W. Verheyen, "Fleximodal Contracts and the CMR: the Belgian approach" (2012) 18 JIML 5; R. de Wit, "Minimal Music: Multimodal Transport Including a Maritime Leg under the Rotterdam Rules" in R. Thomas (ed.), *The Carriage of Goods by Sea Under the Rotterdam Rules* (2010) and G. van der Ziel, "Multimodal aspects of the Rotterdam Rules" in *CMI Yearbook, 2009*.

54 In addition to the books by Grönfors and Andersen Roost mentioned, several other books and articles written in Swedish, Danish and Norwegian are included: U. Fabricius, *Lov om Fragtaftaler ved international vejtransport (CMR)* (2005); K. Grönfors, "Fraktavtalet och den allmänna avtalsrätten" (1988) SvJT 181-202; K. Grönfors, *Fraktavtalet under etthundra år* (1986); K. Grönfors, *Tolkning av fraktavtal* (1989); J. Heidbrink, *Logistikavtalet* (2005); C. Rune, "Haag-Visby-Reglerna" (1969) SvJT 12-26 ; V. Ulfbeck and S. Taiger Ivø, "Optioner og ansvar i transportaftaler" (2008) Erhvervsjuridisk tidskrift 4; P. Vestergaard Pedersen, *Transportret*, 2008 *et al.* In addition, several Nordic court decisions are discussed: see the bibliography.

55 Of the books mentioned, my work seems to be closest to Grönfors work, published in 1968.

56 United Nations Convention on the Law of Treaties, Vienna 1969 (the "Vienna Convention" or the "Vienna Convention on the Law of Treaties"). The convention is generally held to be recorded customary international law, thus binding on treaties predating the Vienna Convention as well as upon states that are not signatories to the convention (R.K. Gardiner, *Treaty Interpretation* (2015) pp. 13–14).

to settle whether it provides for carriage by [road], must be answered in order to interpret the scope of application of conventions such as the CMR.

As it will be concluded that sufficient definitions of the contract of carriage are not contained in the relevant conventions themselves, definitions must be sought in the underlying law. Thus, the general law of contracts must be consulted in order to define what makes a contract a contract for the carriage of goods by [road].[57] However, the uniformity of uniform law is easily undermined by resort to national law in the interpretation of a treaty. Thus, uniformity is best preserved if the interpreter seeks to extract principles that are common, or at least as common as possible, between the state parties to the convention interpreted.

The question of applicability of transport of goods conventions to multimodal transport contracts is of utmost importance. The legal insecurity that exists today operates to the detriment of carriers, shippers and consumers as well as to the whole market considering the significance of the shipment of goods.

1.2.2 Reflection on interpretation of uniform law[58]

Discussions on the applicability of unimodal conventions to multimodal contracts of carriage concern interpretation of international treaties. When interpretation of transport law conventions is discussed within the legal field of transport law, interpretation often focuses on the very words of the treaty, as if the words will eventually reveal their true meaning if only they are repeated enough. To some extent the Vienna Convention on the Law of Treaties is invoked, but often without too much depth as regards understanding of the latter convention.[59] Such a linguistic approach to understanding the terms of the treaties does not appear to be supported within the legal field of general treaty interpretation.[60] On the other hand, discussions regarding the rules of interpretation of international treaties carried out in the legal field of international law do not always separate uniform law from other types of international treaty, thus ignoring any special considerations that may be called for in respect of treaties that regulate the relationship between private parties.[61]

57 In relation to the harmonization of law within the European Union (EU), it has been proposed that the EU seems to perceive the contract of carriage as too particular to be included in attempts to harmonize contract law (E. Eftestøl-Wilhelmsson, *European Sustainable Carriage of Goods* (2016) p. 52).

58 Interpretation of treaties in general and uniform law in particular, and the interpretative data that may be taken into account is the subject of section 4.2 below.

59 See e.g. M. Hoeks, *Multimodal Transport Law* (2010) p. 134*ff.*; L. Andersen Roost, *Multimodale Transporter* (2012) pp. 141–142 and Swedish Supreme Court NJA 2016 s. 900 (Thai Air), in particular para. 9. For a critique of the position of English courts see R. Gardiner, "Treaty Interpretation in the English Courts since *Fothergill v Monarch Airlines* (1980)" ((1995) 44(3) Int'l and Comp LQ 620–628, at p. 623.

60 For a detailed discussion, cf. section 4.2.2 below.

61 Cf. for example Linderfalk, who categorically subsumes the interpretation of all treaties, *traité-loi* as well as *traité-contrat*, to the rules of interpretation of the Vienna Convention (U. Linderfalk, *On the Interpretation of Treaties* (2007) p. 3). For a different approach, see F. Enderlein, "Uni form Law and its Application by Judges and Arbitrators" in *International Uniform Law in Practice*, published by UNIDROIT (1988) pp. 329–353, at pp. 333 and 336.

However, any interpreter of an international treaty, in the more traditional form or in the form of uniform law, is obliged to apply the rules of treaty interpretation of international law.[62] As these have been recorded in the Vienna Convention, which has been ratified by a large number of states and is further considered binding on non-signatory states due to its status as recorded customary international law, the rules thus recorded will be the rules referred to in the following.[63]

In the current work an attempt will therefore be made to carefully apply the rules of interpretation of the Vienna Convention to the articles of applicability of the uniform law regulating the carrier's liability found in the CMR convention, the COTIF–CIM convention, the Montreal Convention and the Hague–Visby Rules.[64] Further, the special considerations necessary when interpreting uniform law are discussed.[65] The Vienna Convention promotes the autonomy of a treaty, referring the interpreter to understand a specific term in the context of the entire treaty. However, no treaty, and especially not a treaty of uniform law, is drafted in a vacuum but exists in a (legal) context. In relation to the term "contract" it will be discussed if, and in such case how, national law can be used to define that term.[66]

1.2.3 Reflections on the legal method

It has been held that the jurist is incapable of describing the legal method. The legal method is a craft, or an art, which can only be learned but never taught and accordingly it cannot be defined.[67]

The legal dogmatic method provides a method, which is used not only in research but also in the practical work of a lawyer. Traditionally, its aim has been

62 See e.g. van Damme, who holds that although article 31–33 of the Vienna Convention may be non-mandatory in the sense that the parties to a treaty can agree on other rules of interpretation, international customary rules are not (I. van Damme, *Treaty Interpretation by the WTO Appellate Body* (2009) p. 71).

63 The Vienna Convention has been ratified by 114 states. It is further considered to be a codification of existing international law, thus being generally binding (M. Ruud and G. Ulfstein, *Innføring i Folkerett* (2011) p. 81) as well as applicable to international treaties pre-dating the convention (U. Linderfalk; "Is Treaty Interpretation an Art or Science? International Law and Rational Decision Making" (2015) 26(1) EJIL 169–189, at p. 169). These features of the convention were emphasized by the drafting committee (I. van Damme, *Treaty Interpretation by the WTO Appellate Body* (2009) p. 38 with references). The rules of treaty interpretation of the Vienna Convention are discussed in section 4.2.2 below.

64 Naturally, the international law of treaty interpretation is neither undisputed (as to its content) nor uncomplicated, which is inter alia shown by the amount of literature on the subject (see e.g. I. van Damme, *Treaty Interpretation by the WTO Appellate Body* (2009), U. Linderfalk, *On the Interpretation of Treaties* (2007) and R. Gardiner, *Treaty Interpretation* (2015). For an overview of literature between 2006 and 2009, see M. Waibel, "Demystifying the Art of Interpretation" (2011) 22(2) EJIL 571–588). However, for the purposes of this work, i.e. to apply the rules of treaty interpretation at all, and in a structured manner, the consideration of other principles than those embedded in the Vienna Convention or of the various approaches to the subject, falls outside the scope.

65 F. Enderlein, "Uniform Law and its Application by Judges and Arbitrators" in *International Uniform Law in Practice*, published by UNIDROIT (1988) 329–353, at pp. 333 and 330 *ff.*

66 Cf. Swedish Supreme Court NJA 2016 s. 900, paras 11–16.

67 J. Samuelsson, *Tolkningslärans gåta* (2011) pp. 73–74.

to settle the contents of the law. However, as the view changes of what the object of research is, the legal dogmatic method changes too. A mere description of the law as it stands would no longer be undertaken as a research task, but it would appear that analysis, discussion and critique is a natural part of any dogmatic research today.[68] There is certainly a perceived need to put new labels on these variations, possibly to distance academic work from practical application of the legal method.[69] However, it seems natural that, although the method used is the same, the work of a researcher must be different from the work of a practising lawyer and that the academic must "stand sure"[70] in the knowledge that legal research differs from practical legal work. Accordingly, the art of jurisprudence is not merely descriptive, but analytical, reflective and critical.[71]

For the sake of clarity, it is pointed out that although Chapter 5 contains comparisons between the material rules relating to the formation and interpretation of contracts of two legal systems, the English common law and the (mainly) Nordic civil law, it is not a question of a comparative study in a methodological aspect.[72] When comparative law is employed as a method it is used to justify scientific conclusions and not merely, as in this work, as a research object that is used to give the further discussions a less abstract sense.[73] Because it is suggested that the question of applicability of certain rules to contracts of carriage by [road] should be answered only after the actual contract of carriage has been analysed in respect of whether it constitutes a contract to which the rules apply, interpretation of the actual contract of carriage becomes central. Further, because the conclusion that is drawn in section 5.2 below is that questions regarding formation and interpretation of contracts fall outside the scope of the conventions subject to the current research, these questions can only be answered with resort to national law. In a thesis which purports to analyse the rules of the conventions in question at a de-national level, i.e. from the perspective of the text of the conventions without regard to the national systems where the rules are applied, this conclusion is not without implications. Therefore, in order to proceed with the analysis and in order to prevent the discussion from being too abstract, it is related to

68 P. Blume, *Juridisk Metodelære* (2004) pp. 150–151.

69 Accordingly, Olsen discusses "pragmatic legal science" and "constructive legal science" as variations to the legal dogmatic method (L. Olsen, "Rättsvetenskapliga perspektiv" (2004) SvJT 105).

70 I was neé Andersson and, during a trip to Scotland together with my father, my father found the motto of the Anderson clan to be "stand sure". At the time, he perceived a need to teach his (teenage) daughter not to stand too sure, but to take on a slightly humbler attitude regarding (her own) knowledge. As life makes us humble, his daughter now relies on the motto the way it was meant.

71 C. Sandgren, "Är rättsdogmatiken dogmatisk?" (2005) 118 (4–5) TfR 648–656.

72 Comparative law can also be used as a point of reference, providing support in legal argumentation or as a source of law (M. Andenas and D. Fairgrieve, "Abstracts and keywords" in M. Andenas and D. Fairgrieve (eds), *Courts and Comparative Law* (2015) pp. 3–22, at p. 20). However, such use is not to be confused with the comparative law method (J. Hage, "Comparative Law as Method and the Method of Comparative Law" in in M. Adams and D. Heirbaut (eds), *The Method and Culture of Comparative Law* (2014) pp. 37–52, at p. 45).

73 Hage specifically points out the common misunderstanding among, in particular, younger researchers that the comparison of legal systems constitutes the use of the comparative method (J. Hage, "Comparative Law as Method and the Method of Comparative Law" in in M. Adams and D. Heirbaut (eds), *The Method and Culture of Comparative Law* (2014) pp. 37–52, at p. 45).

national law of contracts. As is discussed in section 1.3, the choice of English law and Nordic law is based on the seemingly common preconception that English law of contracts is quite distinct from other European (civil) law, and thus to the extent any common features can be found, the conclusions drawn based thereon could have general applicability within Europe.

Thus, the discussion on whether a multimodal contract of carriage that provides for carriage by [road] can be regarded as a contract for carriage by [road] is related to the conclusions drawn regarding the material law of the systems analysed. True, this may be perceived as a justification of the hypothesis contained in the research question. In my perception, however, it is an illustration of how, in this case in a European setting, the interpretation of the term "contract of carriage by [road]" contained in an international treaty could, or should, be made. Neither are the comparisons made in Chapter 5 to be classified as comparative in the disciplinary sense of comparative law, where comparative research is defined not only as a comparison between two or more legal systems and the accounting for similarities and differences, but as including an attempt to explain the reasons for such differences and/or similarities.[74]

1.2.4 Delimitations

The carriage of goods conventions applicable to sea and air transport are essentially global. In terms of land-based transport, the need for global harmonization is not as imminent. As regards Europe, this has led to road and rail transport being regulated by conventions that are basically European, but that also include some near-Eastern and North African states, naturally connected to Europe by road or rail. That is the reason for the first delimitation of this work; as road and rail conventions are not global, it is natural to examine European conventions and disregard any other regime that may apply to states in another region. Europe is the natural focus, and to consider other regional regimes would expand this work beyond what is realistic, not to mention the linguistic difficulties that scrutinizing Asian, African or South American regulation and their case law would entail. Thus, although there certainly are interesting legal questions outside the European perspective, such as the Andean Community regulation on multimodal transport,[75] the Mercosur Partial Agreement for the Facilitation of Multimodal

74 J. Husa, "Research Designs of Comparative Law – Methodology or Heuristics?" in M. Adams and D. Heirbaut (eds), *The Method and Culture of Comparative Law* (2014) pp. 53–68, at p. 54. The method for such comparative research depends, according to Husa, on the individual research project; however, the process is hermeneutic (at p. 56). Bogdan has a less complicated view on comparative law and holds out any comparison between legal systems to constitute the use of a comparative method. However, he points out that the "comparative method" is not a particular technique, "but rather a number of different techniques" (M. Bogdan, *Concise Introduction to Comparative Law* (2013) p. 10). It seems, however, to confuse matters to call something a method if it is not in fact a method.

75 Decision 331 of 4 March 1993, as modified by Decision 393 of 9 July 1996: "International Multimodal Transport".

Transport of Goods[76] and the US federal regulation governing inter-state multimodal transport,[77] these will be left out of the analysis.

As regards the sources referred to, these include Nordic, English and other European to the extent these are available in English. Again, linguistic limitations assert themselves and a critical analysis of the sources referred to will show that they are mainly northern European, which is simply due to a limited availability of academic texts in English from other countries.

For the sake of completeness, the carriage of goods conventions applicable to road, rail, air and sea transports in Europe will be examined and accounted for. The convention that regulates the liability of carriers of inland waterways, the CMNI Convention,[78] has however been left out of the analysis. The reason is its minor applicability from a Nordic perspective and, although I perceive that this work has a wider perspective than Nordic, the addition of this work to an international discussion is in part to add Nordic precedents and doctrine to the picture. Thus, as regards Part II, nothing new could really be added to the already existing accounts.[79] In respect of Part III, the discussion could by all means be relevant in respect of the CMNI, which applies to contracts for transboundary transport by inland waterway.[80] However, the constraints applicable require delimitations to be made and the CMNI has thus been left out.

However, as it is the conventions applicable to contracts for carriage by a certain mode of transport that have caused problems in practice and legal theory, much of the attention will be given to those conventions. The reader will further notice that the carriage of goods by road convention, the CMR convention, will receive much more attention than its rail counterpart, the COTIF–CIM convention. There is an obvious imbalance between the amount of case law relating to the CMR and to the COTIF–CIM. Although rail carriage is to an increasing extent carried out by private companies, the CMR convention is to a larger extent applied between private parties, which may explain the plentiful case law and accompanying doctrine that exists on the convention. Considering the more extensive number of sources that thus exist in relation to the CMR convention than in relation to the COTIF–CIM convention, the former is a more appropriate protagonist than the latter.

76 Partial Agreement for the Facilitation of Multimodal Transport of Goods, 27 April 1995. The member states of Mercosur include Argentina, Brazil, Paraguay and Uruguay (the membership of Venezuela was suspended in December 2016), with Bolivia, Chile, Peru, Colombia, Ecuador and Suriname as associate countries.

77 The Carmack Amendment, 49 USC § 14706 et seq.

78 Budapest Convention on the Contract for the Carriage of Goods by Inland Waterway (CMNI), adopted by the Diplomatic Conference Organized Jointly by CCNR, the Danube Commission and UN/ECE, held in Budapest from 25 September to 3 October 2000.

79 Cf. M. Hoeks, *Multimodal Transport Law* (2010) ch. 7. Hoeks, however, perceived the convention to be of reduced importance due to the (at the time) diminishing transport by inland waterways (at pp. 279–281). The European Commission aims to promote inland waterways as a sustainable alternative to e.g. road transport, but inland waterways remain a marginal transport mode carrying only 4.4 per cent of intra-EU transports in 2015 (EU Transports in Figures, *Statistical Pocket Book 2015* (2015) p. 19), a number which appears to include purely domestic transports as well.

80 CMNI articles 1 and 2.

1.2.5 The legal sources

The current work being one that concerns international law rather than national law, the legal sources used may differ from a purely national survey. Accordingly, in the following some theoretical aspects on the sources used will be discussed.

1.2.5.1 International conventions of uniform law

The focus of this work is international conventions. However, the type of conventions discussed is dissimilar from the type of conventions that is the norm, at least in the perspective of international law. Thus, the original international conventions, or treaties, were agreements between the sovereigns of states (*traité-contrat*).[81]

However, international conventions have developed into agreements on, as I see it, three different layers. Alongside inter-state agreements, for example defining the border between two states, are conventions in which the state parties undertake to grant their citizens certain rights, such as the European Convention on Human Rights. In addition, other international conventions contain material law, relating to the relationship between private parties. These types of convention are often labelled "uniform law conventions" as the purpose thereof is to harmonize the material law applicable in the national systems of the state parties (*traité-loi*).[82] In the current work the term "uniform law" will thus be used for the type of conventions that contain material law, such as conventions regulating the liability of the carrier of goods for goods carried.

Although the binding force of the rules, as towards the parties that are subject to the material law, comes from the enactment thereof into national law,[83] the rules are commonly referred to by the name of the convention, e.g. the Hague–Visby Rules. It may seem misleading to discuss the applicability of the convention, when what is in fact intended is the applicability of the uniform law in its national law costume. However, presumably the national laws implemented in the different contracting states are identical and the discussion is thus facilitated if the convention as such is the subject-matter rather than the various national statutes. To the extent the national laws are not identical, a discussion of the terms of the actual treaty is still meaningful as it is the terms of the actual treaty that the contracting states have undertaken to implement.[84] Further, according to the terms of the conventions it is in fact the terms of the convention as such that

81 In section 4.1 below the relationship between the rules of treaty interpretation and uniform law is discussed.

82 J. Basedow, "The Renaissance of Uniform Law: European Contract Law and its Components" (1998) 18 Legal Stud 121–122.

83 International conventions are only binding on states that agree thereto. Further, conventions only bind state parties whilst the contents thereof only grant rights to, and impose obligations upon, states. Thus, international conventions of uniform law do not, as such, subject private parties to their rules, but obliges each state party to enact the material contents thereof into its national legislation.

84 According to Basedow, uniform law is many times fragmented through its implementation into national law (J. Basedow, "The Renaissance of Uniform Law: European Contract Law and its Components" (1998) 18 Legal Stud 121 at p. 123).

apply where the prerequisites for applicability are fulfilled. As an example, the Montreal Convention provides that "This Convention applies to all international carriage of persons, baggage or cargo performed by aircraft for reward."[85] In addition, legal debate is usually carried out with reference to the conventions as such rather than to national implementations thereof.[86]

1.2.5.2 Precedent as a source of law

Precedent is considered a source of law in civil law systems as well as in common law systems, albeit of dissimilar rank. Whilst the traditional common law approach to precedent is that of a primary source of law, in civil law precedent is subordinate to legislation.[87] Whilst in common law the body of precedent would traditionally compose *the law*, under civil law it is only when the law is unclear that precedent is of relevance; a court applying a clear rule does not create precedents as such, and thus the position of the courts is to fill legal gaps and interpret legal anomalies, which is perhaps less troubling to legal theory.[88] Hence, under civil law the justification of precedent as a source of law can (at least more easily) be left at the legal principle that like cases should be treated alike, which is fundamental to the rule of law.[89]

The tradition of writing judgments is also heterogeneous in different nations. That the English courts write thorough and analytical judgments in which the law is often clearly stated is not surprising considering the place of jurisprudence as a primary source of law. In nations such as Sweden, where precedent is only supplementary to legislation enacted by the Parliament, judgments can be very case-specific, without expressing general principles that can be applied to other cases.[90] However, there seems to be a shift, where supreme courts, which have previously not been too keen on expressing themselves in over-general terms, have taken on the role of developing the law.[91]

---

85 Cf. article 1. In fact, the Montreal Convention does not contain an express obligation for the states that sign the convention to implement it. The preamble states that "The state parties to this convention ... have agreed as follows". In practice this means that each state party must implement the convention into its system of law, but perhaps it would be more correct if the preamble stated that "The state parties to this convention ... have agreed to effect the following provisions as binding law within their territory".

86 See among others M. Hoeks, *Multimodal Transport Law* (2010); L. Andersen Roost, *Multimodale Transporter* (2012); M. Clarke, *Contracts of carriage by air* (2010) p. 7 and M. Clarke and D. Yates, *Contracts of carriage by land and air* (2004) (although the fact that the convention applies due to its statutory enactment in the United Kingdom is explained; cf. regarding the CMR convention at p. 13).

87 J. Cartwright, *Contract Law* (2016) pp. 3–4, 8.

88 In common law systems the justification of precedents is much discussed in legal theory, just as justification of legislation is discussed in legal theory in civil law systems (See e.g. J.F. Horty, "Rules and Reasons in the Theory of Precedent" (2011) Legal Theory 1–33 at p.17.

89 R. Påhlsson, "Skatterättspraxis i utveckling – principer för rättsfallsanalys" (2011) 3 Skattenytt 115.

90 C. Ramberg, "Makten över avtalsrätten" in B. Flodgren *et al.* (eds), *Vänbok till Axel Adlercreutz* (2007) pp. 419–427, at p. 423.

91 With regard to Sweden, see M. Derlén and J. Lindholm, "Judiciell activism eller prejudikatbildning?" (2016) SvJT 143; B. Bengtsson, "Prejudikat eller lagstiftningsreformer?" in H.C. Bugge *et al.* (eds), *Lov, Liv og Lære* (2016) pp. 33–48 and R. Påhlsson, "Skatterättspraxis i utveckling – principer

As mentioned above, courts in different jurisdictions have different traditions in terms of writing judgments. Whilst it seems that courts in common law jurisdictions strive to formulate general rules, courts in other jurisdictions strive to limit the generality of their decisions.[92] Where courts endeavour to create rules that are generally applicable, it must at least be presumed that the court, as such a law maker, analyses the effects of such a general rule not just in the case before it. However, when a court aims merely to try the case before it on the merits and not create generally applicable precedents, the ambition by others, jurisprudence or subsequent courts, to extract non-case specific rules that can also be generally applicable to situations that are not akin to the situation in the settled case may be less successful.[93]

Further, civil cases are characterized by the parties' right and ability to dispose over the case. Hence, a court or tribunal has a limited capacity in that it is restricted by the claims made by the parties. Thus, the claims, as formulated by the respective parties, may prevent the court from settling a legal issue in the way it would prefer.[94] Further, a court may be inclined to decide a matter in a certain way due to compelling reasons, which it may not declare openly. Hence, extracting general rules from precedents should, it is proposed here, be done very subtly and with special caution where the court in question does not itself enounce such generalities. Thus, unless the court expressly enunciates general rules, judgments that contain limited or no background facts to the case and/or limited reference to the claims and legal grounds presented by the parties pose a challenge and should, in my opinion, only with caution be used as precedents.[95] The same applies where judgments contain limited legal reasoning by the court.

för rättsfallsanalys" (2011) 3 Skattenytt 114–115. As regards Norway, see H.P. Graver, "Høyesterett og rettsutviklingen – førti år etter" in H.C. Bugge *et al.* (eds), *Lov, Liv og Lære* (2016) pp. 242–254. Also, in the very limited number of judgments from the German Supreme Court that are analysed in section 3.4.1 a change can be discerned from case-specific settlement of a dispute to a more general discussion of a legal problem.

92 As an example, it has been held that the shift of the Swedish Supreme Court from its previous position as the third instance to a pure prejudicial court has led to a shift in the formulation of judgments (M. Derlén and J. Lindholm, "Judiciell activism eller prejudikatbildning?" (2016) SvJT 143).

93 Kristoffersson holds that in order to extract legal ruls from precedence the judgement must be generalized (E. Kristoffersson, "Att använda prejudikat och annan rättspraxis i rättstillämpningen" (2011) 10 SvSkT 835–849, at p. 839).

94 For example: when the regulations applicable are mandatory, such as the transport conventions considered, the court will obviously have to apply the rules of such conventions where applicable, irrespective of the claims by the parties. However, where the claimant purports that a convention, such as the CMR is not applicable, and the defendant does not oppose thereto, the court will have to apply the convention, as the convention can be voluntarily applied where it is not imperative. Hence, the fact that a court applies a certain convention, such as the CMR, to a road leg of a multimodal contract does not necessarily reflect an opinion by that court that the convention is applicable *ex proprio vigore*.

95 In relation to judgments from courts other than the Supreme Court, Kristoffersson proposes that prejudicial value of a judgment depends on the quality of the legal argumentation therein (E. Kristoffersson, "Att använda prejudikat och annan rättspraxis i rättstillämpningen" (2011) 10 SvSkT 835–849, at p. 837).

Precedents as a source of law therefore must involve evaluation of the judgment, which must be done based on the case's own merits.[96] Ultimately, a case is a judgment of a particular dispute, involving particular circumstances that may or may not speak to the court. Evaluation should thus consider the facts of the case, the claims made by the parties and the reasoning of the court. However, it should also consider what considerations the court may have taken into account, unconsciously or non-openly.[97] In conclusion, the approach, at least from jurisprudence, must not be uncritical and the above considerations taken into account.

1.2.5.3 Doctrine

To a large extent this thesis is based on existing legal doctrine. The analyses are built on the works of other writers, which is related to the actual terms of the treaties scrutinized.

Legal doctrine plays an important role in the practical legal field and to legal development.[98] It can be presumed that legal doctrine is balanced and thought-through and there seems to be good reason for legal doctrine to maintain its practical importance.

Legal doctrine is not seldom referred to as a "legal source".[99] However, the status of legal doctrine has been under constant discussion.[100] Clearly, the answer to whether legal doctrine has the status of a source of law is dependent on what a legal source *is*. To the extent a legal source consists only of such sources of law by which a superior court in a certain legal system considers itself bound, the number of legal sources is extremely limited. In a civil law system, such as any Nordic state, a supreme court would consider itself bound by legislation.[101]

---

96 B.H. Østenstad, "Sårstelldommen (Rt. 2010 s. 612) – prejudikat for kva?" (2014) 53(8) Lov og Rett 484–501, at p. 485.

97 Derlén and Lindholm separates the court's *official method* from its *inofficial method*, where the latter include considerations not openly accounted for in the judgment (M. Derlén and J. Lindholm, "Judiciell activism eller prejudikatbildning?" (2016) SvJT 146).

98 In the case of the Nordic law of contracts, it has been held that docrine is in fact the main legal source (C. Ramberg, "Makten över avtalsrätten" in B. Flodgren *et al.* (eds), *Vänbok till Axel Adlercreutz* (2007) pp. 419–427). Empirically it is clear that the Swedish Supreme Court refers regularly to legal writing: see e.g. NJA 2016 s. 900, NJA 2016 s. 149 and 2014 s. 425.

99 The traditional "legal sources" in Sweden include (in order of status): legislation, preparatory works, precedence and legal doctrine (E. Kristoffersson, "Att använda prejudikat och annan rättspraxis i rättstillämpningen" (2011) 10 SvSkT 835–849, at p. 835).

100 See for example, P.O. Ekelöf; *Är den juridiska doktrinen en teknik eller en vetenskap* (1951).

101 Peczenik classifies legislation as a legal source which must be complied with and precedence, preparatory works, legal principles and international treaties of uniform law as legal sources that should be complied with (A. Peczenik, *Vad är rätt?* (1995) pp. 214–215). In relation to preparatory works, Håstad holds that the courts are bound by the law, but not by its motives (T. Håstad, "Rättstillämpning i strid med lag" in B. Flodgren *et al.* (eds), *Vänbok till Axel Adlercreutz* (2007) pp. 167–180, at p. 167). However, reference thereto by the Supreme Court is common (M. Derlén and J. Lindholm, "Judiciell activism eller prejudikatbildning?" (2016) SvJT 143, at p. 151 fig.3). Kristoffersson holds that Supreme Court precedence must be followed (E. Kristoffersson, "Att använda prejudikat och annan rättspraxis i rättstillämpningen" (2011) 10 SvSkT 835–849, at p. 837); however it is clear that the Supreme Court itself may change previous precedence (Swedish Code of Judicial Procedure RB 3 ch. 6§, see also E. Bylander, "Avgöranden utan plenum i Högsta Domstolen" in (2011/12) 3 JT 503–512).

Preparatory works and precedents, which would normally not be questioned as sources of law, are not entirely binding on the Supreme Court and even legislation, although binding *per se*, is subject to interpretation.

If, on the other hand, a source of law is considered to be something that is actually used in practice to settle the law as is stands, then legal doctrine is certainly a source of law.[102] Thus, to the extent the legal practitioner makes use of the theories provided by legal doctrine as one of several factors to interpret and settle the law, then doctrine is certainly a source of law.[103] That there is an actual interplay between precedent and doctrine can hardly be denied.[104]

1.2.5.4 *Travaux préparatoires*

The teleological method of interpreting legislation has its firm roots in European civil law.[105] As an example, in Nordic civil law the teleological method is firmly settled and thus preparatory work by parliament and government play an important role in the interpretation of legislation.[106] The tradition of respecting the legislator's intentions has led to (or has been fuelled by) preparatory work being published in catalogued order and easily accessible. There is an internal hierarchy where statements in the "propositions" published by the government are superior to statements in the preceding "official inquiry". In Nordic law preparatory work is inferior to legislation, but superior to precedence, in terms of status as a source of law, and there is an established approach to including preparatory work in the interpretation of legislation and settlement of the law as it stands.[107]

In relation to interpretation of international treaties of uniform law, the teleological method has been advocated as a method that promotes autonomous interpretation.[108] Further, the method finds support in the Vienna Convention of

---

102 A. Peczenik, *Vad är rätt?* (1995) p. 210.

103 E.M. Boe, *Rettskildelære under debatt* (2012) p. 320 and A. Peczenik, *Vad är rätt?* (1995) pp. 214–215. See also E. Kristoffersson, "Att använda prejudikat och annan rättspraxis i rättstillämpningen" in (2011) 10 SvSkT 835–849, at p. 836.

104 Cf. T. Eckhoff, *Rettskildelaere* (2001) pp. 271–275. On a critical note it can be asserted that legal doctrine is sometimes self-fulfilling as the exchange between the Supreme Court and Academia concerns not only thoughts but also persons (see e.g. Addendum by Supreme Court Justice S. Lindskog in Swedish Supreme Court T 309–16 (20 December 2016) in which he supports his argumentation on (among other sources) two of his own books).

105 F. Enderlein, "Uniform Law and its Application by Judges and Arbitrators" in *International Uniform Law in Practice*, published by UNIDROIT (1988) 329–353, at p. 332. The method is also sometimes referred to as the historical method of interpretation, which purportedly is part of the Roman legal inheritance (F. Diedrich, "Maintaining Uniformity in International Uniform Law via Autonomous Interpretation: Software Contracts and the CISG" (1996) 8 Pace Int'l L Rev 303 p. 312). In contrast, in English common law the approach is to interpret statutes as narrowly as possible (*ibid.*, at p. 311).

106 A. Peczenik, *Vad är rätt?* (1995) pp. 214–215. However, it is clear that preparatory works are not *binding* on the courts (T. Håstad, "Rättstillämpning i strid med lag" in B. Flodgren *et al.* (eds), *Vänbok till Axel Adlercreutz* (2007) pp. 167–180, at p. 167).

107 Which is shown empirically by Derlén and Lindholm (M. Derlén and J. Lindholm "Judiciell activism eller prejudikatbildning?" (2016) SvJT 143).

108 M. Gebauer, "Uniform Law, General Principles and Autonomous Interpretation" (2000–4) Rev Dr unif 683–705 and M. Clarke, *International Carriage of Goods by Road: CMR* (2014) p. 7*ff.*, with refence to *Buchanan v Babco* [1977] QB 208, 213. Cf. also section 4.2.3 below.

the Law of Treaties as the preparatory work of a treaty is considered (at least) a secondary source of interpretation.[109] However, under international law it is clear that a supplementary means of interpretation such as preparatory work must be published and easily available in order to constitute a permitted source of interpretation.[110] This severely limits the use of such sources since, at least historically, the protocols of diplomatic conferences, during which conventions were drafted, were not published.[111] As regards newer conventions, accessibility may be better.[112] Another important limitation to the use of preparatory works of international conventions is that this preparatory work must be used with the awareness that is usually consists merely of protocols of the discussions that have taken place, and as such communicates both the prevailing opinion but also the minority view and is a diplomatic summary of what has been noted by the state representatives.[113]

In conclusion, although the teleological method of interpretation unquestionably fits well with the purposes of uniform law, resort to preparatory work of international conventions containing uniform law must be cautious, and the interpreter must be aware of the limitations of preparatory work available.

1.2.5.5 References

Not long ago a researcher was limited to the sources found in the local university library, with the possibility to gather additional material through a research expedition to some well-assorted library at another university.[114] In addition sources could be traced through references.[115]

109 U. Linderfalk, *On the Interpretation of Treaties* (2007) p. 238; J. Schelin, "Methods of Interpreting the CMR convention" [2002] TransportR 382–385, at p. 382.

110 *Fothergill v Monarch Airlines Ltd* [1980] 2 All ER 696.

111 Accordingly, the protocols of the CMR negotiations have not been published, although they are accessible at the Library of the United Nations in Geneva (these records have therefore not been considered in the current work). The transcripts of the diplomatic conferences leading to the acceptance of the Hague and the Hague–Visby Rules have subsequently been published in M. Sturley, *The Legislative History of the Carriage of Goods by Sea Act and The Travaux préparatoires of the Hague rules*, vols 1–3 (1990) as well as in F. Berlingieri, *The Travaux préparatoires of the International Convention for the Unification of Certain Rules of Law Relating to Bills of Lading of 25 August 1924, the Hague Rules, and of the protocols of 23 February 1968 and 21 December 1979, the Hague–Visby Rules* (1997).

112 All protocols from the Working Group sessions during which the Rotterdam Rules were negotiated are published on the UNCITRAL website in all official languages of the UN. Although actually easily accessible, there is no index showing in which of the protocols the various articles have been discussed, which limits practical accessibility.

113 K. Grönfors; "Om Konventionstolkning" (1957) SvJT 16–21, at p. 20; L. Sisula Tulokas, "Om konventionstolkning – att äta kakan och ha den kvar" (1987) 132 Marius 3–4; M. Clarke, *International Carriage of Goods by Road: CMR* (2014) p. 9. Diedrich holds that the main goal of "historical interpretation of international uniform law ... [is to find] the actual intentions of the international legislature based on at least a majority vote.", ruling out unofficially published *travaux préparatoires* (F. Diedrich; "Maintaining Uniformity in International Uniform Law via Autonomous Interpretation: Software Contracts and the CISG" (1996) 8 Pace Int'l L Rev 303 at p. 321).

114 For a discussion of the gathering of sources in the pre-digitalized era, see H. Eek *et al.*, *Juridikens Källmaterial* (1982).

115 H. Eek *et al.*, *Juridikens Källmaterial* (1982) p. 182.

However, the sources of available information have developed rapidly; today a researcher has theoretical access to all available sources in the entire world, although there may be linguistic limitations to the possibility of actual consideration thereof. This vast well of information must be approached in some way. Naturally, not all relevant sources can be studied; there are time as well as intellectual restrictions.[116] Further there are limitations to what can be considered reasonable. So how should this issue be approached?

Sources in the form of legal literature have two functions. The first is to orient the researcher within the subject that is undertaken; various books and articles are read, and the researcher develops an understanding for the subject and makes preliminary conclusions. The second function is to support the writings that are thereafter undertaken; books and articles are used to substantiate statements and conclusions. The literature used in this second phase consists of parts of the literature used in the first phase; it consists of the books and articles that the writer considers relevant of all the literature read as some of that will be important for the general understanding, but not specific enough to be used as reference. Although there may be differences in relation thereto, it is pointed out here that in the current work, the list of references only contains the literature actually referred to.

1.3 Mapping the intended route

The research questions posed above thus aim to settle the applicability of existing unimodal conventions regulating the carrier's liability for goods carried to carriage under multimodal contracts of carriage. However, in order to place the analysis in its legal setting, first the legal context will be accounted for. Thus, the conventions discussed in the current work will be presented and the rules regulating the carrier's liability in those conventions will be briefly discussed. Thereafter the background to the research questions will be presented. Such background consists not only of precedence and doctrine relating to the applicability of unimodal conventions to multimodal transport, but also of theory relating to the network system, i.e. application of the unimodal conventions *ex proprio vigore* to the respective modal legs of a multimodal transport, and the uniform system, i.e. a separate system regulating the multimodal carrier's liability. In addition, some of the existing conventions contain rules extending the scope of the convention to other modes of transport, rules which thus complicates the application of the network system. These rules will accordingly be presented and analysed.

Part II contains the actual analysis. It is perceived that, in relation to the primary research question, the articles defining the scope of application of the respective conventions must be interpreted. As mentioned, treaty interpretation is subject to

116 Cf. e.g. M. Waibel, "Demystifying the Art of Interpretation" (2011) 22(2) EJIL 571–588, at p. 583.

rules of international law, regulating treaty interpretation.[117] These rules are vital to the intended interpretation and will therefore be thoroughly discussed and analysed, after which they will be methodically applied to the treaty terms in question. The aim is to define the scope of application of the conventions discussed.

As will be clear from the account of the ongoing legal discussion given in section 3.4 below, it is in relation to the contractual approach to applicability that the main objections to applicability of the conventions in question to carriage under multimodal contracts have been made. It is concluded in Chapter 4 that the wording of the scopes of applicability of the conventions concerned does not prevent applicability to carriage under multimodal contracts of carriage. Accordingly, it is concluded that the applicability thereof depends on the definition of the contract of carriage of goods by [road]. Although the contract of carriage may be defined in the convention itself, the definition thus included does not seem to concern the definition of the contract of carriage by [road] in respect of how to settle whether it is a contract of carriage *by [road]*.[118] Thus, such definition must be sought in a wider context, which, it is asserted, is the context of the general law of contracts.[119]

Because the multimodal contract of carriage comes in several shapes, which could pose different obstacles in relation to applicability of the unimodal conventions in question, an attempt is made to account for these variations as well as categorizing them into two categories. Whilst the "clear contract of carriage" raises questions related to formation of contracts, the "unclear contract of carriage" raises questions related to interpretation of contracts.[120]

Contract interpretation plays an important role in the current work, as will be evident below. As suggested below in Chapter 5, the question of what constitutes a contract of carriage by [road] is best answered through an analysis of the contents of the particular contract of carriage in question. However, because the interpretation of a contract necessarily will relate to the specific contract, it is not always easily subsumed into theoretical "rules" or guidelines.[121] In order to bring the discussion to a less abstract level, the law of contracts of, on the one hand, English common law and, on the other hand, Nordic civil law, will be used as

117 Enderlein argues that rules of interpretation of national law (as distinguished from interpretation in conformity with national law) are better suited for the interpretation of uniform law than the rules of treaty interpretation. However, he concludes that there does not seem to be a significant divergence between articles 31–33 of the Vienna Convention and rules of interpretation of national law (F. Enderlein, "Uniform Law and its Application by Judges and Arbitrators" in *International Uniform Law in Practice*, published by UNIDROIT (1988) pp. 329–353, at pp. 333 and 336).

118 See Grönfors who holds that, with the exemption of the COTIF–CIM convention that (in previous versions) provided a mechanism for contract formation, all uniform law conventions leave contract formation to national law (K. Grönfors, *Fraktavtalet under etthundra år* (1989) p. 33.

119 "General law of contracts" denotes the law of contracts, within a national system, that applies to contracts in general, i.e. formation of contracts, construction and interpretation as well as invalidation thereof.

120 Cf. sections 5.3, 5.5 and 5.6 below.

121 The question of interpretation emerges thus only in relation to the problematic case. The text in itself does not create any questions of interpretation, other than hypothetical ones – i.e. in formulating a question of interpretation it is presupposed, in one way or another, a situation to which the rules are to be applied (my translation). J. Samuelsson, *Tolkningslärans gåta* (2011) p. 168 (n. 517).

illustration. Thus, by relating the discussion to the rules of contract interpretation of these two legal systems, the discussion is made less abstract. Nevertheless, the discussion will still be abstract in relation to the fact that there is no actual contract of carriage to be interpreted.

When national law is resorted to,[122] there is an obvious threat to the sought-after harmonization of uniform law. Although a judge in a national court seeking to interpret the scope of applicability of e.g. the CMR convention is not bound by any other law than that of the law governing the contract at hand, it would be desirable if that judge would extend the horizon and consider the aim of harmonization subsumed into the treaty of uniform law.[123] Thus, in order to preserve uniformity, when applying national law harmonization would benefit if the judge seeks to apply rules that are not unique to the national system at hand, but shared with other systems.[124] In a European perspective, compilations such as the Draft Common Frame of Reference (DCFR) could serve as a source of the common European core.[125] Because compilations like the DCFR are model rules, *de lege ferenda* rather than *de lege lata* their usefulness is limited by the fact that the national judge is bound by material (actual) national law.[126] However, to examine the underlying law of, in the current case, contracts in every single state party to a particular convention would be an overwhelming task for a national judge as well as in the current work. In the latter case, the natural starting point is the Nordic law of contracts.[127] Nordic law is usually referred to as a member of the legal family of civil law, which is contrasted with the legal family of common law. It is often assumed that between civil law and common law there is a demarcation line, in particular in relation to the law of contracts.[128] However, more recently

122 In avoidance of any misunderstanding, it is stressed here that national (material) law is not to be used to interpret or define the terms of a treaty *as such*. However, when a treaty rests on the existence of certain legal figures, such as a contract, the definition of which falls outside the scope of the treaty, the definition of that legal figure is only found in the underlying national legal system, cf. section 5.2 below. See also F. Enderlein, "Uniform Law and its Application by Judges and Arbitrators" in *International Uniform Law in Practice*, published by UNIDROIT (1988) pp. 329–353, at p. 342 *ff.* and Swedish Supreme Court NJA 2016 s. 900 (Thai Air) pp. 9–10.

123 Swedish Supreme Court NJA 2014 s. 425, at p. 7.

124 "Most important is the comparative interpretation ..." (F. Enderlein, "Uniform Law and its Application by Judges and Arbitrators" in *International Uniform Law in Practice*, published by UNIDROIT (1988) pp. 329–353, at p. 335).

125 C. von Bar and E. Clive (eds), *Principles, Definitions and Model Rules of European Private Law, Draft Common Frame of Reference ("DCFR")* (2009). For the same purpose, as regards common law, reference may be had to the US Restatement (Second) of Contracts. However, in the current work the analysis is delimited to a European context, and in respect of the law of contracts, American law differs from English law (J. Cartwright, *Contract Law* (2016) pp. 10–11).

126 Although the common principles of the DCFR have been extracted through extensive scholarly research, the Model Rules are just that, model rules; *de lege ferenda* rather than *de lege lata*.

127 The Nordic states of Norway, Denmark, Finland, Iceland and Sweden have Contracts Acts which are, albeit implemented as national legislation in each state, common to the extent that the legislation was drafted through Nordic cooperation; cf. section 5.5.1 below.

128 G. McMeel and H.C. Grigoleit, "Interpretation of Contracts" in G. Dannemann and S. Vogenauer (eds), *The Common European Sales Law in Context* (2013) pp. 341–372, at p. 341; J. Rosengren, "Engelsk avtalstolkning i ett svenskt perspektiv" (2010) SvJT 1–22, at p. 1 with further references.

a rapprochement seems to have taken place, with the result of diminishing dissimilarities.[129] It is assumed that where common features can be found between the two legal families that are found in Europe, such similarities can serve as a starting point of a discussion on a more general level than can be achieved by reference to a purely national system only. Thus, to the extent any common features can be found, these will form the basis of the following analysis of what constitutes a contract of carriage and what make such a contract one for carriage by [road].

In the final chapter, some general conclusions will be drawn. An attempt will be made to turn the perspective. Thus, against the background of the status quo, a theory of the applicability of unimodal conventions to transport under multimodal contracts of carriage is developed. Based on the foregoing analysis, it will be held that because the conventions in question apply to contracts of carriage by [road], and because such contracts are not defined in the terms of the conventions as regards their conclusion and interpretation, the latter remains subject to national law. Further, it is asserted that because the implication of "by [road]" is not defined either, it is the contract of carriage that needs to be scrutinized in order to settle whether a certain contract is for carriage "by [road]". This theory will be held, not to be prevented by the terms of applicability of the conventions in question, although, as will be discussed, the application of the network system is by no means hassle-free. Lastly, the research questions will be revisited and answered.

129 See e.g. G. McMeel, "Language and the Law Revisited: An Intellectual History of Con tractual Interpretation" (2005) 34 Comm L World Rev 256 at pp. 285–286; J. Rosengren, "Engelsk avtalstolkning i ett svenskt perspektiv" (2010) SvJT 1–22, at p. 22.

PART II

CURRENT LAW AND THEORY

CHAPTER 2

The carrier's liability under current regimes

The purpose of the current chapter is to give a general presentation of the regimes governing the carrier's liability for carriage of goods that are relevant from the perspective of the current thesis.[1] Whilst there are multimodal dimensions of these regimes, which will be discussed in Chapter 3, et seq., the contemporary legal approach to transport is essentially unimodal. Although attempts are made to escape these unimodal constraints,[2] multimodal transport is inevitably dissembled into its unimodal segments. The unimodal approach is caused by, but also the reason for, the fact that the regulatory regimes classify transport based on the transport mode used. The research questions posed in the current work[3] fall back on this unimodal approach – the relationship between the multimodal practice and the unimodal regulations. Accordingly, in order to present the reader with a background, and legal context, to the research questions, the rules governing the carriers' liability for carriage by road, rail, air and sea will be presented. In order to present the conventions in a setting, first a very brief historical resume will be given.

2.1 Background

Commercial carriage of goods and merchandise has a long history.[4] The transport agreement, that is a contract for the carriage of goods from one place to another, has developed through history to become what today could be described as a service agreement. Whilst the details of the development of the carrier's liability for goods carried is lost to history, there are, as will be briefly recounted in the following sections, nevertheless points in history that seem to have affected modern maritime law.

In a European perspective, maritime law has its first traces in ancient Hellenistic and Roman law.[5] The liability of the carrier under Roman law has been

1 As laid out in section 1.2.4 above, although the perspective is European, the conventions discussed have been selected based on its influence on Nordic jurisprudence.

2 For a fairly recent attempt, see F. Lorenzon, "Multimodal Transport Evolving: Freedom and Regulation Three Decades after the 1980 MTO Convention" in M. Clarke (ed.), *Maritime Law Evolving* (2013), 163–180.

3 Cf. section 1.1.2 above.

4 The first maritime routes are thought to have been construed by the Mesopotamians in the twelfth century BC (P. Rousseau, *Histoire des transportes* (1961) pp. 24–25).

5 In the trade of ancient Greece and the Roman Empire, maritime transport was of utter importance and it is often presumed that some form of rules, legislative or customary, were applied

described as close to an insurance undertaking.[6] This strict liability seems to have been the influence of the law of bailment found in Anglo-Saxon law, which in turn is the foundation of the common law concepts of common and private carriers.[7] However, it has been held that it is not before the middle ages that the maritime law developed into a legal field *sui generis*, the rules of which have eventually developed into modern maritime law.[8]

Thus, in the thirteenth century the contract for the transport of goods was a risk-sharing agreement, under which the shipowner and the merchants whose goods were carried by the ship in question, shared the risk that the vessel, and the goods carried onboard, might be wrecked during the voyage.[9] The system, developed by Italian mercantile city states,[10] was based on the idea that the stake held by the ship owner in the "common adventure" that a voyage by sea constituted, by far exceeded the stake held by the merchants. The merchants, for their part, would make large profits if the voyage was successful, and it was considered that they should share the ship owner's risk accordingly. The maritime law applied by the Italian mercantile city states purportedly spread via Spain to France and further to the northern maritime areas, such as the Scandinavian countries and the Hansaetic towns.[11] Also, England embraced the common maritime law, referred to as (inter alia) the laws of Oléron.[12]

It seems thus that since post-Roman times, the carrier has not been liable in full for the shipper's loss of, or damage to, goods, although the degree of the carrier's liability may have changed over time. During the liberal era of the late nineteenth century, the carrier's liability reached its peak and the carrier was sometimes

(Gilmore and Black, *The Law of Admiralty* (1975) pp. 3–4). Thus, a "Rhodian Law" is sometimes claimed to have existed in 900 BC, although the proof therefore is rather vague (Gilmore and Black, *The Law of Admiralty* (1975) pp. 3–4). The "Justinian Digest", a compilation of Roman law by the order of emperor Justinian I from the sixth century, is sometimes referred to as the first European maritime law, although the proposition that the Romans applied a general system of maritime law is not undisputed (Gilmore and Black, *The Law of Admiralty* (1975) pp. 3–4).

6 R. Zimmermann, *The Law of Obligations* (1996) p. 515. It has been proposed that Roman law has had no particular impact on the modern maritime law (Cf. Hambro, *Den privata sjörätten* (1881) p. 2). However, some maritime particularities clearly have their roots in the Digest – for example the system of general average as well as the concept of bailment.

7 L. Gorton, *The Concept of the Common Carrier in Anglo-American Law* (1971) p. 61.

8 F. Schmidt *et al.*, *Huvudlinjer i svensk frakträtt* (1955) p. 11 and C.F. Hambro; *Den privata sjörätten* (1881) p. 2.

9 Whilst the first collection of maritime decisions is claimed to be the *Decisions of Trani* collected in 1063, in the thirteenth century, there seems to have been a rather settled maritime system, applied in the maritime Italian city-states (*Repubbliche marinare*). These maritime laws were purportedly first written down as the Amalfian code (late twelfth century), which however is not preserved (see however, T. Twiss (ed), *The Black Book of Admiralty* (1871) vol. 4, p. 3).

10 Cf. T. Twiss (ed), *The Black Book of Admiralty* (1871) vol. 4, p. 3.

11 During the twelfth century the Consolado del Mare was promulgated, presumably in Barcelona. In the north-western parts of Europe similar rules were applied, written down, presumably also during the twelfth century, e.g. as the Rôles d'Oléron and the Laws of Wisby (T. Twiss (ed.), *The Black Book of Admiralty* (1871) vol. 4, p. 265 and H. Flanders, *A Treatise on Maritime Law* (1852) p. 15 *ff.*). These rules have purportedly had a great impact on modern maritime law (C.F. Hambro; *Den privata sjörätten* (1881) p. 2 and Gilmore and Black; *The Law of Admiralty* (1975) p. 7).

12 It has been purported that the laws were not only brought to England by, but compiled at the order of, King Richard I (cf. T. Twiss (ed.), *The Black Book of Admiralty* (1873) vol. 2, p. li).

referred to as insurer of the goods.[13] However, although the liability was strict *per se*, in many parts of the world contractual liberty was virtually unrestricted and ship owners disclaimed any liability for damage to goods carried.[14] In this context, the first attempts were made to create an international regulation of the ship owners' liability.[15] The compromises between ship owner interests and shipper interests that were reached at this time eventually resulted in the so-called Hague Rules.[16] The compromise, although imposing liability for goods carried on the ship owners, limited the ship owner's liability both in monetary terms and through far-reaching exemptions. These limitations are still found in maritime regulations, with only slight alterations, and may seem difficult to justify in relation to the liability borne by other service providers in general.

The liability of ship owners has since been the model, or norm, when the liabilities of operators of other transport modes were laid down in international conventions during the twentieth century.[17] Thus, also in carriage by road, rail[18] and air, carriers enjoy a limited liability for damage to goods carried.[19]

2.2 The conventions relevant to the study

The need for international, or at least uniform, regulation of international trade has long been recognized. As discussed, since ancient times common, or similar, maritime rules seem to have been applied in large parts of Europe. Since the early

13 M. Sturley, "The History of the COGSA and the Hague Rules" (1991) 22 J Mar L & Com 1–57, at p. 5.

14 M. Sturley, "The History of the COGSA and the Hague Rules" (1991) 22 J Mar L & Com 1–57, at p. 5; S. Dor, *Bill of Lading Clauses & the International Convention of Brussels, 1924 (Hague Rules)* (1969) p. 13*ff.* The strict liability of carriers seems to have emanated from the law of bailment, i.e. the liability of those temporarily holding property for someone else, applied in English and German legal tradition and with roots in Roman law (L. Gorton, *The Concept of the Common Carrier in Anglo-American Law* (1971) p. 60 *ff.*).

15 The drafting of what eventually became the Hague Rules was initiated already in 1882 by the International Law Association, which adopted a model bill of lading which, although it never itself came to be widely applied, influenced the drafting of the Hague Rules (M. Sturley, "The History of the COGSA and the Hague Rules" (1991) 22 J Mar L & Com 1–57, at pp. 7–8).

16 International Convention for the Unification of Certain Rules of Law relating to Bills of Lading, drafted in Brussels in 1924.

17 M. Milde, "Liability in international carriage by air: the new Montreal Convention" (1999) 4 Unif L Rev 835 at p. 838.

18 The earliest European convention is actually the CIM, governing the rail carrier's liability from 1890. However, at the time the railways in Europe were predominately state owned and the carriers under an obligation to accept goods for carriage under tariffs settled by state authorities. The main concern of the drafters of the 1890 convention seems to have been the internal division of the liability between the state-owned railways due to the fact that a change of carrier was inevitable in international railway carriage. Further, the convention contains no general monetary limitation of liability. Thus, although some of the limitations of the actual liability are familiar, it differs quite substantially from the later conventions; cf. K. Grönfors, "Transport Law" in *International Uniform Law in Practice*, published by UNIDROIT (1988) pp. 393–394.

19 As will be accounted for in sections 2.5, 2.6 and 2.7 below, the liability as such of the carriers of other modes of transport differs somewhat. However, the main feature laid down in the Hague Rules imposing a rather strict liability on the carrier *per se*, with extensive monetary limitations, is reflected in the CMR convention, the Montreal Convention and the COTIF–CIM convention.

twentieth century the international regulation of transport of goods, by sea as well as by other modes, has been dominated by international conventions, at least as far as Europe is concerned. The legal context of the liability of carriers of goods is thus intergovernmental. The conventions in question, which will be accounted for below, are private law conventions, which are drafted formulating rules to be applied between private subjects, commonly referred to as uniform law.

2.2.1 The Hague–Visby Rules

Maritime transport is by its nature international and, as recounted above, it has historically been subject to transnational rules or customs. The carriers' liability was relatively strict, imposing on many occasions a strict liability.[20] During the twentieth century an increasing imbalance in power between carriers and shippers had developed, which had led carriers to waive almost all liability that would normally rest upon them.[21] Whilst such contractual exonerations were accepted in Europe and within the Commonwealth, they were disapproved by US courts as well as by Japanese legislation, thus undermining of the previous homogenous liability system.[22] Accordingly, the legal relationship between the shipper and the sea carrier became among the first to be considered urgent to regulate on an intergovernmental level.

In 1877, the first international maritime agreement, the so-called York–Antwerp Rules on general average, was drafted by the Association for the Reform and Codification of the Law of Nations (eventually International Law Association).[23] In 1882, the same association adopted a standard form for the carriage of goods (a bill of lading), which, despite the fact that it never gained recognition or impact as a standard document, would play an important role in relation to the convention that would eventually dominate the transport of goods by sea – the Hague Rules.

In 1893, the USA adopted national legislation regulating the maritime carrier's liability for goods carried, the so-called Harter Act. As non-American ship owners performed most transports to and from America at that time, the legislation aimed at protecting American shippers.[24] After Australia, New Zealand and Canada had adopted similar regulations it seemed likely, during the early 1920s, that many other maritime nations would follow their lead and adopt similar national legislation.[25] This may have been the reason that the international community took action and in 1921 the International Law Association drafted a standard document that eventually became the Hague Rules.[26] The regime is based primarily

20 M. Sturley, "The History of the COGSA and the Hague Rules" (1991) 22 JMLC 1–57, at p. 5.
21 M. Clarke, *Aspects of the Hague Rules* (1976) pp. 3–4.
22 M. Sturley, *ibid.* at pp. 5–6.
23 This document, agreed by the association's delegates from various states, never, in contrast to other documents prepared by the association, took the form of an international treaty, but has been very successful in its application.
24 M. Clarke, *Aspects of the Hague Rules* (1976) pp. 3–4.
25 M. Sturley, "The History of the COGSA and the Hague Rules" (1991) 22 JMLC 1–57, at pp. 15–16.
26 M. Sturley, *ibid.* at pp. 17–18.

on Canadian national legislation, which in turn bears many similarities to the text drafted by the Association for the Reform and Codification of the Law of Nations in 1882.

In 1922, the Hague Rules were discussed at the Comité Maritime International, CMI, Shipping Conference in London, and were then redrafted by the shipping industry to a form fit for adoption as legislation. In August 1924 the Hague Rules Convention was opened for signatories. In Great Britain, the Hague Rules were adopted as national legislation even before being opened for signatories. Other shipping nations were more hesitant, and it was not until the USA ratified the convention in 1937 that it gained general acceptance. Today, 75 nations are parties to the Hague Rules.[27] The Scandinavian states adapted their national legislation to the convention in the 1930s.[28]

In 1968 an attempt to adapt the Hague Rules to the new freight unit, the container, and to modify some weaknesses, such as the decrease of the monetary limitation caused by inflation, which had been revealed,[29] was made through the so-called Brussels Protocol.[30] Of the nations that ratified the Hague Rules, only 30 have acceded to the Brussels Protocol.[31] This entails that the two conventions exist parallel to each other and that some of the nations that have ratified the Brussels Protocol but not denounced the Hague Rules are still obliged to apply the older Hague Rules in relation to those states, such as the USA, that have not acceded to the amendment.[32] The Scandinavian states have all ratified the protocol and renounced the original convention.[33]

2.2.2 The Hamburg Rules

The Brussels Protocol thus never became universally accepted. Furthermore, eventually, many newly liberated ex-colonies regarded the Hague/ Hague–Visby Rules as overly protective of the shipping interests of the developed states.[34] Under the auspices of the United Nations, a new convention was drafted, the so-called Hamburg Rules,[35] which was adopted at a diplomatic conference in 1978. In the Hamburg Rules the carrier's liability was approached in a new way,

27 *CMI Yearbook 2015* p. 449 *ff.* It should be noted that another 14 nations have ratified the convention but eventually denounced it.

28 See Swedish *Travaux Préparatoires*, SOU 1972: 10 p. 29. It should be noted that in relation to the maritime codes, Iceland have not been part of the cooperation, but only Norway, Denmark, Finland and Sweden.

29 CMI, *The Travaux Préparatoires of the Hague Rules and of the Hague–Visby Rules* (1997) (Antwerp) p. 52*ff.*

30 Protocol to Amend the International Convention for the Unification of Certain Rules of Law relating to Bills of Lading, 1968, which was signed in Visby, hence the Hague–Visby Rules.

31 *CMI Yearbook 2015* pp. 455–456. It should be noted that some of the states that are parties to the Brussels Protocol of 1968 (the Visby Rules) have denounced the original convention.

32 M. Clarke, *Aspects of the Hague Rules* (1976) p. 107.

33 *CMI Yearbook 2015* p. 449 *ff.*

34 E. Selvig, *The Hamburg Rules, Marius no 31B* (1978) p. 11.

35 United Nations Convention on the Carriage of Goods by Sea (The Hamburg Rules) Hamburg, 30 March 1978.

through presumed liability for goods transported.[36] Further, many of the, even in 1978, outdated rules in the Hague/ Hague–Visby Rules were modernized. The Hamburg Rules entered into force in 1992 when 20 states had ratified the convention. However, the 34 states that are parties to the convention represent only approximately 4 per cent of the world's shipping activities, and among them none of the world's leading maritime nations are represented.[37] None of the Nordic states have ratified the Hamburg Rules, but have adapted their Maritime Codes to them, as far as permitted by international law considering the states' obligations in relation to the Hague–Visby Rules.[38]

2.2.3 The Rotterdam Rules

During its 29th session in 1996 the UN Committee on International Trade Law, UNCITRAL, observed that the existing legal regimes relating to international transport of goods by sea were unsatisfactory and ambiguous, primarily as regards division of liability between the carrier and the shipper. Further, since the moderinizations of the Hague Rules had not gained complete support and the rules applied in most nations thus appeared somewhat outdated, there was an apprehension that national or regional alternatives would submerge. UNCITRAL therefore requested the CMI to gather information regarding existing international customs in order to survey the desirability of a new international legal regime.[39] The CMI concluded its work on a draft international convention for the carriage of goods by sea in 2001, which was presented to UNCITRAL.[40]

Beginning at the 2002 spring meeting of UNCITRAL Working Group III, the draft convention was considered at two fortnightly sessions annually (in Vienna and New York respectively) for six years (in total 25 weeks of work) until a draft convention could be submitted to the UNCITRAL Commission in 2008.[41] The convention was adopted by the UN General Assembly in December 2008 under the title of the "United Nations Convention on Contracts for the International Carriage of Goods Wholly or Partly by Sea".[42] In September 2009, the convention was opened for signatures during an official signing ceremony in Rotterdam.[43]

According to its drafters, the Rotterdam Rules seeks to pragmatically regulate questions of liability that are intimately connected with international transport of

36 E. Selvig, *ibid.* p. 21.

37 World Shipping Council (www.worldshipping.org/industry-issues/cargo-liability/background (accessed on 15 March 2017) and UNCITRAL (www.uncitral.org/uncitral/en/uncitral_texts/transport_goods/Hamburg_status.html) (accessed on 15 March 2017).

38 K. Grönfors, "Styckegodstransport enligt nya sjölagen" (1995) SvJT 323, at p. 325, H. Tiberg and J. Schelin, *On Maritime and Transport Law* (2016) p. 135. Cf. Swedish Maritime Code of 1994, SFS (1994:1009), ch. 13.

39 A. Diamond, "The Rotterdam Rules" (2009) 4 LMCLQ 445–536, at p. 446.

40 *CMI Yearbook 2009* p. 253.

41 A. Diamond, "The Rotterdam Rules" in (2009) 4 LMCLQ 445–536, at p. 447.

42 The General Assembly recommended that the convention should be referred to as "the Rotterdam Rules", which is the title that will be used throughout this work.

43 *CMI Yearbook 2009* p. 254.

goods by sea. In relation to the Hague Rules, which today is the most widespread liability regime, many of the attempts to modernize that convention that were undertaken through adoption of the Brussels Protocol[44] and the Hamburg Rules, have been incorporated in the Rotterdam Rules. In addition, the rules of the new convention have been adapted to the twenty-first century, e.g. through the introduction of electronic transport documents.[45]

2.2.4 The CMR convention

The break-through in international road transport came after the Second World War. At the initiative of the UN organ UNIDROIT (International Institution for the Unification of Private Law) negotiations were initiated with the aim of creating unity on legal issues relating to transport of goods by road. The negotiations were held within the UN European Economic Commission (ECE) and the resulting convention therefore came to be adopted mainly by European states. The convention is, however, open to all states, and in addition to the 38 European states that have ratified the convention, 15 near east and north African states have acceded to it.

The CMR convention was adopted in 1956 and, although the road transport has developed considerably since, no major revisions of the convention has taken place. In 1972 an attempt was made to revise the convention, albeit without success.[46] The convention is nevertheless applied throughout the member states without being held as out-of-date.[47] The CMR convention was enacted as Swedish legislation in 1969[48] and the terms thereof have been copied into legislation governing domestic road transport as well.[49]

2.2.5 The COTIF–CIM convention

In the mid-nineteenth century an increasing number of railways were built for engine-powered trains (horse-powered trains have existed since ancient times)

44 The Protocol to Amend the International Convention for the Unification of Certain Rules of Law Relating to Bills of Lading adopted in 1968. The Hague Rules as amended by the Brussels Protocol are generally referred to as the Hague–Visby Rules.

45 Among the modern features reflected in the Rotterdam Rules are containerization of sea freight, radical improvements in communication between the ship and its owner and modern navigational equipment. Among the changes in relation to the Hague–Visby Rules is the elimination of the navigational fault liability exemption. Another special feature of the Rotterdam Rules is extension of the period of applicability from tackle-to-tackle (Hague–Visby Rules) and port-to-port (Hamburg Rules) to door-to-door, which means that the Rotterdam Rules cover the transport from the agreed place of loading to the place of delivery even if the transport includes transport by modes other than by sea. The Rotterdam Rules has thus been called a "maritime plus" convention.

46 In 1978 a protocol substituting the gold franc for the special drawing right as the currency for calculating the carrier's limitation of liability was agreed (K.F. Haak, *The Liability of the Carrier under the CMR* (1986) p. 10.

47 As discussed below, the CMR convention served as model for the revision of the COTIF–CIM convention in 1999, which serves to prove its vitality.

48 SFS (1969:12).

49 SFS (1974:610).

and in 1890 a convention for the unification of the regulation relating to transport of goods by railway was adopted in Bern.[50] The convention was revised several times, but in 1980 an entirely new convention, the Convention Concerning International Carriage by Rail of 9 May 1980, COTIF, was adopted.[51] Through the convention the intergovernmental organization COTIF was created and the actual uniform law is contained in appendixes; CIM concerning transport of goods, CIV concerning transport of passengers. The COTIF convention is acceded to by over 40 states of which the majority are European, north African and near eastern.[52] However, at the time that the 1980 convention entered into force in 1985, a comprehensive change from state-owned railway companies to privately owned operators had appeared in the market and many of the provisions in the 1980 convention were already becoming obsolete.[53] Thus, in 1999 a protocol was adopted where this change is reflected.[54] The drafting of the 1999 COTIF–CIM was largely influenced by the CMR convention especially as regards the liability of the carrier.

The regulation of international carriage by rail has, since the first convention in 1890, undergone a change from an agreement on the internal division of liability between different national (state-owned) operators to a system of division of liability between the carrier and the cargo owner.

2.2.6 The Montreal Convention

The Montreal Convention, which regulates the liability of the carrier for carriage of goods as well as passengers and their luggage by air, was adopted at a diplomatic conference in 1999. It was drafted to replace the Warsaw Convention, which had been regulating the liability of air carriers since 1929. The Warsaw Convention had been adopted at a very early stage, years before air carriage had become a common way of transportation and had played a very important role in the unification of not just liability, but of practical matters relating to air carriage such as passenger tickets and air way bills. The Warsaw Convention was amended several times and eventually the air carrier liability system constituted a somewhat complicated net of conventions and protocols.[55]

Accordingly, a new convention was drafted, beginning in 1995, resulting in the 1999 Montreal Convention. The convention, which entered into force in 2003,

50 Convention Internationale sur le Transport de Merchandises par Chemins de Fer, 14 October 1890.

51 SOU 2014:26 p. 43.

52 The COTIF Convention was enacted as Swedish legislation in 1985 (SFS 1985:193).

53 SOU 2014:26 p. 44. The deregulation of railway transport was in fact triggered by a ruling by the European Court of Justice in 1985 (C 13/83, 22 May 1985) and the subsequent Council Directive 91/440/EEC: see the Consolidated Explanatory Report, OTIF General Assembly AG 12/13 Add. 5 30.09.2015.

54 The 1999 protocol entered into force in 2006. In Sweden it was enacted in 20015 (SFS 2015:338).

55 For a comprehensive account of the drafting history of the Montreal Convention, see M. Milde, "Liability in international carriage by air: the new Montreal Convention" (1999) 4 Unif L Rev 835.

was adapted for electronic data transfer, which today has resulted in e-tickets and electronic air waybills.[56] There are 104 state parties to the convention and it is thus by far the most global liability system in the international carriage of goods.

2.3 The sea carrier's liability under current regimes

Carriage of goods by sea is categorized into carriage under charter parties and carriage under transport documents, such as bills of lading. The former is usually claimed to be "ship-focused" in that it is the vessel that is the subject of the transport agreement, whilst the latter is focused on the goods to be carried.[57] Carriage of goods under charter parties will not be dealt with, one of the reasons being that it seems unlikely that goods carried under a charter party are subject to multimodal transport, unless a bill of lading is issued under the charter party, in which case the following liability rules are applicable in any case.[58]

2.3.1 The Hague–Visby Rules

The Hague–Visby Rules applies to contracts for the carriage of goods by sea in so far as the contract prescribes the issuing of a bill of lading as a transport document for the carriage.[59] Thus, the rules are not applicable where the use of a non-negotiable transport document, such as a sea waybill, is anticipated.[60] The rules do not apply to the carriage of live animals or to carriage of goods on deck, where such carriage is contractually agreed.[61] The liability of the sea carrier for the goods carried appears implicitly in the rules, in so far that there is no explicit statement regarding the carrier's liability for the state of the cargo.[62] The rules, however, subject the carrier to a duty to properly and carefully care for the goods.[63] The liability of the carrier is shaped by the limitations of liability

56 M. Milde, "Liability in international carriage by air: the new Montreal Convention" (1999) 4 Unif L Rev 835 at p. 851, although Milde at that time noted that entirely "ticket-less" travel would unlikely be widely used.

57 S. Johansson, *An outline of transport law* (2014) p. 52, H. Tiberg and J. Schelin, *On Maritime and Transport Law* (2016) pp. 135–136.

58 Hague–Visby Rules article I (b).

59 In this section the liability rules of the Hague–Visby Rules are discussed. For a discussion on the relationship between the contract of carriage and the transport document as well as a thorough analysis of the *applicability* of the Hague–Visby Rules cf. section 4.5, in particular subsection 4.5.1, below.

60 G. Treitel and F. Reynolds, *Carver on Bills of Lading* (2011) p. 635, E. Selvig, *The Hamburg Rules, Marius no 31B* (1978) p. 2. For a seemingly diverging opinion, cf. F. Smeele, *Passieve legitimatie uit cognossement* (1998) p. 92.

61 Article I(c).

62 Whilst e.g. the CMR convention states that "The carrier shall be liable for the total or partial loss of the goods and for damage thereto", the Hague–Visby Rules obliges the carrier to take care of the goods, but then merely states when the carrier is not liable. Even if the result is similar, the technique is different.

63 Article III.2 of Hague–Visby Rules states that "Subject to the provisions of Article IV, the carrier shall properly and carefully load, handle, stow, carry, keep, care for, and discharge the goods carried."

available and thus the material content thereof, in relation to the cargo, appears *e contrario* to article IV.2, which reads: "Neither the carrier nor the ship shall be responsible for loss or damage arising or resulting from…", indicating that where none of the exemptions from liability is applicable, the carrier is in fact liable for loss and damage.

"Carriage of goods" is defined as the period during which the goods are present on the vessel including the loading thereon and discharge therefrom.[64] The liability thus covers the entire loading and discharge operations, but not pre- or post-storage.[65] It may be discussed whether this provision indicates that the carrier is also under an obligation to load and discharge the goods, which would appear to be supported by the language of article III.2 ("the carrier shall properly and carefully load […] and discharge the goods carried"), or whether the carrier is under such an obligation only when these duties follow from the contract of carriage.[66] It seems that the latter interpretation would fit better with the contractual scope of the convention.[67]

The safety of the cargo is to a large degree dependent on the condition of the vehicle, i.e. the vessel. Accordingly, the liability of the sea carrier under the Hague–Visby Rules is based on a duty imposed on the carrier in relation to the vessel obliging the carrier to exercise due diligence in making sure that the vessel is seaworthy.[68] Failing to do so results in the carrier's disability to invoke the exemptions from liability provided in article IV.2. The seaworthiness requirement relates to the condition of the vessel at the initiation of the

64 Article I(e) reads: "'Carriage of goods' covers the period from the time when the goods are loaded on to the time they are discharged from the ship." The common suggestion that the Hague–Visby Rules are applicable "tackle-to-tackle", i.e. from the time the goods are attached to the ship's tackle until they are detached during unloading, emanates from earlier drafts of the Hague Rules. It is, in fact, that earlier version that was adopted in England as national law, which may explain the longevity of the expression, see e.g. Swedish Supreme court NJA 2016 s. 149, at p. 6 and F. Sejersted, *Haagreglerne* (1976) p. 40. See also O. Bokareva, *Multimodal Transportation under the Rotterdam Rules* (2015) p. 62. In relation to English law this entails an extension in relation to the common law rule, which provides that the shipper is liable for the goods during lifting, and that the liability shifts to the carrier when the goods crosses the ship's rail (G. Treitel and F. Reynolds, *Carver on Bills of Lading* (2011) p. 657). The Scandinavian countries, on the other hand, have extended the period of liability of the sea carrier to include the time during which the goods are in the custody of the carrier in the port of loading and the port of discharge; see SMC 13:24 (cf. section 5.2.1 below regarding the exhaustiveness of uniform law).

65 R. Aikens *et al.*, *Bills of Lading* (2016) p. 313 and F. Sejersted, *Haagreglerne* (1976) p. 41; a conclusion that is supported by the wording of article III.2. However, nothing prevents the carrier from being liable on other grounds, should his undertakings in relation to the goods extend beyond the carriage as such.

66 G. Treitel and F. Reynolds, *Carver on Bills of Lading* (2011) p. 657.

67 Although the convention applies to carriage by sea, which is defined as the period between loading and discharge, it is the contract of carriage that is the actual subject of the rules. Despite the fact that article III.2 seems to require the carrier to perform these operations, where the contract of carriage in fact has a more limited scope than the rules, the applicability of the rules would seem to be delimited by the contract. Article I(e) could in fact be read as to entail that unless the bill of lading covers loading and discharge operations, the bill of lading does not relate to carriage by sea and the contract is disqualified under the rules, although this would seem to be an incorrect application of the rules.

68 Article IV.1.

voyage.[69] Unseaworthiness that is not initial and occurs during the voyage does not preclude exoneration from liability, as also does not initial unseaworthiness that was not caused by the carrier's want of due diligence.

Albeit the legal basis for the liability of the carrier under the Hague–Visby Rules is not explicitly stated, the system of liability is often considered to be fault-based.[70] The rules impose on the carrier several duties that are to be performed prudently; the goods are to be handled (etc.) carefully and properly, the carrier must exercise due diligence in making the ship seaworthy etc. The liability is accordingly related to a prudent behaviour, i.e. liability for negligence. However, because the liability is formulated in terms of an exemption for the non-negligence of the carrier, including servants etc., the liability could just as well be considered presumed.[71]

In relation to possible damage to the cargo, the carrier may excuse himself from liability where the cause of the damage is one of the causes enumerated in article IV.2. The clause includes traditional exonerations relating to force majeure as well as causes that involve the shipper rather than the carrier, such as insufficient packing and inherent vice of the goods.[72] Further, more particular to the element on which the transport is carried out, the carrier is not liable for damage caused by an attempt to save life or property at sea. Of a more far-reaching kind is the exemption for navigational error; the carrier is not liable for damage caused by negligent navigation or management of the ship performed by the master or the carrier's servants.[73] Hence, the exemption does not apply to faults or negligent actions performed by the carrier himself. However, where the carrier is also the master, it seems that he may avail himself of the exemption in relation to

69 Whether or not there must be causation between damage and unseaworthiness has been subject to different interpretation, but it seems clear that the rules are to be construed to mean that there must be causation between damage and unseaworthiness (N.J. Margetson, *The system of liability* (2008) p. 67*ff*.; G. Treitel and F. Reynolds, *Carver on Bills of Lading* (2011) pp. 669–670).

70 D.R. Thomas, "An appraisal of the liability regime established under the new UN Convention" (2008) 14 JIML 496. See however Treitel and Reynolds who do not find the legal basis of liability to be obvious (G. Treitel and F. Reynolds, *Carver on Bills of Lading* (2011) pp. 978–979). See further below.

71 The Hamburg Rules, which is said to be a presumed liability system, provides that:

> The carrier is liable for loss resulting from loss of or damage to the goods, as well as from delay in delivery, if the occurrence which caused the loss, damage or delay took place while the goods were in his charge as defined in Article 4, unless the carrier proves that he, his servants or agents took all measures that could reasonably be required to avoid the occurrence and its consequences.
>
> (article 5.1)

Even if presumed liability, which is defined as liability for negligence with a reversed burden of proof, is really a version of fault-based liability, it is often seen as a step between strict liability and fault-based liability (P. Bäckdén, "The Land Carrier's Liability – strict with exemptions or presumed?" (2011) 5 ETL 503–511, at p. 506.

72 See the statement of the Norwegian law commission (NOU 1972:11 p. 14 – in English translation in T. Falkanger *et al.*, *Scandinavian Maritime Law* (2008) pp. 277–278 (the citation is omitted in later editions)) to the effect that the exemptions from liability found in letters c–p are superfluous as they are merely examples (and as such unsystematic and incomplete) of what in fact follows from the culpa rule found in letter q.

73 Article VI.2.

actions undertaken in his capacity of master.[74] Further, in relation to this so-called nautical fault, it is important to note that it is only errors and omissions related to the management of the ship, as opposed to the management of the cargo, that free the carrier from liability. Errors and omissions related to the management of the ship are not seldom difficult to distinguish from cargo management.[75] The classic example is that lashing of the cargo is done both to protect the cargo from damage but also as shifting cargo may compromise the safety of the ship.[76]

The carrier is further exonerated from liability due to fire onboard the ship. However, this exemption contains an exemption of its own; if the fire is caused by the "actual fault or privity" of the carrier, the exemption may not be invoked. It should be noted that in relation to the fire exemption, no identification is made between the carrier and the master or any of the carrier's employees.[77] Thus it is only fire caused by the carrier in person that prevents exemption from liability.[78] However, as mentioned, should the cause of the damage be related to the lack of due diligence in relation to the making the ship seaworthy, the carrier may not invoke any exoneration.

There is no general statement in the convention to the effect that the carrier is liable for his agents and servants. As with many other provisions, the general rule must be deduced from its exemptions. Thus, under article IV.2(q) the carrier is not liable for any cause of damage or loss to the cargo that is not caused by the fault or neglect of his agents or servants. Hence, where an agent or servant has caused damage or loss through his fault or neglect, the carrier is *e contrario* liable for such damage.[79] In cases of gross negligence[80] the carrier may not avail himself of any exemptions from or limitation of liability.

74 T. Falkanger *et al.*, *Sjørett* (2016) p. 291.

75 G. Treitel and F. Reynolds, *Carver on Bills of Lading* (2011) p. 706*ff.*

76 See e.g. the Danish case FED 2000.3023 SH (Vindmølletransporterne) dealing with the carriage of wind turbines. See also T. Falkanger *et al.*, *Sjørett* (2016) p. 291*ff.* and S. Johansson, *An Outline of Transport Law* (2014) p. 88.

77 As mentioned, under the nautical fault exemption, the carrier as such is not enumerated among those whose negligence frees the carrier from liability, thus where damage is caused by the carrier (and not in a capacity of master or servant), the exemption is not invokable. The most prominent difference would seem to lie in the placement of the burden of proof; under the nautical fault exemption the carrier will have to show that his employees have acted negligently, whilst under the fire exemption the claimant will have to show that the fire was caused by the management. For a brief discussion on identification, see S. Johansson, *An Outline of Transport Law* (2014) p. 119 *ff.*

78 Obviously, where the owner is a company some form of identification must be made. It has been held that it is only the immediate circle of decision makers, such as the board ("the directing mind and will" of the carrier), that constitutes "the carrier" in such a case (N.J. Margetson, *The system of liability* (2008) p. 119*ff.*), although as regards large corporations the circle seems to have been extended somewhat to include e.g. a traffic manager (G. Treitel and F. Reynolds, *Carver on Bills of Lading* (2011) p. 709).

79 Hence, the claim that the Hague–Visby Rules is a fault-based regime, which has been asserted as something different from the presumed fault regime of the Hamburg Rules, can be questioned. Considering the evidential value of the B/L as regards the condition of the goods and that damage not caused by the carrier's negligence is formulated as an exemption from liability, with the burden of proof resting on the carrier, it seems that the Hague–Visby Rules also presumes the carrier to be liable for damage occurring.

80 Article IVbis.4: "an act or omission of the servant or agent done with the intent to cause damage or recklessly and with knowledge that damage would probably result".

The compensation payable by the carrier is the value of the goods at the port of discharge and is limited to 666.67 SDR per package or 2 SDR per kilo of gross weight of the goods lost or damaged, whichever is the higher.[81] In relation to the so-called global limitation, available to ship owners under the 1976 LLMC Convention,[82] article VIII allows for the application of such limitation, limiting the total amount payable in relation to one incident, where available.

2.3.2 The Scandinavian maritime codes

The Scandinavian countries,[83] which, in this case include Denmark, Finland, Norway and Sweden, have virtually identical maritime codes as regards the carrier's liability for goods carried.[84] These four countries are all parties to the Hague–Visby Rules and thus their maritime codes reflect that convention. However, without having acceded to the Hamburg Rules, the Scandinavian countries have adapted their maritime codes thereto as far as possible considering their obligations in relation to the Hague–Visby Rules. Accordingly, the Scandinavian maritime codes apply to contracts of carriage of goods by sea, without the issuing of a bill of lading being a prerequisite.[85] Further, the liability of the carrier is extended beyond actual carriage (tackle-to-tackle) and includes the period during which the carrier has the goods in his care in the port of loading and the port of discharge (port-to-port).[86] In correspondence with the Hague–Visby Rules, the carrier is liable for loss of or damage to the goods caused by his own negligence or willful conduct as well as for such actions by anyone acting in the service of the ship. The contracting carrier is liable for any subcarriers to whom the carriage is assigned in part or in full. The burden of proof is reversed and hence the carrier is presumed liable unless he disproves negligence. In addition to loss or damage, the carrier is liable for damage caused by delay in delivery of the goods.

Limitation of the carrier's liability includes nautical fault (including errors in the management of the ship) as well as the fire exception. Even though the exemptions from liability correspond to those in the Hague–Visby Rules, the

81 The limitation of the compensation payable, should the ship owner be liable for damage *per se*, is often referred to as "limitation of liability" although, as has been noted, it is not a question of limitation of the actual liability, but a quantitative limitation of the payable amount (O. Bokareva, *Multimodal Transportation under the Rotterdam Rules* (2015) p. 139).

82 The Convention on Limitation of Liability for Maritime Claims (LLMC), adopted on 19 November 1976.

83 Whilst the Nordic countries include Denmark (including Greenland and Faro Islands), Finland (including Åland), Iceland, Norway and Sweden, "Scandinavia" is a geographical term for Denmark, Norway and Sweden.

84 P. Vestergaard Pedersen; *Transportrett* (2008) p. 453.

85 Recently, the Swedish Maritime Code was altered to conform to the Regulation (EC) No 593/2008 of the European Parliament and of the Council of 17 June 2008 on the law applicable to contractual obligations (Rome I); see Prop. 2013/14:243. These changes relate to the applicability of the code that exceeded the applicability provided for in the Hague–Visby Rules.

86 Sweden/Finland ch. 13 §24, Norway/Denmark §274. In a recent judgment from the Swedish Supreme Court the fact that the applicability of the code, in terms of the period during which the carrier is liable, is based on the Hamburg Rules rather than the Hague–Visby Rules were brought to its head in relation to interpretation of the rules in question (NJA 2016 s. 149).

exemptions, such as force majeure, damage caused by the shipper etc. are not enumerated, but follows from general *culpa* liability.[87] The carrier's liability extends to goods carried on deck, as long as such carriage is contractually agreed.[88] Whilst the carriage of live animals is not exempted from the code (cf. Hague–Visby Rules article I(c)), the carrier is not liable for any damage "dependent on the particular risks inherent in such carriage".[89] Where damage is caused by insufficient care in making sure that the ship is seaworthy before the initiation of the voyage, the carrier may not claim exemption from liability. The monetary limitations correspond to the Hague–Visby Rules. In cases of gross negligence, the carrier may not avail himself of any exemptions from or limitation of liability.[90]

2.4 The sea carrier's liability under the Rotterdam Rules

Although both the Hague–Visby Rules and the Rotterdam Rules apply to maritime transports, there are considerable differences between the two conventions. The Rotterdam Rules apply to contracts of carriage, where the place of receipt of the goods by the carrier and the place of delivery are in different states, of which at least one is a contracting state.[91] A contract of carriage regards the carriage of goods from one place to another against the payment of freight.[92] Further, a contract of carriage must include carriage by sea in order to qualify as a contract of carriage under the Rotterdam Rules, but it may also include carriage by other modes of transport in addition to the sea carriage.[93] In such a case, it is not enough that the carriage as a whole is international, but the sea carriage leg must also be international.[94] There is no requirement for its application that any certain kind of transport document must be issued.

87 The carrier is liable for damage resulting from the goods being lost or damaged whilst in its custody ... unless he proves that neither his fault or neglect nor the fault or neglect of any one for who he is responsible has caused or contributed to the damage (Sw/Fi: ch. 13 §25, No/Dk: §275) (translation by H. Tiberg and J. Schelin, *The Swedish Maritime Code* (2015) p. 129).

88 According to ch. 13 § 13/ § 263, "Goods may be carried on deck only if it is allowed by the contract of carriage, follows from any custom or usage of the trade in question or is required by any law or statutory provision." Where goods are carried on deck in breach of this provision, the carrier is liable without exemptions where the damage or loss is solely caused by the carriage on deck. If goods are carried on deck in breach of an explicit agreement to carry under deck, the carrier may not invoke any limitation of liability (Sw/Fi: ch. 13 §34, No/Dk: § 284).

89 Sw/Fi: ch. 13 §27, No/Dk: § 277.

90 The prerequisite corresponds to the Hague–Visby Rules: "The right of limitation is not available for a person proved to have caused the damage or loss intentionally or by gross negligence and with knowledge that such damage or loss would probably arise" (Sw: ch. 13 §33, No/Dk: § 283) (translation by H. Tiberg and J. Schelin, *The Swedish Maritime Code* (2015) p. 133).

91 Article 5. However, the applicability convention does not depend on the nationality of the parties, the vessel etc.

92 The convention is not applicable to charter parties or other contracts "for the use of a vessel or space thereon" (cf. article 6).

93 Article 1.

94 The following prerequisites for applicability can be extracted: (1) there must be a contract; (2) in which the carrier undertakes to carry goods; (3) the carriage must be for reward; (4) the carriage must be international; (5) the place of taking over, the place of delivery, the port of loading or the port

As the Rotterdam Rules may apply to a non-maritime carrier, the parties that are caught by the liability provisions of the rules on the carrier side can be placed in one of three groups: contracting carriers (including land and air carriers); "maritime performing parties" and "non-maritime performing parties".[95] Whilst the non-maritime performing party has no independent liability under the convention, the liability of the maritime performing party equals the liability of the carrier as such.[96] However, the carrier is liable for the entire carriage as contracted for, whilst the maritime performing party is only liable for loss or damage that occurs during its period of responsibility.[97] The carrier, and thus a maritime performing party, is liable for any acts or omissions by sub-contractors, the master and crew of the ship as well as any of its employees.[98]

The liability of the carrier under the Rotterdam Rules has been described as a qualified presumed fault regime.[99] On the whole, the liability regime of the convention is a somewhat complicated scheme for allocating the burden of proof. The primary burden of proof falls upon the claimant who must prove that the loss or damage occurred during the carrier's period of responsibility, subject to which the carrier is presumed liable for such loss or damage.[100] This presumed liability may be rebutted by the carrier by proving that the cause of the damage is not attributable to his, or any person's for whom he is responsible, fault. The carrier may also be exempted from liability if he shows that the damage was caused by one of the events enumerated in article 17.3, which includes force majeure events, acts and omissions on the part of the shipper, insufficient packing, an attempt to save life at sea as well as fire on the ship. Notable in this respect is that the nautical fault exemption has been discarded. Whilst the carrier, when relying on the general exemption in section 2, i.e. proves absence of fault, is conclusively freed of liability, the exemption in section 3 operates rather more complicatedly. Thus, where the carrier relies on one of the exemptions in article 17.3, he is only prima facie relieved from liability. Accordingly, the burden of proof shifts to the claimant who may still prove either (1) that the loss or damage was in fact caused by the carrier's neglect or (2) that the loss or damage was caused by the

of discharge must be in a contracting state; (6) the contract must stipulate carriage by sea; and (7) the sea carriage must in itself be international as must the entire carriage.

95 Carriers include only contracting carriers whilst subcarriers can be either maritime or non-maritime performing parties depending on the mode of transport operated. Performing parties further include sub-contracted parties performing loading, unloading, handling, stowage, care etc. of the goods; see article 1 paras 5–7.

96 Article 19.

97 Thus, it is the contracting carrier that bears the liability for any unlocalized damage; see M. Sturley *et al.*, *The Rotterdam Rules* (2010) p. 142.

98 Article 18.

99 D.R. Thomas, "An appraisal of the liability regime established under the new UN Convention" (2008) 14 JIML 496. Lorenzon, on the other hand, labels the liability regime under the Rotterdam Rules as "a fault-based regime with a reversed burden of proof" (F. Lorenzon, "Liability of the Carrier for Loss, Damage or Delay" in Y. Baatz *et al.*, *The Rotterdam Rules a practical annotation* (2009) p. 49.

100 The period of liability extends from the time that the carrier receives the goods for carriage until the goods are delivered according to article 12.

unseaworthiness of the vessel. In the latter case the carrier may still disprove unseaworthiness.[101]

Last, but not least, the claimant may hold the carrier liable for loss or damage under the carrier's obligation to provide a seaworthy vessel.[102] In relation to the Hague–Visby Rules, the carrier's duty to furnish a seaworthy ship has been fundamentally altered. In accordance with the current Hague–Visby Regime, the duty is a duty to exercise due diligence to make the ship seaworthy. However, under the Rotterdam Rules, the duty, still a duty to exercise due diligence, has been extended in time so that it is a continuous obligation including the voyage by sea.[103] As under the Hague–Visby Rules, the seaworthiness obligation is relative; the vessel must be in a physical condition to meet the perils that may be expected on the particular voyage; bunkers must be sufficient for the particular voyage and the vessel must be properly equipped for the particular voyage and so on.[104] However, the carrier is responsible also for unseaworthiness that occurs during the voyage.

The seaworthiness obligation is further developed in paragraphs (b) and (c) of article 14, which, in addition to the obligation to provide a seaworthy ship, obliges the carrier to properly crew, equip and supply the ship and to make and keep the holds fit for the carriage of goods.[105] Notably, any containers supplied by the carrier are included in the cargoworthiness obligation under paragraph c). The provisions in article 14 mirror the Hague–Visby Rules, with the additions mentioned, so that current case law can be preserved.[106] As regards novelties, the addition of containers to the cargoworthiness provision should not cause problems in practice whereas the continuous obligation in respect of the ship's seaworthiness will have to be explored by the courts particularly as regards the point in time where the carrier's obligation ends. It has been claimed that the seaworthiness obligation under the Rotterdam Rules will include discharge of the cargo in the port of unloading and presumably end there.[107]

Whilst the carriage on deck is entirely excluded from the scope of applicability of the Hague–Visby Rules, thus entitling the carrier to exclude any and all

101 Article 17.4. The provision is indeed complicated and rather makes the "English nightmare" of article 2 of the CMR convention seem like a day-dream. For a very pedagogical account of article 17.4, see J. Clarke and J. Thomson, "Exclusions of Liability" in R. Thomas (ed.), *The Carriage of Goods by Sea Under the Rotterdam Rules* (2010), pp. 141–162, at pp. 144–145.

102 Article 17.5.

103 Article 14: the carrier is bound before, at the beginning of, *and during* the voyage by sea to exercise due diligence to: (a) Make *and keep* the ship seaworthy … (emphasis added).

104 T. Nikaki, "The Obligations of the Carrier to Provide Seawothy Ships and Exercise Care" in R. Thomas (ed.), *A New Convention for the Carriage of Goods by Sea – The Rotterdam Rules*, pp. 89–110, at pp. 102–103.

105 Paragraphs (b) and (c) do not technically define the seaworthiness, but it contains obligations that under the Hague–Visby Rules are encompassed by the seaworthiness (and what is sometimes referred to as cargoworthiness).

106 M. Sturley *et al.*, *The Rotterdam Rules* (2010) p. 83. See also T. Nikaki, "The Obligations of the Carrier to Provide Seawothy Ships and Exercise Care" in R. Thomas (ed.), *A New Convention for the Carriage of Goods by Sea – The Rotterdam Rules* (2009) pp. 89–110, at p. 103.

107 T. Nikaki, *ibid.*, at p. 107.

liability, carriage on deck has been fundamentally changed by containerization. The change of practice has been reflected in the Rotterdam Rules and the carriage of cargo on deck is subject to the convention *per se*. According to article 25.1 such carriage is permitted on three occasions:

> if: (a) Such carriage is required by law; (b) They are carried in or on containers or vehicles that are fit for deck carriage, and the decks are specially fitted to carry such containers or vehicles; or (c) The carriage on deck is in accordance with the contract of carriage, or the customs, usages or practices of the trade in question.

In these situations, the carrier is thus liable for loss or damage with the exception for loss or damage that occurs as a consequence of the special risks related to carriage on deck.[108] On the other hand, if goods are carried on deck in other circumstances than those enumerated, the carrier may neither invoke that the damage is caused by the special risks related to deck cargo, nor any defences provided by article 17, as described above. If the goods are carried on deck in breach of an express agreement to carry under deck, the carrier even loses the right to limitation of liability.

In concurrence with previous regulations, limitation of liability is available to the carrier. The limitation, in case of damage to, or loss of, the goods, is set at 875 SDR[109] per package or shipping unit/ 3 SDR per kilo.[110] Should the value of the goods have been declared in the contract of carriage, the limitation does not apply and likewise if the parties have expressly agreed upon a higher limitation. If the goods are consolidated, that unit counts as a shipping unit unless the number of (smaller) packages is stated in the contract particulars.[111]

In case of delay the same limitation applies, except in cases of pure economic loss where the limitation is set at 2.5 times the freight payable.[112] As mentioned above, the right to limitation is not available where the goods have been carried on deck against an express agreement for under-deck carriage.[113] The right of limitation is also denied a carrier who personally caused the damage intentionally or recklessly and with the knowledge that such damage would probably result.[114]

2.5 The road carrier's liability under the CMR convention

As mentioned above, the applicability of the CMR convention to road transport is based on there being a contract between the shipper and the carrier for the

108 Article 25.2.

109 Special Drawing Rights, article 59.3.

110 Article 59.1.

111 Article 59.2.

112 Article 60. According to the article, loss or damage to the goods caused by delay, is to be compensated under the general rule in article 22. However, it is not entirely clear from the wording of article 60 that in cases other than when delay causes consequential losses, the limitation of liability is subject to article 59, although this is clearly the intention of the drafters (M. Tsimplis, "Limits of Liability" in Y. Baatz *et al.*, *The Rotterdam Rules a practical annotation* (2009) pp. 181–194, at p. 188.

113 Article 25.5.

114 Article 61.

carriage of goods by road.[115] The liability of the carrier under the CMR convention has been described as strict with an exemption for force majeure.[116] However, I am inclined to join the authors challenging this assertion and describe the liability as based on presumed negligence.[117] The carrier is liable for any loss of, or damage to, the goods whilst in his custody[118] unless the carrier can show that the loss or damage was caused by an event beyond his control.[119] This presumed liability may be rebutted by the carrier, who then bears the burden of proving that the damage was caused by one of the events enumerated in article 17.2.[120] In addition, the carrier may be relieved of liability if the damage was caused by any of the special risks listed in article 17.4, such as the use of unsheeted

115 With the additional prerequisite that the carriage is performed by a vehicle and that the service is performed against a reward.

116 S. Johansson, *An Outline of Transport Law* (2014) pp. 88–89.

117 R. de Wit, *Multimodal Transport* (1995) p. 96. Clarke describes the liability of the carrier as "less than absolutely strict but greater than that of an ordinary duty of reasonable care." (M. Clarke, *International carriage of goods: CMR* (2014) p. 183). Although from the view of the liable party they may homogenous, strict liability and presumed liability are in fact two heterogeneous legal concepts. Whilst strict liability acts as a risk-placing instrument, the presumption of liability is a procedural rule distributing the burden of proof. Presumed liability may be severe and the possibilities of the defendant to rebut the presumption are limited. It may on the other hand be less severe and only prevent the defendant from exonerating himself in cases of wilful misconduct. Thus, presumed liability is not a measure of the severity of liability. Strict liability in its purest form is, as the name indicates, liability without regard to the circumstances leading up to the damage; the defendant is liable even if there is no fault on his part. Any contributory action on the part of the claimant can be considered in the award of damages (which may be set to zero) without affecting the liability of the defendant as such. For an exploration of the subject in relation to land carriage, see P. Bäckdén, "The Carrier's Liability – Strict with exemptions or presumed?" (2011) XLVI (5) ETL 509.

118 Article 17.1: "The carrier shall be liable for the total or partial loss of the goods and for damage thereto occurring between the time when he takes over the goods and the time of delivery, as well as for any delay in delivery." The carrier's liability lasts from the time that the goods are taken over until they are delivered and includes loading and unloading. The implication of "takes over" in relation to carriage by road was scrutinized in *Quantum Corporation v Plane Trucking* ([2002] 2 Lloyd's Rep 25) where carriage by air and carriage by road were performed by the same carrier, who thus never literally took over the goods at the beginning of the carriage by road leg as they had already been taken over from the consignor at the beginning of the carriage by air. Mance LJ concluded that: "The place of taking over and delivery of the goods under article 1(1) are to be read as referring to the start and the end of the contractually provided or permitted road leg" (at para. 59).

119 In article 17.2, this is expressed as.

> The carrier shall, however, be relieved of liability if the loss, damage or delay was caused by the wrongful act or neglect of the claimant, by the instructions of the claimant given otherwise than as the result of a wrongful act or neglect on the part of the carrier, by inherent vice of the goods or through circumstances which the carrier could not avoid and the consequences of which he was unable to prevent.

Liability, which is strict, disregards the actual cause of damage and whether this is within the inflicting party's control or not. Liability, which is based on presumed negligence, is still fault-based liability. Theoretically, the liability of the tortfeasor may not be different from other fault-based liability; it is just the burden of proof that is reversed. However, in practice this makes an obvious difference as proof of the cause of damage may be difficult to produce.

120 Cf. Swedish Supreme Court NJA 2016 s. 563 p. 6.

vehicles.[121] However, where the damage is caused by the defectiveness of the vehicle, the carrier may not invoke any exemption of liability.[122]

Under article 30, the goods are presumed to have been delivered to the consignee in good order, that is, without having been subject to damage or loss. This presumption may be rebutted by the claimant, who then must prove that the goods were damaged or lost during the carrier's period of liability. If the claimant thus establishes that the goods were damaged or lost during carriage, the carrier is liable for such damage in accordance with article 17.1 and may, in such case, resort to the defences provided. Accordingly, the carrier may invoke the special risks enumerated in article 17.4 and, if such a risk is applicable, then that risk is presumed to have caused the damage or loss, leaving the carrier without fault.[123] Alternatively, the carrier may defend himself by establishing that the cause of the damage was beyond his control.[124]

Invoking the defence of unavoidable circumstances, the carrier is faced with the challenge of proving that the damage was indeed caused "through circumstances which [he] could not avoid and the consequences of which he was unable to prevent". The implication of unavoidable circumstances is sometime equated to force majeure.[125] However, not only does the force majeure term have somewhat different implications in different states,[126] which makes it an impractical term to use, but it is considered to include causes of damage that are not force majeure events.[127] In order to avoid damage or loss, a carrier must perform his contractual duties, such as stowing the cargo, driving the vehicle and so on, with a certain amount of care. As regards ordinary liability for negligence, the duty of care that must be exercised by the inflicting party has many times been described as that of a normally diligent and careful man: *bonus pater familias*. However, the reading of article 17.2 suggests that the standard of care required by the carrier in order to avoid liability under the CMR convention goes beyond the normal standard. Thus it has been defined as one of "utmost care",[128] which in practice implies that a carrier is only exonerated from damage that occurs despite having taken the measures and precautions that can be taken without being financially

121 In this respect the Rotterdam Rules bears resemblance to the CMR convention; the carriage of goods in a manner unprotected from weather etc (i.e. on deck or on uncovered trailers) is subject to the rules *per se*, but the special risks inherent in such manner of carriage is beyond the carrier's liability; cf. above.

122 Cf. Swedish Supreme Court NJA 2016 s. 563, where the fitness of a vehicle's tank was considered covered by article 17.3 and that therefore the failure to properly clean the tank was subject to the rule *per se*.

123 Again, this presumption is rebuttable by the claimant; cf. article 18.4.

124 Article 17.2.

125 K. Haak, *The Liability of the Carrier under the CMR* (1986) pp. 143–144, A. Messent and D. Glass, *CMR: Contracts for the international carriage of goods by road* (2000) p. 121 (although this appears not to be the view of the authors but a reference of existing views).

126 A. Messent and D. Glass, *ibid.*, at p. 122.

127 M. Clarke, *International carriage of goods: CMR* (2014) p. 227, A. Messent and D. Glass, *ibid.*, at p. 122*ff*, with reference to e.g. *Silber v Islander Trucking* [1985] 2 Lloyd's Rep 243.

128 *Silber v Islander Trucking* [1985] 2 Lloyd's Rep 243.

extravagant or beyond the bounds of common sense.[129] Since it thus seems that a carrier is expected to take precautions beyond what can be expected from the ordinary man, perhaps the standard of care can be described as that of *melior pater familias*. However, in comparison to an ordinary man, *pater familias*, the fact that the carrier is not an ordinary man but a professional carrier affects the precautionary measures that are expected of him.

In conclusion, a carrier by road under the CMR convention is liable for all causes of damage to, or loss of, the goods unless such cause could have been avoided had he exercised utmost care. In exercising utmost care the carrier has to take all precautions that are economically and practically defensible in order to avoid causes of damage that are realistically foreseeable. It has been asserted that the demands on the carrier to foresee and avoid possible causes of damage have been set so high that unavoidable circumstances are seldom successfully invoked unless the cause of damage also constitutes exoneration on another ground.[130]

The carrier is expressly liable for the acts and omissions of his "agents and servants and any other person of whose services he makes use for the performance of the carriage".[131] Such liability includes liability not only for employees but also for sub-carriers. In the case of successive carriage, article 36 allows the claimant to bring any claims for damages against the first carrier, the last carrier and the carrier during whose carriage the goods were damaged or lost, either separately or jointly and severally.[132]

The compensation payable by the carrier is the value of the goods at the place of taking over and is limited to 8.33 SDRs per kilo.[133] In case of delay, the compensation payable is limited to the sum of the carriage charges.[134] The right to invoke the defences of article 17, as well as the right of limitation of liability, is forfeited where the carrier has caused the damage through willful misconduct or, and this statement has caused a rather non-uniform application of the rules, to such default on the carrier's part that according to the law of the court seized of the case is equivalent to willful misconduct.[135]

2.6 The rail carrier's liability under the COTIF–CIM convention

The COTIF–CIM convention is applicable to "every contract of carriage of goods by rail for reward".[136] Thus, the carriage by rail convention also adopts

129 A. Messent and D. Glass, *ibid.*, at p. 124. European case law to this effect seems to be somewhat coherent (M. Clarke, *ibid.*, at p. 230).

130 M. Clarke, *ibid.*, at p. 230.

131 Under the Hague–Visby Rules, such liability for servants etc. only appears *e contrario*, whilst under the Rotterdam Rules there is an express provision to this effect; cf. sections 2.3.1 and 2.4 above.

132 Article 36.

133 Article 23.3.

134 Article 23.4.

135 Article 29.1.

136 Article 1 §1 of the Uniform Rules Concerning the Contract of International Carriage of Goods by Rail.

the contractual approach to applicability.[137] Unlike the CMR, the COTIF–CIM is only applicable when both the place of taking over and the place of delivery are in different states, both of which are parties to the convention.

The contract of carriage is, to some extent, defined in the COTIF–CIM convention. Thus, a contract of carriage is an undertaking by the carrier to carry goods for reward to the place of destination and deliver them there to the consignee: article 6 §1.[138]

The basis of the carrier's liability is virtually identical to that of the CMR; the carrier is liable for any damage to the goods that occur whilst in his custody, that is from the time he takes over the goods until the time of delivery. The burden of proving that loss or damage has occurred falls on the claimant.[139] The carrier is relieved of liability if the damage can be assumed to have been caused by one of the privileged causes enumerated in article 23 § 3[140] or can be proved to have been caused by one of the non-privileged causes in article 23 §2 relating to the sender, the inherent vice of the goods or "circumstances which the carrier could not avoid and the consequences of which he was unable to prevent".[141] The nature of the carrier's liability has been discussed also in relation to carriage by rail. It has been claimed that if the concept of unavoidable circumstances excludes all acts and omissions relating to internal railway operations, liability must be considered as strict.[142] Today, it can hardly be questioned that the concept of unavoidable circumstances, as chiseled into control-based liability,[143] generally excludes all causes of damage relating to the internal organization of the carrier.[144] It can, however, be questioned whether a liability that is enforced with

137 Before 1999, the CIM was applicable to "all consignments of goods for carriage under a through consignment note made out for a route over the territories of at least two States" (article 1 of the Uniform Rules Concerning the Contract for International Carriage of Goods by Rail (CIM). See also the 1970 version which applied to "the carriage of goods consigned under a through consignment note made out for carriage over the territories of at least two of the Contracting States" (article 1 of the International Convention Concerning the Carriage of Goods by Rail (CIM), signed at Berne 1970).

138 Which can be compared to regulation of the formation of the contract of carriage in previous versions of the convention, cf. COTIF–CIM convention 1980 article 11.1.

139 M. Clarke and D. Yates, *Contracts of Carriage by Land and Air* (2004) p. 242. In this context it may be noticed that the issue of parties entitled to claim against the carrier is specifically regulated in the convention: article 44.

140 Including carriage in open wagons, absence or inadequacy of packaging, loading of the goods by the consignor or unloading by the consignee, the carriage of live animals etc.

141 SOU 2014:26 p. 75.

142 J. Haenni, "Carriage by Rail" in R. Rodière (ed.), *International Encyclopedia of Comparative Law*, vol. XII, ch. 2 (1972) p. 112.

143 J. Schelin, *Lastskadeansvaret* (2015) p. 33, J. Heidbrink, *Logistikavtalet* (2005) p. 140 *ff.*

144 O. Mestad, *Om force majeure og risikofordelning i kontrakt* (1991) p. 281. The concept of unavoidable circumstances could be compared to the formulation of the exemption from liability rule in the United Nations Convention on Contracts for the International Sale of Goods ("CISG", done at Vienna, 11 April 1980), article 79(1):

> A party is not liable for a failure to perform any of his obligations if he proves that the failure was due to an impediment beyond his control and that he could not reasonably be expected to have taken the impediment into account at the time of the conclusion of the contract or to have avoided or overcome it or its consequences.

exemptions can be at all regarded as strict.[145] However the rail carrier's liability under the COTIF–CIM convention is labelled, what is clear is that it is stricter than liability in general.[146] As the wording of article 23 §2 is identical to that of article 17.2 of the CMR convention, the considerations elaborated above regarding that article are also relevant in relation to the COTIF–CIM convention.[147]

The carrier's liability is limited to 17 SDRs per kilo.[148] In case of loss due to delay, the compensation payable by the carrier is limited to four times the carriage charges.[149] The right of limitation may be lost if the loss or damage results from an act or omission, committed by the carrier intentionally or recklessly and with the knowledge that such damage would probably result.[150]

2.7 The air carrier's liability under the Montreal Convention

The Montreal Convention is, according to its article 1, applicable to international carriage of cargo by aircraft.[151] Prima facie there is hence no requirement of a contract of carriage.[152] It would, however, seem to be a rare occurrence that carriage for reward is performed without prior agreement.[153] However, irrespectively of how the article is interpreted, there is a clear difference between the Montreal Convention and conventions, such as the CMR, applicable to the contract of carriage as such.

The liability of the air carrier is presumed.[154] The list of defences available to the carrier is condensed in relation to the above accounted for conventions and comprise neither any force majeure/act of God exemption in its normal, general sense, nor any general exoneration for the absence of negligence on the part of the carrier. Instead,

---

Article 79 can be broken down into four prerequisites: the prerequisite of an *impediment*; the prerequisite of the impediment being *beyond the party's control*; the prerequisite of *unpredictability* of the impediment and the prerequisite of *non-avoidance* (J. Ramberg and J. Herre, *Internationella Köplagen* (CISG), 2009, p. 558).

145 See e.g. *Black's Law Dictionary* where strict liability is defined as "Liability that does not depend on proof of negligence or intent to harm" (B. Garner (ed.), *Black's Law Dictionary* (10th edn, 2014)).

146 J. Ramberg, "The Law of Carriage of Goods – Attempts at Harmonization" (1973) 17 Scandinavian Stud L 211, at pp. 223–224.

147 The formulation in the CMR convention is taken from COTIF-CIM convention verbatim, and so it may be presumed that the draftsmen of the former convention sought the same implication as under the latter convention. However, previous to the 1952 version of the COTIF-CIM convention, the term "force majeure" was used and it was not intended that the implication was to be affected by the reformulation (A. Messent and D. Glass, *CMR: Contracts for the international carriage of goods by road* (2000) p. 121).

148 Article 30§2.

149 Article 33§1.

150 Article 36.

151 A definition of aircraft can be found in the Standards and Recommended Practices of ICAO; cf. P. Dempsey and M. Milde, *International Air Carrier Liability* (2005) p. 68. Note that it is not explicitly required that the transportation is carried out in the air.

152 E. Giemulla, *Montreal Convention (Commentary)* article 1–3 (2006).

153 For a further discussion on the scope of application of the Montreal Convention, see section 4.4 below.

154 Article 18.1.

the defences comprise inherent vice of the goods, packaging performed by the shipper, armed conflicts and customs handling of the cargo.[155] In addition, the carrier is exonerated from liability if and to the extent cargo interests caused or contributed to the damage.[156] Thus, although not entirely strict, the liability of the carrier is in fact stricter than the liability of the road carrier,[157] which has been described as strict with exemptions.[158] The exemptions available are all causes of damage where the fault rests on a party other than the carrier, in which case the carrier has accordingly not caused the damage, negligently or otherwise.[159] However, with the omission of a general exemption to the effect that the carrier is exonerated when neither it nor its agents and servants have been negligent, liability is quite severe and approaches the burden in terms of risk that rests on a strictly liable party.[160]

The carrier is liable for goods whilst in his care.[161] However, the period of carriage by air does not extend to carriage by other modes unless such carriage is carried out within the airport. Where carriage by another mode of transport has been undertaken "for the purpose of loading, delivery or transhipment", any damage is presumed to have been caused during carriage by air.[162] If the carrier in breach of the contract of carriage substitutes the carriage by air undertaken for another mode of transport, the carrier is liable under the Montreal Convention.[163]

As regards the carrier's liability for the acts and omissions of its agents and servants, there is no explicit statement to this effect. However, it should follow from general liability (the carrier is liable for damage to the goods whilst in his custody) and the available exonerations (which do not include damage not caused by the carrier's own negligence) that the carrier is liable for damage caused by its servants and agents. Any such servants and agents that are subject to a direct claim may avail themselves of the defences and limits of liability available to the carrier if the servant has acted within the scope of his employment.[164]

---

155 Article 18.2.

156 Article 20.

157 J. Ramberg, "The Law of Carriage of Goods – Attempts at Harmonization" (1973) 17 Scandinavian Stud L 211 at pp. 224–225.

158 S. Johansson, *An Outline of Transport Law* (2014) pp. 88–89.

159 Likewise, the exoneration available under article 20 relates to conduct on the part of the claimant:

> If the carrier proves that the damage was caused or contributed to by the negligence or other wrongful act or omission of the person claiming compensation, or the person from whom he or she derives his or her rights, the carrier shall be wholly or partly exonerated from its liability to the claimant to the extent that such negligence or wrongful act or omission caused or contributed to the damage.

160 Milde claims that the liability of the air carrier is strict and distinguishes strict liability from absolute liability (M. Milde, "Liability in international carriage by air: the new Montreal Convention" (1999) 4 Unif L Rev 835 at p. 855). In my opinion, hybrids like that will only serve to confuse and undermine the concept of strict liability.

161 Article 18.3: "The carriage by air within the meaning of paragraph 1 of this Article comprises the period during which the cargo is in the charge of the carrier."

162 For a more detailed discussion, see section 3.3.1 below.

163 Article 18.4. For a further discussion on the applicability of the Montreal Convention to air carriage under multimodal contracts of carriage, see section 4.4.2 below.

164 Article 43.

The liability of the contracting carrier in relation to successive carriage and sub-carriage as well as the liability of successive carriers and sub-carriers is regulated separately. In relation to sub-carriers (code-sharing) where the shipper has no contractual relationship with the sub-carrier, who is the actual carrier, and the contracting carrier does not perform any carriage, the claimant may claim against either party for loss of or damage to the cargo.[165] The special provision has been considered necessary due to the fact that US courts had interpreted "carrier" as being the performing carrier rather than the contracting carrier, which would enable claims against the contracting carrier.[166] Successive carriage is defined as carriage *to be performed* by various successive carriers, which indicates that it must have been anticipated by the parties to the contract of carriage, that the carriage was to be performed accordingly. If such carriage has been considered as one carriage by the parties, and is subject to a single contract, the entire carriage is subject to the Montreal Convention even if any separate leg of the carriage is domestic.[167] Further, the consignor may take action against the first carrier as well as against the carrier during whose custody of the goods these were damaged and the consignee may take action against the last carrier as well as against the carrier during whose custody of the goods the damage occurred.[168]

The Montreal Convention contains explicit regulation of multimodal transport. The convention adopts the network system and under article 38 the convention is to apply to an air leg of a multimodal transport. However, the convention must be applicable *per se* to that leg, which e.g. means that the air leg must be international, and it does not suffice that the entire multimodal transport is international.[169]

The liability of the carrier is limited to 19 SDRs per kilo, unless a special declaration has been made by the consignor.[170] In relation to cargo, the right of limitation is not subject to any exceptions.[171] In the case of delay, the limitation of liability is the same as in case of damage or loss; however the carrier may avoid liability subject to proof that all measures were taken in order to avoid damage.[172]

2.8 Conclusion

In the current chapter the regulatory systems that are the subject of the current thesis have been presented. These regulatory systems, which have been drafted as uniform law, have as their immediate focus the liability of carriers for goods carried, although the regulations do contain rules on other issues as well.

165 Article 39.

166 P. Dempsey and M. Milde, *International air carrier liability* (2005) p. 232 and E. Giemulla, *Montreal Convention (Commentary)* article 1–22 (2006).

167 Article 1.3.

168 Article 36.3.

169 P. Dempsey and M. Milde, *ibid.*, at p. 230.

170 Article 22.3.

171 E. Giemulla, *ibid.* article 22–22 (2010). However, the carrier may however lose the right to limitation in cases of willful misconduct where passengers or baggage have been injured, damaged or lost under article 22.5.

172 Article 19.

It can be concluded that the systems of liability present similarities as well as dissimilarities. Abstracting general rules may show that the carrier's liability under the different regimes is similar; however, such general rules, being detached from its context, do not really reflect the reality.[173] Thus, albeit the liability is similar, the routes to the destination differ and thus, in effect, the situation for a claimant under the different regimes is heterogenous. It may be that the effect of the fact that the regulations are heterogenous is exaggerated within the legal field; in practice, carriers may not be very occupied with the legal "details" and shippers undoubtedly do not adapt the choice of mode of transport based on the legal limits of the carrier's liability. However, from a legal point of view, the dissimilarities may lead to situations in which the outcome is highly unpredictable.

In the following chapter, further background to the research questions will be presented; how do the current unimodal liability systems fit together and how do they fit the multimodal contract of carriage. As will be discussed, the applicability of the conventions in question has been the subject of analysis in doctrine as well as legal precedence. The focus of the following chapter is the current status of the relationship between the unimodal conventions accounted for above and the multimodal contract of carriage, a status quo that is to some extent characterized by a rigid approach to the understanding of the terms of uniform law, as will be further explored in Chapter 5. The aim of the following account and discussion is accordingly to put the analysis in Part III in its relevant context. The route to be followed commences with a presentation of the basic problem, and continues through an account of the two systems generally presented as the options in terms of regulating the carrier's liability for carriage under multimodal contracts of carriage. Albeit, these systems are not directly relevant for the research questions posed, the necessity of scrutinizing the applicability of unimodal conventions rests on the absence of a uniform system, whilst the imperfect fit of these conventions to multimodal transport is apparent from the problems that follow from the network system. From there, a slight deviation into the multimodal aspects of the existing conventions is purported, to further understand the consequences of applying the unimodal conventions to transport under multimodal contracts. The last port to be called is the above-mentioned precedence and legal discourse, which is presented and to some extent analysed. The final destination is an understanding of the relevant context in which the research questions are undertaken.

173 J. Merryman, "On the Convergence (and Divergence) of the Civil Law and the Common Law" (1981) 17 Stan J Int'l L 357 at pp. 378–379.

CHAPTER 3

Application of unimodal conventions in a multimodal context – status quo

From the general presentation of the liability regimes in force above, it appears that the regulation of the carrier's liability is basically unimodal. In the current chapter, the relationship between the unimodal conventions presented above, and the multimodal contract of carriage, will be discussed. The attempts to reconcile the two spans from extending the rules of a unimodal regime to other modes of transport under certain conditions to interpreting the scope of application of the regimes, via national (or potentially regional) solutions.

The multimodal contract of carriage is not easily fit into the existing unimodal costumes. In relation to the regulation of the multimodal contract of carriage, different "systems" of regulation have developed, which will be discussed below. The mere fact that the regulations are unimodal, and contracts are multimodal, entails gaps as well as overlaps, which in turn add to legal unpredictability. The network and uniform systems will be presented and discussed in section 3.2 below.

As mentioned, to some extent the drafters of the unimodal regulations have attempted to solve the "problem" of multimodal contracts of carriage. Accordingly, the unimodal conventions discussed to some extent contain rules that extend the applicability of the unimodal rules to other modes than the mode primarily regulated by the convention. These multimodal extensions, as well as the risks of competition, are discussed in section 3.3.

At the other extreme, the emergence of multimodal contracts has triggered the question of whether the unimodal conventions are at all applicable to multimodal contracts of carriage. This legal question constitutes the core of the analysis of the current work. Whilst an independent analysis will be undertaken in Chapter 4, the legal development in precedence and doctrine must be accounted for, a task that is undertaken in section 3.4. This legal development has been perpetuated by developments within the trade, developments that have triggered a re-evaluation of legal rules, many of which were adopted when this development was partly unforeseen.

In between the two approaches thus available to the "multimodal problem" lay the individual attempts to provide legal foreseeability with the national legal system. In a European context such national solutions are found in the Netherlands and in Germany. Because of their close relationship to the network and uniform systems, these two jurisdictions will be accounted for in section 3.2.

The different parts of the current chapter, as well as the previous, all form the background to the actual research questions. Without the background of the existing legal discussion, applicable national solutions and the outcome in leading precedence, the research undertaken in the next part (Part III) would be disengaged and somewhat incomprehensible.

3.1 The basic problem

In a European setting, all international conventions in force today that govern the carrier's liability for goods carried are unimodal. This is by no means an artificial segmentation of transports, which perhaps today could be described as overwhelmingly multimodal, but a reflection of what transport used to look like: unimodal.[1] In fact, all conventions discussed in this work are "designed to stand alone".[2] The containerization of trade is usually credited (or blamed) for the emergence of multimodal transport. Most likely, other factors, such as the willingness of carriers to contract for other modes than those operated by themselves, have affected development as well. In any event it seems to be clear that contracts for the carriage of goods have changed and that today a contract of carriage often includes more than one mode of transport. This fact, together with the fact that many of the unimodal conventions apply to contracts of carriage, rather than to actual performance by a particular mode of transport, have given rise to legal discussion. As regards liability for multimodal carriage, the discussion concerns whether a contract of carriage that provides for carriage by more than one mode is to be regarded as a contract for several carriages by different modes, or whether a multimodal contract is nothing but a multimodal contract (sometimes referred to as a contract *sui generis*), which cannot be broken down into unimodal parts.

The outcome of that discussion may be that the existing systems that govern the carrier's liability for goods carried do not apply if goods are carried under multimodal contracts of carriage. Obviously, such non-applicability can be healed through contractual measures through which the rules are made applicable to a certain contract or through national legislation that applies the rules also to multimodal contracts of carriage. However, from the point of view of the uniform law, such solutions must be considered inadequate. The unimodal conventions in force are mandatorily applicable (to the extent they are applicable *ex proprio vigore*) and thus trusting to the goodwill of the carrier to insert a reference clause in its standard conditions of carriage does not amount to the protection that the rules sets out to award cargo interests. Further, national solutions are exactly what is sought to be avoided by uniform law and thus albeit national legislation may be preferable to freedom of contract (from the perspective of the mandatorily applicable uniform law), it cannot replace the enforcement of the actual uniform law.

3.2 Two alternative systems

In terms of regulating multimodal carriage, generally two different systems are considered relevant: the network system and the uniform system. Whilst the uniform system would provide a single uniform regulation for the entire multimodal

1 Which recalls a comic strip by Bill Watterson where Calvin's dad explains that TV did not use to be black and white; it was full colour but reflected the world as it then was (i.e. black and white).

2 S. Mankabady, "The Multimodal Transport of Goods Convention: A Challenge to Unimodal Transport Conventions" [1983] 32 Int'l & Comp LQ 120–140, at p. 120.

carriage, the network system makes use of the existing unimodal regulations and stitches them together into a net.

3.2.1 The uniform system

There are several reasons for implementing a uniform system, i.e. regulation that governs multimodal transport as such and applies the same liability rules to all legs of the transport.[3]

One advantage is clearly foreseeability: under a uniform system the entire transport will be governed by one single liability system instead of various systems under the network system. A uniform system will also reduce disputes connected with the fact that it is often difficult to establish during which transport mode damage has been caused. The main disadvantage with the uniform system as such is that the contracting carrier subcontracts on a unimodal basis and the liability of the performing carrier is regulated by a unimodal set of rules, be it an international convention or national legislation, and recourse by the contracting carrier to the performing carrier is therefore not "back-to-back".[4]

However, the real feasibility of the uniform system is to a large extent dependent on the status of the multimodal contract of carriage and the applicability of the unimodal conventions thereto. If the contract for multimodal carriage is regarded as a contract *sui generis*, as has been asserted, none of the existing unimodal conventions, it is argued, would be applicable.[5] Thus, such a viewpoint opens up for a special liability system applicable to contracts for multimodal carriage, a uniform system.[6] However, if the unimodal liability systems are considered applicable to the legs of a multimodal contract of carriage, then enactment of a uniform system will cause constant conflict between the uniform system and existing regulations. Although national uniform systems exist, there is to date no international regime regulating the carriers' liability in relation to multimodal contracts of carriage in force.[7]

In the 1970s a convention governing the international multimodal carriage of goods was drafted under the auspices of the UN.[8] The Multimodal Convention

3 C. Hancock, "Multimodal transport and the new UN Convention on the carriage of goods" in (2008) JIML 484–495, at p. 488.

4 C. Hancock, *ibid.* at p. 488 and E. Eftestøl-Wilhelmsson, *European Sustainable Carriage of Goods* (2016) p. 65.

5 E. Selvig, "Multimodal transport: the 1980 U.N. Convention: papers of a one day seminar: Southampton University, Faculty of Law, 12th September 1980", at p. A3, para. 2.

6 J. Ramberg, "Is Multimodal Transport a Contract *sui generis* also within the Field of EU Competition?" in H-J. Bull and H. Stemshaug (eds), *EC Shipping* (1997) pp. 163–168, at pp. 166–167.

7 Some states, such as Germany and the Netherlands, have implemented national regulations on multimodal transport; cf. section 3.2.3 below. The United Nations Convention on International Multimodal Transport of Goods, adopted in Geneva 1980 ("the Multimodal Convention"), see further below, has not yet received the necessary number of acceding states to enter into force. The general opinion seems to be that it will never enter into force.

8 The United Nations Convention on International Multimodal Transport of Goods, adopted in Geneva 1980 ("the Multimodal Convention"). The work by the UNCTAD began in the early 1970s, although discussion on the need of a multimodal regulation had been initiated already in the early years of the twentieth century (R. de Wit, *Multimodal Transport* (1995) p. 147*ff.* and F. Lorenzon,

provides a uniform system to "contracts of multimodal transport between places in two States",[9] where "multimodal transport" connotes "the carriage of goods by at least two different modes of transport on the basis of a multimodal transport contract".[10] Under the convention, the contracting carrier ("multimodal transport operator") is liable for loss of and damage to the goods carried, as well as for delay in delivery thereof, subject to limitation of liability as well as grounds for losing the right to limit liability. The uniform system is, however, disharmonized by the introduction of article 19, which provides that localized damage shall be determined by reference to any applicable international convention or mandatory national law.[11]

Considering the net of existing regulations on unimodal transport, in order to introduce an absolute uniform system (in contrast to the modified uniform system provided in the Multimodal Convention and in the Rotterdam Rules) the relationship thereto of the unimodal conventions must be settled. As will be discussed in section 3.4 below, one solution is to consider these conventions not applicable to multimodal contracts of carriage. As will be shown in Chapter 4, such a conclusion can only be drawn from an analysis of the articles of application of the conventions themselves. Another proposed solution is to consider the multimodal contract of carriage a transport contract *sui generis*, to which the unimodal conventions are not applicable not due to the interpretation of their terms of application but due to the categorization of the multimodal contract of carriage.[12] This theory will be considered in the following section.

3.2.1.1 Contract categories and contracts *sui generis*

As mentioned, the multimodal contract of carriage, i.e. a contract for the carriage of goods where transport by several modes has been contracted for and covered by a single contract, is sometimes argued to be a contract different from other transport contracts.[13] The basis of the theory on the *sui generis* character of the

---

"Multimodal Transport Evolving: Freedom and Regulation Three Decades after the 1980 MTO Convention" in M. Clarke (ed.), *Maritime Law Evolving* (2013) pp. 163–180, at pp. 168–169).

9 Article 2.

10 Whilst "multimodal transport" is not actually defined, "international multimodal transport" is defined in article 1 as:

> the carriage of goods by at least two different modes of transport on the basis of a multimodal transport contract from a place in one country at which the goods are taken in charge by the multimodal transport operator to a place designated for delivery situated in a different country.

11 This rule appears somewhat contradictory as the entire convention seems to rest on the precondition that no unimodal conventions are applicable to carriage under multimodal transport contracts; cf. below. In fact, although "[t]he relationship of the Multimodal Convention to the existing modal transportation regimes was a persistent and continuous issue throughout the negotiations [of the convention]" (W. Driscoll and P. Larsen, "The Convention on International Multimodal Transport of Goods" (1982–1983) 57 Tul L Rev 193 at p. 209), that relationship does not seem to have been primarily the possible risk of simultaneously applicable conventions (*ibid.* p. 209 *ff.*).

12 Lorenzon proposes the idea that the container could be considered as the transport mode (F. Lorenzon, "Multimodal Transport Evolving: Freedom and Regulation Three Decades after the 1980 MTO Convention" in M. Clarke (ed.), *Maritime Law Evolving* (2013), 163–180, at p. 177), which appears to be an elegant solution to the "multimodal problem".

13 E. Selvig, "Multimodal transport: the 1980 U.N. Convention: papers of a one day seminar: Southampton University, Faculty of Law, 12th September 1980", at p. A3, para. 2.

multimodal transport contract is not entirely clear.[14] However, the conceptual idea is a precondition for a uniform system, such as the Multimodal Convention, and the simple explanation of the *sui generis* theory could be that it emanated out of necessity in order to avoid conflicts with unimodal conventions.[15] However, although, naturally, the adoption of a convention governing multimodal transport would have entailed the abandonment of the pure network system, and the initiation of the drafting process of that convention could be seen as an indication that the drafters considered the networks system inapplicable, the drafting history suggests otherwise. The rationale for the drafting of a multimodal convention seems to have been the disadvantages of the network system rather than the perception of the multimodal contract of carriage as a contract of carriage *sui generis*.[16] Consequently, the theory was likewise an issue of concern in drafting the Rotterdam Rules.[17]

However, even if that was the rationale, the *sui generis* theory must rest on arguments of a more solid kind. Accordingly, one argument that has been asserted to support the theory is that under a multimodal contract of carriage, the contracting carrier never undertakes to perform the contract by any particular mode, or combination of modes, which entails that the contract is not actually a contract of carriage.[18] However, even if that argument is accepted,[19] it only

---

14 D. Glass, *Freight Forwarding and Multimodal Transport Contracts* (2012) p. 336.

15 In relation to the drafting of the Multimodal Convention, E. Selvig holds that:

> The prevailing view so far has been that the multimodal contract is a new and distinct type of contract, which must be distinguished from the various contracts of unimodal carriage. ... Hence, as long as the unimodal conventions apply only to contracts for carriage by a particular mode of transport, the multimodal contract falls outside their scope, and a new multimodal convention does not conflict with the existing unimodal conventions.
>
> (E. Selvig, "Multimodal transport: the 1980 U.N. Convention: papers of a one day seminar: Southampton University, Faculty of Law, 12th September 1980", at p. A17, para. 12).

The EU seems to be of the opinion that it could avoid the possible applicability of the unimodal conventions to multimodal contracts of carriage by *declaring* the multimodal contract to be a contract *sui generis* (E. Eftestøl-Wilhelmsson, *European Sustainable Carriage of Goods* (2016) p. 86). However, it is held here that such declaration would not be relevant in respect of the applicability of the unimodal conventions unless the declaration is made by all state parties to the respective convention (cf. the Vienna Convention on the Law of Treaties, article 31.3(a)).

16 UNCTAD, United Nations Conference on a Convention on International Multimodal Transport, vol. II, Draft Convention and Reports of the Conference, TD/MT/CONF/17/add.1 (1981) p. 1. Accordingly, article 19 of the convention gives precedence to applicable unimodal rules where the damage is localized, a rule which would have been abundant under the *sui generis* theory, at least in a European perspective. Further, the network system, in its "modified" form, is in fact the system prescribed in the convention.

17 Working Group III, A/CN.9/WG.III/WP.29; Transport Law: preparation of a draft instrument on the carriage of goods [by sea] note by the secretariat. There has, however, been uncertainty enough among the drafters of the Multimodal Convention as well as of the Rotterdam Rules, as articles have been included attempting to avoid possible conflicts with existing unimodal conventions; see article 30(4) of the Multimodal Convention and articles 26 and 82 of the Rotterdam Rules.

18 J. Ramberg, *The Law of Transport Operators* (2005), pp. 19 and 25.

19 As will be discussed in section 5.4 below, a general prerequisite for the contract of carriage is that the carrier undertakes to carry and also where such an undertaking does not specify the mode of transport, there is nevertheless an undertaking to carry.

applies to undefined contracts of carriage and not the clear mode-to-mode contracts and accordingly it does not explain the *sui generis* theory as regards such multimodal contracts where the carrier actually undertakes to carry the goods by a specified combination of modes. Another argument for the theory seems to be based on the proposition that the unimodal conventions that apply to contracts of carriage by a particular mode of transport do not apply to contracts for carriage by that mode and, in addition, one or more other modes of transport.[20] Accordingly, as such unimodal conventions do not apply to multimodal contracts, these must be regarded as a contractual type of their own.[21] If these circumstances are accepted as enough for declaring the CMR convention not applicable to a road leg of a multimodal contract, then this could in turn lead to the conclusion that the multimodal contract is a contract *sui generis*, simply because the unimodal conventions do not apply. However, to the extent the *sui generis* theory is used to enhance the argumentation of non-applicability of unimodal conventions, the theory is both part of the argumentation and a result of it, which indicates that the theory has become an independent creature without sufficient connection to its own justification. Thus, the argumentation is circular.

The practice of referring certain types of contract to different categories is not particular to transport law.[22] Accordingly contracts in general are regularly referred to different categories of contracts. The basis for such categorization is often the different legal consequences that the different types of contract entail.[23] Thus a purchase agreement, a rental agreement and a pledge agreement are examples of contracts that belong to different categories of contract. The categorization of contracts is derived from Roman law and is mainly applied in civil law systems. The categorization of contracts is purportedly based on the legal consequences that follow from the agreement, consequences that normally follow from supplementary law – mandatory or non-mandatory.[24] Somewhat more simplified: a contract category is "a collection of legal problems and their corresponding solutions, which are realized in relation to regularly occurring conduct".[25] Accordingly, the legal consequence that a rented item remains in the ownership of the lessor under a rental agreement, and that ownership of an item is transferred to the buyer under a purchase agreement, is not necessarily explicit in the agreement itself. Clearly, categorization of contracts facilitates legal problem solving and demarcates the relevant legal rules applicable.[26]

---

20 German Federal Supreme Court BGH 17 July 2008, I ZR 181/05 and Dutch Supreme Court, Hoge Raad, 1 June 2012, nr.10/05322.

21 Cf. Hoeks, who does not agree with the theory. Further, Hoeks concludes that the main argument asserted in Dutch legal theory is that the multimodal contract of carriage to a large extent includes services other than transport (M. Hoeks, *Multimodal Transport Law* (2010) pp. 75–77). The arguments purported will be discussed further in section 3.4 below.

22 J. Sundberg, "Avtalstyper och typavtal" (1961) SvJT 11–30, J. Hellner *et al.*, *Speciell avtalsrätt II Kontraktsrätt, 1 häftet* (2015) p. 23 *ff.*

23 J. Heidbrink, *Logistikavtalet* (2005) p. 28.

24 J. Sundberg, *ibid.*, at p. 12.

25 J. Heidbrink, *ibid.*, p. 27 (my translation from the Swedish original).

26 J. Heidbrink, *ibid.*, p. 30.

Where a certain contract contains elements from more than one category of contracts, it is often referred to as a "mixed contract", a term that indicates that the solution to a contractual dispute under the contract may vary depending on to which category the part of the contract in dispute refers.[27] Historically, the contract of carriage was considered a mixed agreement; partly a contract for hire and partly a contract for bailment.[28] During the late twentieth century, the contract of carriage seems to have gained status as a contract category of its own, a contract *sui generis*.[29]

At some point the mixed agreement may become frequent enough to form a new contract category. This development can be triggered either by legislation or by legal theory. Where a type of contract is "awarded" its own legislation, the status of the type of contract forming a new category may seem rather matter of fact, but the mere fact that a certain type of contract is regulated by special legislation does not necessarily mean that it forms a category *sui generis*.[30] More common is referral of a type of contract to a new category in legal theory. Even in 1961, Sundberg asserted that jurisprudence seemed to prefer to "invent" a new contract category, *sui generis*, rather than subordinating a new type of contract under existing categories.[31] However, the raison d'être of categorization would soon be frustrated if every type of contract that does not immediately fit into an existing category is referred to its own category *sui generis*.[32]

Generally, the contract of carriage is thus referred to as a contract category, although it seems that some hesitation remains.[33] The category comprises all types of contract of carriage, with a possible two sub-categories: contracts of carriage of goods and charter parties.[34] The point of departure must therefore be that to the extent the contract of carriage is considered a contract *sui generis*, it is one category and one category only.[35] The contract of carriage can no longer be

27 K. Grönfors, "Fraktavtalet och den allmänna avtalsrätten" (1988) SvJT 1988 181–202, at p. 182.

28 M. Hoeks, *Intermodal Transport Law* (2010) p. 41 with reference to Napoleon's Code Civil.

29 M. Hoeks, *ibid.* at pp. 41–42. See however Hammarsjköld, who puts much effort into sorting the contract of carriage into the existing categories (H. Hammarskjöld, *Om fraktavtalet och dess viktigaste rättsföljder* (1886)).

30 For example, the sales agreement is subject to various statutes, depending on the status of the parties (e.g. consumer–tradesman), the place of entering into the contract (e.g. distance- and doorstep sales), the object of the sale (e.g. real estate, financial instruments). These still remain in the contract category of sales, albeit perhaps as sub-categories.

31 J. Sundberg, *ibid* at p. 26, see also K. Grönfors, *ibid.* at pp. 182–183.

32 J. Heidbrink, *ibid.*, at p. 31 and J. Hellner *et al.*, *Speciell avtalsrätt II Kontraktsrätt 1:a häftet* (2016) p. 24.

33 That the categorization of the contract of carriage as a contract *sui generis* is still not universally embraced appears from Hoeks statement "Nevertheless, most legal systems have recognized that the contract of carriage should be construed as a special kind of contract, in need of its specific rules" (M. Hoeks, *Intermodal Transport Law* (2010) p. 42).

34 K. Grönfors; *Tolkning av fraktavtal* (1989) p. 55.

35 Thus, the contract of carriage is referred to as a single category, see H. Hammarskjöld, *Om fraktavtalet och dess viktigaste rättsföljder* (1886); J. Sundberg, "Avtalstyper och typavtal" (1961) SvJT 11–30; K. Grönfors, *Fraktavtalet under etthundra år* (1986); K. Grönfors; *Tolkning av fraktavtal* (1989) p. 55; J. Hellner *et al.*, *Speciell avtalsrätt II Kontraktsrätt 1:a häftet* (2016) ch. 5; M. Hoeks, *Intermodal Transport Law* (2010) p. 42. See, however, Haenni, who holds the contract of

considered a mixed agreement, as the legal rules pertaining thereto are unique; for example the liability of the carrier is divergent from that of any other bailee.[36] In consequence with the prerequisites for a contract category, the contract of carriage is thus undoubtedly a contract category.[37] The categorization could, however, be proposed to be taken one step further; indeed there are heterogenous rules for different modes of transport. However, many of the existing contract categories can be divided into sub-categories.[38] On an abstract level, the similarities between different contracts of carriage are sufficient to fit them into one category.[39]

As mentioned, at some point the assertion was made that the multimodal contract of carriage was to be considered as a contract *sui generis*. The appeal in declaring a type of contract a contract *sui generis*, forming its own category, is obviously that the mould into which the contract type is to be fitted can be tailored perfectly to fit the contract type. On the other hand, it is clear that the benefits sought by categorization of contracts as such are eliminated if every type of contract is awarded its own category. Although it is appealing, perhaps because fitting a new type of contract into existing categories requires a great deal of effort, inventing new categories of contracts should be done with hesitation and only after consideration of the consequences. As has been shown by other authors, fitting the multimodal contract of carriage into the existing category and the unimodal regulations associated with that category is possible, although not easily done.[40] It is certainly a *modus operandi*, which should be preferred to the more effortless referral of a new contract type to a new category. Moreover, due to the scope of application of the unimodal conventions discussed in the current work, the mere fact that the multimodal contract of carriage is considered a contract *sui generis* does not necessarily affect the applicability of those conventions.[41]

Accordingly, the contract of carriage seems to have developed in a most generic way; initially the general type of contract – the contract of carriage – was regarded as a mixed contract. Later, it gained status as a contract *sui generis*. Eventually, sub categories developed, and a difference was perceived between contracts of carriage depending on by which mode the transport was to be carried out. When the multimodal contract of carriage appeared, it was conceived as a mixed contract; a mix between the sub-categories of the contract of carriage. Its

---

carriage by rail to be a contract *sui generis* (J. Haenni in *International Encyclopedia of Comparative Law*, vol. XII, *Law of Transport*, ch. 2, "Carriage by Rail", p. 10).

36 Thus, the fact that contracts of carriage are subject to particular legislation renders it a contract category according to J. Hellner *et al.*, *ibid.*, at p. 23.

37 J. Heidbrink, *Logistikavtalet* (2005) pp. 27–29.

38 For example, the purchase agreement, where there are ordinary purchase agreements, the consumer purchase agreement, agreements for the purchase of real estate etc.

39 J. Heidbrink, *ibid.*, at p. 31.

40 M. Hoeks, *Intermodal Transport Law* (2010) ch. 4.

41 The scope of application of the unimodal conventions are analysed in sections 4.3–4.6 below, where the conclusion will be drawn that the terms of these treaties do not prevent applicability to carriage under multimodal contracts of carriage. In Chapter 5, it will be concluded that an agreement to carry goods by [road] constitutes a contract of carriage by [road] even if that agreement in contained in a multimodal contract of carriage.

struggle for independence may be only natural, but prevention of that development is not merely reactionary but a necessity if the categorization of contracts is to be useful, considering the plethora of new types of contract emerging in modern trade, all claiming their *sui generis* independence.

3.2.2 The network system

A multimodal transport is, as a matter of fact, made up of two or several segments, or legs, of transport by various modes of transport.[42] For example, a multimodal transport from Frankfurt to Atlanta could be carried out by rail between Frankfurt and Rotterdam, by sea between Rotterdam and Baltimore and by road between Baltimore and Atlanta. Thus, another way of looking at the multimodal transport contract is that it consists of two or more contracts for unimodal carriage. In the absence of an international uniform system in force, this network approach is necessary for multimodal transports to be subject to any regulation as regards carriers' liability.

Under the network system each leg of the transport would be governed by the rules applicable to that particular mode: the COTIF–CIM convention to the rail transport between Frankfurt and Rotterdam; the Hague Rules[43] to the sea transport between Rotterdam and Baltimore and national US legislation to the road transport between Baltimore and Atlanta. Hence, the network system may seem quite straightforward. However, the system entails some serious problems.[44] First of all, it presupposes that it is known where, i.e. during which leg of the multimodal transport, the goods were damaged or lost.[45] Secondly, where unimodal regulations contain extensions of their applicability to other modes of transport, such as article 1 § 3 and § 4 of the COTIF–CIM convention, it may be difficult to establish which convention is to apply. Lastly, it is not obvious that the international regulations that adopt the contractual approach to applicability apply to transports carried out under a multimodal contract. Whilst the latter issue will be discussed in section 3.4 below, the two former issues will be the subject of this section.

3.2.2.1 Localization of damage and delay

The conventions discussed in this work regulate, among other things, the carrier's liability for goods during carriage by a certain mode, such as road, rail, sea

42 Door-to-door Transport, *CMI Yearbook 2000*, pp. 118–121, at p. 119, available at (www.comitemaritime.org/Uploads/Yearbooks/Yearbook+2000.pdf); R. De Wit, "Minimal music: multimodal transport including a maritime leg under the Rotterdam Rules" in R. Thomas (ed.), *The Carriage of Goods by Sea Under the Rotterdam Rules* (2010) p. 91.

43 The USA has not acceded to the Visby protocol and is thus only bound by the original Hague Rules.

44 E. Røsæg, "The network principle – An eligible solution or a necessary evil?" in J. Schelin (ed.), *Future Logistics and Transport Law* (2005), pp. 71–78.

45 C. Hancock, "Multimodal transport and the new UN Convention on the carriage of goods" (2008) JIML 484–495, at p. 488; O. Bokareva, *Multimodal Transportation under the Rotterdam Rules* (2015) p. 80.

and air. Due to the scope of application of the international conventions governing carrier's liability, localization of damage and delay is absolutely essential. As an example, the Montreal Convention applies to "international carriage of … goods by aircraft" and subjects the carrier by air to liability as contained in the convention. Thus, the convention only applies to damage (and delay) that occurs during carriage by air. From this follows that in order to apply such a unimodal convention to damage that occurs during multimodal transport, it must be known where the damage occurred, i.e. during which leg of the transport. Due to the scope of application of the current unimodal conventions, none of them is applicable unless the damage is localized.[46]

It is clear that when goods are carried in closed units, such as containers, the prospects of identifying at what point during carriage damage has occurred are limited. Thus, "a locked and sealed container will leave the shipper's premises and arrive, still locked and sealed, at the consignee's premises" and any damage will not be revealed until it is opened by the consignee.[47] In exceptional cases, such as if the goods have been exposed to salt water, or if a collision or other recorded accident has taken place, localizing the damage may be possible. But in the majority of cases there are no indications as to where the damage might have occurred (it is not even certain that the damage has occurred during one particular leg, but may have occurred gradually). In these cases, the network system gives rise to problems. As mentioned, the unimodal conventions presuppose that loss or damage occurred during the transport leg governed by each convention. Thus, unless it can be proved (by the claimant) that loss or damage occurred during a specific leg, no convention is applicable. This would mean that in the majority of cases where containerized goods are damaged, the claimant could be left to general legislation on bailment or similar. The network system hence clearly needs fallback liability rules in cases of non-localized damage.

Accordingly, although the damage undoubtedly has occurred during multimodal transport and the contracting carrier is unquestionably liable for the damage, the problem arises on what basis liability is to be settled. Where none of the unimodal conventions can be applied due to the unknown place and time of the occurrence of the damage, the basis of liability would have to be settled in accordance with other rules.[48]

3.2.2.2 "Terminal-problems", the seam of the network system

Thus, the network system leads to liability gaps in situations where the damage cannot be localized. However, the network system may also lead to another, similar, but reversed, problem. Most unimodal conventions regulate not only the

---

46 M. Hoeks, *Multimodal Transport Law* (2010) p. 17.

47 R. de Wit, *Multimodal Transport* (1995) p. 139.

48 In this case settlement of liability in accordance with e.g. national rules would not seem to trigger the question of the preemptiveness of the liability conventions as it is not a question of the particular damage not being regulated by a convention that applies to the transport operation as such. To the contrary, it is the very inapplicability of the conventions as such that necessitates the application of national law.

carrier's liability during transport as such, but also the carrier's liability during loading and unloading.[49] As unloading from one mode may be loading onto the next mode of transport, asserting the applicable liability regime may prove difficult should damage (or delay for that matter) occur during reloading. It is not unlikely that two conventions turn out to be simultaneously applicable.[50] Multimodal transport is sometimes claimed to be "seamless". However, from a legal point of view there are considerable seams, seams that may entail considerable legal obstacles – "itching seams".

As can be concluded from the previous sections, unimodal conventions are heterogenous as regards liability imposed on the carrier. Even in cases where the liabilities as such are virtually identical, such as under the CMR and the COTIF–CIM, the amounts of limitation of liability differ. For the multimodal contracting carrier, as well as for the sender in some respects, it is important to establish under which liability system the contracting carrier is to reimburse the sender, as this will affect the likelihood of recovering in full from the actual carrier, who in fact caused the damage.

The majority of the conventions discussed subject the carrier to liability for damage to goods from the time that the carrier takes over the goods from the consignor until delivery to the consignee, i.e. during the time the goods are in the care of the carrier.[51] This means that the carrier is liable for the goods during loading operations as well as during storage of the goods as long as the goods have not yet been delivered to the consignee. Prima facie it could appear that this uniformity facilitates settlement of liability and in some respects it does, as will be shown below regarding the Hague–Visby Rules. However, it complicates localization of damage, which is absolutely necessary in order to apply the right set of rules.[52] As an example, if goods are temporarily stored between carriage by road and carriage by rail, both the CMR convention and the COTIF–CIM convention could apply to damage that occurs. As the liability discussed is the liability of the contracting (multimodal) carrier towards the cargo interests, the goods are continuously in the care of that carrier from the point in time when they are first taken over and delivery so that take over between road and rail carriage

49 The CMR convention article 17.1; the Montreal Convention article 18.3 and the COTIF–CIM convention article 23 §1.

50 If the goods are loaded straight from a trailer onto a rail car, without being stored or even put down onto the ground, the same movement is undoubtedly both unloading from the truck and loading onto the rail car. Should the goods be put down onto the ground, it would perhaps theoretically be possible to establish a line between road and rail carriage, but it would clearly be a highly artificial approach.

51 Accordingly, the CMR convention article 17.1, the COTIF–CIM convention article 23 §1, the Montreal Convention article 18.3 and the Rotterdam Rules subject the carrier to their respective liability system from the time the goods are taken over by the carrier until the time of delivery.

52 It follows *e contrario* from the scope of application of the respective conventions that any damage must be localized in order for the rules to apply, as they apply to damage that occurs during transport by a particular mode of transport (R. de Wit, *Multimodal Transport* (1995) p. 139). Further, on a more theoretical level, the application of the "wrong" rules entails breach of its international obligations by the state in which a judgment is given, as it has then not applied the rules of the convention that actually applies.

must thus be artificially settled. If the contracting carrier employs sub-carrier(s) for either or both transports, the line between the two modes may be easier to settle as it could be settled based on the taking over of the goods by the rail sub-carrier. However, if the contracting carrier performs both transports, or if storage is performed by neither the carrier by road nor the carrier by rail, settlement is more complicated. It would seem that the most sensible solution would be to consider for what purpose the goods were stored: for carriage by road or for carriage by rail. Further, the actual location of the storage, i.e. at a rail yard or at a road carriage terminal, could contribute to settlement as well.

Similar issues arise when goods are not temporarily stored but loaded directly from one mode of transport to the next. In that situation, unloading from one mode is loading onto the next mode of transport. Accordingly, if the goods are loaded straight from a trailer onto a rail car, without being stored or even put down onto the ground, the same movement is undoubtedly both unloading from the truck and loading onto the rail car. As both the CMR convention and the COTIF–CIM convention apply to loading/unloading operations, both conventions are prima facie applicable should damage occur during such operations.[53] In a case judged by the Austrian Supreme Court in 1995, it was held that damage occurring during reloading from road to rail transport, under a multimodal contract of carriage, was to be subject to carriage by road liability rules based on the fact that the sub-carrier by rail had not yet accepted the goods from the sub-carrier by road.[54] This solution seems to reflect the prerequisite of the COTIF–CIM convention that the rail carrier is liable for the goods from the time they have been taken over. However, it does not assist in settlement when one carrier performs both legs of the transport.

Further, it has been held that the network system entails gaps in liability for damage that occurs during storage between two transport movements.[55] However, under a multimodal contract of carriage, the contracting carrier takes over the goods from the initial consignor and delivers them to the final consignee, either itself or through sub-contracted carriers. Thus, the contracting carrier no doubt has continuous liability for the goods. On the other hand, should none of the liability conventions be applicable the liability of the contracting multimodal carrier would be governed by national rules, such as the liability of a bailee or similar.

Under all conventions discussed, with the exception of the Hague–Visby Rules, the carrier is subject to liability during the entire time that the goods are in the care of the carrier. Therefore, the problem of settling which of two possible conventions is applicable is likely to be more common than the problem discussed here. However, where carriage by sea is part of a multimodal transport,

53 Should the goods be put down onto the ground, it would perhaps theoretically be possible to establish a line between road and rail carriage, but it would definitely be a highly artificial approach and even if it is possible to artificially draw a line between the unloading operation and the reloading operation, that line may be possible to draw only after extensive litigation.

54 A. Schmid, "Austria: carriage of goods – rail and road" (1995) 3(10) Int ILR G199–200.

55 R. De Wit, *Multimodal Transport* (1995) pp. 140–141.

the Hague–Visby Rules may cause a liability gap, at least to the extent that liability cannot be based on either convention. Where carriage by sea is combined with carriage by road or rail, storage of the goods may be covered by the land carrier's liability. As mentioned above this could be the case if the goods are damaged during storage in a port, where they are awaiting onward carriage by road. In that case they are stored for the purposes of road transport and it would seem natural to consider the contracting carrier to be in charge of the goods in the capacity of road carrier. Thus, liability can be settled according to the CMR convention. In accordance with the above-mentioned judgment from the Austrian Supreme Court, damage could further be allocated to the road transport leg if the sub-carrier by road, to the extent one exists, has accepted the goods from the carrier by sea. However, when the goods are stored in a port awaiting sea carriage, it may be more difficult to base the contracting carrier's liability on the rules of an international convention, at least if that carriage by sea convention is the Hague–Visby Rules, which limit the sea carrier's liability to the time loading operations are initiated.[56] Thus, in this particular instance there may be a gap in liability, at least as far as liability based on international conventions regulating the carrier's liability is concerned.[57] This liability gap is eliminated in the Hamburg Rules as well as in the Rotterdam Rules. The Scandinavian maritime codes, in line with their general adaptation to the Hamburg Rules, extend the sea carrier's period of liability to the period between receipt of the goods in the port of loading to delivery of the goods in the port of discharge.[58]

3.2.2.3 The modified network system

In order to avoid problems caused by unlocalized damage, as well as gradually occurring damage and delay, and to seal possible gaps in uniform law described above, the modified network system is often promoted as a solution.[59] The modified network system is modified in that it supplements the ordinary network system with a "catch-all" provision. Hence, any damage that is not regulated by mandatory uniform law is regulated by a general liability rule. The most obvious benefit of this modification is foreseeability: the parties do not risk any liability being governed by national legislation of which they have no knowledge.

A modified network system could obviously be imposed through uniform law, but in the absence of such law nothing prevents the parties from contractually

56 The Hague–Visby Rules are generally considered to subject the carrier to liability for the goods from "tackle-to-tackle", i.e. from the time the loading of the goods on to the ship is initiated until their discharge is completed. This conclusion is based on article 1(e), which confines "carriage of goods" to the period from loading to discharge, which thus limits the scope of application of the rules to this period (cf. F. Berlingieri, "A comparative analysis of the Hague–Visby Rules, the Hamburg Rules and the Rotterdam Rules"; published at www.uncitral.org/pdf/english/workinggroups/wg_3/Berlingieri_paper_comparing_RR_Hamb_HVR.pdf. See also F. Sejersted, *Haagreglerne* (1976) p. 40.

57 It may not be too far-fetched to assume that the contract of carriage contains a "catch-all" provision providing for application of e.g. the CMR convention where no other mandatory rules apply. However, this does not eliminate the fact that a legal gap exists.

58 Cf. *The Swedish Maritime Code* (SFS 1994:1009) ch. 13:24.

59 R. De Wit, *Multimodal Transport* (1995) pp. 142–143.

agreeing to it.[60] Further, the Dutch and German national systems described in section 3.2.3 below are essentially modified network systems.

3.2.2.4 Unauthorized substitution

It is generally held that unauthorized substitution of the agreed mode of transport does not affect the applicable rules.[61] This conclusion is based on the prerequisite of the existence of a contract of carriage found in several of the conventions discussed; if the carrier, without being authorized to do so in the contract, substitutes the mode of transport, no contract exists for the mode by which the goods are carried.[62] It has even been held that the carrier may not invoke the liability rules of the transport mode by which the goods were actually carried *to the detriment* of cargo interests, if the substitution constitutes a breach of contract.[63] Where the carrier substitutes the mode of transport without contractual consent, Danish doctrine has held that the cargo interests would be allowed to choose the liability rules to be applied; either those applicable to the mode of transport contracted for, or those applicable to the mode of transport actually used.[64] In fact, it has even been held by the Danish Supreme Court that even where substitution is contractually permitted, the cargo owner may invoke the legal rules pertaining to the substituted for mode of transport, whilst at the same time the court held that a contract of carriage is not affected by invocation of an option to substitute mode of transport and thus remains a contract for the carriage of goods by the mode that was initially agreed upon.[65] The effect would thus be that the cargo owner could choose the most favourable liability rules where substitution has taken place, contractually permitted or not. However, the predominant view appears to be that in the case of unauthorized substitution, the liability rules of the agreed mode of transport are applicable. This conclusion is also the view most consistent with the scope of application of the sea and land conventions, which

---

60 See for example the FIATA Multimodal B/L, article 6.

61 V. Ulfbeck and S. Taiger Ivø, "Optioner og ansvar i transportaftaler" (2008) 4 Erhvervsjuridisk Tidsskrift 331–343, at p. 333, J. Heidbrink, *Logistikavtalet* (2005) pp. 50–51, M. Hoeks, *Multimodal Transport Law* (2010) p. 83, L. Andersen Roost, *Multimodale transporter* (2012) p. 75, U. Fabricuis, *Lov om fraktaftaler ved international vejtransport* (2005) p. 39 with further references, P. Vestergaard Pedersen, *Transportret* (2008) pp. 942–943.

62 See V. Ulfbeck and S. Taiger Ivø, "Optioner og ansvar i transportaftaler" (2008) 4 Erhvervsjuridisk tidskrift 331–343, at p. 333.

63 L. Andersen Roost, *Multimodale transporter* (2012) p. 75.

64 Fabricus holds that a carrier who substitutes a mode of transport without contractual consent cannot achieve a more favourable position through invoking the rules for that other mode of transport. The cargo interest can thus claim against the carrier under the CMR although no road carriage was ever performed. In addition, the cargo interest can claim indemnification under general contract law for breach of contract (U. Fabricuis, *Lov om fraktaftaler ved international vejtransport* (2005) p. 41). See also V. Ulfbeck and S. Taiger Ivø, *ibid.*, at p. 341.

65 See V. Ulfbeck and S. Taiger Ivø, *ibid.*, at p. 340 and Danish Supreme Court U.2008.1638H, at p. 1652. The statement by the Danish Supreme Court, which was made *obiter*, would appear to be based on equity, although no justification is actually provided by the court. Certainly, it could appear just to allow the cargo interests to benefit from a choice as the carrier in fact had committed a breach of contract. However, the possible losses suffered by the cargo interests would have to be indemnified under a claim for breach of contract.

by their wording apply to contracts of carriage by a certain mode.[66] As regards carriage by air, the Montreal Convention explicitly applies to carriage that should have been carried out by air but is substituted for another mode without the consent of the consignee.[67]

Although the rules pertaining to a particular mode of transport are best adapted to the preconditions of that mode of transport, there seems to be no justification for allowing the carrier to invoke rules that apply to a mode of transport used in breach of the contract of carriage, and certainly not where those rules are more beneficial to the carrier compared to the rules that would otherwise apply. There is certainly more appeal in allowing the cargo interests to choose the set of rules that provide the preferred outcome. However, with the exception of the Montreal Convention, there are no legal preconditions for such a right to choose. Conventions that adhere to the contractual approach to applicability, such as the CMR and the COTIF–CIM, as well as the Hague–Visby Rules in fact, would not apply autonomously to carriage carried out in breach of a contract.[68] The discussion conducted, and conclusions drawn above, regarding the effects of invoking an option to substitute mode of transport are only valid as regards contractually allowed for substitution. Where the carrier substitutes without contractual permission, there is no basis for claiming the existence of a contract for carriage by [road], a contract that must exist in order for these conventions to be autonomously applicable. Performance alone does not trigger such applicability.[69]

3.2.3 The systems applied in national legislations

In view of the increasing dominance of multimodal transport solutions, and against the background of the increasing uncertainty as regards the applicability of certain unimodal transport of goods conventions to unimodal legs of a multimodal transport, together with the fact that no multimodal transport convention has yet been accepted, there is an obvious opportunity for national solutions. However only two such examples of national legislation seem to be in place; in Germany and in the Netherlands.[70]

3.2.3.1 German national legislation

In Germany, modernized national transport legislation was enacted in 1998. The regulation is found in the German Commercial Code, the Handelsgesetzbuch (HGB), and is to a large extent modelled after the CMR convention. The code unifies transportation by road, rail, inner waterways and air as well as multimodal

66 Cf. sections 4.3, 4.5 and 4.6 below.
67 Article 18.4.
68 K. Haak, *The Liability of the Carrier under the CMR* (1986) p. 44 (fn. 22).
69 See further section 5.7 below.
70 M. Hoeks, *Multimodal Transport Law* (2010) p. 456 and E. Eftestøl-Wilhelmsson, *European Sustainable Carriage of Goods* (2016) pp. 24–27. Also, England can be regarded as having clear law on the topic in accordance with the *Quantum* case decided by the Court of Appeal in 2002 (*Quantum Corporation Inc v Plane Trucking Ltd* [2002] 2 Lloyd's Rep 25).

transportation under one common set of rules.[71] As regards multimodal transport the definition thereof is transport of goods by more than one mode of transport carried out subject to one single transport contract.[72] In order to qualify as a mode of transport under the code, it must be subject to separate liability regimes *per se*. That is, had separate unimodal contracts been entered into, those unimodal contracts should be subject to different liability regimes, in order for the transport mode to be regarded as a separate mode of transport.[73] Hence, for example, loading carried out by forklift is not considered a mode of transport and will thus not cause a transport contract to be regarded as a multimodal contract.[74] According to the HGB a contract of multimodal carriage is then subject to the general rules on transport on carrier's liability unless it is subject to regulation in an international convention. In this respect it is only international conventions that actually regulate multimodal transport that will be acknowledged.[75] The German legislation is based on the presumption that the existing unimodal conventions, such as the Hague–Visby Rules, the CMR convention and the COTIF–CIM convention, do not apply to multimodal transport to a larger degree than is explicit in those conventions (see section 3.4 below). Therefore, from the point of view of the HGB, unimodal conventions are not autonomously applicable to the (unimodal) parts of a multimodal transport.

Where it can be established during which transport leg, i.e. during which mode of transport, loss or damage occurred, the HGB stipulate a network approach under a hypothetical contract formula. Hence, the liability system that would have been applied had the carrier and the sender entered into a separate agreement

---

71 Even though maritime transport is covered by separate legislation (also found in the HGB), multimodal transport is always subject to the same rules whether it includes maritime transport or not.

72 L. Andersen Roost, *Multimodale Transporter* (2012) p. 229.

73 HGB §452 reads:

> If carriage of goods is performed by various modes of transport on the basis of a single contract of carriage, and if, had separate contracts been concluded between the parties for each part of the carriage which involved one mode of transport (leg of carriage), at least two of these contracts would have been subject to different legal rules, the provisions of the first subsection shall apply to the contract, unless the following special provisions or applicable international conventions provide otherwise. This also applies if part of the carriage is performed by sea.
>
> a) If it has been established that the loss, damage or event which caused delay in delivery occurred on a specific stage of the carriage, the liability of the carrier shall, contrary to the provisions of the first subsection, be determined in accordance with the legal provisions which would apply to a contact of carriage covering this stage. [...].
>
> b) [...].
>
> (this translation appears in M. Hoeks, *Multimodal Transport Law* (2010) pp. 463 and 465)

By the "first subsection" is indicated the general provisions of transport law, i.e. HGB Book 4, section 4 (M. Hoeks, *ibid.*, at p. 462).

74 L. Andersen Roost, *ibid.* at pp. 230–231. Which regulation these unimodal parts of the multimodal transport would be subject to is decided in accordance with German international private law, i.e. mainly the Rome I Regulation (Regulation (EC) No. 593/2008 of the European Parliament and of the Council of 17 June 2008 on the law applicable to contractual obligations).

75 However, unimodal international transports that in all respects fulfil the criteria of applicability of the respective conventions will always be subject to such convention.

on a unimodal basis, will be applied to settle the carrier's liability.[76] Accordingly, the network system is imposed with mandatory force[77] through the hypothetical contract formula, thus avoiding the problem of the autonomous applicability of unimodal conventions.[78]

In conclusion, and as regards international multimodal transport, it may be held that German legislation provides for a network system with a fallback regulation for non-localized loss, damage and delay.[79] It also clearly assumes that unimodal transport conventions, such as the COTIF–CIM and the CMR, are not autonomously applicable to carriage carried out under a multimodal transport contract.

3.2.3.2 Dutch national legislation

The Netherlands also has national legislation regulating multimodal transport. Dutch regulation of multimodal, or combined, transport subsumes multimodal transport contracts that are subject to Dutch law to the network system.[80] However, the legislation imposes the network system only to the extent the relevant unimodal regimes are *applicable* to a multimodal transport leg.[81] This entails that the question of applicability of the unimodal conventions to multimodal transport contracts is not avoided, but has to be considered before the network system can be applied.[82] The legislation indicates that the position taken by the Dutch legislator must have been that mode-based regulations, such as the CMR convention, apply to transport carried out under a multimodal contract as otherwise the statute in question serves no purpose.[83] The fallback provision concerning non-localized loss, damage or delay entails that the liability regulation, applicable to each leg

76 The general transportation rules regulate not only the carrier's liability but also issues such as the waybill, loading and unloading, packaging, payment, time-limits, arbitration, liens and the like. However, it is only the liability rules of the other unimodal transport regulation that supersedes these general rules (L. Andersen Roost, *Multimodale Transporter* (2012) pp. 221–222 and pp. 232–233).

77 It is stressed that this mandatory force is limited to the jurisdictional force of German national legislation and does (naturally) not make the conventions so applied applicable by their own force.

78 The same approach was taken by the drafters of the Rotterdam Rules, cf. section 3.3.1.4 above.

79 E. Eftestøl-Wilhelmsson, *European Sustainable Carriage of Goods* (2016) p. 27.

80 M. Hoeks, *Multimodal Transport Law* (2010) p. 456 and M. Spanjaart, "GODAFOSS: the applicability of the CMR within multimodal contracts of carriage" in (2012) 7TranspR 278–282, at p. 278.

81 Article 8:41 of the Dutch Civil Code provides: "In a contract of combined carriage of goods, each part of the carriage is governed by the judicial rules applicable to that part" (translation by Spanjaart (M. Spanjaart, *ibid.*, at p. 278)). See also M. Hoeks, *ibid.* at pp. 456–457.

82 Since in international transport this could cause severe problems, it has been held that the same hypothetical contract formula as applied in German law (as well as in article 2 of the CMR and in the Rotterdam Rules) is to be applied in order to identify the appropriate rules (M. Spanjaart, *ibid.*, at p. 278). However, it is not clear what this proposal is based on. Further, Hoeks is of the opposite opinion, i.e. that the statute requires the autonomous applicability of the conventions concerned (M. Hoeks, *ibid.* at pp. 456–457).

83 M. Hoeks, *Multimodal Transport Law* (2010) p. 458. However, this view is undermined by the Dutch Supreme Court's decision in the *Godafoss* case (Dutch Supreme Court, Hoge Raad, 1 June 2012, nr.10/05322). It could obviously be argued that where the unimodal conventions are autonomously applicable the statute is also somewhat superfluous; see M. Hoeks, *ibid.*, at p. 457.

of the multimodal transport, that provides the highest amount of reimbursement for the cargo interests is to apply.[84]

Although national legislation could be used to impose a uniform system, at least on a national level, it appears that the desire was instead to enforce the network system. As a legal situation where states would enforce national uniform systems on multimodal transport would entail the severe undermining of the legal foreseeability attempted by the system of uniform law governing carriers' liability, it is certainly wise that so far states do not seem too eager to establish such systems.

3.2.4 Conclusions

The rationale behind the network system is to a large extent the lack of a uniform system; although the need for a uniform system that regulates multimodal transport in its entirely has been long recognized, no international convention has yet entered the scene. The network system is, however, based on the precondition that the unimodal conventions are applicable to the unimodal legs of a multimodal transport.[85] As will be discussed in detail below, the applicability of conventions governing land-based transport, which adhere to the contractual approach to applicability, to transports carried out under a multimodal (or non-unimodal) contract has been disputed. Obviously, the position that these unimodal conventions are only applicable to unimodal contracts seriously undermines the network system. It does not seem possible to predict the outcome of this discussion; the only thing that seems to be certain is that there is no uniform application of the CMR convention in this respect and that case law in the member states is heterogeneous. A point of note is that states that have imposed national legislation that covers multimodal transport regulate such transport through the network system, albeit providing a fallback for non-localized damage.

On the other hand, should the unimodal conventions that apply to contracts of carriage by a certain mode be considered autonomously applicable to carriage under multimodal contracts of carriage, a situation may arise where two conventions are simultaneously applicable to a certain transport. This is caused by the fact that most unimodal conventions extend their applicability to transport by other modes under certain circumstances. The issue of overlapping conventions is by no means new; theoretically, a conflict could arise between the CMR convention and the Hague–Visby Rules or the COTIF–CIM convention when piggy-back transport of a road vehicle is international. In reality it does not, however, seem to have caused insurmountable problems, perhaps because

84 Article 8:42 (1) and 8:43 of the Dutch Civil Code in translation by M. Spanjaart, "GODAFOSS: the applicability of the CMR within multimodal contracts of carriage" (2012) 7 TranspR 278–282, at p. 279. M. Hoeks, *ibid.*, at p. 459. Note that this provision only refers to the *liability* of the carrier; see M. Hoeks, *ibid.*, at p. 459.

85 Again, this statement relates to an international level; the gaps possibly created can be solved contractually or through national legislation, which however, in the perspective of uniform law, seems to be unsatisfactory.

such multimodal transport has been considered road transport rather than multimodal and the contract, as well as the transport documents, has been considered by the parties to be for carriage by road. However, where the contract is purely multimodal, i.e. undefined as no mode of transport appears as the agreed mode of transport, the problem resembles the above-discussed application problem. In such an undefined contract, an international piggy-back transport of a trailer by rail, e.g. through the Simplon tunnel between Switzerland and Italy or through the Channel tunnel between England and France, could theoretically be governed by both the COTIF–CIM convention and the CMR convention.

The preceding review has also shown that the network system does entail several problems, which perhaps could be referred to as application issues, that is problems connected with application of the network system. Many of these problems would be solved by the implementation of a uniform system. i.e. a liability system governing multimodal transport *per se*.

Applying a uniform system would indeed provide a solution to these problems and in the absence of a uniform multimodal convention the same result could perhaps be achieved contractually. However, to the extent the conventions discussed are autonomously applicable, the rules thereof would apply mandatorily and any contractual agreement regarding settlement of the carrier's liability that infringes on the rules of the conventions would accordingly be set aside.

In the absence of a uniform system, the consequence of not allowing the network system to apply through the autonomous applicability of the unimodal liability rules is freedom of contract. Although the position of the contracting consignor as the weaker party in relation to the contracting carrier, which has traditionally been the starting point of all existing liability rules, may be discussed, the step between mandatorily applicable uniform rules and complete freedom of contract is a long one. Thus, whilst the carrier contracting for a unimodal international transport would be forced to subscribe to such mandatory rules, contracting for multimodal carriage would allow the same carrier to impose any contractual terms on the contracting consignor. The difference in foreseeability on the part of the contracting consignor cannot be justified by the difference in the two forms of transport, which is non-significant. In effect, the network system would, despite the flaws discussed above, provide greater foreseeability for the cargo interests than the non-applicability of such system.

3.3 Multimodal aspects of the unimodal conventions

As mentioned in the introduction to the current chapter, all conventions discussed, except for the Hague–Visby Rules, provide to a certain extent for the extension of its unimodal rules to transport by other modes. Thus, each system is self-contained, and it appears that the extent thereof is limited to the multimodality that could be foreseen at the time of drafting of each convention. As multimodality has expanded and transport patterns have changed, it could be questioned whether these extensions facilitate the settling of the carrier's liability or if they constitute an obstacle to the network system.

Further, to the extent that the unimodal conventions discussed are considered to be applicable *ex proprio vigore* to carriage under multimodal contracts, the multimodal extensions of the unimodal conventions would risk to conflict with the unimodal rules governing the mode of transport to which a convention is extended. As these risks are intimately connected to the overriding research question (to what extent can unimodal transport of goods conventions be applied to transport carried out under a multimodal transport contract?), they will be analysed below.

3.3.1 Extended scope of applicability of unimodal conventions

To some extent, most unimodal conventions include a multimodal feature, however distinctive in their respective scopes. Whilst the Montreal Convention relating to carriage by air applies a minimal approach to inclusion of transport by other modes within its ambit, the CMR convention and the COTIF–CIM convention are more generous with their applicability to transport by other modes.

3.3.1.1 The CMR convention

As elaborated above, the CMR convention applies to contracts for the carriage of goods by road. Under certain circumstances, however, the convention also applies to carriage by other modes of transport. Thus, article 2.1, states:

> Where the vehicle containing the goods is carried over part of the journey by sea, rail, inland waterways or air, and, except where the provisions of article 14 are applicable, the goods are not unloaded from the vehicle, this Convention shall nevertheless apply to the whole of the carriage. Provided that to the extent it is proved that any loss, damage or delay in delivery of the goods which occurs during the carriage by the other means of transport was not caused by act or omission of the carrier by road, but by some event which could only occurred in the course of and by reason of the carriage by that other means of transport, the liability of the carrier by road shall be determined not by this convention but in the manner in which the liability of the carrier by the other means of transport would have been determined if a contract for the carriage the goods alone had been made by the sender with the carrier by the other means of transport in accordance with the conditions prescribed by law for the carriage of goods by that means of transport. If, however, there are no such prescribed conditions, the liability of the carrier by road shall be determined by this convention.

The article can be said to be divided into two parts: the general rule and the exception. The general rule is that where goods are carried (1) under a contract for carriage by road and (2) without being unloaded from the road vehicle, (3) which is carried by another mode of transport – the CMR applies to such "mode on mode" carriage. In practice, this means that ro/ro carriage (trailers carried by ferry e.g. over the Öresund sound) and piggy-back transport of trailers by train (e.g. under the English Channel) falls under the application of the CMR convention so that the liability of the road carrier towards the sender/consignee is covered by a single liability regime. It should be noted in this regard that the mode-on-mode transport must be carried out under a contract of carriage by road and not by a separate contract.

Application of the general rule inevitably means that the road carrier's liability to the sender/consignee will differ from the liability regime under which the road carrier will be able to recover from the actual carrier, such as a sea carrier or railway. The general rule further entails that damage or loss that occurred during a transport by another mode than by road will be assessed under a liability regime unfamiliar with the special risks of that mode of transport.

For this reason, an exception provides the road carrier with a right, under certain circumstances, to rely on the defences and limitations of liability available to the actual carrier, such as those found in the Hague–Visby Rules or the COTIF–CIM convention. Thus, article 2.1 of the CMR convention stipulates that where a damage or loss has occurred (1) during the carriage by the other means of transport, (2) due to an event particular to that other mode of transport and (3) where there is no fault on the part of the road carrier, the road carrier may rely on the (4) mandatory rules applicable had there been a separate contract between the sender and the actual carrier for that leg of the transport. Whilst the first prerequisite may be difficult in practice, for the same reasons as localizing damage in general, it does not seem to cause legal concern. However, when damage or loss occurs at the intersection of two modes, such as during the loading of the road vehicle onto a ship,[86] the question may arise whether the carriage by another mode of transport has commenced. Conversely, what is legally not as unproblematic is the carriage as such and whether the carriage by another means of transport than road must have been contractually agreed. Whereas in some instances piggy-back transport, although not expressly agreed between the parties, must have been envisaged by the parties and thus implied in the carriage contract, for example in carriage from Scandinavia to the continent or from the UK to the continent, in some instances it has neither been expressly nor impliedly agreed between the parties. On this point, Messent and Glass conclude that where carriage by another mode has been done without the prior consent of the sender, then the carrier cannot evade CMR liability.[87] Accordingly, they hold, the exception in article 2.1 is only applicable where it has been agreed that the road vehicle is to be carried by another mode of transport during part of the carriage.[88]

The second prerequisite, prescribing that the loss or damage must have been caused by an "event which could only have occurred in the course of and by reason of the carriage by that other means of transport", seems to channel the carrier's liability so that risks that are particular to a certain mode of transport are governed by the rules adapted to such risks. First of all, the condition that the damage or loss must have occurred "in the course of" the carriage by the other means of transport seems to reiterate the previous prerequisite that the damage or loss must have

86 *Thermo Engineers Ltd. v Ferrymasters Ltd.* [1981] 1 Lloyd's Rep 200.

87 A. Messent and D. Glass, *CMR: Contracts for the international carriage of goods by road* (2000) p. 49. This is an uncontroversial statement; cf. section 3.2.2.4 above.

88 See also U. Fabricius, *Lov om fragtaftler ved international vejtransport* (2005) p. 69.

occurred during the carriage by the other means of transport.[89] That said, the condition in question is qualified by the criterion that the event causing the damage or loss "could only" have occurred in the course of the carriage by the other mode of transport. Thus, it is not enough that the damage or loss occurs during the transport by another means of transport, but the event must be particular to the operation of that mode of transport. The other condition, that the damage or loss must have been caused by an event that could "only" occur "by reason of" the carriage by the other means of transport may seem straightforward but has caused legal disagreements. As the reason behind the exception in article 2.1 seems to be that causes of damage that are particular to a certain mode of transport should be governed by the rules specifically applicable to that mode of transport, it would be easy to conclude that damage caused "only" "by reason of" a certain mode of transport must have been caused by an event particular to that mode. Clarke exemplifies this line of reasoning by equating "only" "by reason of" with "perils of the sea" in cases of ro-ro carriage by sea.[90] However, this interpretation of the article has been rejected in case law. Thus, in 1981 the collision of a trailer with a bulk head of a ship was held by an English court to be "by reason of" the carriage by sea, as a collision with *a bulk head of a ship* can only occur during carriage by sea.[91] Thus, the English courts have taken a wide approach where almost any event occurring on e.g. a vessel is particular to carriage by sea. Such an approach benefits the contracting carrier, as most claims against him will be fully recoverable from the actual carrier. A narrower approach, where "event" is construed as referring to a collision with an overhead obstruction rather than a bulk head of a ship, on the other hand promotes the uniform applicability of the CMR convention to the entire carriage in line with the general rule in article 2.1. This narrower approach was taken by a Dutch appellate court in 1989,[92] as well as by a Danish district court in 1993.[93] However, the wider approach seems to have established itself among scholars.[94] It seems, however, that had the intention of the drafters been that the exemption should apply where the *actual event* rather than the *type of event*[95] is particular to the other mode of transport, article 2.1 is indeed overly complicated in its drafting as then this second prerequisite would seem redundant altogether.[96]

The third condition prescribes that the loss or damage must not have been caused by the contracting carrier, which means that where the damage has been

89 A. Messent and D. Glass, *ibid.*, at p. 53.

90 M. Clarke; *International Carriage of Goods by Road: CMR* (2014) p. 43, which, however, he admits is incoherent with *Thermo Engineers Ltd. v Ferrymasters Ltd.* [1981] 1 Lloyd's Rep 200.

91 *Thermo Engineers Ltd. v Ferrymasters Ltd.* [1981] 1 Lloyd's Rep 200. The cargo interests proposed that the collision was to be equated with any collision with an overhead obstacle such as a bridge, and so was not to be considered particular to carriage by sea.

92 *Enka AG v Estron BV*, Hague Court of Appeal, reported in 1990 I Unif L Rev o.s. 242 1990.

93 Københavns Byret den 05.10.1993, E 1309/92, discussed in U. Fabricius, *Lov om fragtaftler ved international vejtransport* (2005) p. 77.

94 J. Ramberg, "Deviation from the Legal Regime of the CMR" in J. Theunis (ed.), *International Carriage of Goods by Road (CMR)* (1987) pp. 19–30, at p. 27.

95 J. Ramberg, *ibid.*, at p. 27.

96 M. Clarke, *ibid.*, at p. 44.

caused by the carrier by road the CMR convention always applies. This prerequisite must be distinguished from article 3 according to which the contracting carrier is liable for persons whose services he makes use of in the performance of his duties. Although the contracting carrier answers for the actions of the actual carrier, in the current respect the "carrier" must be limited to road carriers, thus not including the subcarrier carrying out the carriage by sea, as the third prerequisite would otherwise make no sense. However, it is not suggested that "the carrier" in article 2.1 is to be equated to the carrier in article 29 regarding loss of right of limitation.[97] Rather, the carrier in article 2.1 should be interpreted to mean the carrier and his servants in a narrow sense, that is his employees or servants carrying out *the carriage by road*.[98]

As a final condition, the CMR convention only gives preference to conditions prescribed by law that would have been applicable had the sender made a separate contract for carriage by the other mode. This condition is the subject of some confusion since the English and French (equally authentic) texts are somewhat incoherent. Whilst the English text reads "conditions prescribed by law", the French text reads "dispositions impératives de la loi", i.e. "mandatory provisions of law". This has led to some discussion, although there seems to be no real question that the CMR convention only gives preference to mandatory legislation.[99] It could be noted that where no mandatory rules govern a contract of carriage, the hypothetical contract envisaged becomes perhaps a bit too hypothetical as to its contents. However, it may well be that this confusion is based on a civil law perspective. Clarke equals conditions prescribed by law with compulsory rules without even mentioning the incoherence between the English and French texts, which indicates that to an English lawyer "conditions prescribed by law" concerns mandatory rules.[100] Also Messent and Glass assume that the CMR convention only succumbs to mandatory legislation and strongly object to the findings in *Thermo Engineers Ltd. v Ferrymasters Ltd*[101] that the hypothetical contract should consider such permitted variations that the parties could and would have made.[102] However, it should be noted that the discussion does not cover mandatory v optional legislation, which may suggest that this is rather a civil law distinction.

As regards the hypothetical contract between the sender and the actual carrier, this provision might cause some problems in application. As regards piggy-back transport by rail, the COTIF–CIM convention applies with mandatory force to contracts for the carriage of goods by rail, which would have been the type of contract the sender and the carrier by rail had made. However, as regards piggy-back transport by sea, ro-ro transport, the fact that may cause problems is that

97 Article 29.2.

98 U. Fabricius, *Lov om fragtaftler ved international vejtransport* (2005) p. 75; A. Messent and D. Glass; *CMR: Contracts for the international carriage of goods by road* (2000) p. 52.

99 U. Fabricius *ibid.*, at p. 81.

100 M. Clarke, *International Carriage of Goods by Road: CMR* (2014) p. 45.

101 *Thermo Engineers Ltd. v Ferrymasters Ltd.* [1981] 1 Lloyd's Rep 200.

102 A. Messent and D. Glass *ibid.* at pp. 54–59.

the rules applicable to transport by sea, the Hague or Hague–Visby Rules, only applies where the contract of carriage provides for the issuing of a bill of lading. There is no doubt that not all transport of goods by sea is subject to bills of lading. In ro-ro transport, i.e. relatively short crossings by ferry, it could be assumed that most carriage is carried out without a bill of lading. The question thus becomes: should a court applying article 2.1 assume that a separate contract between the sender and the actual carrier would have prescribed for the issuing of a bill of lading, as only then do the provisions adapted to sea transport apply,[103] or should the court consider that most ro-ro transport is not performed under a bill of lading. In a Belgian case,[104] the court concluded that since no bill of lading had been issued for the transport, as contracted between the road carrier and the sea carrier, no bill of lading would have been issued under a hypothetical contract directly between the sender and the sea carrier. Fabricius concludes that if the non-issuance of a bill of lading for the actual carriage disqualifies application of the Hague–Visby Rules in accordance with CMR article 2.1, the exemption rule loses most of its importance.[105] However, the type of contract actually entered into between the contracting carrier and the carrier by sea is adapted to the fact that during ro-ro transport the goods remain in the possession of the carrier by road, which makes a bill of lading redundant. Had, on the other hand, a separate contract for carriage by sea been entered into by the shipper and the sea carrier it is not obvious that such a contract would have been for the goods *and* the vehicle, why thus the use of a bill of lading may be more likely.

3.3.1.2 The COTIF–CIM convention

The COTIF Convention and its Annex b – CIM – applies to carriage of goods by rail between approximately 40 states. Like the CMR convention, the COTIF–CIM convention applies to carriage by other modes of transport than rail in certain specific cases (article 1):

> § 3 When international carriage being the subject of a single contract includes carriage by road or inland waterway in internal traffic of a Member State as a supplement to trans-frontier carriage by rail, these Uniform Rules shall apply.
>
> § 4 When international carriage being the subject of a single contract of carriage includes carriage by sea or transfrontier carriage by inland waterway as a supplement to carriage by rail, these Uniform Rules shall apply if the carriage by sea or inland waterway is performed on services included in the list of services provided for in Article 24 § 1 of the Convention.

Thus, the COTIF–CIM convention may be applicable to road carriage as well as carriage by sea, but never to air carriage. The prerequisites for applicability of the convention to road carriage and to sea carriage differ, but the common denominator is that the carriage by road or sea must be carried out under the contract

103 If no mandatory rules apply, the CMR will govern the carriage as stated in the general rule despite the damage or loss being particular to carriage by sea.

104 Hof Van Beroep te Antwerpen, 15 March 1989, reported in (1989) ETL 574.

105 U. Fabricius, *Lov om fragtaftler ved international vejtransport* (2005) p. 84.

of carriage by rail, i.e. the transport is subject to a single contract. Further, the carriage by road or sea must be supplemental to the carriage by rail. Hoeks concludes that the COTIF–CIM convention applies to feeder transport, such as pickup and delivery services, and defines supplemental carriage as carriage of "lesser import than the rail stage".[106] However, there seems to be no ground for restricting the applicability of article 1 §§ 3 and 4 in such a way. The only prerequisites imposed are in fact that the contract is one for carriage by rail and that the carriage by road, sea or inland waterway is carried out as a supplement to such international carriage by rail, supplemental carriage being carriage that completes the transport contract. What makes a particular carriage supplemental does not seem to be elaborated and there seem to be no quantifiable restrictions such as distance in kilometres or time. As long as the contract is one for carriage by rail (and is deemed as such when scrutinized), the supplemental carriage can be both long and time-consuming. If carriage of goods from Kiruna in northern Sweden to Narvik in northern Norway is complemented by carriage by road to Tromsø (there is no railway north of Narvik), the carriage by road being 250 kilometres compared to the 170 kilometres by rail, such carriage by road could very well be deemed supplemental to the international carriage by rail.

In addition, the effect of article 1 §§ 3 and 4 is limited by the prerequisite that, as regards transport by road, such transport will be subject to the COTIF–CIM convention, only if it is domestic,[107] and as regards transport by sea and trans frontier carriage by inland waterway, such transport must be carried out on lines included in a special list published by the OTIF in order to be subject to the convention.

3.3.1.3 The Montreal Convention

The Montreal Convention from 1999 applies to carriage by aircraft.[108] It does not prima facie extend to carriage by other modes.[109] However, according to article 18, the carrier's liability comprises carriage by air, which commences when the carrier takes charge over the goods.[110] This entails that the air carrier's liability under the convention may comprise carriage by other modes. However, according to article 18.4 the period of carriage by air will never extend to carriage

106 M. Hoeks, *Multimodal Transport Law* (2010) p. 264.

107 The application was limited to domestic road transport as the drafters wanted to avoid conflicts with the CMR convention – which in turn, according to Hoeks, indicates that the COTIF–CIM convention is meant to apply to rail stages of a multimodal transport (M. Hoeks, *ibid.*, at p. 267).

108 It is actually not explicitly stated that the carriage must be by *air*. Aircraft is defined in Standards and Recommended Practises of the ICAO as "Any machine that can derive support in the atmosphere from the reactions of the air other than the reactions of the air against the earth's surface", thus implying that all machines that *can* thus derive their support, seemingly including carriage by such machine on land, although this would not seem to be a common feature. However, in article 18.3 the carrier's period of liability is limited to carriage by air. In article 18.3 a reference is made to article 1, which seems somewhat awkward: "The carriage by air within the meaning of paragraph 1 of this Article comprises the period during which the cargo is in the charge of the carrier.", as no mention of *carriage by air* is made in article 1.

109 Article 1.

110 Article 18:1 and 18:3.

by another mode unless such carriage takes place within the boundaries of the airport. Thus the convention's applicability to other modes of transport is rather insignificant.[111] Although, where carriage by another mode of transport (expressly defined as carriage by land, sea or inland waterway) takes place under the same contract as the carriage by air for the purposes of loading, delivery or transhipment, any damage sustained by the goods is presumed to have been caused during carriage by air.[112] Thus, unless a known accident or other event has occurred, or for other reasons it is obvious that the damage did not occur during carriage by air, the carrier is liable under the Montreal Convention. The burden of proof seems to rest with the party wishing to invoke another liability regime.

The Montreal Convention has, however, two interesting features as regards its applicability, with implications for multimodal carriage. First, although the convention presupposes a contract of carriage, it is prima facie applicable to *carriage by aircraft* rather than to *contracts* for such carriage.[113] Further, from article 38 it follows, *e contrario*, that the convention applies to air carriage as long as it falls within article 1.[114] This entails that it is always applicable to the air leg of a multimodal carriage, as long as the place of departure and the place of destination *according to the contract* are situated in two different states that are parties to the convention.[115] The question is whether it is the (original) place of departure and (final) place of destination according to the multimodal contract of carriage or the place of departure and place of destination of the air carriage, that are relevant. Whilst the latter seems more logical, it would exempt from the scope of the convention carriage by air under multimodal contracts where such carriage has not been expressly agreed.[116] The former interpretation departs from the reference in article 38 to article 1, which requires carriage by air under a multimodal contract

111 Such movements within an airport or port would probably not even be defined as transport; see K. Grönfors, *Fraktavtalet under etthundra år* (1986) p. 95.

112 Giemulla holds that this presumption only applies to air carriers (E. Giemulla, *Montreal Convention Suppl.* 9 (December 2014), article 38, p. 4). According to article 40, the carrier, i.e. the contracting carrier, is liable for any sub-carrier employed. There is no reason to conclude that such sub-carriers do not include sub-carriers by road that perform transhipment as prescribed in article 18.4. However, the presumption is only eligible where damage is not localized to such transhipment, and thus it cannot be invoked towards a sub-carrier by road. On the other hand, there is no prerequisite that the carriage by air, to which the convention applies, is performed under a contract of carriage by air (cf. section 4.4.1 below), which is why the contracting carrier does not necessarily have to be a carrier by air. Thus, Giemulla's statement should perhaps be rephrased to the effect that the presumption in article 18.4 only applies between the contracting carrier and the cargo interests.

113 Article 1, cf. section 4.4.1 below.

114 Article 38.1: "In the case of combined carriage performed partly by air and partly by any other mode of carriage, the provisions of this Convention shall, subject to paragraph 4 of Article 18, apply only to the carriage by air, provided that the carriage by air falls within the terms of Article 1."

115 Hoeks claims that application of the Montreal Convention to international air carriage, which forms part of a larger multimodal transport is "crystal clear" (M. Hoeks, *Multimodal Transport Law* (2010) p. 258). The applicability of the Montreal Convention to the air leg of a multimodal contract is also clear from article 38.1, *e contrario*, which article also reiterates the necessity that the carriage fulfils the prerequisites of article 1.

116 Article 1.1–1.2 entails that carriage by air is subject to the convention where the place of departure and the place of destination as they appear from the contract of carriage are situated in two different contracting states.

of carriage to be comprised by article 1 in order for the convention to apply to the air leg. Because article 1.2 refers to the place of departure and place of destination under the contract of carriage, rather than the contract of carriage by air, it may seem obvious to consider the (original) place of departure and (final) place of destination according to the multimodal contract of carriage as the relevant places. However, the effect of such interpretation could be that carriage by air between two non-contracting states will be subject to the convention. As an example, if goods are carried under a multimodal contract from state A to state D, which are both parties to the Montreal Convention, but where the actual carriage by air takes place between states B and C (i.e. the goods are sent by road or rail from A to B and from C to D), which are not parties to the Montreal Convention, the convention would still apply. Such an application could hardly be accepted, as the convention then would claim applicability in relation to non-contracting states.[117] On the other hand, under an undefined contract of carriage, which is eventually carried out in part by air, and in part by some other mode of transport, there may not be a contractually agreed place of departure and place of destination in relation to the carriage by air.[118] Although the term "place of departure" brings to mind carriage by air and in particular carriage of passengers by air, it does not by its plain meaning exclude carriage by any other mode. Accordingly, it should not, *per se*, prevent the convention from applying to carriage by air where such carriage takes place either as substitution for another mode of transport or where it takes place under a contract, which does not specify the mode(s) of transport to be used. In order to apply the Montreal Convention to air carriage under a multimodal contract, in instances other than where the contract contains clear regulation of the modes of transport to be used and the places of reloading are stated in the contract (and fulfil the requirements of article 1.2), application of the convention is not without obstacles.[119]

Where carriage by air is performed as successive carriage, article 1.3 prescribes that such carriage shall be deemed undivided carriage to the extent it is regarded by the parties as a single operation. For the purposes of article 1.2, this means that as long as the original place of departure and the final place of destination fulfil the geographical requirements set out, the entire carriage is subject to the convention. Hence even purely domestic carriage may be subject to mandatory

117 For further analysis of the problem in relation to the CMR convention, see section 4.3.2 below.

118 As regards the geographical precondition, several other scenarios can be imagined. Under an undefined contract of carriage, air carriage takes place as one of several modes of transport. The original place of loading and discharge are both situated in states parties to the Montreal Convention, but neither the place of departure or place of destination of the air carriage are mentioned in the transport contract. Is the prerequisite of article 1.2 fulfilled? Or again, where, under a multimodal contract prescribing carriage by road–sea–road, carriage by sea is substituted for carriage by air due to time constraints. If the place of loading onto the ship and the place of discharge from the ship, which coincides with the place of departure and destination of the air carriage, are situated in states parties to the Montreal Convention, are the prerequisites in article 1.2 fulfilled?

119 Surprisingly, the issue is discussed neither by Giemulla (E. Giemulla, *Montreal Convention Suppl.* 6 (January 2010), article 1) nor by Dempsey and Milde (P. Dempsey and M. Milde, *International Air Carrier Liability; The Montreal Convention of 1999* (2005)).

application of the convention, i.e. when it is performed as a part of a larger, international, carriage.[120] Where, in a successive carriage, which is regarded by the parties as a single operation, one of the air legs is substituted for e.g. road transport, the question is how this affects application of the Montreal Convention as regards the requirements of article 1.2. Will the Montreal Convention be applicable only if the original place of departure and the final place of delivery fulfil the geographical requirements, but not the places between which the goods are trucked (i.e. the goods are shipped by air from A to B, by road from B to C and by air from C to D and only A and D are situated in contracting states)? Under article 18.4, as reviewed above, if the trucking service can be deemed as transshipment, the presumption of any damage having occurred during carriage by air applies. However, this is a presumption of liability only and does not affect applicability of the convention, i.e. article 18.4 does not render the trucking service part of the air carriage.[121]

In addition, where the carrier substitutes carriage by aircraft for carriage by some other mode without the consent of the consignor, the convention expressly applies, which is in line with the general consensus regarding e.g. the CMR convention. Parties to a carriage by air contract that also includes other modes of transport are free to contractually agree on the application of the Montreal Convention to the entire contract.[122]

To conclude, the Montreal Convention in principle does not apply to carriage by any other mode of transport. Where carriage by another mode of transport takes place as a loading operation or transshipment, the contracting carrier is presumed liable under the convention. Application of the convention to air carriage carried out as a part of a multimodal contract is unquestionable, where the contract prescribes for air carriage and the contract thus contains an agreed place of departure and destination for the air carriage.

As regards substitution of another mode of transport for carriage by air, and carriage by air under an undefined contract of carriage, such carriage is, according to Giemulla, subject to the convention.[123] The unclear element in this respect is the geographical scope of application, which is incorporated into article 38 through its reference to article 1. As long as there is a contractually agreed place of departure and destination for the air carriage, the applicability of the convention is clear and unproblematic. However, where no such places are contractually agreed the question is whether the contract actually falls within article 1.

As regards undefined contracts of carriage, i.e. contracts where the mode of transport is left to the carrier to decide, there are two scenarios. The first is if the carriage is carried out as a unimodal transport by air, then such carriage should be subject to the Montreal Convention as long as the place of departure

120 Which is also expressly stated in article 1.3.

121 On the other hand, where such carriage takes place within the boundaries of an airport, the carriage by another mode is deemed part of the air carriage, according to article 18.4.

122 Article 38.2. This obviously requires that no other mandatory regime claims applicability to the transport by that other mode(s) of transport.

123 E. Giemulla, *Montreal Convention Suppl. 9* (December 2014), article 38–3.

and destination of the air carriage under the transport contract are situated in two different contracting states. The other scenario is where such an undefined contract is carried out as a multimodal transport. As the parties then have only agreed on the original place of loading and the final place of destination of the goods, and if the carriage neither begins with nor ends with carriage by air, there is no agreed place of loading or destination that is related to the carriage by air, which is why the prerequisite of article 1.2 does not seem to be satisfied. It could be argued that the place of departure and place of destination should be considered to relate to the original place of loading and destination under the multimodal contract, as the terms "place of departure" and "place of destination" do not exclude such interpretation. Considering the scope of application of the convention to carriage by air rather than to contracts therefore, the impact of the convention would be severely circumscribed and, in reality, the scope of its application would be contractual, if article 38 were to be limited to carriage by air with a contractually agreed place of departure and place of destination. The consequences of such interpretation have been thoroughly analysed in relation to the CMR convention.[124]

3.3.1.4 The Rotterdam Rules

The Rotterdam Rules attempts to multimodalize a unimodal regime. Application of the convention to transports other than carriage by sea, and the relationship between the convention and other unimodal regimes, appears from three articles: 1, 26 and 82. Whilst article 1 is the key to this particular Pandora's box, articles 26 and 82 reseal it, leaving but a slight opening.

In the following, articles 1, 26 and 82 will be examined. Their material application affects applicability of the rules at large and their interaction determines the applicability of the Rotterdam Rules to other modes of transport than maritime transports.

The application of the Rotterdam Rules in general

The Rotterdam Rules apply to contracts of carriage where the place of receipt and the place of delivery, as well as the port of loading and the port of discharge, are in different states.[125] A contract of carriage is defined as a contract for carriage by sea, which may include carriage by other means of transport as well. The convention thus applies first and foremost to carriage by sea, although to the extent that the contract of carriage also prescribes for carriage by other modes of transport, these movements will be subject to the convention. As a starting point the convention thus applies to entire multimodal transports. The scope of application of the Rotterdam Rules is further discussed in section 4.6 below.

124 See e.g. UK Court of Appeal, *Quantum Corporation Inc v Plane Trucking Ltd* [2002] 2 Lloyd's Rep 25 as well as M. Hoeks, *Multimodal Transport Law* (2010) p. 180*ff*. Cf. also section 4.3.2 below.

125 Article 5.

3.3.1.5 Article 26 – the limited network system

As discussed previously, international conventions on the liability of carriers of goods have historically been unimodal. This has reflected the fact that carriage of goods has been contracted on a unimodal basis. Any attempt to extend the applicability of a convention beyond unimodality is therefore bound to cause problems of conflict between transport conventions. Although both the CMR convention and the COTIF–CIM convention extend beyond road/rail, neither the CMR convention nor the COTIF–CIM convention deals with such potential conflicts. The Rotterdam Rules, however, venture into the jurisdiction of existing conventions to such degree that possible problems of conflict could not be ignored.

Even the first draft of the Rotterdam Rules included a provision corresponding to what eventually became article 26.[126] The working group was thus concerned at an early stage with possible conflicts between the draft convention and existing transport conventions.[127] When article [26] was considered in full for the first time, there seems to have been quite a broad consensus that the limited network system staged by article [26] was enough to prevent any conflicts with unimodal conventions.[128] Although the Rotterdam Rules are clearly based on the presumption that unimodal conventions that apply to contracts for the carriage of goods, i.e. the contractual approach to applicability, do not apply to the separate legs of a multimodal transport, in the second draft of article [26][129] it was nevertheless complemented by a pure conflict of conventions rule.[130] Despite some indecisiveness, article [26] has been maintained throughout all drafts as well as in the final version of the Rotterdam Rules.[131] With the exception of various linguistic redrafts, the only major change to article [26] in its final version compared to the first draft is the inclusion of the hypothetical contract formula instead of the prerequisite of application *ex proprio vigore* of the land or air conventions.

In its final appearance article 26 provides that:

> When loss of or damage to goods, or an event or circumstance causing a delay in their delivery, occurs during the carrier's period of responsibility but solely before their loading onto the ship or solely after their discharge from the ship, the provisions of this Convention do not prevail over those provisions of another international instrument that, at the time of such loss, damage or event or circumstance causing delay:
>
> (a) Pursuant to the provisions of such international instrument would have applied to all or any of the carrier's activities if the shipper had made a separate and

126 A/CN.9/WG.III/WP.21 p. 21, Working Group III, 9th session, 2002. The article was at the time labelled article 4.2.1. In the following, it will be referred to as article [26].

127 A/CN.9/510 pp. 10–11 (paras 28–31).

128 The view that article 26 was superfluous as there could be no conflicts with purely unimodal conventions was also expressed, as was the view that article 26 would not suffice to prevent conflicts as it only gives preference to parts of conflicting conventions. A/CN.9/526 p. 68 (para 246), 11th session, 2007.

129 A/CN.9/WG.III/WP.32, article 8.

130 Article 83.

131 It was not until the draft prepared for the 19th session that the brackets in which the article had been placed were removed, A/CN.9/WG.III/WP.81, article 26.

direct contract with the carrier in respect of the particular stage of carriage where the loss of, damage to goods, or an event or circumstance causing delay in their delivery occurred;

(b) Specifically provide for the carrier's liability, limitation of liability, or time for suit; and

(c) Cannot be departed from by contract either at all or to the detriment of the shipper under that instrument.

The reading of article 26 hence implies that the Rotterdam Rules are in fact not truly multimodal in their limited maritime scope but leave room for the application of other unimodal liability regimes under certain circumstances. Although article 26 imposes the liability rules of other liability regulations, which might conflict with the Rotterdam Rules, it is generally considered that article 26 is not a conflict of conventions rule as such. However, a truly multimodal convention would risk causing incompatible obligations for a signatory state that is also party to one or more unimodal conventions as such a uniform system would apply to all parts of a multimodal transport whereas the unimodal conventions may be considered to apply to the separate legs of such transport. Accordingly, in order to avoid such collision of obligations, article 26 is the rule that modifies the uniform system of article 1 and establishes a network system.[132] Thus, where damage has been localized to a non-sea leg it is not the liability rules of the Rotterdam Rules that are to be applied.

However, article 26 does not yield to other liability systems, but *incorporates* the liability etc. rules of such other conventions that may be applicable to, and that are indeed better suited to govern, parts of a multimodal transport that are not carried out by sea *by reference*.[133] However, it does not incorporate all parts of those other international instruments but only rules relating to liability, limitation of liability and time for suit, which will be discussed below.

Accordingly, article 26 does not provide a conflict of conventions rule, as a conflict is not avoided only because the rules of the conflicting convention are incorporated into the rules.[134] However, article 26 adapts the Rotterdam Rules to liability systems that are better suited to the mode of transport during which the damage has occurred, as well as protecting the contracting carrier in relation to the recourse claim against the actual carrier, which will be back to back.

Localized damage

There are several reasons for adapting the uniform system set out in article 1. One is the risk, which is inherent in uniform systems, that the Rotterdam Rules will be in conflict with other, mainly unimodal, conventions. Another is the discrepancy

132 Originally, article 26 was considered to comprise all that was necessary in terms of conflict of conventions. Eventually, however, article 82 was included, which is a true conflict of conventions rule.

133 G. van der Ziel, "Multimodal aspects of the Rotterdam Rules" in *CMI Yearbook 2009*, p. 310 and U. Lind Rasmussen, "Additional Provisions Relating to Particular Stages of Carriage" in A. von Ziegler *et al.* (eds), *The Rotterdam Rules 2008* (2010) p. 145.

134 To the same extent as, theoretically, a conflict is not avoided even if two competing conventions contain the exact same rules on liability.

between the liability of the contracting carrier and the actual carrier, which will be faced by the contracting carrier. Whereas the former is dealt with in article 82, the latter is the subject of article 26. As the original purpose of article 26 was to solve both issues, the rationale behind article 26, once article 82 had been included in the convention, is not entirely clear. It has been held that its only purpose is to make the limited network liability system part of the Rotterdam Rules.[135] In turn, the main purpose of the limited network liability system, is presumed to be to ensure that the contracting carrier's recourse claim against the actual carrier is back-to-back.[136] As regards the network system, on the other hand, one of the problems thereof is the regulatory gap faced by damage, which cannot be localized to a certain unimodal leg. Thus, the combination of the uniform system and the network system seems to solve the basic problems of both systems.

Accordingly, damage that is localized to have occurred solely during a non-maritime leg of the transport will, subject to the other prerequisites discussed below, be regulated by such unimodal rules that regulate the mode in question. This means that damage that occurs during the maritime leg is always subject to the Rotterdam Rules. Additionally, progressive damage, which occurs gradually during several legs of the transport (including the maritime leg), is always subject to the Rotterdam Rules, as well as non-localized damage.[137]

Hypothetical contract

At a rather late stage of drafting, article 26 was redrafted to exclude the prerequisite of applicability *ex proprio vigore* of the conflicting regulation to the benefit of the hypothetical contract formula. As article 26 was previously drafted, only regulations that actually claimed applicability (by their own force) would fulfil the prerequisites that would trigger article 26. This would obviously mean that each case would have to be tried on its merits in relation to the applicability rules of a specific regulation. This would entail issues such as the applicability of unimodal conventions to multimodal contracts and thus lead to severe difficulties and certainly reduce the prospects of foreseeability.

On the other hand, the hypothetical contract formula prescribes that, were the shipper to have made a separate contract with a carrier for the particular leg of the carriage and had that contract been subject to a unimodal regime, the same regime will be applied to the thus localized damage. The hypothetical contract formula has previously caused some problems in practice, e.g. under article 2

135 U. Lind Rasmussen, *ibid.*, at p. 144.

136 U. Lind Rasmussen, *ibid.*, at p. 144.

137 As discussed previously, unimodal regulations are by their nature only applicable to localized damage, as they apply to transport of goods by a certain mode, and where the damage cannot be localized the regulation does not claim applicability. As regards gradually occurring damage, similarly this is not attributable solely to one unimodal leg of the transport and thus the unimodal conventions are not autonomously applicable thereto. However, Diamond seems to claim otherwise as he argues that article [26] assists if it can be shown that loss or damage occurred solely before loading or after discharge, but that where the damage is progressive or non-localized, two international instruments may both apply with potentially conflicting results (A. Diamond, "The Next Sea Carriage Convention" [2008] LMCLQ 135–187, at p. 144).

of the CMR convention, mainly, it seems, due to the fact that the Hague–Visby Rules presupposes a bill of lading for applicability.[138] This has been the source of some criticism regarding article 26, but it may be suggested that such problems are insignificant in relation to the problems that would have arisen had the article not been redrafted.

RULES RELATING TO THE CARRIER'S LIABILITY

It is generally held that section (b) of article 26 entails that it is not the entire convention designated in section (a) that is to be applied to the damage but only the rules thereof that regulate the carrier's liability, limitation of liability and time for suit.[139] The conclusion follows from the wording that the Rotterdam Rules "do not prevail over *those provisions* of another international instrument that … specifically provide for the carrier's liability, limitation of liability, or time for suit" (emphasis added).

MANDATORY INTERNATIONAL INSTRUMENT

Finally, the regime thus applicable to the hypothetical contract must be scrutinized under two prerequisites. Firstly, such regime must be an international instrument. The term "international instrument" has been chosen deliberately in order to include not only international conventions, but also regional instruments that do not classify as conventions, e.g. directives issued by the European Union. Such international instrument must, obviously, be in force at the time of occurrence of the damage but it does not have to have been in force at the time of the entry into force of the Rotterdam Rules. Secondly, the liability rules thus applicable must be mandatory, at least in relation to the shipper.

3.3.1.6 Article 82 – relation to other unimodal regimes

Even though the Rotterdam Rules are a novelty as regards their extended multimodal application, as has been shown previously in the current chapter, other unimodal regimes contain multimodal features, although these are limited in their scope compared to the Rotterdam Rules.

The existing regimes that were considered to pose a risk of conflicting with application of the Rotterdam Rules are mainly European; both the CMR convention and the COTIF–CIM convention contain rules that extend their application to transport by other modes.[140] These regulations are rather limited in their application in relation to article 1 of the Rotterdam Rules, but nevertheless could cause a conflict with the rules.

Whereas article 26 was originally drafted to deal with possible conflicts where the Rotterdam Rules regulate transport by modes other than sea and thus interfere

138 Cf. section 4.5.1 below.

139 M. Sturley *et al.*, *The Rotterdam Rules* (2010) p. 69; U. Lind Rasmussen, "Additional Provisions Relating to Particular Stages of Carriage" in A. von Ziegler *et al.* (eds), *The Rotterdam Rules 2008* (2010) p. 149 and A. Diamond, "The Rotterdam Rules" [2010] LMCLQ 445–536 at. p. 456.

140 As does the European Budapest Convention on the Contract for the Carriage of goods by Inland Waterway (CMNI), Budapest 2001. However, this is not discussed in the current work.

with various unimodal transport conventions, advocates of the kind of regulation now found in article 82 realized the conflicts that would occur as far as sea transport is concerned due to the fact that other unimodal conventions regulate sea transport ancillary to the land or air transports that those conventions mainly regulate. The problem of conflicting conventions thus targeted by article 86 is indeed not a problem caused by the multimodality of the Rotterdam Rules but by the multimodality of other conventions, which in some cases claim applicability to sea transports. The problem should therefore not be a novelty and has thus been discussed in relation to the Hague–Visby Rules as well as the COTIF–CIM convention.[141]

For this reason, it was considered, although at a late stage of drafting, that the Rotterdam Rules ought to contain a rule explicitly regulating the relation of the convention to existing unimodal regimes that contain a multimodal feature. Thus article 82 was included in the convention. The article is divided into sub-paragraphs, each dealing with a specific mode of transport, and reads:

> Nothing in this Convention affects the application of any of the following international conventions in force at the time this Convention enters into force, including any future amendment to such conventions, that regulate the liability of the carrier for loss of or damage to the goods:
>
> (*a*) Any convention governing the carriage of goods by air to the extent that such convention according to its provisions applies to any part of the contract of carriage;
> (*b*) Any convention governing the carriage of goods by road to the extent that such convention according to its provisions applies to the carriage of goods that remain loaded on a road cargo vehicle carried on board a ship;
> (*c*) Any convention governing the carriage of goods by rail to the extent that such convention according to its provisions applies to carriage of goods by sea as a supplement to the carriage by rail; or
> (*d*) Any convention governing the carriage of goods by inland water-ways to the extent that such convention according to its provisions applies to a carriage of goods without trans-shipment both by inland waterways and sea.

Paragraph (a) – Montreal Convention

It was the possible conflict between the Montreal Convention and the Rotterdam Rules that triggered the inclusion of a conflict of conventions article in

141 Hoeks discusses the problem and in relation to sea transport she concludes that the problem of conflicts between the CMR and the Hague–Visby Rules is not too imminent as sea transports affected by article 2 of the CMR is mainly short sea shipping where bills of lading are not usually issued and that the Hague–Visby Rules are only applicable to shipping where such a document is issued (M. Hoeks, *Multimodal Transport Law* (2010) ch. 9.1). However, this is perhaps to simplify the applicability of the Hague–Visby Rules somewhat too much. As bills of lading are, to an increasing degree, being abandoned in favour of non-negotiable documents, the applicability of the widely supported Hague–Visby Rules, which was drafted during times when bills of lading were the norm, has been claimed not to be dependent upon the issuing of a B/L (W. Tetley, *Marine Cargo Claims*, vol. 1 (2008) at pp. 17–18). As will be discussed in section 4.5 the general opinion seems however to be that the Hague–Visby Rules applies to carriage by sea under contracts where a bill of lading is contemplated.

line with what later became article 82. It had previously been pointed out that the maritime plus approach of the new convention could conflict with earlier unimodal conventions, but it was considered that any such conflicts were sufficiently avoided through what later became article 26.[142] And although possible conflicts caused by the fact that some unimodal conventions do contain multimodal aspects had been pointed out by the delegates from states bound by the CMR and COTIF–CIM conventions,[143] it was only at a very late stage in the drafting process that they seem to have convinced the working group of the conflicts likely to occur, which would possibly prevent states party to the said conventions from becoming parties to the new convention.[144] It was most likely not the severity of the possible conflicts between the Rotterdam Rules and the Montreal Convention that triggered the drafting of a new conflict of conventions article, but the fact that, although the working group considered "the combination of air and sea transport in the same carriage … to be rare",[145] such conflict would affect most state parties due to the universality of the Montreal Convention.

The Montreal Convention is in practice only applicable to carriage by air.[146] However, the convention has two multimodal features, which should perhaps more accurately be labelled clarifications to the scope of application. Thus article 18.4 clarifies that if carriage takes place by other modes of transport that is carried out as a part of the contract for carriage by air ("for the purpose of loading, delivery or transhipment"), any damage that occurs during transport is *presumed* to have been caused during the carriage by air. Further, article 18.4 clarifies that any carriage by other modes that takes place contrary to the contract of carriage is regarded as carriage by air. The former evidences that the drafters of the Montreal Convention sought to avoid the legal vacuum that non-localized damage in multimodal transport could end up in. Thus, it does not mean that the Montreal Convention trespasses into the domains of another unimodal convention, as any damage that is localized to a land or sea leg of a multimodal transport is subject to such other liability system as is applicable *ex proprio vigore*. Hence, with the exception of transport within the boundaries of the airport (which would very unlikely be international and thus subject to any international convention), the

142 Report of Working Group III (Transport Law) on the work of its eighteenth session (Vienna 6–17 November 2006), A/CN.9/616 pp. 49–52.

143 It seems that the non-European delegates to the working group were somewhat tired of the protracted discussions of conflict between the new convention and the European unimodal transport conventions and pointed out that "the Rotterdam Rules were intended for worldwide use and that typically European reservations as to conflicts of conventions could not go on to unduly burden the negotiations, nor could they be allowed to unnecessarily encumber the new Convention's wording" (R. de Wit, "Minimal music: multimodal transport including a maritime leg under the Rotterdam Rules" in R. Thomas (ed.), *The Carriage of Goods by Sea Under the Rotterdam Rules* (2010) at p. 99).

144 Report of Working Group III (Transport Law) on the work of its twentieth session (Vienna 15–25 October 2007), A/CN.9/642, p. 52.

145 Report of Working Group III (Transport Law) on the work of its eighteenth session (Vienna 6–17 November 2006), A/CN.9/616 p. 55.

146 Articles 1 and 38, cf. section 4.4.2 below.

Montreal Convention could hardly be said to have any multimodal features.[147] The effect of article 82 of the Rotterdam Rules in this respect will thus be fairly limited.

However, section (a) of article 82 will have the effect that the Rotterdam Rules will never be applicable to an international air leg of a multimodal transport. As mentioned, whilst article 26 only prevents the existence of irreconcilable liabilities it does not prevent the simultaneous applicability of two conventions. However, article 82 yields to other conventions to the extent they apply *ex proprio vigore*. Thus, as the Montreal Convention applies to actual carriage by air, irrespective of the type of carriage contract such carriage is subject to, article 82 (a) will effectively prevent the application of the Rotterdam Rules to air carriage. An interesting issue is the interaction between article 26 of the Rotterdam Rules and article 18 of the Montreal Convention, which both provide fallback rules as regards unlocalized damage. In a carriage by sea and air (however unlikely) the Rotterdam Rules would apply to the carriage by sea, but article 82 would yield to the Montreal Convention as far as the carriage by air is concerned. If damage occurs during transport, but it is not clear whether during the carriage by air or the carriage by sea, article 26 of the Rotterdam Rules would seem to provide the applicability of that convention to the damage, whilst article 18 of the Montreal Convention would provide for the applicability of that convention. However, it would seem that due to article 82, the Rotterdam Rules would yield to the Montreal Convention as soon as that convention claims applicability.

Paragraph (b) – the CMR convention

In article 82 (b), exemption from the applicability of the Rotterdam Rules to certain international transport by road regimes is made. The drafting of the exemption makes quite clear that it is the CMR convention that the exemption aims at. The CMR convention extends its applicability to transport by other modes than by road in certain cases where the goods remain loaded on the truck and the truck as such is carried by another means of transport, for example a ro-ro ferry.[148] Due to this extension of the CMR convention to sea transport in some instances, application of the Rotterdam Rules to carriage by sea could be in conflict with the CMR convention as far as ro-ro transport is concerned.

Accordingly, the CMR convention applies to carriage by sea when the goods remain loaded on the road vehicle. Thus, where damage occurs during sea–road transport and the sea leg is carried out as ro-ro transport of the road vehicle, both

147 As Hoeks comments, there is one minor risk of conflict between the Montreal Convention and the land carriage conventions (the COTIF–CIM convention only in cases where an airport contains a railway station) and that is where an international land transport ends within an airport and damage to the goods occurs during unloading/ transhipment, and the land carriage convention accordingly will be applicable as well as the Montreal Convention according to its article 18.4 (M. Hoeks, *Multimodal Transport Law* (2010) p. 364).

148 Further, the damage must be particular to that other mode of transport and must not have been caused by the acts or omissions of the carrier by road; see further article 2 of the CMR convention. It may be noted that for article 2 to apply, the damage must hence be localized to the maritime leg of the transport.

the CMR convention and the Rotterdam Rules would prima facie be applicable. If the damage is localized to the sea transport, article 26 of the Rotterdam Rules does not prevent a conflict, which, as mentioned, is intended to avoid conflict when damage or loss is located to the land or air leg. However, article 82 would seem to solve the problem by allowing the CMR convention to prevail over the Rotterdam Rules.

Article 82 seems to set out two preconditions as far as transport by road is concerned. The first is applicability *ex proprio vigore*. As regards transport by road, this means that where an international convention regulating transport by road also regulates transport by sea, it is only, in contrast with article 26, when that convention claims applicability by its own force that article 82 can be applied.[149] As it has been claimed that the CMR does not apply to multimodal contracts, the CMR might not claim applicability to ro-ro transport of a road vehicle. If ro-ro transport, which complies with the prerequisites of article 2 of the CMR convention, is carried out under a multimodal contract of carriage, including other modes of transport where the goods are in fact unloaded from the road vehicle, the applicability of the CMR may be questioned. If the CMR does not claim applicability (a question that must be answered by the applying court and the answer to which clearly depends on where that court is situated), article 82 is not effectuated and the Rotterdam Rules would apply to the ro-ro transport by sea even though it is combined with road transport and the goods are not unloaded during the sea traverse. The same dilemma occurs where the goods are unloaded during the sea traverse. As article 2 of the CMR convention is not applicable, it could be argued that the CMR does not apply even to the road transport. Whilst the CMR convention applies as long as the road transport starts in one country and ends in another, the Rotterdam Rules demand that the sea transport is international. Where the sea traverse under a road contract is national and the goods are unloaded from the road vehicle neither the CMR convention nor the Rotterdam Rules claims applicability.

Furthermore, article 82 sets out that such other "convention governing the carriage of goods by road to the extent that such convention according to its provisions applies to the carriage of goods that remain loaded on a road cargo vehicle carried on board a ship". The question is what conclusions can be drawn from the wording "to the extent that". It has been suggested that the wording indicates that the road transport convention is only to take precedence in relation to a sea leg, and not the ancillary land transport, although that such intention lies behind the article would seem unlikely.[150] The intended interpretation is thus suggested to be that the entire convention on land or air transport takes precedence.[151] Hence the wording in question would only be

149 And rightfully so, as otherwise there is no conflict of applicability.

150 C. Hancock, "Multimodal Transport and the New UN Convention on the Carriage of Goods" (2008) 14 JIML 484 and 493 and A. Diamond, "The Next Sea Carriage Convention?" (2008) LMCLQ 135, at pp. 142–143.

151 C. Hancock, "A new convention for the carriage of goods by sea" in R. Thomas (ed.), *The Rotterdam Rules* (2009) p. 48 and G. van der Ziel, "Multimodal Aspects of the Rotterdam Rules" in *CMI Yearbook 2009*, p. 310.

intended to identify such conventions that take precedence over the Rotterdam Rules. However, it seems that the wording of article 82 (b) also contains another ambiguity. Thus, the wording "to the extent that", could either mean that any carriage by road convention that regulates ro-ro sea carriage takes precedence over the Rotterdam Rules or that it is only when such a convention claims applicability to the sea transport in question in accordance with its regulation of ro-ro sea carriage that the Rotterdam Rules denounce its applicability. The question could perhaps be summarized as whether on a general level article 82 (b) identifies conventions that take precedence or whether it is case-specific and sets forth prerequisites that must be fulfilled in the particular case. For example; the CMR convention regulates sea transport when goods remain loaded on a road vehicle and thus fulfils the prerequisites in article 82 (b). If, in a certain case, the goods are actually unloaded during the sea traverse, the CMR convention does not claim applicability to the sea transport. As the convention "according to its provisions applies to the carriage of goods that remain loaded on a road cargo vehicle carried on board a ship" in general, the result could be that the CMR convention takes precedence over the Rotterdam Rules as a whole due to article 82 (b) but refrains from regulating the liability of any damage localized to the sea leg. Naturally, the sea transport might in the end be regulated by the Rotterdam Rules anyway, but the multimodal aspect of the rules is ineffectual. However, it seems that the intention of the drafters was that article 82 (b) is to give precedence to another convention when such convention "applies to the carriage of goods" when the goods in a particular case actually "remain loaded on a road cargo vehicle carried on board a ship". This is logically the intention behind the regulation and thus it is only when the CMR claims applicability to the whole road and sea transport that the Rotterdam Rules step back.[152] There are, so to speak, two sides of the conflict coin: one is possible conflicts due to the multimodal aspects of the Rotterdam Rules (i.e. that the rules regulate land and air transports also regulated by unimodal conventions) and the other is the multimodal aspects of otherwise unimodal land and air conventions (i.e. when such conventions regulate sea transport). It is only the latter that is dealt with in article 82.

Paragraph (c) – COTIF–CIM convention

The COTIF–CIM convention also contains a "multimodal clause" as the rules of the convention are extended to transport by other modes of transport that are performed as a supplement to rail carriage.[153] Hence the formulation in article 82 (c) clearly aims at avoiding conflicts of application between the Rotterdam Rules and the COTIF–CIM convention.

152 H. Honka, "General Provisions" in A. von Ziegler *et al.* (eds), *The Rotterdam Rules 2008* (2010) p. 352.

153 In addition, there is a prerequisite that the transport is included in a list of services kept by the OTIF; cf. article 1 §4.

To a large extent, the same considerations as regards paragraph (b), i.e. the CMR convention, assert themselves in relation to paragraph (c).

THE SCOPE OF APPLICATION OF ARTICLE 82

Another question triggered by article 82 is whether the other conventions, i.e. the Montreal Convention, the CMR convention and the COTIF–CIM convention are to be applied only as far as their liability rules are concerned or if article 82 gives complete precedence to these other conventions.

The purpose of the article, i.e. to avoid any conflict with those other conventions, indicates that article 82 is to give precedence to the other convention in its entirely.[154] A comparison with article 26 supports this conclusion, as article 26 expressly states that only rules regarding liability, limitation thereof and time for suit are to be applied in cases that fall under that article. The non-existence of such an explicit restriction suggests that the drafters did not intend to limit application of the CMR convention *et al.* to certain parts thereof.

3.3.1.7 Conclusion

As should be clear from the current chapter, there is on the one hand a question of whether the network system is enforceable by its own force (i.e. due to the mandatory force of the scope of application of the respective conventions) due to uncertainty as regards applicability to multimodal contracts of carriage of the liability conventions applicable to contracts of carriage. On the other hand, as discussed in the current section, some of the liability conventions extend their applicability to carriage by other modes, under certain conditions. The most extensive current example is article 2 of the CMR convention, although should the convention enter into force, the Rotterdam Rules will extend to entire multimodal contracts of carriage, as long as there is an international sea leg.

The Montreal Convention does not in practice extend into the spheres of application of either the CMR convention or the COTIF–CIM convention. Further, article 2 of the CMR is not likely to compete with applicability of the Montreal Convention; piggy-back transport of a road vehicle (laden with goods) by aircraft is hardly a common feature in private transport business. As regards the COTIF–CIM convention, it is never applicable to carriage by air (even if it were supplemental to carriage by rail). Thus, the Montreal Convention is relatively unaffected by the multimodal aspects of the current conventions, although it certainly applies to carriage by air under a multimodal contract of carriage. In addition, it would seem that to the extent international carriage by sea is supplemented by international carriage by air, the Rotterdam Rules will give precedence to the Montreal Convention.

In respect of land carriage, the situation is different. Both the CMR convention and the COTIF–CIM convention contain multimodal aspects and, whilst the COTIF–CIM convention actively seeks to prevent conflict with the CMR

154 C. Hancock, "A new convention for the carriage of goods by sea" in R. Thomas (ed.), *The Rotterdam Rules* (2009) p. 48.

convention by limiting its applicability in a multimodal aspect to domestic transport of goods by road, the CMR applies to piggy-back transport by rail even if it is trans frontier and thus covered by COTIF–CIM. As there is no exception in the COTIF–CIM convention as regards piggy-back transport of vehicles where transport is subject to the CMR convention, both conventions could be applicable to damage occurring during the rail transport. One solution would be to regard a piggy-back transport as an extension of the unimodal transport and thus not as a multimodal transport, as the drafters of the CMR convention certainly did. Another is to advocate the non-applicability to multimodal contracts of the unimodal conventions that apply to contracts of carriage, and thus no conflict would arise between the CMR convention and the COTIF–CIM convention as the COTIF–CIM convention would not be applicable. On the other hand, in relation to the multimodal aspects of the unimodal conventions there does not seem to have been much conflict in practice.

3.3.2 The relationship between the unimodal conventions

As discussed above, the majority of the unimodal conventions subject to analysis in this work contain some multimodal feature. Hence these unimodal conventions to some extent trespass onto each other's territory by their extended applicability to other modes of transport. Thus, whilst the COTIF–CIM convention only extends to domestic supplementary transport by road and therefore will not infringe on any other convention, the CMR convention, by way of its article 2, may infringe on the Hague–Visby Rules as well as on the COTIF–CIM convention. This is to some extent a general issue within multimodal transport, but provided that the unimodal conventions are considered mandatorily applicable to carriage under multimodal contracts and the network system is employed by its own force, the possible conflicts are increased. In a European setting, based on the conventions currently in force, the number of possible conflicts is limited. However, the Rotterdam Rules certainly could infringe on the existing unimodal conventions, a problem that has been addressed in that convention.

3.3.2.1 The Rotterdam Rules

The multimodal, the maritime plus, application of the Rotterdam Rules extends the new convention to areas that are traditionally governed by other conventions. The extent of such infringement depends on the view that is taken regarding the applicability of these unimodal conventions *ex proprio vigore* in relation to multimodal transport contracts.[155]

As mentioned previously, the drafters of unimodal conventions that venture into the core legal areas of other unimodal conventions, such as the CMR and the COTIF–CIM, do not seem to have been overly concerned with possible

155 Cf. section 3.4 below and R. de Wit, "Minimal music: multimodal transport including a maritime leg under the Rotterdam Rules" in R. Thomas (ed.), *The Carriage of Goods by Sea Under the Rotterdam Rules* (2010) p. 99.

conflicts caused. Yet those conventions have been ratified by many states, including states bound by conventions affected by these multimodal features. However, the drafters of the Rotterdam Rules clearly were, or at least became, concerned with the effects that the multimodal application of the Rotterdam Rules would bring. During the UNCITRAL negotiations, Working Group III was called on to address the issue of "potential conflict with other mandatory transport conventions".[156] The concern seems to have been that the potential risk of conflict would reduce the number of state parties to the new convention.

The Rotterdam Rules and the Montreal Convention

The primary reason for the drafters of the Rotterdam Rules to regulate possible conflicts between those rules and the carriage by air convention, the Montreal Convention, was that the Montreal Convention is applicable to *carriage* by air, rather than to *contracts* for such carriages and, in particular, it is explicitly applicable to air carriage performed under a multimodal contract. Thus, the Montreal Convention is undoubtedly applicable to air carriage that takes place in addition to international carriage by sea.[157] The Montreal Convention, on the other hand, will most unlikely claim any applicability to such international sea transport that makes up the core of the Rotterdam Rules' area of applicability.[158] Hence, the risk of competition between the two conventions only stems from the scope of application of the Rotterdam Rules.

For this reason, article 82(a) is drafted differently from the remaining subparagraphs (b)–(d), which are drafted to respond to the multimodal aspects of the land and inner waterways conventions. Accordingly, article 82(a) simply gives precedence to the Montreal Convention where it is applicable *ex proprio vigore*. Considering the almost universal adherence to the Montreal Convention, this means that the Rotterdam Rules will, in practice, never be applicable to international air carriage.

The Rotterdam Rules and the CMR convention

It seems quite clear that the drafters of the Rotterdam Rules did not consider unimodal conventions applicable to contracts for the carriage of goods by a certain mode of transport, to be applicable to parts of a multimodal transport carried out by the transport mode in question.[159] Thus initially they saw no possible conflicts between the Rotterdam Rules and other conventions, e.g. the CMR convention and the COTIF–CIM convention. However, at a late stage of the negotiations

156 A/CN.9/526 p. 59; see also A/CN.9/WG.III/WP.26.

157 It was recognized by the working group that the combination of sea and air transport ought to be rare: A/CN.9/642 p. 52 (para. 229).

158 The multimodal aspects of the Montreal Convention have been elaborated above. The only theoretical conflict based on the multimodal aspects of the Montreal Convention would be if an international sea transport preceded an international air transport and the goods were unloaded from the vessel within the limits of the airport; a highly theoretical scenario, which is unlikely to occur in practice.

159 A/CN.9/616 p. 50 (para. 220).

the possible conflict embedded in the fact that those conventions possess multimodal features, albeit of lesser reach than the Rotterdam Rules, was appreciated. These conflicts would not be solved by the existing article 26, as that article incorporates the liability rules of other unimodal regulations into the Rotterdam Rules rather than giving precedence to such conventions.[160] Hence article 82 was extended to deal not only with the Montreal Convention but also with the CMR convention and the COTIF–CIM convention (as well as the CMNI Convention, which is, not subject to discussion in this work).[161]

Whilst the CMR convention applies to contracts for the carriage of goods by road, the Rotterdam Rules apply to contracts that provide for carriage by sea and in addition may provide for carriage by other modes. It has been established previously that the relation between the sea leg and other legs performed by other modes, such as by road, are unimportant and that, as long as the sea leg is international, the Rotterdam Rules apply, even where the carriage by another mode could be regarded as dominant in relation to the sea leg. As one of the prerequisites for application of the Rotterdam Rules is that the sea transport is international, and the same prerequisite applies under the CMR convention (i.e. that the road transport is international) it is only the two following combinations of sea and road carriage that will possibly cause a conflict between the two conventions: (1) international sea transport in combination with international road transport and (2) international sea transport in combination with domestic road transport if the sea transport is a ro-ro transport of the road vehicle.

In the case of an international transport, carried out by road and (an international traverse by) ro-ro ferry, both the Rotterdam Rules and the CMR convention seem to claim applicability. If the point of departure taken is the CMR, that convention would govern the whole transport under its articles 1 and 2. However, as the contract provides for international carriage by sea, the point of departure could also be taken in the Rotterdam Rules. The Rotterdam Rules would prima facie apply in accordance with its articles 1 and 5 and if the damage is localized to the sea transport the Rotterdam Rules remain applicable as article 26 does not come into play. If the sea transport were not a ro-ro transport and the goods are unloaded from the road vehicle during the sea traverse, no conflict with the CMR convention would arise as far as sea transport is concerned.[162] However, where

160 Although article 26 of the Rotterdam Rules is often referred to as a "network rule" (see e.g. M. Sturley *et al.*, *The Rotterdam Rules* (2010) p. 74), it is, in fact, not. Article 26 incorporates the liability rules of other mode specific rules into the convention, which clearly adapts the liability rules of the Rotterdam Rules to each particular mode of transport, but it is still the Rotterdam Rules that actually apply and not the mode specific rules. This would appear to be the reason for the perceived need for article 82.

161 Or "they who must not be named" (R. de Wit, "Minimal music: multimodal transport including a maritime leg under the Rotterdam" in R. Thomas (ed.), *The Carriage of Goods by Sea Under the Rotterdam Rules* (2010) p. 99).

162 As has been elaborated previously, where the road transport, which includes a ro-ro sea traverse, is included in a larger multimodal contract, it could be argued that the CMR convention does not apply, and article 82 is accordingly not effectuated as the CMR convention then would not be applicable by its own force (and there is no conflict between the Rotterdam Rules and the CMR convention).

the goods are carried by ro-ro sea transport and the goods are thus not unloaded from the road vehicle, a possible conflict with the CMR convention arises, as both the Rotterdam Rules and the CMR convention claim applicability to the entire transport. In order to avoid conflict, the situation is addressed by article 82(b).

Article 82 of the Rotterdam Rules is, as mentioned, drafted to eliminate the risk of conflict between the Rotterdam Rules, among others, and the CMR convention.[163] However, the scope of article 82(b) is not entirely clear. There seem to be three ways to read article 82(b): either the Rotterdam Rules give precedence to the CMR convention in every case where the CMR claims applicability, or the Rotterdam Rules only give priority to the CMR convention where CMR claims applicability through its article 2, i.e. where the transport by road includes ro-ro transport by sea.[164] The third reading, which would seem to be the least likely to have been intended by the drafters but perhaps the reading that is most true to the wording of article 82(b), is that the Rotterdam Rules give priority to the CMR where the contract of carriage provides for carriage by road and ro-ro transportation by sea, but only during the sea stage.[165] The first interpretation of the article in question is based on the fact that the CMR convention includes a provision that makes the convention applicable "to the carriage of goods that remain loaded on a road cargo vehicle carried on board a ship" and the provision found in article 82(b) is understood as pointing out the relevant conventions rather than describing under what conditions the other convention is to prevail. The second interpretation entails an understanding of "to the extent", which indicates that the convention "according to its provisions applies to the carriage of goods that remain loaded on a road cargo vehicle carried on board a ship" *in the particular case*, i.e. only when article 2 of the CMR convention comes into play will the Rotterdam Rules yield. The third suggested interpretation is rather literal but is nevertheless entirely plausible.

As neither subsequent agreements nor subsequent practice have emerged in relation to the Rotterdam Rules, article 31.2–3 of the Vienna Convention will not give the interpreter much guidance. Therefore, an interpretation of article 82(b) of the Rotterdam Rules must primarily resort to article 31.1 as a source of interpretation. Accordingly, article 82(b) should be given its ordinary meaning, which would seem to comprise all three suggested readings, in its context, which thus primarily consists of the text of the treaty, in the light of the object and purpose of the treaty. Starting with the object and purpose of the Rotterdam Rules, these include promoting of legal certainty, improving the efficiency of international carriage of goods and facilitating new access opportunities for previously remote parties and markets, thus promoting trade and economic development, both domestically and internationally, which is believed to be achieved through

163 Although it has been claimed that it does not entirely fulfil that purpose (E. Røsæg, "Conflicts of Conventions in the Rotterdam Rules" (2009) 15 JIML 238–248).

164 E. Røsæg, *ibid.*, at p. 246.

165 A. Diamond, "The Rotterdam Rules" [2009] LMCLQ 445, at p. 454.

the adoption of uniform rules to govern international contracts of carriage wholly or partly by sea.[166] The object and purpose of the rules would accordingly seem to be best promoted through a narrow interpretation of article 82(b), including as many contracts of carriage as possible under the ambit of the rules. However, the object and purpose will on the other hand, as with a wider perspective, best be promoted through ratification of the treaty by as many states as possible, an object that may be counteracted by a narrow interpretation of article 82(b).[167] The context would obviously include the other articles of the Rotterdam Rules, but arguably also the conventions to which article 82(b) refers. Thus, if the only potential perceived conflict with the CMR convention is the latter conventions application to mode-on-mode transport, because the starting point is taken that the CMR convention does not apply to road movements under a multimodal contract, then the first interpretation accounted for above, would not in practice entail any different result than the second interpretation (and therefore not even be considered). Therefore, to a certain extent, interpretation of the CMR convention is relevant for interpretation of article 82(b) and although it is obvious that the drafters did not perceive the CMR convention as a possible conflict with multimodal transport where the goods are unloaded from the road vehicle for an international sea traverse, even if the road carriage is international an objective interpretation would have to be based on an independent investigation of the issue. Considering the discussion accounted for in section 3.4 below, it is far from certain that the CMR convention does not apply autonomously to road transport carried out under a multimodal contract of carriage. Therefore, an interpretation of article 82(b) cannot be based on an assumption that it is certain that the CMR convention does not pose a problem in such a case. Any interpretation of article 82(b) must, to the contrary, take the possible application of the CMR convention into account. Accordingly, it is held here that the first interpretation, i.e. that the Rotterdam Rules give precedence to the CMR convention in every case where it claims (autonomous) applicability, is preferable to the second interpretation, i.e. that the Rotterdam Rules only give priority to the CMR convention where it (the CMR) claims applicability through its article 2, as the latter will entail the risk that the Rotterdam Rules conflict with the CMR convention. The third reading of the term would appear, although consistent with the ordinary meaning of the term, to be clearly inconsistent with the context as well as the object and purpose of the treaty.

On the other hand, in order for the CMR convention to be autonomously applicable to road transport carried out under a multimodal contract of carriage, which falls under the ambit of the Rotterdam Rules, the damage would have been located to the road leg. Where the damage is thus located, article 26 of the Rotterdam Rules provides that the liability of the CMR convention is triggered. Article 26 does however only trigger the liability rules applicable to road transport, to the detriment of rules not regulating the carrier's liability, whilst article 82(b) would

166 Cf. Preamble of the Rotterdam Rules.
167 M. Sturley *et al.*, *The Rotterdam Rules* (2010) p. 71.

give way for the CMR entirely and *de facto*.[168] Although it seems obvious that it is article 26 that is intended for such a situation, there is nothing in article 82 that indicates that the article is subsidiary to article 26. The conclusion would then be that although article 26 applies the liability rules of a certain unimodal carriage convention when damage is localized to such part of the multimodal carriage, *if* that other unimodal convention is one of the conventions referred to in article 82, it can be applied in its entirety through article 82.

Where transport, combining international road carriage with international ro-ro carriage by sea, involves damage to goods, which cannot be localized, both the CMR convention and the Rotterdam Rules claim applicability to the liability issue. Article 26 of the Rotterdam Rules does not change the competing applicability, as the damage is not localized. However, article 82(b) would give precedence to the CMR convention, which then governs liability under its article 2. On the other hand, should the damage be localized to the sea leg of the transport, the CMR initially claims applicability as it is only when the damage is both localized and mode-specific that the CMR convention under its article 2 refers to the law applicable to sea transport. In this scenario, the Rotterdam Rules also claims applicability. However, as the damage occurred during maritime ro-ro transport, there is no question that article 82(b) gives precedence to the CMR convention.

To the extent that the CMR convention, in a particular case, is not considered to be autonomously applicable to a road transport under a multimodal contract of carriage, under which the goods are unloaded from the truck for the sea traverse, no conflict arises between the CMR convention and the Rotterdam Rules and the latter can be applied in accordance with its articles 1 and 5. In this case the Rotterdam Rules will apply *per se* to the whole contract, which includes international sea transport and, in addition, transport by road. Should the damage be localized to the road leg, article 26 incorporates the liability rules of the CMR, as the CMR would have applied had the shipper made "a separate and direct contract" with the road carrier for carriage of goods by road. Thus, the liability rules of the CMR convention, albeit not the actual convention, would be applied to a road leg of a multimodal transport to which under this scenario the convention is not applicable *ex proprio vigore*.

As elaborated previously, at the time when the drafters of the Rotterdam Rules were made aware that article 26 was not sufficient to deal with possible conflicts between the Rotterdam Rules and other conventions, it was the Montreal Convention that it was first concerned with. As the Montreal Convention does not, to any significant degree, contain any multimodal regulations that could interfere with the Rotterdam Rules, the question is why the drafters did not settle with article 26. Obviously, it was other aspects of the conventions referred to in subparagraphs (b)-(d) of article 82 that worried them. That is, the fact that those

168 It has been argued above, and is argued here, that article 26 merely incorporates the liability rules of other unimodal liability systems into the Rotterdam Rules, but where the other set of rules is autonomously applicable, article 26 does not solve the conflict of simultaneously applicable conventions.

conventions extend their applicability to other modes of transport, significantly in comparison with the Montreal Convention although less significantly in comparison with the Rotterdam Rules. Article 26 does not prevent conflicts between concurring regulations. It refers to the liability etc. rules of other, unimodal, conventions that would have been applicable had the additional land, air or inner waterway leg been subject to a unimodal contract. Looking at the convention as a whole, the rationale behind article 26 as it stands in its final version would be to reduce the occasions where the contracting carrier has to take the financial consequences of the non-identical liability limits of the various unimodal conventions. However, incorporating the liability etc. rules of competing regulations does not avoid potential legal conflict. Possibly, the number of occasions when a court has to deal with an alleged conflict is reduced as the incentive for disputes is largely eliminated, but theoretically the two simultaneously applicable regulations do still pose a legal dilemma.[169]

3.3.2.2 The CMR convention

The possible conflicts that could be caused by the extension of the CMR convention to mode-on-mode transport are little discussed. The effect of article 2 of the CMR convention is, as regards the conventions discussed here, in practice only relevant in relation to the Hague–Visby Rules and the COTIF–CIM convention. As mentioned previously, there are plenty of international ro-ro ferry crossings in Europe and a couple of international mode-on-mode rail trajectories, of which the English Channel tunnel probably has the most impact.

The CMR and the Hague–Visby Rules

A conflict between the CMR convention and the Hague–Visby Rules would only arise if the Hague–Visby Rules are applicable to a ro-ro transport to which article 2 of the CMR applies. As both these conventions rely on the existence of a contract of carriage by the mode in question, again the crucial point is the contract of carriage.

Article 2 of the CMR convention extends the applicability of the CMR convention to transport by other modes. The starting point is article 1 and the prerequisite of a contract of carriage by road that is found in that article. The type of contract presupposed in article 2 is not entirely clear. In many cases it would seem that a ro-ro ferry crossing would not appear from the contract of carriage.[170] On the other hand, such an intermediary transport may be inevitable and thus

169 Sturley *et al.* conclude that "the limited network system largely eliminates the concern over any potential conflict of conventions" (M. Sturley *et al., The Rotterdam Rules* (2010) p. 71). With reference to the discussion above, it seems that article 26 eliminates much conflict in practice, but in theory the state parties still face concurring obligations, not at least as regards rules not relating to the carrier's liability, limitation of liability and time for suit, as well as regards non-mandatory rules.

170 Considering that article 2 was drafted to enable the United Kingdom to become a state party, it seems clear that at least an implicit agreement as regards mode-on-mode transport must be accepted, as no contract of carriage by road between the European continental states and the United Kingdom could be carried out without sea transport, later supplemented by the possibility of rail mode-on-mode transport through the Channel Tunnel.

implied in the contract, which would actually make the contract a multimodal contract rather than a unimodal contract of carriage. The type of contract envisaged in article 2 was not considered by the drafters of the convention as multimodal, mainly due to the fact that the goods are not unloaded from the road vehicle.[171] This would entail that even where ro-ro transport is explicit or implicit from the contract of carriage none of the assertions made regarding the applicability of the CMR convention to road transport under a multimodal contract of carriage would be relevant.[172]

However, in relation to possible conflict between the CMR convention and the Hague–Visby Rules it is contracts of carriage where the sea crossing appears as part of the contract that are of interest. In fact, should carriage by sea appear from the contract of carriage in such a way that a contract of carriage by sea could be considered to exist, the Hague–Visby Rules could potentially claim autonomous applicability to the sea leg. Again, it is the contract of carriage that is the focus of attention; if the contract of carriage provides for carriage by road as well as carriage by sea there is a potential conflict. In respect of the Hague–Visby Rules the risk of conflict has been held to be prevented by the fact that the rules for its applicability require an undertaking by the carrier to issue a bill of lading, which is not very often used in the kind of short sea shipping where ro-ro transport of trucks is common.[173] However, once again it is important to keep in mind the different levels of contractual relationships. In respect of multimodal transport, it is the relationship between the contracting carrier and the contracting consignor that is subject to analysis and whether the sea carrier issues a bill of lading for the sea transport or not is a matter that relates to the contract between the contracting carrier and the sea carrier, which is unquestionably a contract of carriage by sea. Indeed, the contracting carrier may have issued a bill of lading for the entire transport, and to the extent the contract of carriage refers to carriage by sea, the bill of lading issued may very well "relate to the carriage of goods by sea". Accordingly, it is arguable that where a contract of carriage provides for carriage by road and ro-ro transport by sea and the carrier issues a bill of lading for the entire transport, the prerequisite found in article 1 of the Hague–Visby Rules is fulfilled.

It seems that to the drafters of the CMR convention, the sea traverse, in the relationship between the contracting carrier and the contracting consignor, simply could not be considered carriage by sea for the reason that the goods remained

171 Commentary on the convention of 19 May 1956 on the contract for the international carriage of goods by road (CMR) (GE.75–30686), prepared by R. Loewe and published by the UN in 1975, p. 17.

172 However, one of the arguments asserted by Koller, in advocating the non-applicability of the CMR to road carriage under a multimodal contract of carriage, is that article 2 deals with multimodal transport to the effect of pre-empting the applicability of the convention to any other forms of multimodal transport (I. Koller, "Quantum Corporation Inc. v. Plane Trucking Limited und die Anwendbarkeit der CMR auf die Beförderung mit verschiedenartigen Transportmitteln" in (2003) 2 TransportR 45–50).

173 R. Herber, "The European Legal Experience with Multimodalism" (1989–1990) 64 Tul L Rev 611 at p. 618.

on the road vehicle. Ro-ro transport, it was considered, was in fact a transport carried out at two levels simultaneously; in the relation between the contacting carrier and the sea carrier it is a carriage by sea of the vehicle, and in the relation between the contracting carrier and the contracting consignor it is carriage by, if not road, at least road vehicle.[174] As the contract of carriage would thus not be considered to contain a contract of carriage by sea, there would be no potential conflict between the CMR convention and any carriage by sea convention.[175]

It appears that generally, when article 2 of the CMR convention is discussed, it is not the autonomous applicability of e.g. the Hague–Visby Rules that is considered but the prerequisite in article 2 which provides that

> the liability of the carrier by road shall be determined not by [the CMR] convention but in the manner in which the liability of the carrier by the other means of transport would have been determined if a contract for the carriage the goods alone had been made by the sender with the carrier by the other means of transport in accordance with the conditions prescribed by law for the carriage of goods by that means of transport.[176]

The discussion often concerns whether the Hague–Visby Rules would have applied to such a hypothetical contract considering the custom to issue seaway-bills rather than bills of lading in short sea shipping as well as the fact that trailers are generally deck cargo in ro-ro transport.[177] The actual conditions under which short sea shipping takes place could, on the other hand, be a reason for the absence of a risk of competition between the CMR convention and the Hague–Visby Rules. At this point, it is important to keep the separate relationships in mind. Thus, the Hague–Visby Rules could be considered autonomously applicable to ro-ro sea carriage where such sea carriage appears from the contract of carriage between the contracting carrier and the contracting consignor, i.e.

---

174 Commentary on the convention of 19 May 1956 on the contract for the international carriage of goods by road (CMR) (GE.75–30686), prepared by R. Loewe and published by the UN in 1975, p. 17.

175 Grönfors holds that due to the fact that at the time of drafting of the Hague Rules, integrated transport was unforeseen, the applicability of these rules must be made flexible and should thus not be considered to compete with the applicability of the CMR to ro-ro transports (K. Grönfors, *Successiva Transporter* (1968) p. 268).

176 See e.g. D. Glass, "Article 2 of the CMR convention – a reappraisal" (2000) JBL 562–586.

177 Haak comments on four Dutch cases that deal with the issue; *The Baltic Ferry* from 1989, *The Gabriele Wehr* from 1990, *The Duke of Yare* from 1995 and *The St Clair* from 2001, of which *The Gabriele Wehr* and *The St Clair* were decided by the Dutch Supreme Court. In none of these cases did the courts discuss the applicability of the Hague–Visby Rules *per se*, but in *The Gabriele Wehr* the Supreme Court held that in relation to article 2 of the CMR it is the Hague–Visby Rules that are referred to, and that possible escapes from these mandatory rules, such as the non-issuing of a bill of lading or the fact that trailers are usually carried on deck, should be disregarded and furthermore the hypothetical contract is to be assumed to be made on terms which subjects the contract to these rules. There is no indication, to my understanding, that the same principles would apply as regards autonomous application of the Hague–Visby Rules. In *The Duke of Yare*, decided by the District Court of Rotterdam, a bill of lading was in fact issued for the ro-ro carriage over the English Channel. However, there is no indication of the conditions of the contract of carriage by road, i.e. the court does not seem to have been concerned with the possible autonomous applicability of the Hague–Visby Rules (K. Haak, "Ro-Ro Transport under CMR, Art 2: The Dutch Solution" [2005] LMCLQ 308).

the "road carriage contract" and under which a bill of lading is to be issued. In this respect, the practices normally applied in ro-ro carriage are of less importance. Those practices become important under article 2 of the CMR convention, when the hypothetical terms of the hypothetical contract are to be settled.[178] However, considering the decreasing use of bills of lading in sea carriage, it has been argued that the Hague–Visby Rules should also be considered applicable where the transport document is non-negotiable.[179] Should this interpretation be accepted, the Hague–Visby Rules would be autonomously applicable wherever the contract of carriage, explicitly or implicitly, envisages carriage by sea.[180] This would obviously entail that article 2 of the CMR convention would regularly be in conflict with the Hague–Visby Rules, should the contract of carriage be considered to provide for carriage by sea.[181]

It has been held that one motive for inclusion of the reference to the rules that would govern the hypothetical contract in article 2 of the CMR convention was to reduce conflicts between the terms of the convention and national or international law.[182] This appears to be an indication that the drafters actually considered possible conflict with other conventions, although it must be pointed out that the mere fact that the rules of the two competing conventions are identical does not actually eliminate the conflict as the question of which of the (identical *per se*) rules prevails.

The CMR convention and the COTIF–CIM convention

Mode-on-mode carriage of road vehicles on rail carriages may not be as common as ro-ro carriage of such vehicles by sea. However, there exist a few tunnels where this type of carriage appears. The rail tunnel under the English Channel, connecting the United Kingdom with France, ought to be the most common example where such carriage in addition is international. The Simplon Tunnel between Switzerland and Italy also provides for carriage of road vehicles by rail.

As the COTIF–CIM convention applies to international contracts of carriage by rail the risk of conflict between the CMR convention article 2 and the

178 In this regard it is often discussed whether the terms of the actual contract of carriage by sea, made between the road carrier and the sea carrier, are to be considered as an indication of what the hypothetical contract may have looked like (K. Haak, "Ro-Ro Transport under CMR, Art 2: The Dutch Solution" [2005] LMCLQ 308 and D. Glass, "Article 2 of the CMR – a reappraisal" (2000) JBL 562–586). However, to the extent a separate contract had been made between the contracting consignor and the sea carrier, it would not likely have been for ro-ro carriage and thus the terms would likely diverge from those of the existing ro-ro contract.

179 D. Glass, *ibid.*, at p. 572, with reference to *Browner International Transport Ltd v Monarch SS Co. Ltd* [1989] 2 Lloyd's Rep 185, and H. Karan, *The Carrier's Liability under International Maritime Conventions* (2004) pp. 140–141. See also F. Sejersted, *Haagreglerne* (1976) p. 34 and W. Tetley, *Marine Cargo Claims* (2008) pp. 17–18. For the opposite view see Prop. 1993/94:195, p. 152 and J. Wilson, *Carriage of Goods by Sea* (2010) p. 176.

180 H. Karan, *ibid.* at pp. 140–141.

181 In order to avoid such conflict, Grönfors suggests that article 2 of the CMR convention could be regarded, as one of several possible interpretations, as a localization of damage clause, which thus localizes the damage to the road leg (to which the liability rules of the CMR convention applies) or to the sea leg (to which the Hague Rules applies) (K. Grönfors, *Successiva Transporter* (1968) p. 268).

182 D. Glass, *ibid.*, at p. 569.

COTIF–CIM convention would appear to be imminent. However, if there is little discussion regarding possible conflict between the CMR convention and the Hague–Visby Rules, discussion on the possible conflict between the CMR convention and the COTIF–CIM convention is even more absent.[183] Considering the palpable difference in the limitation of liability, there would seem to be grounds for litigation.

Obviously, many of the issues discussed in the previous section reappears in relation to the COTIF–CIM convention and the discussion would thus to a large extent mirror that discussion. The COTIF–CIM convention requires for its application the existence of a contract for the international carriage of goods by rail. Although the issuing of a consignment note is a mandatory obligation that rests on the carrier, the absence thereof does not limit the applicability of the convention. Thus, there would seem to be a risk of conflict between the CMR convention and the COTIF–CIM convention as soon as the contract of carriage analysed (i.e. the (multimodal) contract between the contracting carrier and the contracting consignor) explicitly or implicitly provides for carriage by rail.

3.3.2.3 The COTIF–CIM convention

The COTIF–CIM convention applies to a fairly large extent to ro-ro traffic although it operates in a different way from the CMR convention. Hence, the COTIF–CIM convention applies to carriage by sea to the extent that such carriage is performed by one of the ferry lines listed in the CIM list of lines published by the OTIF.[184] According to article 1 §4 of the COTIF–CIM convention the prerequisites are that the carriage is subject to one single contract and that the carriage by sea is carried out as a supplement to carriage by rail. The term "supplement" should not be understood as referring to the importance of the sea carriage in relation to the rail carriage. The prerequisite of a single contract of carriage is straightforward. The list of lines to which the COTIF–CIM convention applies has a somewhat complicated structure, but it can be concluded that the lines included are fairly limited. However, to the extent a line is found in the list, the implications in relation to the Hague–Visby Rules will mirror the implications discussed above in relation to the CMR convention. The COTIF–CIM convention does not, in contrast to the CMR, require for its applicability to these other modes of transport that the goods are not unloaded from the rail carriage, although it is presumed that the lines included in the mentioned list allow for ro-ro transportation of rail carriages. However, the fact that the goods are unloaded would not technically prevent the applicability of the COTIF–CIM convention. Another dissimilarity with the CMR convention is that the COTIF–CIM convention does not provide that liability in certain circumstances is to be

183 M. Clarke, *International Carriage of Goods by Road: CMR* (2014) p. 38.

184 In addition to pure carriage by rail, the COTIF–CIM convention applies to domestic transport by road which is supplementary to carriage by rail, as well as to carriage by sea and inland waterway to the extent such carriage is supplementary to carriage by rail, and the line listed by the OTIF (Article 1, §§ 3–4).

decided by the carriage by sea convention, as provided by article 2 of the CMR convention, which seems wise considering the problems of applicability that article has caused.

In conclusion, the rules relating to the extension of the CMR convention and the COTIF–CIM convention to other modes of transport seem to pose an inherent risk of possible conflicts between those two conventions, as well as in relation to the Hague–Visby Rules. Curiously, there is not much discussion regarding these possible conflicts. On the other hand, there is not much indication that the expansion of these unimodal conventions to other modes of transport causes many problems or disputes in practice either. The reason for the latter state of affairs can only be speculated on. One likely reason is financial: if, for example, goods transported by road are damaged during ro-ro transport by sea it seems likely that the damage is limited to one truck load, e.g. a container. Thus, the difference in limitation amounts between the CMR convention, under which the contracting carrier reimburses the contracting consignee, and the Hague–Visby Rules, under which the contracting carrier seeks recourse against the sea carrier, is perhaps not sufficient for the contracting carrier to assert the applicability of the latter convention against the contracting consignee but is borne by the contracting carrier as a business risk.

3.4 The legal background to the research questions

There is a seemingly increasing tendency to consider the conventions that apply to contracts for carriage of goods by a certain mode not to be applicable to contracts that provide for transport by more than one mode. This entails a rejection of the network system as that system is based on the application of each unimodal set of rules to the separate legs of a multimodal transport.[185] As there is no international uniform system in place, the alternative to the network system is currently to allow the contractual terms to be enforceable, i.e. to accept a state of freedom of contract. However, there are also cases where the court applies the whole transport the liability provisions applicable to one of the transport modes by which the goods are carried: the so-called overall characterization theory, a form of unified system.[186]

At the time of the emergence of multimodal contracts of carriage, the network system seems to have been applied without much discussion,[187] and it was only

185 This conclusion relates to the mandatory imposition of the network system on an international level, i.e. the network system that presents itself if the unimodal conventions are regarded as applicable by their own force to transport under a multimodal contract of carriage. There are other ways to impose a network system, e.g. contractually or though national legislation, in which case the scope of application of the unimodal conventions would not need to be scrutinized.

186 See e.g. *Quantum Corporation Inc v Plane Trucking Ltd* [2002] 2 Lloyd's Rep 25 paras 60–62 and Danish Supreme Court HD 23 April 2008 (U.2008.1638H).

187 Commentary on the convention of 19 May 1956 on the contract for the international carriage of goods by road (CMR) (GE.75-30686), prepared by R. Loewe and published by the UN in 1975, p. 8. However, in 1968 Fitzpatrick discusses the applicability of the CMR to road legs of multimodal transport (P.G. Fitzpatrick, "Combined Transport and the CMR convention" (1968) JBL 311–319).

later, at the time of drafting the Multimodal Convention in 1980, that the first proposals regarding the status of the multimodal contract of carriage as a contract *sui generis* seem to have been made. The ensuing discussion in legal doctrine was fuelled in 2002 by the English *Quantum* case and further in 2008 by a judgment from the German Supreme Court. In the following, I will analyse the legal status regarding the applicability of unimodal conventions to multimodal contracts of carriage, and whether the network system has any legal support in European adjudication.

3.4.1 Precedent

German national legislation, which thus imposes the network system via the hypothetical contract formula, prevents the immediate collapse of the network system although it does not entail a long-lasting solution. Further, the German legislation appears to be rather solitary and in the remaining European states the existence of a network system depends on the interpretation of the scope of applicability of existing unimodal conventions, an interpretation that is left with the national courts.

Accordingly, the following judgments from several European national courts, relate to possible application of the network system. In order to be mandatorily enforceable, the network system presupposes the autonomous applicability of the unimodal conventions to the legs of a multimodal contract of carriage. All judgments referenced below relate to the CMR convention, although not all include actual consideration of the applicability of the convention. Several judgments relate to questions of the jurisdiction or competence of the court, which means that even if the question of application of the CMR convention is analysed, the consequences in respect of the network system may not have been considered by the court in question. Because it is perceived that there has previously been a rather uniform application of the network system by European courts, which has eventually been undermined and even turned over, the judgments analysed below will be presented chronologically rather than based on the nationality of the court that decided the case. Further, although some national tendencies can be discerned, the international aspect is enhanced by such presentation.

3.4.1.1 Danish Maritime and Commercial Court 19 January 1984 (U.1984.577S)

A shipment of prawns was shipped from Hirtshals in Denmark to London. The leg between Hirtshals and Århus was carried out by truck, after which the truck was shipped on a ro-ro ferry to Middlesbrough and thereafter again by truck (the goods thus seems never to have been reloaded). On arrival in London the consignee claimed that 27 out of the 6,000 boxes were missing. During which part of the transport the loss was caused does not seem to have been investigated. The claimants alleged that Danish national CMR legislation was applicable: however, the court applied the Hague–Visby Rules as the transport was covered by a through bill of lading. The court found that it was not clear that the parties had entered into a contract for the carriage of goods by road, which prevented application of the CMR convention. It further found that the bill of lading referred to the Hague–Visby Rules and prescribed those rules to be applicable to the whole transport. The court also considered the whole transport to be of a sea transport character, as the two containers that contained the 6,000 boxes were never unloaded from the chassis onto which they were loaded at the place of loading in Hirtshals, and that the dominant part of the transport was sea transport.[188] There is no indication in the judgment that, had the court found that the parties had entered into a carriage by road contract, it would not have applied the CMR convention, which would have covered the whole transport due to its article 2.[189]

3.4.1.2 German Federal Supreme Court BGH 24 June 1987

This case concerned carriage of a shipment of tools from Neunkirchen, Germany to Portadown in Northern Ireland. After the shipment had been carried by road from Neunkirchen to Rotterdam, it was reloaded onto a vessel, which carried it to the port of Belfast. From Belfast it was supposed to be carried by road to its final destination, but due to unpaid freight the carrier exercised his right of stoppage and eventually returned the goods to the shipper in Germany. Against the carrier's claim for freight the shipper alleged damage to the goods. In order to settle the basis for the carrier's liability, the German Supreme Court placed the burden of proof as to where the damage occurred on the carrier. It further held that for non-localized damage the carrier would answer under the liability regime that would have been applicable had each leg of the transport been governed by a separate contract, which is the least favourable to the carrier. The German Supreme Court held that the road carriage from Neunkirchen to Rotterdam was subject to the CMR convention on the basis that the carriage was an international transport by road, which was subject to a CMR waybill.

It has been claimed that the judgment establishes that under German law, where a transport is subject to a multimodal contract of carriage, the carrier's liability is governed by the liability rules that would have been applicable to the (localized) damage had each mode of transport been governed by separate unimodal contracts.[190]

---

188 It is notable that the facts that the court considers support the characterization of the transport as sea transport are those found in CMR article 2, which according to that convention characterizes a transport as road transport.

189 Against the background of the sea transport being the dominating mode of transport, in terms of it being the mode of transport envisaged by the shipper, and as it is the mere fact that the containers are not unloaded from the trailer chassis that would have made the CMR convention applicable, the outcome, although remarkable at first glance, is probably correct. Where the CMR convention does not claim applicability to the road transport the parties are free to agree to apply the Hague–Visby Rules.

190 L. Andersen Roost; *Multimodale Transporter* (2012) p. 208, with reference to Herber, "Zur Berücksichtigung des Tailstreckenrechts bei Multimodalem Transportvertrag" in *Festschrift für Henning Piper* (1996) p. 877. The German Supreme Court seems also to have applied the network principle in its judgment of 30 September 1993 in I ZR 258/91, where it applied the CMR to a road stretch under a multimodal contract, which included road and inland waterway transport.

3.4.1.3 German Federal Supreme Court BGH 17 May 1989, I ZR 211/87

This case involved transport from Stuttgart in Germany to Algiers in Algeria under an air carriage contract as well as multiple layers of subcarriers. The contracted for air carriage was for part of the carriage, from Stuttgart to Frankfurt airport, substituted for road carriage. The goods were damaged during the carriage by road. Although the owner of the goods, which comprised electronic devices, claimed that the carriage by road constituted a breach of the contract of carriage, the German Supreme Court did not find it necessary to establish whether substitution was permitted or not. In either case, a permitted substitution or a culpable breach of contract, damages should, according to the court, be calculated in accordance with the national rules relating to carriage of goods by road. In the latter case, the court concluded that a party in breach of its obligations may not invoke its own breach of contract in order to gain a better position than had it performed its obligations in accordance with the contract. The carrier must then bear at least the risks and obligations connected with the mode of transport chosen. It is not clear however whether the court would in that case consider the national legislation on road transport applicable or merely have the carrier answer to the owner of the goods as if that legislation was applicable.

It has been concluded from the case that had the carriage by road been international, and permitted under the contract, the CMR convention would have been applied to the road leg.[191] However, this conclusion may be challenged as the German national legislation applicable to the road transport, the KVO[192] "applies to commercial long-distance freight transport"[193] and does not indicate application to a transport contract in the sense prescribed by the CMR convention. Thus, the crucial point of the CMR convention, applicability to contracts of carriage, which the Supreme Court later found incompatible with multimodal contracts of carriage, was never scrutinized by the Supreme Court in this case.

3.4.1.4 Dutch District Court of Rotterdam, Rb Rotterdam, 28 October 1999, the *Resolution Bay*

The case concerned frozen meat being transported from an inland point in New Zealand to Antwerp in Belgium via the ports of Port Chalmers and Rotterdam, between which the goods were carried by sea. From Rotterdam to Antwerp the goods were carried by road and whilst the contract did not specify that the goods were to be carried by road from the Netherlands to Belgium, it did allow for the goods to be so carried.[194] The District Court of Rotterdam was faced with

191 M. Hoeks, *Multimodal Transport Law* (2010) p. 170.

192 Kraftverkehrsordnung für den Güterfernverkehr mit Kraftfahrzeugen of 23 December 1958. This legislation was replaced in 1998 by the TRG, inserted in the fifth book of the Handelsgesetzbuch, HGB.

193 §1 (1) Die Kraftverkehrsordnung gilt für den gewerblichen Güterfernverkehr im Sinne von §3 des Güterkraftverkehrsgesetzes ("The road transport regulation applies to commercial long-distance freight transport within the meaning of §3 Road Haulage Act") (my translation).

194 It is not clear from the case whether it was stipulated or agreed between the parties that the goods were to be unloaded from the ship in Rotterdam, in which case it would not be too far-fetched to construe the contract as including a road transport from Rotterdam to the final destination.

the question of its own competence; if the CMR convention were applicable, as indeed the claimants maintained, the court would have competence over the dispute in accordance with CMR article 31. The crucial question was thus whether the goods were *taken over* by the road carrier in Rotterdam in the sense stipulated by the CMR convention. Without any in-depth analysis the court concluded that the contracting carrier, P&O, and/or its representative took delivery of the goods from the sea carrier for transport by road in Rotterdam and that this therefore was to be considered the place of taking over the goods as stated in the CMR convention article 1. Thereafter, the court without hesitation applied the CMR convention to the international road leg of a multimodal transport. Hence, the case does not concern the applicability as such of the CMR convention to the road legs of a larger, multimodal, transport, but jurisdiction according to article 31.[195] Clearly, jurisdiction according to article 31 presupposes applicability of the convention as such. However, the Rotterdam District Court does not seem to have been too preoccupied with the issue. At the same time, the question whether the place of taking over the goods by the road carrier can be a place other than the initial taking over the goods by the carrier from the shipper is also relevant to questions of applicability as such. Here the court concluded that as the carrier had opted to carry out the transport between Rotterdam and Antwerp by road, which it was contractually permitted to do, the carrier, or its representative, had taken over the goods in Rotterdam in the sense stipulated by the CMR convention article 1.

3.4.1.5 UK Court of Appeal – *Quantum Corporation Inc v Plane Trucking Ltd* [2002] 2 Lloyd's Rep 25

Under a contract of carriage by air, Air France had undertaken to carry goods from Singapore to Dublin, Ireland. According to the contract, the goods would be transhipped in Paris. From Paris, the transport was carried out by a trucking service, i.e. by road, during which carriage the goods were stolen. The contract of carriage indicated that the transport from Paris to Dublin was to be carried out by flight AF9408, which in fact identified the very trucking service that was used. Similar consignments had been transported several times before, under the same type of contract and by the same means of transport (i.e. air carriage to Paris and road carriage therefrom). The claimants asserted that the road carriage was subject to the CMR convention, whilst the defendants claimed that no mandatory regime was applicable and that therefore its own standard terms were applicable (alternatively that the Warsaw Convention was applicable under the overall characterization test). The court held that, for the applicability of the CMR convention, it is not necessary that the contract of carriage is an express and unconditional undertaking to carry by road and that the CMR convention

However, as Antwerp is a major port the consignor could very well have been of the understanding that the goods were to be carried by sea to Antwerp.

195 It seems that the claimants asserted that the CMR is not applicable, although it is not clear on what ground. It could be that the reason purported was that the place of taking over was in New Zealand, which is not party to the CMR, an assertion that is dealt with by the court in relation to article 31.

applies to the road leg of a multimodal contract. Thus, where a change of transport modes is contractually allowed, or even, as in this case, presupposed, the fact that the goods were carried by road meant that a contract for the carriage of goods by road was involved. The court further concluded that as regards the place of taking over the goods, under a multimodal transport, that is to be understood as the place where the goods were taken over for road carriage. In its conclusions the court relied on precedent from various European countries, which to that date was fairly unanimous in applying the CMR to road carriage although the contract of carriage also provides for carriage by (an)other mode(s).

3.4.1.6 Belgian Supreme Court, Cour de Cassation, 8 November 2004, C.03.0510.N[196]

In resemblance to the German Federal Supreme Court, the Belgian Supreme Court, Le Cour de Cassation, reviews the legal aspects of the judgment appealed and, should it find the legal considerations made by the lower court erroneous, returns the case to the lower court for reconsideration. The present case concerned a courier service for computer devices from Londerzeel in Belgium to Belm in Germany, undertaken by TNT Express. The goods were damaged whilst still in Belgium. The claimant asserted that the damage should be reimbursed in full whilst the carrier claimed that the damage was subject to limitation under the CMR convention either because the CMR convention was autonomously applicable to the carriage or because the carrier's general conditions incorporated the rules of the CMR.[197] The lower court, whose judgment was upheld by the Supreme Court, considered that the agreement between the shipper and the carrier was not a contract for the carriage of goods by road, as required for the applicability of the CMR convention. The contract did not either explicitly or implicitly specify how the goods were to be transported but left the transport arrangements entirely to the carrier. Indeed, the court regarded the contract as a service agreement, rather than as a carriage contract. A transport contract, the lower court held, is characterized by an initial consensus on the transport mode to be used for the transport. The contract at issue did not give the carrier a right to substitute the mode of transport, but left the choice entirely to TNT Express as the service provider. On appeal, the Supreme Court, in its judgment, emphasized the absolute requirement in the CMR convention that the parties have entered into a contract for carriage by road; i.e. that at the time of entering into the contract the parties expect the goods to be carried by road, either because of their express agreement or that it so appears from the circumstances. The effect of the judgment is that the Supreme Court confirms the requirement of article 1 of the CMR convention that the convention is only applicable to contracts of carriage

196 This summary is based on a detailed summary of the judgments by the lower court and the Supreme Court in P. Vestergaard Pedersen, *Transportret* (2008) pp. 944–950.

197 As regards this secondary ground, the court found that the general conditions referred to "The CMR convention or the Warsaw convention whichever is applicable", which thus according to the court required autonomous applicability of the CMR convention anyway.

by road (and not to the actual carriage by such mode). However, the judgment does not approach the issue of autonomous applicability of the CMR convention to contracts that provide for carriage by road and in addition carriage by other mode(s), and accordingly it does not prevent such applicability.[198] However, the judgment does prevent the application of the network system to undefined contracts of carriage.

3.4.1.7 Danish Supreme Court HD 23 April 2008 (U.2008.1638H)

A cargo of frozen roe was contracted to be carried from Denmark to Japan. The contract, which covered the entire transport from Billund in Denmark to Narita in Japan, was a contract for carriage by air. However, the carrier shipped the goods from Billund to Frankfurt airport by road (a so-called "trucking service") in accordance with an option to do so in the contract. Due to a road accident, the goods were damaged during road transport. The claimant asserted that the carrier was liable according to the national carriage by air statute, whilst the defendant claimed that the carriage was subject to the CMR convention and therefore time-barred. The court held that the contract for the entire transport was in fact a contract for carriage by air, and as such it was governed by the rules relating to air carriage. Invoking an option to carry by road did not, according to the court, change the characteristics of the contract.[199] However, the court stated, *obiter dictum*, that the fact that an option to carry by another mode is invoked will have the consequence that the cargo owner in relation to the contracting carrier may invoke the liability rules relating to the mode of transport by which the transport was in fact carried out. It seems quite clear that the shipper expected the carriage to be performed by air in its entirety and that, thus, although in fact containing an option for the carrier to substitute the mode of transport, this option was "small print" rather than an anticipated alternative. As the Supreme Court bases its conclusions on the overall consideration of the of the contract of carriage, which it concludes is a contract for carriage by air, it does not discuss the applicability as such of the CMR convention to the carriage by road.[200] In relation to the outcome of the case, it should be borne in mind that had the Supreme Court considered the CMR convention applicable to the transport, the claim would have been time-barred.

198 The conclusion by Vestergaard Pedersen, namely that the judgment entails that the CMR convention is not applicable to multimodal transport contracts (P. Vestergaard Pedersen, *Transportret* (2008) pp. 945–946), thus seems too far-reaching, as the court does not seem to express its views on multimodal contracts that include an express agreement to carry goods by road.

199 Under the Montreal Convention, article 18.4, such trucking of the cargo is to be considered air carriage if the carrier does not enjoy the contractual right of substitution of the mode of transport, i.e. if the trucking constitutes a breach of contract.

200 It has correctly been pointed out by Ulfbeck and Taiger Ivø that the Danish Supreme Court only considers whether performance affects the characteristics of a transport contract when the carrier has utilized an option to substitute the mode of transport and that thus it has not been considered in precedents whether the CMR convention would be considered applicable to road carriage under a multimodal contract. However, according to Ulfbeck and Taiger Ivø, the prevailing view in Denmark is that it is not (V. Ulfbeck and S. Taiger Ivø, "Optioner og ansvar i transportaftaler" (2008) 4 Erhvervsjuridisk Tidsskrift 331–343, at p. 338).

3.4.1.8 German Federal Supreme Court BGH 17 July 2008, I ZR 181/05

A Japanese freight forwarder had contracted to carry 24 containers of copying machines from the manufacturer in Japan to its German subsidiary in Mönchengladbach. The containers were carried by sea from Tokyo to Rotterdam, and from Rotterdam they were intended to be carried by road. During road transport, whilst still in the port of Rotterdam, the contents of one container were damaged due to a road accident. The carrier, the Japanese freight forwarder, contested the jurisdiction of the German courts. The Court of Appeal found that the German courts had jurisdiction based on article 31 of the CMR convention, which it found applicable, according to its article 1, to road carriage under a multimodal contract of carriage.

The German Supreme Court thus deviated from what was generally considered to be its precedence and, in line with the general opinion in German legal writing,[201] found that the CMR convention was not applicable to a road leg of a multimodal carriage. In so finding it concluded that article 1.1 of the CMR convention did not provide for application of the convention to multimodal contracts, as a contract for multimodal carriage was, in fact, not a contract for carriage by road (only).[202] Further it held that article 2 was exclusive in the way that the CMR convention only applied to piggy-pack multimodal carriage; article 2 regulated a particular form of multimodal transport and the inclusion of that regulation in the convention was to be understood systemically as an indication that the CMR convention was not applicable to other forms of multimodal transport.[203] In addition, the court pointed to the fact that the protocol of signatories to the CMR convention included an undertaking by the state parties to the convention to negotiate a separate convention on multimodal transport contracts, and that German governmental consideration relating to ratification of the CMR convention assumed that the convention was not applicable to multimodal transport other than according to its article 2. The court continued by holding that the aim of the convention, to harmonize international carriage of goods by road, was not prevented by the interpretation it suggested and that such an interpretation was not contrary to previous Supreme Court decisions as they did not concern applicability of the CMR convention in cases when German law was not the appropriate law. Lastly, the court attempted to undermine the legal basis of the judgment of the English Court of Appeal in the *Quantum* case on the same ground, namely that the German

201 M. Hoeks, *Multimodal Transport Law* (2010) p. 174, with references to Koller, Herber, Ramming, Basedow, Thume and others. See in particular I. Koller, "Quantum Corporation Inc. v. Plane Trucking Limited und die Anwendbarkeit der CMR auf die Beförderung mit verschiedenartigen Transportmitteln" (2003) 2 TransportR 45–50.

202 This seems to be in line with the opinion of the German legislator who, when adopting new legislation on transport of goods in 1998, considered multimodal transport to be a mode of transport of its own, along with the more traditional modes (L. Andersen Roost, *Multimodale Transporter* (2012) p. 214).

203 Note in this respect that mode-on-mode transport does not seem to have been perceived as multimodal transport by the drafters of the CMR (Commentary on the convention of 19 May 1956 on the contract for the international carriage of goods by road (CMR) (GE.75–30686), prepared by R. Loewe and published by the UN in 1975, p. 17).

cases referred to in that case did not concern the autonomous application of the CMR convention to multimodal contracts.

The German Supreme Court is a pure auditing court, which decides on the legal issue and reverts to the Court of Appeal to re-evaluate the dispute based on the Supreme Court's findings.[204] It hence does not try the factual circumstances of the case. As such it makes general statements about applicable law and hence generates generally applicable rules. Its statement that "Eine Zuständigkeit der deutschen Gerichte für die Entscheidung des Rechtsstreits besteht nicht, weil die CMR grundsätzlich nicht auf multimodale Frachtverträge anwendbar ist"[205] is a clear and general statement, which leaves little room for German courts to distinguish future cases.

3.4.1.9 Dutch Supreme Court, Hoge Raad, 1 June 2012, nr.10/05322, the *Godafoss*

Similar to the *Resolution Bay* from 1999, this case concerned the competence of the District Court of Rotterdam, which in 2007 rendered a decision said to be a virtual copy of the *Resolution Bay*.[206] The facts of the case concerned a shipment of fish from Iceland to Italy via Rotterdam, from where the goods were carried by road and stolen before reaching its final destination. The contract of carriage contained an exclusive forum clause nominating the Icelandic courts, which clause would be valid unless the CMR convention was autonomously applicable to the road leg of the transport. The case was eventually tried by the Dutch Supreme Court. In its judgment, the Supreme Court divided the matter into two questions: (1) Whether the CMR convention generally applies to multimodal carriage, which is not mode-on-mode transport under article 2 of the convention, and (assuming the answer to this first question is "no") (2) Whether the CMR convention applies if the damage to or loss of the goods occurs during carriage by road. Based on arguments such as the existence of article 2 and the fact that the signatories to the CMR convention undertook to negotiate a multimodal convention, the court answered the first question in the negative.[207] Although the court seemed to indicate that application of the CMR convention to "every contract for the carriage of goods in vehicles for reward" included application to carriage by road carried out under a multimodal contract, the second question was also answered in the negative as it is considered to entail too much legal uncertainty if questions of jurisdiction can be answered only after it was clear during which leg of a multimodal transport the damage has occurred, and it thus was clear which

204 L. Andersen Roost, *Multimodale Transportaftaler* (2012) p. 204.

205 At para. 16.2: "Jurisdiction for German courts in settling legal disputes is absent as the CMR in principle is not applicable to multimodal contracts of carriage" (my translation).

206 M. Spanjaart, "GODAFOSS: the applicability of the CMR within multimodal contracts of carriage" (2012) 7 TranspR 278–282, at p. 280.

207 An answer which is obvious although on other grounds; the applicability of the CMR convention to an entire multimodal contract is prevented by the fact that to the extent such a contract is not carried out by road, it cannot in any way be said to be a contract for the carriage of goods by road, unless the carriage by another mode is a mode-on-mode transport without transhipment of the goods.

regulation applied to the dispute. The court further emphasised that a road leg of a multimodal carriage of goods was not the same as an independent contract for the carriage of goods by road, which however somewhat contradicted its finding that the reading of article 1.1 was an argument for the applicability of the CMR convention to a road leg. A point of interest is the statement by the Supreme Court that "a regime in which the applicable rules change with the specific legs of the transport, does not work"[208] as this is the exact system prescribed by national Dutch legislation in relation to multimodal transport.[209]

The Dutch Supreme Court clearly approaches the questions it puts forward in a very general way and with the intention of enunciating a general rule. The judgment is given after the judgment by the BGH in 2008, and the Dutch Supreme Court is clearly affected by the German decision. It rejects the judgment of the English Court of Appeal referenced above, as being based on judgments, which, in contrast to what the English court assumed, did not unequivocally support autonomous application of the CMR convention.

3.4.2 Views expressed in jurisprudence

At first instance, the *Quantum* case was decided by the Commercial Court in 2001.[210] Based on two considerations, the court considered the CMR convention not to be applicable to the road stretch from Paris to Dublin. First, the court considered that the carriage contract was predominantly one for carriage by air, which led to the conclusion that it was not a contract for carriage by road. Secondly, based on construction problems as regards the requirement that the goods are taken over in a contracting state, which the Commercial Court understood as physical taking over and which had already occurred in Singapore, the court considered the CMR convention not suitable for application to road carriage under a multimodal contract of carriage. The case was criticized by Malcolm Clarke.[211] Clarke held that the predominant view among European commentators was that the CMR convention is indeed applicable to multimodal movement when the road part falls under article 1.[212] Clarke further rejects the overall consideration of the carriage contract made by the court, which was based on the fact that the air leg was longer than the road leg, with the argument that: "[it] is like saying that a 'bloody Mary' should be classified as a non-alcoholic drink because it contains more tomato juice than vodka". Clarke further submits that "taking over" the goods does not necessarily have to be a physical taking over, as contracting carriers that sub-contract the whole carriage, and thus never take physical possession of the goods, are also liable under the convention. He dismisses as irrelevant the

208 Translation by Spanjaart (M. Spanjaart, "GODAFOSS: the applicability of the CMR within multimodal contracts of carriage" (2012) 7 TranspR 278–282, at p. 282).

209 Article 8:41 of the Dutch Civil Code.

210 *Quantum Corp Inc v Plane Trucking Ltd* [2001] 1 All ER (Comm) 916 (QBD (Comm)).

211 M. Clarke, "A Multimodal mix-up" (2002) JBL 210–217.

212 Clarke refers to Bugden, Glass, Theunis, Tilche, Basedow, Herber/Piper and Haak; M. Clarke, *ibid.*, in fnn. 10–14.

argument put forward by the Commercial Court that as the intention of the drafters of the CMR convention was to conclude a multimodal transport convention they thus did not intend the CMR convention to be applicable to multimodal transport. He rebuts that as the convention could apply and considering the failure to implement a multimodal transport convention, it is likely that the drafters would have wanted the CMR convention to apply to multimodal transports, had they known of future events. Clarke concluded his argumentation by holding that "uniform law is not to be frozen in time … [it] must be interpreted and developed dynamically".[213]

The *Quantum* case was subsequently tried by the Court of Appeal, whose judgment is discussed above.[214] The Court of Appeal reversed the Commercial Court judgment, to a large extent based on the same arguments put forward by Clarke, but the court also referred to precedents from other European jurisdictions. The Court of Appeal's judgment, although presumably applauded by Clarke,[215] is criticized by Ingo Koller.[216] Accordingly, Koller holds that article 1 of the CMR convention should be read as referring to contracts for the carriage by road only, and not in combination with other modes of transport. Such an interpretation is, according to Koller, supported by the French wording of article 1, holding the convention applicable to a *contrat de transport*.[217] He further asserted that article 2 of the CMR convention is intended to regulate the only form of multimodal transport to which the convention is applicable, a conclusion which he also supported on the fact that the drafters of the convention clearly intended that multimodal transport should eventually be governed by its own liability rules and thus only had unimodal road transport contracts in mind as the subjects of the CMR convention.[218] Koller submits that the main objection to applying the CMR to a part of a multimodal transport were articles 3 and following, which did not fit a road leg of a multimodal transport.

The *Quantum* case has also been criticized by Per Vestergaard Pedersen, who claims that the view held by the English court, namely that a contract of carriage containing an option for the carrier to substitute the agreed mode of transport for another should be classified as a contract for the mode by which the transport is carried out, to the extent the carrier utilizes his contractual right to do so, could never be accepted under Scandinavian law. Vestergaard Pedersen proposes that

213 M. Clarke, *Ibid*.

214 *Quantum Corporation Inc v Plane Trucking Ltd* [2002] 2 Lloyd's Rep 25.

215 Although the Court of Appeal was obviously inspired by the arguments brought forward by Clarke in relation to the judgment by the Commercial Court, Clarke is restrained in his commentary to the Court of Appeal judgment (M. Clarke, "The line in law between land and sea" (2003) JBL 522–524).

216 I. Koller, "Quantum Corporation Inc. v. Plane Trucking Limited und die Anwendbarkeit der CMR auf die Beförderung mit verschiedenartigen Transportmitteln" (2003) 2 TransportR 45–50.

217 The convention has been authenticated in two languages, English and French.

218 It should be noted in this respect that the drafters of the CMR convention do not seem to have regarded mode-on-mode transport as multimodal transport, but rather as unimodal due to the fact that the goods remain loaded on the road vehicle: see Commentary on the convention of 19 May 1956 on the contract for the international carriage of goods by road (CMR) (GE.75–30686), prepared by R. Loewe and published by the UN in 1975, p. 17.

it follows from general rules on contract classification that a contract will not change characteristics because it is fulfilled differently than agreed.[219]

Against the propositions made by Koller, Krijn Haak and Marian Hoeks argue that the applicability of the CMR convention to a road leg of a multimodal transport is supported by near-unanimous legal discussion.[220] They hold that the key to application of the CMR convention lies in article 1, which does not literally demand that carriage is undertaken exclusively by road, only that it contains a road stage. As regards the place of taking over the goods, which according to article 1.1 have to be situated in a contracting state, this should, they assert, be "read as referring to the start of the contractually provided or permitted *road leg*".[221] This, Haak and Hoeks argue, is supported both by the fact that the most important feature of "taking over" is that it annotates the geographical scope of the convention and also by the fact that a physical taking over is not necessary in other situations, such as sub-contracting where the contracting carrier under article 34 is liable for the entire carriage. Haak and Hoeks further claim that article 2 should not be taken as proof of the non-applicability of the CMR convention to road transport under a multimodal transport contract. Instead, article 2 should be read *e contrario*; if no transhipment takes place, the CMR convention is applicable to the whole carriage, including the sea leg; but if, however, transhipment takes place the CMR convention is not applicable to the sea leg, but to the road legs that precede and succeed the sea transport.[222]

In 2008 what, according to Haak and Hoeks, appeared as near consensus, was turned on its head by the German Supreme Court.[223] The German Court of Appeal (Oberlandesgericht Düsseldorf) whose judgment was overturned by the BGH in its 2008 decision, had concluded, in line with what up until 2008 was considered precedent in Germany, that the CMR was applicable to the road carriage between Rotterdam and Mönchengladbach and that the German courts thus

219 P. Vestergaard Pedersen, *Transportret* (2008) pp. 953–955. However, Vestergaard Pedersen seems to have missed the crucial point in Mance LJ's reasoning; that the substitution of mode of transport occurs under a contractual right to do so. Thus, the contract is not simply one for carriage of goods by e.g. air, but one for carriage of goods by air *or any other mode that the carrier deems appropriate*. Further, it appears that, to the contrary of Vestergaard Pedersen's statement, contracts are not to be classified by their prima facie appearance, but by their material contents. Hence a contract which, according to e.g. its heading, is purported to be a contract for carriage by air is not regarded as such a contract if its contents reveal that the goods are in fact to be carried by road. To the same end, a contract presenting itself as a contract for carriage by air should not be regarded as such if it contains an option for the carrier to substitute mode of transport, in which case it should be classified as a *contract for carriage by air with an option for the carrier to substitute mode of transport*.

220 K. Haak and M. Hoeks, "Intermodal transport under unimodal arrangements" (2003) 5 TransportR 89–102.

221 K. Haak and M. Hoeks, *ibid*., at p. 95.

222 Haak and Hoeks argue that the expanding of the application of the convention to sea transport in some cases is placed after the general application article for a reason; first article 1 claims applicability to all road transport whereafter article 2 expands application to other modes of transport under certain prerequisites. This, they claim is a far larger step than to "expand" the application to road carriage that takes place under a multimodal contract. K. Haak and M. Hoeks, *ibid*., at p. 96.

223 German Federal Supreme Court BGH 17 July 2008, I ZR 181/05, referenced above in section 3.4.1.

had jurisdiction over the dispute. After the BGH decision in July 2008 a crack appeared in what had seemed to be uniform international case law. For this, the BGH's decision is criticized by Peter Laurijssen, who holds that the door to legal uncertainty was re-opened by the BGH.[224] Laurijssen holds that the network system previously applied promoted legal uniformity, sought by the drafters of the CMR convention, and provided legal certainty whilst the approach initiated by the BGH would lead to forum shopping and subversion of the mandatory regulation of the convention.

In her doctoral dissertation, Marian Hoeks thoroughly analyses the arguments on which the German Supreme Court based its decision in 2008.[225] As summarized above, the BGH's main arguments against direct applicability of the CMR convention to road transport carried out under a multimodal transport contract, were (1) that article 1 of the convention indicated that the convention was applicable to contracts for the carriage of goods by road, and only by road; (2) that article 2 of the convention dealt with multimodal transport and should be understood as exclusive, indicating that the convention is not applicable to multimodal transport other than mode-on-mode transport; and (3) that the protocol of signature to the convention clearly obliged the state parties to negotiate a multimodal convention and thus did not intend the CMR convention to apply to road transport carried out under a multimodal transport contract.

The first argument, mainly supported on the French reading of article 1.1,[226] is dismissed by Hoeks as inadequate. Hoeks points out that the translation of the French *de* is "of" and that a contract *of* carriage of goods by road is not very different from a contract *for* the carriage of goods by road. Hoeks further points out the obligation laid down in the Vienna Convention of the Law of Treaties that where two equally authentic versions of a convention disclose a difference in meaning, the meaning that best promotes the object and purpose of the treaty shall be adopted. That objective is best achieved, claims Hoeks, by allowing for applicability of the CMR convention to carriage of goods by road under a multimodal contract, as the objective and purpose of the convention is to create uniformity.[227]

As regards the second argument, Hoeks holds that article 2 in fact does not deal with multimodal transport at all, and hence does not provide for the only multimodal carriage covered by the convention.[228] Instead, article 2 expands the

224 P. Laurijssen, "Quantum Corporation Inc. v. Plane Trucking Ltd. revisited by the German Supreme Court: considerations on the German Federal High Court's decision of 17 July 2008" (2009) 44(2) ETL 143–149.

225 M. Hoeks, *Multimodal Transport Law* (2010).

226 Article 1.1 reads:

> La présente Convention s'applique à tout contrat de transport de marchandises par route à titre onéreux au moyen de véhicules, lorsque le lieu de la prise en charge de la marchandise et le lieu prévu pour la livraison, tels qu'ils sont indiqués au contrat, sont situés dans deux pays différents dont l'un au moins est un pays contractant. Il en est ainsi quels que soient le domicile et la nationalité des parties.

227 M. Hoeks, *Multimodal Transport Law* (2010) pp. 175–176.

228 M. Hoeks *ibid.* at pp. 177–180.

scope of the CMR convention to cover other modes of transportation and, Hoeks argues, "is placed after article 1 to show that it serves as an enlargement of the scope of application of the CMR as found in Article 1".[229] To apply the CMR convention to a road leg of a multimodal contract does not extend the convention to other modes of transport, but merely applies the road regime to road carriage, according to Hoeks.[230]

In relation to the third argument put forward by the BGH regarding the protocol of signature, Hoeks points to the fact that the signatories also undertook to negotiate a convention applicable to furniture removal, but whilst such carriage has been explicitly excluded from the scope of the convention,[231] multimodal transport was not.[232] Further, Hoeks asserts that the drafters probably would have preferred the CMR convention to be applicable to road carriage under a multimodal contract, had they known that after 50 years with explosive utilization of containers and multimodal transport, no multimodal transport convention would not yet be in force.[233]

Hoeks also rebuts the argument, which convinced the English Commercial Court but was rejected by the Court of Appeal in *Quantum*,[234] that the road carrier may not "take over" the goods from the consignor or "deliver" the goods to the consignee as required in article 17, which prescribes the period of the carrier's liability, as well as in articles 1 and 31.[235] That the period of the road carrier's liability only comprises the period during which the road carrier has the goods in its care, as opposed to the whole period between taking over the goods from the initial consignor to the delivery thereof to the final consignee, which hence under a multimodal contract comprises other modes of transport, is unquestionable.[236] However, the question is whether "taking over" and "delivery" must be from the original consignor/consignee or if taking over from the previous carrier and/or delivery to the succeeding carrier suffices to initiate the road carrier's liability. Hoeks notes that the term "delivery" is used in various articles of the convention, although with different purpose. Therefore, it is consistent with the objective of the convention to interpret the term differently depending on the purpose of the article in which it is found.[237] Consequently Hoeks proposes that where "delivery" refers to a point in time, such as in article 32, which prescribes a period of

229 M. Hoeks, *ibid.*, at p. 180.

230 In the reading of the CMR convention suggested by the BGH in 2008, article 2 would entail that the CMR convention either applies to a whole multimodal transport because the goods are not unloaded from the truck, or not at all, not even to the road transport, as the goods are unloaded from the vehicle. However, the reading of article 2 ("this Convention shall *nevertheless* apply to the *whole* of the carriage") (emphasis added) clearly indicates that the drafters assumed that the CMR convention would apply to the road carriage, should the goods be unloaded during the e.g. sea traverse.

231 Article 1.4 (c).

232 M. Hoeks, *ibid.* at pp. 176–177.

233 M. Hoeks, *ibid.*, at p. 178.

234 UK Court of Appeal, *Quantum Corporation Inc v Plane Trucking Ltd* [2002] 2 Lloyd's Rep 25.

235 M. Hoeks, *Multimodal Transport Law* (2010) p. 180.

236 M. Hoeks, *ibid.* at pp. 180–181.

237 M. Hoeks, *ibid.*, at p. 183.

limitation for action relating to the carrier's liability, it should be interpreted as final delivery, i.e. delivery to the consignee. When, on the other hand, "delivery" refers to a place, as in article 31 on jurisdiction (which also prescribes jurisdiction at the place of "taking over" the goods), it should be interpreted as the place of (taking over and) delivery by the road carrier, which do not necessarily involve the (original consignor or) final consignee.

The judgment rendered by the Danish Supreme Court in 2008 mainly concerned the legal implications of the invocation by the carrier of an option to carry the goods by another mode of transport than was initially agreed with the sender.[238] Accordingly, the Danish Supreme Court held that performance did not alter the characteristics of the transport contract, even if it was contractually permitted. The conclusion has been held to be in line with the discussion in Danish doctrine that followed the judgment by the English Commercial Court in the *Quantum* case and, according to Vibe Ulfbeck and Stinne Taiger Ivø, the judgment is unsurprising.[239] However, the authors propose the judgment would probably have had a different outcome had the carrier informed the sender of the change of transport mode, e.g. by issuing a CMR waybill that the sender had accepted.[240] The authors criticize the *obiter dictum* of the Supreme Court in which it held that, in a case of substitution, the sender would be allowed to choose between the liability regime governing the agreed mode of transport and the regime governing the mode of transport actually used. According to Ulfbeck and Ivø, application of such a right is non-uniform in relation to other CMR states and the area of its application unclear. As regards multimodal transport, the authors hold that the Supreme Court judgment does not have any relevance to clear multimodal transport contracts (i.e. contracts where the modes of transport have been expressly agreed).[241] On the other hand, the judgment has clear relevance to undefined contracts (i.e. contracts in which the mode or modes of transport has not been expressly agreed at all), which as a result is not governed by any liability regime at all.[242] Lissi Andersen Roost holds that the judgment seems to be based on the presumption that an option to substitute mode of transport is always to the benefit of the carrier, which she considers to be an incorrect assumption.[243]

The judgment rendered by the Dutch Supreme Court in June 2012, the *Godafoss* case,[244] followed the German Supreme Court case from 2008 and has hence been welcomed by some and criticized by others. The case has been commented on in *Transportrecht* by Martin Spanjaart without much critique as to the

238 Danish Supreme Court, HD 23 April 2008 (U.2008.1638H).

239 V. Ulfbeck and S. Taiger Ivø, "Optioner och ansvar i transportaftaler" (2008) 4 Erhvervsjuridisk Tidsskrift 331–343, at p. 336.

240 V. Ulfbeck and S. Taiger Ivø, *ibid.*, at p. 337.

241 V. Ulfbeck and S. Taiger Ivø, *ibid* at p. 338.

242 V. Ulfbeck and S. Taiger Ivø, *ibid.*, at p. 337. The authors assert, based on Danish doctrine, that neither undefined nor clear multimodal contracts are subject to any mandatory liability regime.

243 L. Andersen Roost, *Multimodale Transportaftaler* (2012) p. 61.

244 Dutch Supreme Court, Hoge Raad, 1 June 2012, nr.10/05322.

outcome of the case as such, but rather as to the arguments therefore.[245] Arguments, such as the wording of article 2 of the CMR convention and the existence of an undertaking to negotiate a multimodal convention, are held to be vague as they have also been used to promote the opposite construction, namely that the CMR convention is applicable to road carriage under a multimodal contract. Rather, the argument, "almost obiter dictum outlined by the Court of Appeal [...] and followed by the Supreme Court",[246] regarding the jurisdictional consequences is held by the author to be significant. As mentioned, the *Godafoss* case concerned jurisdiction under article 31 of the CMR convention, and difficulties can easily be identified where the application of unimodal conventions, together with their rules on jurisdiction, change with every leg of the multimodal transport. Any such problems are avoided by the Dutch Supreme Court as no mandatory regulation will henceforward prevent enforcement of the parties' jurisdiction agreement. Another weakness in the *Godafoss* case pointed out is the unclearness as to application of the case *ratio*; does the decision apply only to jurisdiction or to application of the entire CMR convention in general?[247] The author draws the conclusion that the *Godafoss* case should not be considered to hold that the CMR convention is not applicable to road carriage under a multimodal contract at all.[248]

The *TNT Express* judgment given by the Belgian Supreme Court and referenced above has subsequently been confirmed in Belgian precedent.[249] As held by Wouter Verheyen, interpretation of the *TNT Express* judgment by the lower courts has been rather narrow.[250] Thus, the Brussels Court of Appeal, whilst considering whether the parties had made an agreement regarding the mode of transport, seemed to have required such an agreement to be explicit or at least confirmed in the transport document. Although the transport mode according to Verheyen was clearly implied, due to the short distance of fewer than 100 kilometres, and because same-day-delivery was agreed, the Court of Appeal found the contract of carriage not to provide for carriage by road.[251] As mentioned above, the Belgian precedents only concern "undefined contracts of carriage".[252] However, as these types of contract are increasingly common, the effect may be

245 M. Spanjaart, "GODAFOSS: the applicability of the CMR within multimodal contracts of carriage" (2012) 7 TransportR 278–282.

246 M. Spanjaart, *ibid.*, at p. 282.

247 M. Spanjaart, *ibid.*, at p. 282.

248 This conclusion is based on the fact that the network system is applied in Dutch national legislation, which legislation would be undermined should the Supreme Court case be considered to entail the non-applicability of the CMR convention. This problem has been solved by the German Supreme Court by its distinction between the autonomous application of the CMR and its application triggered by national legislation.

249 *NV DPD Belgium v P.J. Timmermans*, Court of Appeal Antwerp, 31 October 2011, 2010/AR/875; (2013) ETL 3 and *NV De Post v NV Gebroeders Lauwe David*, Court of Appeal Brussels, 2 September 2011, 2008/AR/1077.

250 W. Verheyen, "Fleximodal Contracts and the CMR: the Belgian Approach" (2010) 18 JIML 364–371.

251 W. Verheyen, *ibid.*, at p. 367.

252 Cf. section 3.4.1 above.

far-reaching.[253] Verheyen holds that the judgment by the Supreme Court opens the possibility of implicit agreements regarding mode of transport to affect characterization of the contract of carriage, although the lower courts seem to have closed that door.[254] Verheyen is not sceptical of the decisions, but seems to agree with the Belgian courts that the contractual scope of application of the CMR convention is respected by the decisions. Verheyen asserts that the approach taken by the English Court of Appeal in the *Quantum* case makes the CMR applicable to actual carriage rather than to contracts of carriage.[255] Verheyen concludes that under Belgian precedent, the CMR convention may be applied to road legs of a multimodal contract of carriage.[256]

3.4.3 Conclusions

In conclusion it seems that a shift in approach has begun. The pragmatic view, well supported by the argumentation in *Quantum*, is gradually superseded by the somewhat more theoretical approach where the CMR convention is not applied to a road leg of a multimodal transport. This indicates that the multimodal contract of carriage is viewed as a contract *sui generis* rather than a contract for carriage by several modes. The consequence is that the network system cannot be applied, and parties are left in a vacuum of non-regulation where freedom of contract is a fact and detailed contracts a necessity.[257]

However, although the trend seems clear, it is of importance to keep in mind that the precedents that seem to carry this evolution forward do not necessarily deal with the pure issue of the autonomous application of the CMR convention to carriage by road under a multimodal transport contract. In fact, the majority of cases referenced above deal with jurisdiction under article 31 and although consideration of jurisdiction indeed includes consideration of the applicability of the convention, consequential arguments put forward by the deciding courts (obviously) focus on jurisdictional consequences rather than consequences to multimodal transport as such of not applying the network system. In general,

253 W. Verheyen; "The DPD-case: a case for a parcel-specific liability regime?" (2013) ETL 4–13, at p. 11.

254 W. Verheyen, "Fleximodal Contracts and the CMR: the Belgian Approach" (2010) 18 JIML 364–371, at p. 366.

255 W. Verheyen, *ibid.*, at p. 366. This, it is asserted here, is a misunderstanding of the English judgment. According to Verheyen the decision by the Belgian Supreme Court allows for the applicability of the CMR to contracts of carriage where the mode of transport is implicit; it is the lower courts' judgments that have narrowed the application thereof to explicit contracts of carriage. Thus, it would seem that the Belgian Supreme Court and the English Court of Appeal share the same view; the CMR is to be applied to undefined and incorrectly defined contracts of carriage to the extent that the mode of carriage can be derived from the contract; even if it is only implicit.

256 W. Verheyen, "The DPD-case: a case for a parcel-specific liability regime?" (2013) ETL 4–13, at p. 4.

257 As mentioned above, this state of contractual freedom can obviously be "solved" on a national legislative level. However, the raison d'être of uniform law is that the regulation of a specific area of law is to be regulated on an international level, thus avoiding national or regional solutions. It is accordingly held here that national legislation is not an adequate substitution for the applicability *ex proprio vigore* of the network system on an international level.

these cases also lack discussion on the core of the applicability of the CMR convention: the contract for carriage of goods by road. Supported by circumstantial arguments, such as the wording of the signatory protocol, it is concluded that several facts point to the conclusion that the CMR convention was not intended to be applied to road carriage in cases other than where the carriage is subject to a unimodal contract, save for application of article 2. Unfortunately, any analysis of the transport contract in particular in order to judge whether a multimodal transport contract that includes carriage by road could be considered a contract for the carriage of goods by road is missing.

Further, it must be taken into account that the courts are limited by the pleadings formulated by the parties and that they are affected by the circumstances of the individual case. For example, in the Danish Supreme Court case from 2008 described above, the carrier had substituted air carriage for road carriage and although substitution was permitted in the contract of carriage the shipper expected the goods to be carried by air. Had the court found the CMR convention to be applicable, the carrier's arbitrary decision to substitute mode of carriage would have prevented the claimant from holding the carrier liable for damage caused during carriage due to the applicable time bar. Likewise, in the English *Quantum* case from 2002, the carrier's proposition that its own standard terms were applicable would have prevented the claimant from arguing that the theft (to which the road carrier's employees were undisputedly party) amounted to such wilful misconduct as would bar the carrier from limiting its liability under the CMR convention. It is therefore not necessarily the consequences of not applying the CMR convention to road transport under a multimodal transport contract in general that are considered by the court but the consequences in the individual case. Every judgment may hence be fair and logical in the individual case, but at the same time they contribute to a body of precedents, the content of which is used to draw general conclusions on the current law. In the case of applicability of the CMR convention to road carriage under a multimodal contract of carriage, it is doubtful that the majority of the courts have considered the consequences of the individual judgment in relation to that body of precedents.

However, the case settled by the Dutch Supreme Court in 2012 concerned a question of jurisdiction. In this case, the court visualized the larger picture, where jurisdiction would vary with each leg of the transport should the CMR convention be considered to be applicable to the road leg of a multimodal transport[258] and found this scenario undesirable. Although this is the exact result of the network, or *chameleon*, system prescribed in Dutch national legislation, the court made a valuable point, which is the very essence of the problems associated with the network system. Under the network system the liability rules will vary from mode to mode. Unfortunately, this judgment is the exception that proves the rule; analyses as regards the consequences at large of application/non-application of the CMR convention in the respect discussed are rare.

258 Which could also entail that a court first must establish during which leg a consignment was damaged and thereafter declare its own incompetence to try the case.

Legal writing shows an extensive gap and somewhat rigid positions, where every argument has two sides to it and can be used both to prove autonomous application of the CMR convention to road carriage under a multimodal contract as well as disproving it. The review above shows that the arguments asserted are of two kinds. Whilst the argument relating to the correct understanding of the term "contract of carriage by road" concerns the actual meaning of the term in question, the other arguments relate to the context. Although the context is an important factor in the interpretation of treaty terms, it is to some extent secondary, and the distinction between understanding the actual term and the context is not conceded or reflected upon. As regards positioning, there is, to a considerable degree, coherence between the position of national courts and the scholars of that nation.[259]

3.5 Conclusion

That the network system entails problems in its application is apparent and uncontroversial. These problems do not only relate to the issue of unlocalized damage and possible problems connected with reloading of goods between two modes of transport, but also the fact that some of the unimodal conventions contain rules that extend the applicability thereof to other modes of transport under certain preconditions. As has been shown, the uniform system is however not without complexity either, especially not considering the legal uncertainty surrounding the relationship between unimodal conventions and carriage under multimodal contracts of carriage. In essence, it is the risk of dual applicability of a uniform system and unimodal conventions that time and again causes uniform systems to be modified rather than purely uniform. Accordingly, the Multimodal Convention as well as the Rotterdam Rules direct localized damage to the regulations applicable to unimodal transport. Furthermore, interestingly, the national regulations on multimodal transport that exist in Europe favour the network system to a uniform system although, on a purely national level, states are free to diverge from the rules of the unimodal conventions as these are only mandatorily applicable to international transports.

One possible solution to this dilemma could be to consider the multimodal contract of carriage so different from other transport contracts that it constitutes its own contract category; a contract *sui generis*. Besides the fact that it is not entirely uncontroversial that the contract of carriage as such constitutes its own contract category, there seem to be two obstacles to this solution. First of all, the prerequisites for establishing a contract category often adduced, such as the contract type being subject to particular rules or the contract mirroring a frequent

259 This coherence goes both ways; in the UK the Court of Appeal followed the line suggested by Professor Clarke in his critique of the Commercial Court's decision and in Germany the Supreme Court followed the critique by Professor Koller of the English Court of Appeal's judgment in *Quantum*. Thus, the courts seem to a large extent to follow national doctrine. There are, however, examples of the opposite such as in the Netherlands.

business transaction, are not present.[260] Secondly, due to the scope of application the mere fact that the multimodal contract of carriage is considered a contract *sui generis* does not affect the applicability of those conventions, as will be seen in the following chapters.

Another possible solution is, as has been done by scholars and courts as outlined in section 3.4 above, to claim that the unimodal conventions (and in particular the CMR convention) are not, when interpreted, applicable to carriage under multimodal contracts of carriage. This proposition will be subject to scrutiny in section 4.3 below. Further, the scopes of application of the conventions discussed in the current work will be thoroughly interpreted and it will be seen that the crucial element is the actual contract of carriage and its contents.

3.5.1 Moving forward

The purpose of the current chapter has been to place the forthcoming analysis in its theoretical setting. It can be concluded that the overall characteristic of such theoretical setting is legal uncertainty. The legal uncertainty appears to be twofold. On the one hand there is a substantial inadequacy relating to the application of the network system, a system that is far from seamless as described in section 3.2.2 above. On the other hand, there is legal uncertainty caused by legal developments in precedence and doctrine. However, before accepting this latter status quo, the arguments brought forward should be scrutinized. Thus, it may be questioned whether interpretation of the scope of applicability of the CMR convention, being the primary subject of legal discussions, lead to the result thus purported.

The rules in question are contained in treaties of uniform law. The interpretation of treaties is generally referred to the legal discipline of international law, and theory in relation thereto is abundant.[261] Although the Vienna Convention is applicable to interpretation of uniform law, in relation to uniform law regulating international transports, interpretation is many times undertaken without a clear apprehension of treaty interpretation theory (or practice). The Vienna Convention is often mentioned by interpreters of uniform law; however, the interpretation rarely follows the path laid out in the said convention. As the uniform law discussed in the current work, when applied, is actually applied as a matter of national law, it may be near at hand to interpret the rules in a similar fashion as national law is interpreted, i.e. by applying rules of interpretation of national legislation. As will be discussed below, this may not be entirely without merit considering that the subjects of the uniform law are private parties. Further, those who are entrusted with the interpretation of the rules in question generally do not interpret treaties and are not particularly familiar with the international rules that

260 J. Heidbrink, *Logistikavtalet* (2005) p. 28.

261 Regrettably, however, theory of treaty interpretation (within the legal field of international law) does not seem to distinguish between traditional treaties (*traité-contrat*) and treaties of uniform law (*traite-loi*).

regulate that activity. In fact, uniform law is the exception to the rule, and when the uniform law in addition is disguised as national law, it is easily recognized that the Vienna Convention is not strictly adhered to. However, although the rules of uniform law *per se* are applicable between private parties, interpretation thereof should prima facie relate to international rules of treaty interpretation. Thus, the starting point of the following analysis will be the rules of treaty interpretation – first in theory and then practically applied to the articles that determine the scope of application of the conventions subject to analysis.

PART III

ANALYSIS

CHAPTER 4

The scope of application of the unimodal conventions revisited

In the current chapter an attempt will be made to approach the analysis of the scope of application of the unimodal conventions somewhat differently than has previously been done, as outlined in section 3.4 above. This analysis will be made in two steps; the first being an interpretation of the scope of application articles that consider that the uniform laws are actually international treaties and as such subject to international law. This analysis will inevitably lead to the conclusion that the terms of the scopes of application do not *prevent* the application of the unimodal conventions to transport under multimodal contracts of carriage.

In the previous chapter the current application of the CMR convention to carriage by road under multimodal contracts of carriage, as well as the legal discussion in relation thereto, was presented. This status quo constitutes the background to the current part as well as to the primary research question ("To what extent can unimodal transport of goods conventions be applied to transport carried out under multimodal transport contracts?"). The thesis that will be explored is that the scope of application of the CMR convention does not prevent the application thereof to carriage by road under multimodal contracts of carriage. In order to prove this thesis, first of all the scope of application of the conventions discussed in the current work must be settled. Thus, initially, the articles defining the scope of application of the conventions will be interpreted. However, treaty interpretation is subject to rules of international law, and in order to interpret the terms in question the rules of treaty interpretation must be fully understood. Therefore, the current chapter will commence with a discussion of the rules and theories of treaty interpretation. Thereafter these rules will be methodically applied to the scope of application articles of the respective conventions. The aim is to define the scope of application of the transport conventions discussed. The perspective applied is interpretation of the text of the treaties in accordance with treaty interpretation theory. Accordingly, the existing interpretation of the terms in question by courts and scholars discussed in the previous chapter will not be considered indicative, unless so prescribed by treaty interpretation theory.

4.1 Introduction

The purpose of this thesis is to analyse the relationship between multimodal contracts of carriage and unimodal regulations, i.e. the applicability of such conventions to carriage of goods under a multimodal contract of carriage. Although the question is independent, it is closely related to the question of the application of the network system. As mentioned in section 3.2.2 above, the network system is based on the applicability, *ex proprio vigore*, of the unimodal conventions to transport under multimodal contracts of carriage and in the absence of any uniform system the non-applicability of the unimodal conventions will entail a situation where unimodal contracts of carriage are subject to mandatory liability rules, whilst multimodal contracts of carriage are subject to contractual freedom.[1] In the current chapter the articles governing applicability of the unimodal conventions will be scrutinized. The objective is to settle the scope of application of the conventions in question, which is a precondition for settling to what extent these unimodal conventions can be applied to transport carried out under a multimodal transport contract, i.e. the primary research question.

The conventions regulating the carrier's liability are, albeit particular in their nature of uniform law, international treaties, and as such subject to the rules of international law. Therefore, reading and interpreting their scope of application must be with respect to the rules of treaty interpretation, in particular those recorded in the Vienna Convention on the Law of Treaties. Although interpreters of the conventions on the carrier's liability by all means refer to the Vienna Convention, the analysis would, it is asserted, benefit from a more profound analysis with application of the rules of treaty interpretation. That said, it is asserted that the particular character of uniform law, in relation to purely intergovernmental agreements must be taken into account.

In the following, the interpretation of uniform law will be analysed; thereafter the scope of application of the CMR/COTIF–CIM conventions, the Montreal Convention, the Hague–Visby Rules and the Rotterdam Rules, respectively, will be construed.

4.2 Interpretation of uniform law

International conventions, or treaties, are agreements entered into by sovereign states intended to regulate the relationship between those sovereign states. Originally, treaties were agreements between heads of state rather than between states as such.[2] Such treaties could hence be compared to agreements between private parties, which likewise regulate a certain legal relationship between those parties. Interpretation of such international treaties ought therefore not to differ too much from interpretation of private agreements. In 1969 the Vienna Convention on the Law of Treaties was laid down, regulating the formation of treaties as well as the interpretation thereof. Articles 31–33 of the convention regulate interpretation of

1 Unless national legislation is in place to fill the gaps, such as in Germany and the Netherlands, cf. section 3.2.3 above. As mentioned, this is, on an international level, an unsatisfactory solution as it enhances the deharmonization (even if it is the material rules of the uniform law that is applied through the national rules); see e.g. OLG Köln 25 May 2004 (2004) TransportR 359–361 (referenced by M. Hoeks, *Multimodal Transport Law* (2010) pp. 186–187), where the CMR convention was applied to road carriage under a multimodal contract of carriage as the court found English law to be applicable to the contract and the CMR convention was considered applicable to such carriage *under English law*.

2 A.D. McNair, *Law of Treaties* (1986) p. 18.

treaties and, when scrutinized, these rules could very well be rules on interpretation of contracts, at least in a civil law legal system.[3] The Vienna Convention is considered to be recorded customary law, and thus applicable also to treaties predating the convention.[4]

However, increasingly states enter into international conventions that do not primarily regulate the relationship between themselves but instead regulate the relationship between private parties. Such conventions are often referred to as "uniform law" and are in fact draft legislation, which the contracting states undertake to implement into national legislation.[5] As international treaties they grant rights and impose obligations on the states parties to them, but their substance regulates interaction between private subjects.[6] In order for the substantive law contained therein to take force, the state party must implement, or otherwise give effect to, the contents of the treaty into its national legal system. The ways of implementation of such uniform acts into national law vary.[7] Generally, one of two different methods is applied; either the (rather uncommon) monist approach where the convention obtains the status of law through its ratification or (the more common) dualist approach where the rules of the convention must be enacted by parliament to be binding on the subjects of the state.[8] As regards the latter method, a uniform law convention may either be incorporated into the national system through promulgation, i.e. a statue referring to the rules of the convention giving them the force of law.[9] Another method of incorporation is through transformation where the rules of the convention are transformed into national legislation, rules which give effect to the contents of the convention, however not necessarily verbatim. This latter

3 "From the time of Grotius onwards, if not before, successive generations of writers and, more recently, of arbitrators and judges, have elaborated rules for the interpretation of treaties, borrowing mainly from the private law of contract": A.D. McNair, *ibid.* at pp. 364–365.

4 R. Gardiner, *Treaty Interpretation* (2015) pp. 13–14. As customary international law, the rules of treaty interpretation are not only binding on treaties predating the Vienna Convention but also upon states that are not signatories to the convention. In respect of Norway, as well as in general, see M. Ruud and G. Ulfstein, *Innføring i Folkerett* (2011) p. 81.

5 M. Heidemann, *Methodology of Uniform Contract law* (2007) p. 3; M. Gebauer, "Uniform Law, General Principles and Autonomous Interpretation" (2000) 4 Rev Dr unif 683–705; M. Clarke, *International Carriage of Goods by Road: CMR* (2014) p. 3; P. de Meij; "Interpretatie van verdragen van uniform (vervoer) recht" (with summary in English) (1998) ETL 607–647, at p. 644 and K. Zweigert and J. Kropholler, *Sources of international uniform law 1: Private and commercial law* (1971) at p. XVI.

6 M. van Alstine; "Dynamic Treaty Interpretation" (1997–1998) 146 U Pa L Rev 687 at p. 700.

7 M. Roth and R. Happ, "Interpretation of Uniform Law Instruments According to Principles of International Law" (1997) 2 Unif L Rev 700, at p. 700.

8 F. Berlingieri, "Implementation of maritime Conventions: a review of the methods used" (2013) 4 LMCLQ 443–475, at p. 445 and S. Johansson, *An Outline of Transport Law* (2014) pp. 34–35. Because in states employing the monist approach, ratification is subject to approval by Parliament, the difference between the two systems does not appear overwhelming (as an example, whilst ratification of a convention in the USA requires the consent by two-thirds of the Senate, implementation in Sweden requires approval by the majority of the Parliament, i.e. more than 50 per cent).

9 Cf. e.g. Swedish CMR Act, Lag med anledning av Sveriges tillträde till konventionen den 19 maj 1956 om fraktavtalet vid internationell godsbefordran på väg (SFS 1969:12), which simply states that the CMR convention is to have effect as Swedish law.

method seems to be particularly common in relation to the Hague–Visby Rules, due to the fact that this method is explicitly mentioned as a method of incorporation in the rules themselves.[10]

The aim of uniform law is, as its name reveals, to unify and harmonize[11] law in a certain field.[12] For apparent reasons, the areas of law thus made uniform have an international characteristic, which hence is the reason behind the perceived need for harmonization. One area of law which has been regulated by uniform law is international sales of goods, regulated by the CISG convention.[13] Another area is international carriage of goods, which is regulated by international conventions such as the CMR convention, the COTIF–CIM convention, the Montreal Convention and the Hague–Visby Rules. These conventions, as far as they contain material rules regulating the legal relationship between private parties, do not differ from national legislation in terms of impact upon private parties and therefore they must be treated in the same way as national legislation as far as protecting legal certainty for private parties in relation to the state is concerned.[14] Thus, in interpreting uniform law conventions, consideration must be taken of the position of the subject affected by the rules.[15] At the same time, it is important that these uniform rules are applied and interpreted uniformly in order to maintain any harmonization achieved by the rules.[16] In the following, interpretation of legislation and interpretation of treaties as well as the concept of uniform law will briefly be discussed in order to draw conclusions regarding interpretation of uniform law.

---

10 F. Berlingieri, *ibid.*, which contains a survey of the implementation methods in 39 states. Cf. also the Swedish Maritime Code, Sjölagen (SFS 1994:1009), ch. 13.

11 It should be noted that whilst "harmonization" and "unification" are many times used interchangeably, it has been held that the two terms are not synonymous; in a harmonized system the rules are not identical but play together in harmony. In a unified system, the rules (of different states) are identical (O. Bokareva, *Multimodal Transport under the Rotterdam Rules* (2015) p. 197). In the following "harmonization" is used to describe the aim of uniform rules, i.e. that the rules of different states are identical.

12 M. van Alstine, "Dynamic *Treaty Interpretation*" (1997–1998) 146 U Pa L Rev 687 at p. 701.

13 United Nations Convention on Contracts for the International Sale of Goods, Vienna 1980.

14 A convention has no impact at all on private parties until it has been implemented into national law. As national law the rules obviously have the same impact as any other national law. However, in order to preserve uniformity it is usually considered, at least today, that it is the rules of the convention that are interpreted by national courts although the courts really apply national legislation.

15 Roth and Happ hold that the proposition that international law principles are not appropriate for private rights and obligations codified in law-making treaties is based on a confusion of two levels of interpretation. They point to the fact that it is national legislation based on uniform law that is to be interpreted according to international law, not the contract entered into between private parties, which is governed by the law in question (M. Roth and R. Happ, "Interpretation of Uniform Law Instruments According to Principles of International Law" (1997) 2 Unif L Rev 700, at pp. 706–707). It is asserted here that the authors in so arguing have disregarded the fact that uniform law is directed towards private parties and that international law assumes treaties, being mere contracts between states, may therefore not be well suited to uniform law for the reason that interpretation of uniform law must take into account the legal predictability of the private subjects, which must be preserved.

16 F. Berlingieri, "Uniform interpretation of international conventions" (2004) in LMCLQ 153–157, at p. 154 and P. de Meij; "Interpretatie van verdragen van uniform (vervoer) recht" (with summary in English) (1998) ETL 607–647, at p. 645.

4.2.1 *Interpretation of national legislation*

Interpretation of legislation differs from interpretation of contracts.[17] Whilst the wording of a written contract is prima facie evidence of the contents thereof, where the intention of the parties can be established to have been something else, the intention of the parties prevails over the written contract (as it is the intention of the parties that actually constitute the agreement and the written contract is merely evidence thereof).[18] Legislation is not the voluntary meeting of identical intentions between two independent parties, but the one-sided imposition by one party in monopoly, the state, of rules on dependent parties, the citizens of the state. For obvious reasons, therefore, the state cannot say A and later claim that by A it actually meant B, which therefore is what its citizens should have obeyed. Naturally, citizens must be able to assume that the content of a piece of legislation is what is conveyed through the common understanding of the words used. And where the wording of legislation is ambiguous and conveys more than one meaning and thus has to be interpreted, the position of the target of the legislation, the citizen, must always be borne in mind. Interpretation of legislation is thus somewhat stricter than interpretation of contracts and, at least to some extent, surrounded by rules.[19]

The aim, or reason for, interpretation of legislation is the same as for interpretation of contracts: in a particular case it is not clear what the implication of a certain rule is. Interpretation of legislation is usually divided into several ways of interpretation including literal interpretation, teleological interpretation, interpretation by analogy and interpretation *e contrario*.[20] However, whilst the former two could be classified as methods on a more general level, the latter two are perhaps rather explanations of the outcome of the interpretation in the actual case. Literal interpretation is necessarily the primary interpretation by any interpreter.[21] However, as a method of interpretation it emphasizes the impor-

---

17 Interpretation of legislation is certainly, just as has been claimed for interpretation of contracts, an art, which cannot be captured in simple rules. It appears that writings on interpretation of legislation are often tracings and systematizations of how judges proceed. Thus the methods described are infinite and the dimensions that can be applied a challenge to concepts recognized in the scientific field of physics. The above account is thus a mere introduction to the following and will hopefully not be perceived as an offence to the substantive theories on the subject.

18 Cf. section 5.6.1 below.

19 For example, criminal law may never be applied in analogy and tax law should not be interpreted teleological (A. Peczenik, *Juridikens teori och metod* (1995) pp. 55–56).

20 Categorization of interpretation can also be made in other dimensions, such as subjective and objective. For an interesting discussion, see Å. Frändberg, "Statutory Interpretation Against the Background of a General Typology of Interpretation" in D. Prawits (ed.), *Meaning and Interpretation* (2002).

21 One may, for good reasons, ask whether the first reading of a rule or term is really interpretation. In relation to interpretation of treaties, E. De Vattel maintained in 1758 that:

> [I]t is not permissible to interpret what has no need of interpretation. When a deed is worded in clear and precise terms, when its meaning is evident and leads to no absurdity, there is no ground for refusing to accept the meaning which the deed naturally presents.

(Cited by U. Linderfalk, "Tolkning genom sammanjämkning – Om Wienkonventionen om traktaträtten artikel 33(4), och traktattolkningens särskilda lära" (2012) 4 Tidskrift for Rettsvitenskap 458–490, at p. 474)

tance of the written terms of legislation. Teleological interpretation could perhaps be regarded as the opposite of literal interpretation, as it takes into account the meaning of the legislation intended by the legislator.[22]

The guiding principle of interpretation of legislation is foreseeability, which must be balanced with reasonableness. Therefore, although literal interpretation is a reflection of the rule of law, it must not be purported *in absurdum* and where a literal reading of a rule leads to unreasonable results, the method of interpretation must be expanded.[23]

As regards teleological interpretation, this promotes general and flexible legislation. In order to uncover the intention of the legislator, the interpreter may normally use the considerations published by the Parliament. It is thus not a question of inquiring into the personal intentions of any member of government or parliament and, even if such sources were available, they would rarely be accepted as a datum of interpretation.[24] Further, the intention of the legislator as presented in the preparatory work will never under normal circumstances prevail over clear legislation.[25]

Foreseeability is preserved in as much as the intention of the legislator is publicly available, although the method indeed is not easily accessed by the non-legally educated common person. The teleological method of interpretation is commonly applied in European civil law systems, albeit in heterogenous forms.[26] Although the gap between civil law systems and common law systems in general seems to be lessening, it appears that under English law literal interpretation would be preferred to teleological interpretation.[27]

The other two principles of interpretation of legislation mentioned, interpretation by analogy and *e contrario* is interrelated with the doctrine of prohibition of *non liquet*.[28] Accordingly, where the judge, or legal writer for that matter, finds

---

According to the doctrine of clear meaning thus developed, interpretation differs from understanding, and is only necessary when the meaning of a rule or term is ambiguous or obscure. Although I am inclined to agree in substance, in relation to the Vienna Convention, I consider article 31.1 to capture and prescribe the process of understanding rather than interpretation in its strict meaning; a legal rule can never be clear without consideration of the context in which it appears.

22 It should be noted that preparatory works are a means of *interpreting* legislation only, and that clear legislation is not applied in contrary to its clear meaning even if the preparatory works indicate a different objective. This detail seems to have been lost in transition as the understanding of teleogolgical interpretation by the English judiciary has been expressed by Lord Denning as "They ask simply: what is the sensible way of dealing with this situation so as to give effect to the presumed purpose of the legislation? They lay down the law accordingly" (Court of Appeal in *James Buchanan & Co Ltd v Babco Forwarding & Shipping (UK) Ltd* [1976] WL 46847; affirmed by the House of Lords [1977] WL 59036). This statement is thus not correct (cf. A. Peczenik, *Juridikens metodproblem* (1980) p. 111).

23 Å. Frändberg, *Rättsordningens idé* (2005) p. 291.

24 A. Peczenik, *Juridikens metodproblem* (1980) pp. 109–110.

25 See eg. M. Tjernberg, "Regeringsrättens strikta lagtolkning" in (2013) Skattenytt 14.

26 In Scandinavia, the teleological method of interpretation has its firm support in the doctrine of legal sources (in Swedish "*Rättskälleläran*", which defines and ranks legal sources in legislation, preparatory works, precedence and doctrine) according to which preparatory works form the second primary source of law.

27 A. Peczenik, *ibid.* at pp. 116–117.

28 Å. Frändberg, *ibid.*, at p. 222.

a gap in legislation, this gap must be bridged in some way. Under the method of interpretation by analogy, the gap can be bridged by reference to legislation that does not exactly regulate the present case, but regulates cases that are so similar that an analogy, i.e. an application of a non-applicable rule to the non-legislated case, seems justified. An analogy often applied in Swedish law is use of the sanctions available to the aggrieved party under the Sale of Goods Act for breach of other forms of contract.[29]

Under the principle of interpretation *e contrario*, on the other hand, the solution to a dispute is justified by the fact that a certain case, which is contrary to the present dispute, is regulated in a certain way and that therefore the present case is solved in the opposite way. In private law disputes, as opposed to criminal law, an *e contrario* finding may not always be helpful, however. Whilst in criminal law, the fact that a certain act is not covered by a certain rule means that the judge will not find the indictee guilty of a criminal offence, in civil procedure the judge must, as mentioned, find an actual solution to the dispute. To continue the example above: being required to provide a remedy for a contract party who has been exposed to a breach of contract by the other party, an *e contrario* interpretation of the Sale of Goods Act, i.e. that the remedies provided therein do not apply to the type of contract in dispute, would be of little assistance in providing a solution to the dispute.

The interpretation of legislation brings to consideration some of the most important principles of a democratic state such as the rule of law, foreseeability and legal certainty as well as justice. Whilst it is indispensable that a private subject can foresee the consequences of their actions and adjust to the rules laid down by the state as well as that the principle of equality is respected, it is also essential that the exercise of power and the rulings of courts are perceived as just. There is hence a balance between legal certainty and justice.[30] Of the two, however, it would seem that arbitrary rulings, i.e. unforeseeability, are less reconcilable with the rule of law than injustice. In essence, therefore, the application of legislation should primarily be foreseeable, which means that although instances may occur where the legislation must be interpreted, prima facie it should be applicable in accordance with the ordinary meaning conveyed.

4.2.2 The Vienna Convention on the Law of Treaties

The Vienna Convention was drafted in 1969 and applies to the formation and interpretation of treaties. The rules of interpretation found in its articles 31–33

29 The Swedish Contracts Act (SFS 1915:218) regulates the formation of contracts as well as the invalidity of contracts. However it does not regulate breach of contract, which is why the sanctions available under the Sale of Goods Act (SFS 1990:931) are often applied by analogy. See also C. Ramberg, "Avtalslagen 2010" (www.avtalslagen2010.se).

30 Linderfalk considers the balance to be between foreseeability and flexibility (U. Linderfalk, "Doing the right thing for the Right Reason – Why Dynamic or Static Approaches Should be Taken in the Interpretation of Treaties" (2008) 10 International Community Law Review 109–141, at pp. 109–110). However, there is not necessarily an actual difference as "flexible" denotes the ability of legislation to adapt to new phenomena and changing society, which is not remotely different from legislation being applied in a way that is perceived as just.

give practical guidance on factors to be taken into account when interpreting the terms of a treaty.

The rules of treaty interpretation found in the Vienna Convention have an almost global impact. The treaty is ratified by 114 states, which are legally bound to apply the rules of the treaty.[31] Further, the rules are considered to be recorded customary international law,[32] thus binding on all states, including those not signatories to the convention.[33] Also, although the convention expressly renounces its own retroactive application, it is generally considered applicable also to treaties predating the Vienna Convention, at least as far as the rules of treaty interpretation are concerned.[34] Thus any attempt to understand a treaty, whether it is a treaty of uniform law or a more traditional treaty, should consider the rules of interpretation of the Vienna Convention.[35] Accordingly, irrespective of which approach to interpretation, such as autonomous interpretation, is promoted, the interpretation must take into account the rules laid down in articles 31–33.

4.2.2.1 Article 31 – General rule of interpretation

Article 31 of the Vienna Convention is the primary rule of interpretation. It should be noted that the title of article 31 is "General Rule of Interpretation", i.e. in the singular, which indicates that all paragraphs of the article are of equal status.[36]

A relevant question in relation to interpretation of treaties is what actually constitutes interpretation. Interpretation is in itself an ambiguous term, as indeed most terms are, and can be used, on the one hand, to signify the prima facie reading of a text that cannot be performed without an intellectual consideration of the word and the text; it is simply not possible to read a text without considering its meaning. On the other hand interpretation can be used to signify the process that begins when the primary reading of the text conveys no clear or unambiguous meaning to the reader.[37] The former understanding of the word is natural if one

---

31 U. Linderfalk, *On the Interpretation of Treaties* (2007) p. 3.

32 For example, the rules of treaty interpretation summarized by A.D. McNair and published in "Law of Treaties" in 1961, significantly corresponds with the rules of interpretation of the Vienna Convention.

33 I. van Damme, *Treaty Interpretation by the WTO Appellate Body* (2009) p. 38; R.K. Gardiner, *Treaty Interpretation* (2015) pp. 13–14 and M. Ruud and G. Ulfstein, *Innføring i Folkerett* (2011) p. 81. Among the non-signatory states relevant in a European perspective, the Vienna Convention has not been ratified by France and Norway. The reason for the latter not to ratify is related to the supremacy of the national Parliament in relation to formation of treaties.

34 U. Linderfalk, "Is Treaty Interpretation an Art or Science? International law and Rational Decision Making" (2015) 26(1) EJIL 169–189, at p. 169.

35 The rules of the Vienna Convention must, as a matter of international law, be considered (U. Linderfalk, *On the Interpretation of Treaties* (2007) p. 3). However, they are not mandatorily applicable in the ordinary sense of the term. Thus, should the treaty prescribe its own interpretative rules, these should be applied (U. Linderfalk, *ibid.*, at p. 3, fn. 6). It is held here that the mere provision that a treaty is to be interpreted with regard to the object and purpose of the treaty is not enough to depart from international law, as such a provision does not contradict the rules of interpretation of the Vienna Convention.

36 M.E. Villiger, "The Rules of Interpretation: Misgivings, Misunderstandings, Miscarriage? The 'Crucible' Intended by the International Law Commission" in E. Cannizzaro (ed.), *The Law of Treaties Beyond the Vienna Convention* (2011) p. 114.

37 Cf. citation by E. Vattel in fn. 407 above.

assumes the approach described, which is, however, somewhat philosophical, whilst the latter seems to be closer to the ordinary meaning of the word, at least in a legal context.[38]

It has been held that the Vienna Convention presupposes the doctrine of clear meaning, thus that interpretation according to the convention starts only after an ambiguity has been observed.[39] On the other hand, the very first paragraph of article 31 holds that the terms of a treaty are to be given their ordinary meaning, which appears to be closer to interpretation in its meaning of intellectual understanding. Giving the terms of a treaty their ordinary meaning would seem to instruct the interpreter to just read the words thereof as this is what the intellectual purpose of reading is, and the natural way of asserting a meaning to the words read.[40] However, paragraph 1 of article 31 of the Vienna Convention does not in fact prescribe the above-described procedure, but merely that interpretation, *when and to the extent such is carried out*, is to be carried out in accordance with the ordinary meaning of the terms. Hence, there may be no contradiction between the proposition that any and all application presupposes an understanding that intellectually entails interpretation and the proposition that articles 31–33 of the Vienna Convention apply only to interpretation in the stricter sense, that is after an ambiguity has been identified.[41]

Irrespective of whether the Vienna Convention presupposes the doctrine of clear meaning or not, paragraph 1 of article 31 reinforces the importance of interpretation in the sense of understanding; any interpretation must respect the ordinary meaning of the term interpreted. Interpretation in the sense of understanding inevitably draws on the subjective viewpoint of the interpreter; it is the ordinary meaning given to the terms by the interpreter that will form the prima facie understanding of the term. The starting point will therefore vary depending on the understanding of the term by the interpreter. For this reason, it seems that it is the qualification of the term "ordinary meaning" in paragraph 1 of article 31, namely "in their context", which is the important prerequisite in the paragraph. It

38 M. Dascal and J. Wróblewski, "Transparency and Doubt: Understanding and Interpretation in Pragmatics and Law" (1988) 7 Law and Philosophy 203–224, at p. 205.

39 U. Linderfalk, "Tolkning genom sammanjämkning – Om Wienkonventionen om traktaträtten artikel 33(4), och traktattolkningens särskilda lära" (2012) 4 Tidskrift for Rettsvitenskap 458–490, at p. 474. However, in a recent judgment, the Svea Court of Appeal in Sweden held that "The starting point for interpretation is always the *wording* of the treaty. ... If the wording is clear it will also, in principle, be the end point of the interpretation" (my translation). The court thus seems to hold that interpretation includes the reading of the term, and does not presuppose an ambiguity (Svea Court of Appeal, 18 January 2016, T 9128–14). The case concerned the interpretation of an arbitration clause included in a bilateral investment protection treaty between Russia and Spain.

40 R. Gardiner, *Treaty Interpretation* (2015) p. 29.

41 See R. Gardiner, *Treaty Interpretation* (2015) pp. 28–29 disagreeing with the proposition by McNair that application, which is carried out with clear rules, is separate from interpretation that signifies the process that starts after a term has been found to be unclear (A.D. McNair, *Law of Treaties* (1986) p. 365 at n. 1). See also Linderfalk who claims that interpretation according to the Vienna Convention applies only to unclear provisions (U. Linderfalk, "Tolkning genom sammanjämkning – Om Wienkonventionen om traktaträtten artikel 33(4), och traktattolkningens särskilda lära" (2012) 4 Tidskrift for Rettsvitenskap 458–490, at p. 474) (in this respect, see also U. Linderfalk, *On the Interpretation of Treaties* (2007) where he seems to assume that "interpretation" under the Vienna Convention includes the prima facie understanding of a term (ch. 3).)

is not the ordinary meaning of the terms that is to be applied to the interpretation, but the ordinary meaning of the terms in their context.

What constitutes the context is defined in paragraph 2 and includes, in addition to the text (presumably the text of the convention[42]) itself, the preamble and annexes to the convention, any agreement made between all the contracting parties in connection with the conclusion of the treaty and any instrument accepted by all parties as an instrument related to the treaty.[43] The protocol of signatories in connection with the signing of the CMR convention seems to qualify as "context" under the Vienna Convention, as would any other protocol of signatories. However, the documents referred to in paragraph 2 of article 31 would seem to be of lesser importance in relation to the text itself.

It must further be assumed that the "context" includes the fact that uniform law is in fact law. Thus, the terms must be given their ordinary *legal* meaning. In addition, the context must include the particular area of law or business, which the uniform law sets out to regulate, be it sale of goods or transport of goods. The rationale here is that it is obvious that the terms must be understood in the convention as they are understood in the field that the rules regulate. As an example, the term "delivery" as used in the CMR convention must be understood as referring to the handing over of goods from the carrier to the consignee rather than the birth of a child, not (only) because that interpretation follows from what is specified as the context in paragraph 2 of article 31 of the Vienna Convention, but because that is the ordinary meaning of the term in the context of carriage of goods.

When the context has thus been defined in accordance with paragraph 2, the last prerequisite of paragraph 1 asserts that the ordinary meaning of the terms is to be established in light of the *object and purpose* of the treaty. To explain the concept of object and purpose on a general level has proved difficult.[44] First of all, the discussion concerns whether the two terms really are separable. It has, however, been asserted that, despite the apparent similarity between the English words "object" and "purpose", the "object of a treaty is the instrument for the achievement of the treaty's purpose, and this purpose is, in turn, the general result which the parties want to achieve by the treaty".[45] Collectively the two terms point to the reasons for the treaty to exist (its "raison d'être").[46]

---

42 Linderfalk discusses whether the text also includes documents other than the convention, which seems to presume that "text" means at least the text of the entire convention (U. Linderfalk, *On the Interpretation of Treaties* (2007) p. 103).

43 Article 31.2.

44 Linderfalk claims that those who have tried to give the concept a general definition have failed (U. Linderfalk, "On the Meaning of the 'Object and Purpose' Criterion, in the Context of the Vienna Convention on the Law of Treaties, Article 19" in (2003) 72 Nordic J Int'l L 429, at p. 431.

45 Buffard and Zermaneck, "The 'Object and Purpose' of a Treaty: An Enigma?" cited by R. Gardiner, *Treaty Interpretation* (2015) p. 213. Linderfalk holds that:

> Hence, by "the object and purpose" of a treaty we shall understand, firstly, the rights and obligations to which the treaty gives expression – its normative content. Second, we shall understand the state (or states) of affairs envisaged by the parties to be attained by applying the treaty – the telos (or teloi) of the treaty.
> (U. Linderfalk, *ibid.* at pp. 441–442)

46 U. Linderfalk, *On the Interpretation of Treaties* (2007) p. 204.

The settlement of what constitutes the object and purpose of a treaty seems to be somewhat of a black hole in international law theory. The term is frequently used, not only in several articles of the Vienna Convention but in various treaties.[47] Nevertheless, it remains largely undefined as to its actual implication. Whilst interpretation of a certain term entails giving the term a sensible meaning, settling the object and purpose is not about interpreting the term, but about filling the term with content.[48] Such content is inevitably subjective, concerning the goals of the drafters of the treaty.

The sources of information generally referred to as admissible in settling the object and purpose of a treaty bear resemblance with what, according to article 31.2, constitutes the context.[49] Thus, it has been held that the object and purpose of a treaty is to be subsumed from the treaty itself, and that the text of the treaty, including its preamble and annexes, constitutes the primary source of information.[50] However, it has not been purported that the settlement of the object and purpose it limited to certain sources; even reference to supplementary means of interpretation may be had in order to shed light on the object and purpose.[51] In fact, given that the settlement of the object and purpose does not concern interpretation of the term, the sources available to the interpreter to settle the object and purpose ought to be non-restricted.[52] Naturally, the actual treaty, its text and preamble, conveys information as regards its raison d'être to the interpreter; albeit these can only be assumptions and no certain conclusions can be drawn. In relation to uniform law, it would seem that the *travaux préparatoires* would be a source that is likely to contain useful information regarding the object and purpose of the treaty at large as well as specific articles. In conclusion, however, it appears that, except where the object and purpose is explicit in the treaty, the interpreter can only make assumptions in relation thereto, albeit qualified. It should finally be noticed that although one or more object(s) and purpose(s) may be conveyed in the preamble, this is not necessarily the sole object(s) and purpose(s).

Further, it must be established *how* the object and purpose of a treaty is to affect interpretation. It has been held that the object and purpose constitute criteria that guide the interpreter in the choice between two competing meanings of a term; it is the meaning that better serves the object and purpose of the treaty that

47 D. Jonas and T. Saunders, "The Object and Purpose of a Treaty: Three Intepretative Methods" (2010) 43 Vand J Transnat'l L 565, at p. 567 *ff.*

48 It has been purported that a circularity exists here because "a treaty's object and purpose is understood through the treaty's text, but the text is only properly understood when interpreted in light of the treaty's object and purpose" (D. Jonas and T. Saunders, "The Object and Purpose of a Treaty: Three Intepretative Methods" (2010) 43 Vand J Transnat'l L. 565, at p. 581) appears to be a misunderstanding.

49 R. Gardiner, *Treaty Interpretation* (2015) p. 213. It has even been proposed that "categories of evidence that may be referred to in order to establish the context ... of the treaty" apply equally to the settlement of the object and purpose (V. Lowe, *International Law* (2007) p. 74).

50 Gardiner specifically opposes that the object and purpose are to be found in a convention's preamble (only), R. Gardiner, *ibid.*, at p. 213.

51 R. Gardiner, *ibid.*, at p. 215.

52 U. Linderfalk, *On the Interpretation of Treaties* (2007) p. 229 (fn. 10).

should be chosen as the correct interpretation.[53] Accordingly, the settlement of the object and purpose is always made in relation to a specific issue of interpretation.[54] In fact, in the choice between two possible interpretations, the object and purpose of the treaty may in practice guide the interpreter to settle which interpretation does not serve such goal(s). It is further important to bear in mind that the object and purpose are not independent interpretative data but denominators to the "ordinary meaning".[55]

In addition, it appears that the obligation to interpret a treaty in light of the object and purpose embeds two principles. First, it is generally held that it is the requirement to interpret the terms of a treaty in light of the object and purpose of a treaty that is the legal basis for the use of the teleological interpretation method.[56] Secondly, the requirement gives effect to the principle of effectiveness.[57] The principle of effectiveness requires that a treaty is interpreted so that it has an actual effect and that it is interpreted so that all provisions of a treaty have effect.[58] The essence of these two principles is to prevent excavation of the treaty by interpretation. Accordingly, interpretation of a treaty must aim to realize the raison d'être of the treaty as well as of the individual articles.

In relation to the interpretation of uniform law, it may be questionable what the objective of uniform law can add to the interpretation thereof, as the objective of a certain convention is often held to be uniformity. Thus, if uniform law is to be interpreted in light of its objective, such objective must be established to be something more than "uniformity", as otherwise the argumentation will be circular.[59]

Paragraphs 1 and 2 of article 31 are followed by two subsequent paragraphs (3 and 4), which add to the picture. Thus paragraph 3 prescribes that subsequent

---

53 U. Linderfalk; "Tolkning genom sammanjämkning – Om Wienkonventionen om traktaträtten artikel 33(4), och traktattolkningens särskilda lära" in (2012) 4 Tidskrift for Rettsvitenskap 458–490, at p. 489.

54 U. Linderfalk, *On the Interpretation of Treaties* (2007) p. 205 *ff.* Linderfalk holds that the settlement of the object and purpose accordingly most often do not regard the treaty *in extenso*, but in relation to the possible interpretations of a specific term; although, he admits, many times that the object and purpose of the treaty *in extenso* must be established, at least to a relatively high degree of clarity.

55 R. Gardiner, *Treaty Interpretation* (2015) p. 211.

56 U. Linderfalk, *ibid.*, at p. 204. A characteristic of the teleological method of interpretation is the use of legislative history, such as preparatory works. However, given that preparatory works is only a secondary means of interpretation according to the Vienna Convention, the relationship between using the object and purpose of a convention and the use of preparatory works may seem paradoxal. It has been held that the restriction in the use of preparatory works embedded in its despatch to secondary sources, is only intended to regard situations where an interpretation is based on such material (R. Gardiner, *ibid.*, at p. 352*ff.*). Accordingly, examining the preparatory works for interpretative inspiration is purportedly never restricted.

57 U. Linderfalk, *ibid.*, at p. 219.

58 When a treaty is open to two interpretations, of which one does and the other does not enable the treaty to have appropriate effects, good faith and the object and purpose of the treaty demand that the former interpretation should be adopted (Commentary on draft articles, [1966] Yearbook of the ILC, vol. II, p. 219, para. 6).

59 As an example cf. the argumentation by Hoeks, in which she maintains that the disuniformity created by the non-application of the CMR on multimodal transports is contrary to the objective of the convention, which is uniformity (M. Hoeks, *Multimodal Transport Law* (2010) pp. 175–176).

agreements and practice in application of the treaty as well as international law should be taken into account, together with the context, whilst paragraph 4 states that where it can be established that the parties intended a term to convey a certain meaning, that meaning should be given to that term. However, paragraphs 3 and 4 are certainly based on the presumption that is the state parties that have entered into the treaty that are the subjects of the treaty, in which case common intention and subsequent actions are perfectly legitimate factors that affect interpretation – just as in the interpretation of contracts. In relation to uniform law, they may on the other hand be a bit more problematic considering that the subjects of uniform law are not the states parties to the treaty. It is accordingly proposed here that article 31.3 is of limited relevance to the interpretation of uniform law.

It could be questioned whether paragraph 3 (b), which refers to "Any subsequent practice in the application of the treaty which establishes the agreement of the parties regarding its interpretation", is of relevance to the interpretation of uniform law treaties. Subsequent practice in the application of the treaty would indeed seem to include the practice of national courts in interpreting and applying the treaty.[60] However, the crucial point of the paragraph is held to be, not the practice as such, but the prerequisite that such practice "establishes the agreement of the parties regarding its interpretation".[61] Accordingly, the practice as carried out by the parties to the treaty should somehow show that the parties are in agreement regarding the practice. Thus, although reference to subsequent practice by (national) courts in applying and interpreting uniform law would seem to be a crucial instrument in order to preserve uniformity, it is questionable whether the interpretation and application of a treaty by state administration could be classified as subsequent practice as envisaged in the Vienna Convention. First of all, whilst the term "parties" is considered to indicate all parties to the treaty, it is not necessary that all parties must take part in the subsequent practice, but all parties must be presumed to approve of the interpretation in order for an agreement to exist.[62] Secondly, because the application of the treaty never concerns the actual state parties, but rather private parties within the state, and the practice thereof is generally delegated to the national courts of the contracting states, it is difficult to see how such subsequent practice can establish an agreement between the parties in relation to the interpretation thereof. Thus, an agreement between the parties to the treaty cannot be established through the unilateral interpretation of the terms of the treaty of national courts, especially not where such court practice is not uniform. This does not necessarily mean that precedence is of no relevance to the interpretation of the terms of a treaty of uniform law, but its value seems to lie primarily in the strength of the arguments provided in the judgments. It would further not appear too far-fetched that precedence could be allowed to influence

60 Linderfalk holds "practice" to connote "the sum total of a number of applications", which can be the application by anyone, not just the parties themselves. Further, such practice includes both positive and negative application, i.e. non-application of the treaty (U. Linderfalk, *On the Interpretation of Treaties* (2007) pp. 166–167).

61 U. Linderfalk, *ibid.*, p. 166.

62 U. Linderfalk, *ibid* p. 167.

the interpretation through the use of the object and purpose of a treaty, which, in relation to uniform law, is presumed always to include harmonization.

Although articles 31–33 of the Vienna Convention have been extensively discussed, interpreted and even dissected, paragraph 4 of article 31, which reads: "A special meaning shall be given to a term if it is established that the parties so intended", seems to have been left out of analyses to a fairly large extent. The ordinary meaning of the terms seems to be that if the parties to a treaty intended to signify something by a term other than what could be considered to be its meaning (after having applied the previous parts of article 31), then that common intention of the parties is to prevail. The context of the rule is interpretation of unclear or ambiguous terms of a treaty, i.e. how are the terms of a treaty to be understood? The wider context, including the remains of the treaty and its preamble, relates to compilation of customary international law regarding formation, interpretation and termination of treaties as well as settling disputes in relation thereto. Again, the term in question shows that the Vienna Convention is drafted primarily with contractual treaties in mind.[63] The object and purpose of the treaty is not only unity and agreement between states about which rules actually govern their relationships (customary international law is undoubtedly more elusive than rules recorded in a treaty), but also the peaceful relation between states and the commitment of states to their contractual undertakings and the recourse of other states in case of a breach of that commitment by a state. In conclusion, it is asserted that the meaning of the rule contained in paragraph 4 of article 31, interpreted in good faith in accordance with the ordinary meaning of the terms in their context and in the light of its object and purpose, implies simply that if the parties intended something else than can be considered the ordinary meaning of a term in its context etc, the meaning intended by the parties will prevail. It is not enough that such other meaning is proposed; it has to be established. Because the parties may agree on this other meaning of the term, it is not a rule regulating the burden of proof. The rule merely holds that to the extent it is proved (by one of the parties, both or several parties or otherwise), that another meaing was intended that other meaning should prevail. The object and purpose of the rule itself is contractual and relates to the *pacta sunt servanda* rule embedded in the preamble; it is the intention of the contracting parties that will prevail and if that intention has not been correctly recorded in the contract, neither party will be able to benefit therefrom.

4.2.2.2 Article 32 – Supplementary means of interpretation

Where interpretation according to article 31 of the Vienna Convention does not remove the ambiguity of the term or where the result of such interpretation is manifestly absurd or unreasonable, the interpreter may, according to article 32,

63 See for example paragraph 4 of the preamble: "*Noting* that the ... *pacta sunt servanda* rule is universally recognized" (original emphasis) and the fact that throughout the treaty no other parties than state parties are mentioned. This by no means necessarily entails that the convention is not suitable for other types of treaty, but merely an observation on the primary intention of the parties.

resort to supplementary means of interpretation such as the preparatory work. Here, it is clear that such means of interpretation are supplementary to interpretation according to article 31. However, it is, as always, difficult to draw any sharp distinction; in asserting the object and purpose of the terms of a treaty in accordance with article 31.1, consultation of the *travaux préparatoires* may be legitimate. In the English case *Fothergill v Monarch Airlines* it was held that although the literal reading of article 26 of the Warsaw Convention was seemingly clear, the purpose of the convention, as apparent from the *travaux préparatoires*, indicated another interpretation.[64]

Article 32 allows the interpreter to resort to supplementary means of interpretation in two instances; either the interpreter wants to confirm the outcome of an interpretation in accordance with the general rule, or the interpreter considers the interpretation in accordance with the general rule fruitless; the term remains ambiguous or the outcome of the interpretation is manifestly absurd or unreasonable. The possibility for the interpreter to have recourse to supplementary means of interpretation seems to be generous. If the outcome of the general interpretation is unambiguous the interpreter may consult e.g. the *travaux préparatoires* and likewise where the outcome of the general interpretation is ambiguous. In fact, in interpreting the terms of a treaty, it seems that interpreters, such as the International Court of Justice (ICJ) quite freely consult any supplementary means of interpretation.[65] A distinction has been made between consulting the preparatory work and actually basing an interpretation thereon, where the latter case is restricted by article 32.[66] Due to article 32 paragraph 1, the interpreter may always consult the preparatory work, and other supplementary means of interpretation, in order to confirm the outcome of the general interpretation. In order to base an interpretation on supplementary means of interpretation, on the other hand, the outcome of the general interpretation must qualify under paragraphs (a) or (b). It has further been held that a sharp distinction between interpretation under article 31 and article 32 was not the intention of the drafters of the Vienna Convention, but that an examination of the preparatory works of a treaty is an integral part of treaty interpretation.[67] The "supplementarity" of the means of interpretation supplied in article 32 thus lies rather in the fact that they are most of the time to be used cumulatively with the means of interpretation supplied in article 31, than in it being subordinate to article 31.[68]

Although it may have been the intention to shelter the existing practice of consulting preparatory work, and other preparatory sources, as an integral part

64 *Fothergill v Monarch Airlines Ltd* [1980] 2 All ER 696; see especially (ii) as to the use of *travaux préparatoires* per Lord Scarman p. 253.

65 R. Gardiner, *Treaty Interpretation* (2015) p. 348.

66 R. Gardiner, *ibid.*, at p. 354*f.*

67 R. Gardiner, *ibid.*, at p. 355.

68 R. Gardiner, *ibid.*, at p. 355, with reference to H. Waldock, Third Report on the Law of Treaties, 1964, *Yearbook of the ILC*, vol. II. The exception to this assumption is interpretation in accordance with article 32(b), as the means of interpretation supplied in article 31 must be considered preempted. See U. Linderfalk, *On the Interpretation of Treaties* (2007) p. 237.

of interpreting a treaty, the Vienna Convention does in fact require the interpreter to justify the use of such means of interpretation by one of the prerequisites of article 32. The possibility to confirm the meaning resulting from an interpretation in accordance with article 31 seems to be the more open and available prerequisite, always allowing for consultation of the *travaux préparatoires* as long as the interpreter has first settled a meaning of the term in accordance with the general rule of interpretation. One question that presents itself is what if recourse to the preparatory work does not confirm the meaning resulting from the general interpretation? If the preparatory work affirms rather than confirms the meaning that the interpreter has settled according to article 31, the interpreter may face a dilemma. In order to follow the order of events prescribed in article 32, where the preparatory work, or other supplementary means of interpretation, affirms the meaning resulting from the general interpretation, the interpreter cannot simply move to determining the meaning in accordance with such supplementary means of interpretation using paragraphs (a) or (b) of article 32 as the justification for the use of such means. Literally, article 32 only allows the interpreter to base the interpretation on any supplementary means of interpretation where the meaning of the term is ambiguous, obscure, absurd or unreasonable and that meaning has been reached through interpretation according to article 31. Thus, strictly speaking, where the meaning as interpreted in accordance with article 31 is neither ambiguous, obscure, absurd or unreasonable but the ambiguity (etc.) is caused by consulting, for example, the preparatory work, then recourse may not be had to supplementary means of interpretation to determine the meaning. It is not entirely clear how an interpreter is to approach a situation where the preparatory works affirm rather than confirm the meaning as interpreted according to article 31.[69] What seems somewhat clearer is the unlikelihood of the situation appearing in practice, as the preparatory works of a treaty are rather used as an integral part of the process of interpretation than as a strictly secondary source of interpretation.[70] This practice seems to have been well established already at the time of drafting the Vienna Convention, and there is support in the *travaux préparatoires* of that convention that the drafters sought to allow for such practice under the rules of interpretation.[71] That aim does not, however, appear entirely from a reading of articles 31 and 32.

4.2.2.3 Article 33 – Treaties authenticated in several languages

Last, but not least, the Vienna Convention attempts at resolving problems of interpretation of treaties connected with the existence of versions in several languages of equal authenticity.[72] That a treaty is authenticated in more than

69 R. Gardiner, *Treaty Interpretation* (2015), pp. 354–355.
70 R. Gardiner, *ibid.* at pp. 361–362.
71 R. Gardiner, *ibid.* at pp. 349–355.
72 Article 33.

one convention language would appear to be the rule rather than an exception and article 33 is thus of extensive practical importance.[73] It may be questioned whether article 31 or article 33 is the primary rule to apply in relation to treaties authenticated in more than one language. The heading of article 33, "Interpretation of treaties authenticated in two or more languages", seems to indicate that an interpreter of a multilingual treaty should resort directly to article 33. Such an interpretation is further confirmed by article 33.4, which embeds articles 31 and 32.

Paragraphs 1 and 2 of article 33 are somewhat axiomatic, stating that what follows from the treaty itself prevails. Paragraphs 3 and 4 apply to interpretation of treaties that have the dimension of multiple, equally authentic, versions. Basically, terms in different, equally authentic, languages are presumed to have the same meaning and where the two languages disclose differences of meaning, the term is to be interpreted in accordance with articles 31 and 32. Paragraph 3 indicates that where a treaty has been authenticated in more than one language, the interpreter may rely on only one language version, rightfully assuming that all other versions convey the same substantive meaning.[74] This means that there is no obligation in the interpretation of multilingual treaties to consult more than one version. However, where the interpreter has studied more than one language version and revealed a difference in meaning, the assumption that both, or all, versions have the same meaning does not give much assistance. Instead, the so-called reconciliation rule in paragraph 4 is to be applied. The reconciliation rule consists of three steps; first the general and subsidiary rules of interpretation in articles 31 and 32 are to be applied and, secondly, where the treaty itself gives priority to one version, that version is to prevail.[75] The third step is the reconciliation itself, which in essence aims at giving priority to one version over the other(s). The rule indicates that the interpreter should apply the meaning, that better fulfils the object and purpose of the treaty.[76] This entails that the interpreter will have to consider the object and purpose of the treaty twice, albeit in two different aspects.

73 In relation to uniform transport law, a feature that might cause heterogenous interpretation is that whilst the Hague–Visby Rules are authenticated in English as well as French, the Hague Rules are only authenticated in French. Thus, even if identical terms appears in the two treaties (which so many of the terms do), if the English and French versions of the Hague–Visby Rules contain a difference in meaning and, after article 33 has been applied, the interpreter favours the English version, the French version would still have to be applied in relation to the Hague Rules (cf. R. Aikens *et al.*, *Bills of lading* (2016) p. 287).

74 U. Linderfalk, "Tolkning genom sammanjämkning – Om Wienkonventionen om traktaträtten artikel 33(4), och traktattolkningens särskilda lära" (2012) 4 Tidskrift for Rettsvitenskap 458–490, at p. 466.

75 It may (rightfully) be questioned why the term in question is first to be interpreted in accordance with article 31 and 32 before the version so agreed between the parties is given priority; is interpretation necessary when the parties have agreed to give one version priority? Linderfalk argues that a discrepancy between two versions does not exist in the terms of the Vienna Convention before the observed discrepancy has been confirmed through interpretation (U. Linderfalk, *ibid.*, at p. 478).

76 U. Linderfalk, *ibid.*, at p. 481.

4.2.3 Autonomous interpretation of uniform law

Treaties of uniform law constitute international treaties and as such they are subject to the rules of international law, customary or recorded, such as the rules on treaty interpretation accounted for above.[77] However, uniform law is drafted as national legislation and the actual agreement between the states is an undertaking to give force to the terms drafted, within the national legal system. Interpretation of the terms of the treaty thus generally relates to the material uniform rules, rules that may, in their applicable form, constitute national legislation. Accordingly, it has been proposed that the rules of treaty interpretation found in international law do not entirely fit interpretation of uniform law.[78] A traditional view was that uniform rules were to be interpreted according to national law.[79] This could seem to be a logical result of the uniform law having been incorporated into the body of national law. It would, however, entail that uniform law is only uniform when the treaty embedding it enters into force, but as soon as national courts start to interpret it, it will increasingly lose its uniformity as national courts may not interpret the rules homogeneously, especially if they are interpreted as a part of national legislation rather than international uniform law.[80] The question is thus how to interpret the material rules of uniform law.

In order to preserve the uniformity of uniform law, it has been asserted that all interpretation of uniform law must be autonomous and without regard to national law.[81] Accordingly, the term autonomous interpretation has been established, referring to interpretation that does not refer to the meaning of legal terms and concepts in national law but interprets the terms and concepts of a convention in

77 U. Linderfalk, *On the Interpretation of Treaties* (2007) p. 3. The rules of interpretation of treaties recorded in the Vienna Convention on the Law of Treaties are accounted for in the next section.

78 For example, van Alstine holds: "because they regulate purely private relations, the interpretative standards developed for public international law treaties would appear inapposite in the context" (M. van Alstine, "Dynamic Treaty Interpretation" (1997–1998) 146 U Pa L Rev 687, at p. 701). See also P. de Meij, "Interpretatie van verdragen van uniform (vervoer) recht" (with summary in English) (1998) ETL 607–647, with a reference to Trompenaars, *Pluriforme unificatie en uniforme interpretative* (1989) pp. 121–123.

79 See M. Roth and R. Happ, "Interpretation of Uniform Law Instruments According to Principles of International Law" (1997) 2 Unif L Rev 700.

80 F. Berlingieri, "Uniform interpretation of international conventions" (2004) LMCLQ 153–157, at p. 154, M. Gebauer, "Uniform Law, General Principles and Autonomous Interpretation" (2000) 4 Rev Dr unif 683–705, at p. 684, H. Palmer Olsen, "International courts and the doctrinal channels of legal diplomacy" (2015) 6(3–4) Transnational Legal Theory 661–680, at p. 667. Sturley asserts that disharmonization is the result of national courts' endeavour to construe uniform law in consistency with national law, i.e. so that the uniform law, as interpreted, fits into the national system (M. Sturley, "International Uniform Laws in National Courts: the Influence of Domestic Law in Conflicts of Interpretation" (1986–1987) 27 Va J Int-l L 729). This seems a well-founded conclusion, which also illustrates that a national court, in the choice between interpreting uniform law in consistency with international precedence or in consistency with the national legal system, will likely chose the latter. However, it is not only the actual interpretation (in its meaning under the doctrine of clear meaning, cf. section 4.2.2 above) that may cause disuniformity. The mere receipt of a uniform rule into a certain context of national law causes it to assume a certain meaning, affected by that context (J. Merryman, "On the Convergence (and Divergence) of the Civil Law and the Common Law" (1981) 17 Stan J Int'l L 357, at p. 379).

81 M. Gebauer *ibid.* at pp. 683–705.

relation to the convention itself.[82] Accordingly, autonomous interpretation is not a method of interpretation (such as literal, teleological etc.) but a principle that makes some methods, such as systematic and teleological, preferable over others.[83] Thus autonomous interpretation favours interpretative arguments supported by the convention's own system and which realizes the objectives of the convention. In conclusion, the argument is that uniform law must be freed from the national chains that legal terms are often bound by. If uniformity is to be continuous and not only exist at the time the convention enters into force, interpretation thereof has to be independent from national law.[84] Albeit an appealing theory, it does not provide an applicable method unless further explored. Further, the principle appears to have two constraints; first of all, it presupposes an exhaustive coverage of the uniform law and, secondly, its support in international law must be settled before it can be applied.[85]

The notion of autonomous interpretation is somewhat vague. The interpreter is guided towards methods of interpretation that promotes the self-sufficiency of the uniform law, such as literal or teleological (which may sometimes be contradictory) and is encouraged to interpret the terms of uniform law so that the objectives of the convention are realized. As far as legal terms are concerned it is questionable if such terms can be understood at all without reference to national law.[86] Only after the term is understood in a national setting, can the interpreter adjust the interpretation and "free it from its national chains". Such liberation may also require the insight from the part of the interpreter that the term is in fact understood differently in different jurisdictions.[87]

It seems however that such autonomous interpretation presupposes a rather complete system.[88] If interpretation is to be carried out with reference to the internal system of a uniform law only, obviously that system must be able to provide a

82 M. Gebauer, "Uniform Law, General Principles and Autonomous Interpretation" (2000) 4 Rev Dr unif 683–705, at pp. 686–687, G. Lestas, "The Truth in Autonomous Concepts: How To Interpret the ECHR" (2004) 15(2) EJIL 279–305, at p. 282.

83 M. Gebauer, *ibid.* at pp. 686–687.

84 The European Court of Human Rights (ECHR) has expressed its doctrine of "autonomous concepts" as a safeguard against eroding the undertakings made by the contracting states (G. Lestas, *ibid.*, at p. 282).

85 At an early stage in the ECHR's application of the doctrine of autonomous concepts (first introduced in *Engel v the Netherlands*, 8 June 1976 (series A no. 22)) it was criticized by one of the court's judges as entailing a danger that the court arrives at "an abstract qualification which may be philosophically valid, but which has no basis in law" (dissenting opinion of Judge Matscher in *Özturk v Germany* (1984) cited by G. Lestas, *A Theory of Interpretation of the European Convention on Human Rights* (2007) p. 48).

86 The question is if any term can be understood without reference to the national background of the interpreter. Lestas takes the example of the term "tea", which to some include any hot drink made from the infusion of dried leaves in hot water, whilst to some it only includes drinks where the dried leaves from the tea-bush are infused, as other "teas" are called "infusions" (G. Lestas, "The Truth in Autonomous Concepts: How To Interpret the ECHR" (2004) 15(2) EJIL 279–305, at p. 289).

87 Continuing the example above, if the interpreter in unaware of the fact that "tea" does not encompass all hot infusions in some jurisdictions, it is impossible to make an autonomous interpretation of the term.

88 M. Heidemann, "The autonomous interpretation method in international law with particular reference to the proposed European Sales Law II" (2013) 94 Amicus Curiae 28–36, at p. 32.

solution. In respect of private uniform law, the task to draft an exhaustive system appears overwhelming; not even the comprehensive Rotterdam Rules Convention can be claimed to constitute a self-containing system. Especially in relation to older conventions, interpretation without reference to external sources may prove difficult.[89] In fact, these conventions may have been drafted under the presupposition that interpretation would be carried out with reference to national law.

The European Court of Human Rights, which applies its doctrine of autonomous concepts regularly, appears to have a nuanced approach to the autonomy. Thus it has held that the national concept is not irrelevant, but it is certainly not decisive for the interpretation of a term under the European Convention of Human Rights.[90] Because many of the terms are legal concepts, terms that only have a meaning in relation to law, the starting point must be national law.[91] The ECHR thus appears to start its interpretation from the national legal concept and then compare that understanding with the objective of the term in the convention.[92] To the European Court of Justice, as another example, it appears to indicate interpretation free of influence from the definition of a certain term in international law.[93]

Another example is the Convention on Contracts for the International Sale of Goods (CISG),[94] which, although generally considered to require autonomous interpretation of its terms, refers the interpreter to national law as a secondary source of interpretation of matters that fall within the scope of the convention, but not expressly settled.[95] It is thus submitted that although autonomous interpretation is appealing, as regards legal terms, such interpretation must start from a national understanding of such terms and that the non-comprehensiveness of a uniform law convention may prevent interpretation that is altogether autonomous.

Further, the interpretation of treaties is, as was discussed in the previous section, subject to international law. Thus, it would appear that any interpretative principle must rest on the rules of international law in order to be applied. It was held above that the international rules of treaty interpretation are, although binding on states per se, non-mandatory in the sense that a treaty may provide its own rules of interpretation. Accordingly, there are examples of private law conventions, which provide for autonomous interpretation. The most relevant example is article 2 of the Rotterdam Rules, requiring the interpreter to have regard to the international character, and the need to promote uniformity in the application, of the convention. Another example is article 7(1) of the CISG, of which article 2

89 For example, the Hague Rules from 1924 contain a mere 16 articles, whilst the Rotterdam Rules from 2008 contain 96 articles.

90 G. Lestas, "The Truth in Autonomous Concepts: How To Interpret the ECHR" (2004) 15(2) EJIL 279–305, at p. 284.

91 G. Lestas, *ibid.*, at p. 285.

92 G. Lestas, *ibid.*, at p. 281 *ff.*

93 S. Nicolosi, "Disconnecting Humanitarian Law from EU Subsidiary Protection" (2016) 29 Leiden Journal of International Law 463–483, at p. 478.

94 United Nations Convention on Contracts for the International Sale of Goods, Vienna 1980.

95 Article 7(2).

of the Rotterdam Rules is a verbatim copy.[96] An almost identical rule is found in article 3 of the Hamburg Rules. Although this requirement in relation to the interpretation of the conventions does not expressly refer the interpreter to the internal system of the convention, it generally is considered to promote autonomous interpretation.[97] In other cases, interpretation should rest on the international rules of treaty interpretation.[98]

How are those considerations to be taken into account? How is autonomous interpretation to be carried out, maintaining autonomy in the interpretation and at the same time respecting existing rules of international law? It has been suggested that the substantive criteria of the interpretation standard are: the observance of the international character of the norm; the need to promote uniformity in international law; the ordinary meaning of the term; the context of the term within the uniform instrument including its object and purpose; recourse to preparatory materials and; the subsequent agreement and practice.[99] It is obvious that with the exception for the first two, these criteria reflect articles 31 and 32 of the Vienna Convention. In fact, the two first criteria would most often constitute (one of) the objectives and purposes of uniform law and thus all criteria would seem to rest on the rules of treaty interpretation of international law. In fact, it has been claimed that the principle of autonomous interpretation has been perfectly subsumed into the rules of interpretation in the Vienna Convention.[100]

The criteria thus stated give the interpreter guidance, albeit perhaps not overwhelmingly firm. In order to apply the two first criteria the interpreter needs a starting point; a prima facie understanding of the term. Thus, perhaps the third criterium, the ordinary meaning of the term, is the first to be applied. The ordinary meaning of a term was discussed in the previous section and as far as legal terms are concerned it is repeated here that the ordinary meaning thereof unavoidably draws on one national legal system or another. One conclusion could thus be that an autonomous interpretation of a certain (legal) term starts at the ordinary meaning of the term, which would instinctively be the understanding of the term by the interpreter based on that person's national background. The observance of the international character of the norm could entail different things; on the one hand

96 The articles read: "In the interpretation of this Convention, regard is to be had to its international character and to the need to promote uniformity in its application and the observance of good faith in international trade."

97 Gebauer holds that the request to have regard to the international character of the convention requires autonomous interpretation (M. Gebauer, "Uniform Law, General Principles and Autonomous Interpretation" (2000) 4 Rev Dr unif 683–705, at p. 686).

98 It must be stressed that whatever method of interpretation is preferred, international law must not be departed from (U. Linderfalk, *On the Interpretation of Treaties* (2007) p. 3).

99 M. Heidemann, "The autonomous interpretation method in international law with particular reference to the proposed European Sales Law II" (2013) 94 Amicus Curiae 28–36, at p. 33.

100 M. Roth and R. Happ, "Interpretation of Uniform Law Instruments According to Principles of International Law" (1997) 2 Unif L Rev 700, at p. 705. De Meij points to the fact that national courts to a large extent do apply the Vienna Convention to the interpretation of uniform transport law (P. de Meij; "Interpretatie van verdragen van uniform (vervoer) recht" (with summary in English) (1998) ETL 607–647). See also Hoeks who claims that autonomous interpretation is the result of article 31(1) of the Vienna Convention (M. Hoeks, *Multimodal Transport Law* (2010) p. 138).

it could mean that the interpreter should distance the prima facie interpretation from the national law or, on the other hand, that the interpreter should compare the prima facie interpretation with the national understanding of the term in other contracting states. Whilst, the *modus operandi* of the latter is rather concrete, the former is more abstract, although more in line with the concept of autonomous interpretation. However, it is proposed here that the latter *modus operandi* entails the former; where an interpreter starts with the prima facie interpretation known from national law and then compares that understanding with the understanding in other contracting states, the interpretation is distanced from a purely (uni-) national understanding. By reconciling the different national understandings, an international understanding of the term is possible. True, such understanding may be heterogenous and, albeit there is certainly a core of a "lowest common denominator", it is not suggested that this is the interpretation to be applied. However, if the international understanding of the term is related to the object and purpose of the uniform law, the interpreter can decide whether to apply a broad or limited understanding of the term. As a hypothetical example, if the term "cargo" in the Montreal Convention is to be interpreted and it is proposed that by "cargo" is to be understood low value–large volume shipments, as the term "goods" is the correct term to be used for high value-low volume shipments. After an inventory of national definitions, it is apparent that this division is made in some contracting states, whilst in others the term "cargo" would be understood as any shipments. In making an international comparison, the interpreter has taken into account the international character of the Montreal Convention and by comparing the two different interpretations with the object and purpose of the convention, the latter interpretation would surely be the most appropriate.

4.2.4 Interpretation of private uniform law

Regulation by international conventions interferes on three levels: state v state (e.g. a treaty regulating the border between two neighbouring states); state v private subjects (usually entitling private subjects to rights against the state, e.g. the European Convention on Human Rights and its equivalents in other parts of the world); and, lastly, private subject v private subject (e.g. the United Nations Convention on Contracts for the International Sale of Goods, the CISG, or Carrier's liability conventions, such as the CMR convention, the Hague–Visby Rules and the COTIF–CIM convention).

The treaty as such evidently regulates the relationship between the state parties only, but the contents of the treaty may in addition have an effect on either of the two latter levels. The former relation, i.e. between a state and a private party, is one between a stronger party and a weaker, usually vesting rights of the latter in relation to the former. As mentioned, the European Convention on Human Rights (ECHR) is an example of such a convention, which is safeguarded by its own court, the European Court of Human Rights. This court has developed methods of interpretation that aim at preserving the rights of private subjects. An example is autonomous interpretation, which in the sphere of the ECHR denotes

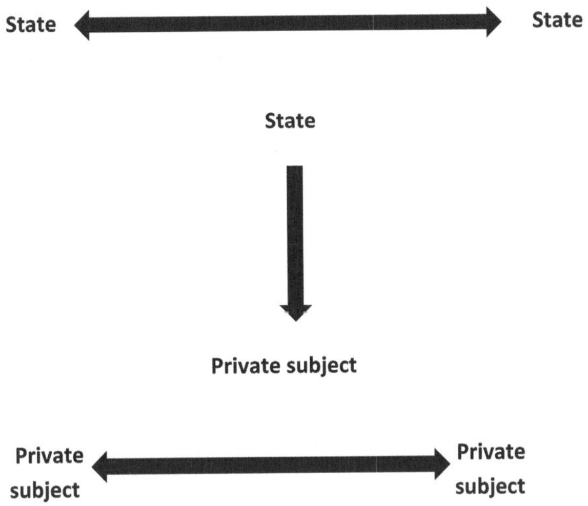

interpretation independently of the national implication of a term. Were the court to permit state parties to apply national interpretation of the terms of the convention, the convention could end up as a mere shell without substance as states could legislate to the effect that the terms of the convention have a meaning that limits the obligations of the state under the convention, thus circumventing the state's original international obligations. It seems also that the court often refers to effective interpretation, which in essence entails realizing the object and purpose of the convention – in the most efficient way.[101] The object and purpose of conventions such as the ECHR is, obviously, protection of human rights in relation to the state and, since a restrictive interpretation protecting the sovereignty of the state seems to have been abandoned in favour of a restrictive interpretation in protection of the private sphere, the enlargement of the rights of individuals at the expense of the state is widely accepted.[102]

In uniform law regulating purely private legal relationships, the perspective is horizontal rather than vertical. But the interpretation of such uniform law also involves the vertical relationship between the private subject and the state. Accordingly, rules of interpretation of treaties that clearly assume the treaty to be a contract between nations may not be immediately suitable for the interpretation

101 L. Crema, "Disappearance and New Sightings of Restrictive Interpretation(s)" (2010) EJIL 21 681–700.

102 Crema asserts that the restrictive interpretation is really a value-oriented rule of interpretation. Value, which is commonly thought worthy of protection, varies. In 1758, E. Vattel enumerated values that ought to motivate an extensive or restrictive interpretation and the common (good) values relate to utility, freedom, stability of society, the validity of acts and human sociality. In the era of nation states these values were substituted for the sovereignty of the state as the prime value (see eg. the Treaty of Lausanne from 1925). In contemporary international law, the protected value is freedom of individuals from abuse by the state (L. Crema, "Disappearance and New Sightings of Restrictive Interpretation(s)" in (2010) 21 EJIL 681–700).

of uniform law.[103] As shown in the previous section, the Vienna Convention contains rules of interpretation that evidently presuppose contractual treaties as the subject-matter of the interpretation. Thus, where the rules of interpretation of treaties focus on data such as the intentions of the parties, the interpreter must not disregard the private subject's right of legal foreseeability. To take paragraph 4 of article 31 of the Vienna Convention as an example: in a bilateral treaty between state Å and state Ö regarding the maritime border between the two states, it is stated that the states undertake to keep an area of 5 kilometres from the border protected from fisheries. In a dispute between the states, state Ö establishes that by the term "fisheries" the states meant all fishing and that not only professional but also non-professional fishing would be disallowed. As this special meaning of the treaty is established, interpretation of the treaty should be in accordance therewith. Now, if the rules established in the treaty instead were uniform law that the states implemented in their national legislation and the ordinary meaning of the word "fishery" (also in the context of the treaty and in light of its object and purpose) is considered to be professional activities it would seem somewhat totalitarian to charge a non-professional fisherman with illegal fishing in the zone in question. The fisherman must, in protection of legal predictability, be able to rely on the objective meaning of the rules (as opposed to the subjective meaning intended by the contracting parties) and even if the state can establish a special meaning in accordance with paragraph 4, it would seem unjust to interpret the rule accordingly.

Even more delicate is the situation where the convention is entered into between two states but the rules regulate the relationship between two private subjects. If the imagined convention above instead regulated the right of private subjects to fish close to the shore infringing the rights of the landowner who enjoyed a right to the resources of the sea that extended 1 kilometre from the land. Thus, either outcome of the interpretation of "fishery" will be detrimental to a private subject. However, allowing the landowner to establish the meanings of the rules as intended by the state parties, but which were not obvious to either party (where in fact both had assumed the meaning of the rule in accordance with its ordinary meaning), would appear arbitrary and contrary to the way other legislation is interpreted.

To clarify: it is not asserted that interpretation of uniform law should be in accordance with national law principles. On the contrary; one of the important objects of uniform rules is harmonization, which can only be achieved through uniform interpretation. However, there is a difference between interpretation of national rules and national rules of interpretation.[104] Whilst interpretation of the terms of a treaty of uniform law in accordance with national law would mean that a certain term would be given the same meaning as in national law, applying

---

103 M. van Alstine, "Dynamic *Treaty Interpretation*" in (1997–1998) 146 U Pa L Rev 687, at p. 708.

104 F. Enderlein, "Uniform Law and its Application by Judges and Arbitrators" in *International Uniform Law in Practice*, published by UNIDROIT (1988) 329–353, at p. 334.

national rules of interpretation means that interpretation rules are adapted to the type of rules that are enacted in a uniform law treaty. All uniform law affects private subjects to the exact same extent as national legislation and the interpretation thereof, by means of the Vienna Convention, autonomous or otherwise, must take into account the rightful claim to legal predictability of these private subjects. The intent of the contracting states, or rather the drafters of the treaty, is not irrelevant, just as it is not irrelevant to the interpretation of legislation.[105] It is a matter for discussion whether literal or teleological interpretation better serves the purpose of legal predictability as regards uniform law. However entirely subjective intent by the contracting parties, not expressed in any publicly available drafting history, should not be allowed to change any clear meaning of the terms of uniform law. On the other hand, some considerations must be made in relation to interpretation of uniform law that is not provided for by national rules of interpretation. Accordingly, the preservation of the uniformity and the harmonization sought by the treaty is not catered for in national rules of interpretation. These considerations are, however, to some extent, catered for in international rules of treaty interpretation.[106] In addition, it cannot be disregarded that the Vienna Convention according to its scope of application applies to treaties of uniform law. Thus, the rules of treaty interpretation contained therein should be applied, although less weight should be given to interpretative data that reflect the subjective intent of the contracting states, which is not expressed in such supplementary means of interpretation envisaged in article 32.

Particular considerations may present themselves when uniform law is perceived as incomplete. Thus, gaps in legislation can either be solved by analogous application of rules that are not immediately applicable to the situation in question, or by an *e contrario* conclusion of the non-applicability of legislation. Based on the presumption that the "princes and rulers", entering into international conventions, can only by their positive actions subject themselves or their states to international law, interpretation by analogy is generally considered not permitted in respect of international conventions. This means that the rules of uniform law cannot be applied to cases other than those explicitly regulated by the convention. This principle borders the *e contrario* method of interpretation, under which a certain conclusion can be drawn from the fact that a certain case is not regulated by a certain provision. In an English judgment, *Shell Chemicals v P&O Roadtanks*, the Court of Appeal held that the fact that liability for wrongful delivery, i.e. delivery of other goods than contractually agreed, did not concern the "liability of the carrier for the loss of or damage to or delay to the consigned goods" entailed that the damage in question fell outside the scope of the convention and thus another basis of liability, e.g. national rules, could be applied to

105 M. van Alstine, "Dynamic *Treaty Interpretation*" (1997–1998) 146 U Pa L Rev 687, at p. 708.

106 As was discussed in section 4.2.2.1 above, although referring to court practice from other contracting states is not directly promoted in the Vienna Convention, such practice, which certainly promotes uniformity, could be supported on the obligation to interpret the terms of a treaty in light of the object and purpose the treaty.

impose liability on the carrier.[107] However, where a certain liability falls within the scope of a convention per se, but is not regulated therein, such non-regulated liability cannot be settled based on other rules.[108] In terms of legislation based on uniform law, this principle thus entails that gaps in legislation are not to be filled, but rather accepted as non-regulated issues.[109]

Interpretation of international treaties comprising uniform law is to be done autonomously, that is, the terms of the treaty should be unaffected by a purely national understanding thereof and as far as possible the basis for interpretation should be the treaty itself. There does not seem to be any contradiction between this proposition and the rules of interpretation set out in the Vienna Convention. Indeed, writers who advocate autonomous interpretation of uniform law do not seem to dismiss the Vienna Convention *per se*.[110]

It is held, however, that some of the rules for interpretation of treaties provided in the Vienna Convention are intended for interpretation of the international contract type of treaty and thus fit less well with considerations that are peculiar to uniform law. Thus, as the subjects of uniform law are private parties rather than state parties, many of the considerations required in interpretation of national law, in particular the individual's right to legal predictability, also assert themselves in the interpretation of uniform law. Accordingly, the interpreter must respect the legitimate expectation of the private subjects that the law stands as it is conveyed through the terms of the uniform law.

Further, there are interpretative data that may serve uniform interpretation but which are not primary sources of interpretation according to the Vienna Convention. Accordingly, it was shown above that application of uniform law by national courts does not easily fit into the sources referred to in article 31. Although it may correctly be claimed that foreign case law is not easily accessible, either intellectually or practically, for the private party subject to uniform law, which obviously limits foreseeability, nevertheless taking into consideration, and referring to, case law in other states – parties to the convention in question – is fundamental to preserving the uniformity of the law. In addition, the preparatory works of international treaties are only secondary sources of interpretation according to the Vienna Convention. However, these are fundamental to teleological interpretation, which, in accordance with the discussion in section 4.2.3 above, appears to be one of the methods of interpretation that promotes autonomous

107 *Shell Chemicals UK Ltd v P&O Roadtanks Ltd.* [1995] 1 Lloyd's Rep 297.

108 For an excellent discussion on this subject, see Lord Hope of Craighead in *Sidhu v British Airways PLC* [1997] 2 WLR 26.

109 This conclusion mirrors the implication of terms into private contracts under English law; cf. section 5.6.1 below. See also Lord Hoffmann's statement in the *Belize Telecom* case:

> If the parties had intended something to happen, the instrument would have said so. Otherwise, the express provisions of the instrument are to continue to operate undisturbed. If the event has caused loss to one or other of the parties, the loss lies where it falls.
>
> (*Attorney General of Belize v Belize Telecom Ltd* [2009] UKPC 10)

110 See for example M. Gebauer, "Uniform Law, General Principles and Autonomous Interpretation" (2000) 4 Rev Dr unif 683–705.

interpretation.[111] In this respect, it thus seems that there is a divergence between the rules of treaty interpretation and the often-promoted doctrine of autonomous interpretation of uniform law.

These propositions do not entail that interpretation should be in accordance with national law. As mentioned, interpretation in accordance with national law would effectively deprive uniform law of its uniformity, a uniformity that is assumed to be beneficial to the private parties subject to it. However, there is a difference between national rules of interpretation and interpretation of national rules. Thus, rules of interpretation that are developed for interpretation of national legislation take into account considerations of legal predictability, and so on, discussed above. Therefore, they may be beneficial for interpretation of uniform law. In order to preserve uniformity, the rules thus applied must, however, be national in the sense that they are particular to the law in the state where the interpretation is carried out. To the extent that they are common between all contracting states, or at least perceived as general, uniformity would not be undermined.[112] It is thus asserted that interpretation of uniform law could be influenced by rules of interpretation of national legislation to the extent such rules are common or general, although such rules should only be restored to where the international rules of treaty interpretation, such as the rules of the Vienna Convention, do not sufficiently serve the values, such as legal predictability, rightly expected by individuals that are subject to the uniform law.

4.2.5 Conclusions

The rules of interpretation of national law and international law have been accounted for and scrutinized in the sections above. Further, the theory of autonomous interpretation has been discussed and, in addition, the relationship between rules of treaty interpretation of international law and private uniform law was analysed.

It is often held that uniform law is to be subject to autonomous interpretation. It was concluded above that any interpretation must respect the rules of treaty interpretation. However, it was also concluded that the criteria for autonomous interpretation that have been advanced rest on the rules of treaty interpretation of the Vienna Convention. In fact, even the more particular criteria, i.e. the observance of the international character of the norm and the need to promote uniformity in international law, is often part of the object and purpose of uniform law and as such enforced by article 31 of the Vienna Convention. It would thus seem that the conclusion that autonomous interpretation is perfectly supported by the Vienna Convention has some merit to it.

111 M. Gebauer, *ibid.* at pp. 686–687.

112 Which probably means that in relation to a mainly European uniform law treaty such as the CMR convention it may be less challenging to find common or general rules than in relation to a worldwide treaty such as the Montreal Convention.

Another possible dilemma with autonomous interpretation is the interpretation of legal terms, which may be difficult to interpret without reference to national law.[113] It was proposed that the interpreter of a legal term is bound to prima facie understand the term according to national law. However, this understanding could be adjusted with the application of the criteria set out for autonomous interpretation. Thus, by comparing the understanding of a certain legal term in one jurisdiction with the understanding thereof in other jurisdictions, a spectrum of possible interpretations may present itself. By relating such possible interpretations to the object and purpose of international harmonization as well as other possible object(s) and purpose(s) of the uniform law, the proper interpretation can be chosen. In addition, the supplementary data of interpretation prescribed for in the Vienna Convention can be applied, among which the use of preparatory works seem to promote autonomous interpretation. However, in summary, the rules of treaty interpretation of the Vienna Convention seem to be a perfectly appropriate starting point for interpretation of uniform law.

Accordingly, in the following sections the scope of application of articles of the conventions discussed will be interpreted with the use of the rules of treaty interpretation of the Vienna Convention. As mentioned initially, this interpretation will primarily be carried out in relation to treaty interpretation theory. Thus, sources that may normally affect interpretation of legislation, such as precedence and doctrine, will only be used as interpretative data to the extent permitted by the rules of treaty interpretation. However, such sources may be used as support in respect of conclusions drawn. Further, as regards the interpretation of the scope of applicability of the CMR convention, the interpretation will be preceded by an analysis of the arguments purported in support of the non-applicability of the convention to transport by road under a multimodal contract of carriage in relation to the rules of treaty interpretation.

4.3 Scope of application of the CMR convention and the COTIF–CIM convention

The scope of application of an international convention of uniform law is usually, for obvious reasons, defined in one of the first, if not the very first, articles of the convention. The scope of application article is naturally the key to the entire convention, and is therefore the first rule to be applied to whatever situation is prima facie believed to come within the sphere of the convention.

As the COTIF–CIM convention from 1999 is modelled after the CMR convention, issues of applicability are common to the two conventions. Whilst the CMR convention is applicable to "every contract for the carriage of goods by road in vehicles for reward", the COTIF–CIM convention applies to "every contract of

113 Willhelm C. Vis, former secretary general of UNCTAD, has held that "uniform rules become part of a given legal system and cannot be interpreted in isolation" (W.C. Vis, "International Unification of Private Law: The Multilateral Approach", *Remarks in Proceedings of the Annual Meeting* (American Society of International Law), vol. 80 (9–12 April 1986) 233–243, at p. 236.

carriage of goods by rail for reward". The thus chosen contractual approach to applicability has been discussed previously. Noteworthy in this respect is that irrespective of how the particular article that defines applicability of the convention has been drafted, on a principle level the contractual approach has been chosen over other types of approach to applicability. Thus, it is the contract of carriage that is the subject of the CMR and the COTIF–CIM conventions, rather than performance of a transport or the transport document.

A crucial issue is naturally what types of contracts are subject to the said conventions. The conventions state that they apply to contracts *for* the carriage of goods by road and contracts *of* carriage of goods by rail respectively. A contract, in order to be subject to either convention, must therefore constitute a contract for the carriage of goods by either road or rail. As discussed previously in section 3.4, there are irreconcilable views on what constitutes such a contract – and what does not. Accordingly, interpretation of the articles of application of the conventions has been claimed to entail the exclusion of contracts other than those that provide for carriage by road and by road only.[114] Thus the applicability of the conventions would be limited to unimodal transport by the respective mode of transport.

The main arguments that are put forward in support of the view that the CMR convention, and they are mainly put forward in relation to the CMR, does not apply to carriage by road that is part of a multimodal undertaking are (1) that article 1 stipulates applicability to contracts for the carriage of goods by road and not to contracts for the carriage of goods by road and some other mode of transport; (2) that article 2 expressly, and exclusively, states under which circumstances the CMR convention is applicable to multimodal transport; and (3) that under a multimodal contract, the road carrier does not "take over the goods" from the consignor and/or does not "deliver the goods" to the consignee as stipulated in article 1, as the road leg only covers part of the transport.[115] These arguments have been meritoriously addressed elsewhere,[116] but in line with the purpose of the current work, in the following these arguments will be thoroughly scrutinized in relation to the rules of interpretation of treaties.

4.3.1 Contracts for the carriage of goods by road – and road only

The scope of applicability of the CMR convention appears from its article 1.1, which holds that the convention "shall apply to every contract for the carriage

114 Although the issue is thus common to both conventions, the debate – and the case law – is to a high degree focused on the CMR convention. One reason for this is probably that carriage by road is to a larger extent carried out as a supplement to another mode of transport, so that the contract is principally for some other mode of transport. Another reason is that it can be assumed that a majority of multimodal contracts contain a road leg and hence road transports to a greater degree form part of a multimodal transport contract. Also, as the COTIF–CIM convention according to its article 1.3 applies to domestic transport carried out by road or inland waterway in connection with carriage by rail, the question of the applicability of the road carrier's liability regimes will often not surface. Thus in the following there will be a bias towards the CMR convention.

115 For a summary of the discussion in legal writing, see section 3.4.2 above.

116 M. Hoeks, *Multimodal Transport Law* (2010) ch. 4.

of goods by road". This scope of applicability is defined by a few additional prerequisites such as the internationality of the transport and the requirement that the transport is carried out against payment of freight, and limited by the exemption of certain types of road transport contract, such as postal consignments.

4.3.1.1 The argument and counterarguments

It has been suggested that a carriage contract cannot be a contract for the carriage by road as required for the applicability of the CMR convention if it also provides for carriage by some other mode.[117] In so arguing, Berlingieri simply states that the drafters, had they wished to include road transport performed under a multimodal contract, would have formulated the article differently.[118] Thus, Berlingieri does not seem to hold that the phrase in question excludes applicability to road transport performed under a multimodal contract, but only that this does not seem to have been the intention of the drafters. Koller, on the other hand, seems to base his argument for this interpretation on linguistics, in making a comparison between the equally authentic French and English texts.[119] Koller's argument refers to the French version of the convention text, which prescribes applicability to a *contrat de transport de merchandise par route* where the first *de* would indicate that *de merchandise par route* are adjectives to *contrat*, which thus excludes contracts of carriage by other modes in addition to carriage by road from the applicability.[120]

In opposition, Hoeks argues that the meaning of *de* in English is "of", and that the difference between a "contract of carriage of goods by road" and a "contract for the carriage of goods by road" is insignificant and a weak foundation to support the entailing restriction of the CMR convention.[121]

In this respect, Clarke argues that there is nothing in the text of article 1 that indicates that the contract must be exclusively (or predominantly) for the carriage of goods by road and that the convention is therefore applicable to road carriage under mode-to-mode contracts.[122] In the *Quantum* judgment, Mance LJ argues that a contract "for" the carriage of goods by road should be interpreted

117 F. Berlingieri, "Door-to-door Transport of Goods; can uniformity be achieved?" in *Liber Amicorum in Honour of Roger Roland* (2003) pp. 37–55, at p. 40; U. Fabricius, *Lov om Fragtaftaler ved international vejtransport* (2005) p. 38; P. Vestergaard Pedersen; *Transportret* (2008) pp. 962–964; and I. Koller; "Quantum Corporation Inc. v. Plane Trucking Limited und die Anwendbarkeit der CMR auf die Beförderung mit verschiedenartigen Transportmitteln" (2003) 2 TransportR 45–50.

118 F. Berlingieri, *ibid.*, at p. 40, fn. 7.

119 I. Koller, "Quantum Corporation Inc. v. Plane Trucking Limited und die Anwendbarkeit der CMR auf die Beförderung mit verschiedenartigen Transportmitteln" (2003) 2 TransportR 45–50.

120 M. Hoeks, *Multimodal Transport Law* (2010) p. 175, with reference to I. Koller, *ibid.*

121 M. Hoeks, *ibid.*, at p. 175 where Hoeks argues that the interpretation of article 1 in this respect must be made in light of the object and purpose of the treaty and that as the effect of non-applicability of the CMR to a road leg of a multimodal contract is freedom of contract instead of the mandatory rules of the conventions that the draftsmen found required to impose on the parties such an interpretation cannot be in conformity with the object and purpose of the treaty.

122 M. Clarke, "A Multimodal Mix Up" (2002) JBL 210–217, at p. 215.

as a contract "permitting for" or "permitting" carriage by road.[123] However, this conclusion is made in relation to contracts that do not prescribe for, but merely permits for, carriage by road.[124]

4.3.1.2 Vienna Convention, article 33

The linguistic argument asserting that *de* in the French version of the text is an attributive genitive to the contract indicating that it must only be for road, and for no other mode of transport in addition to road, is, it is asserted, somewhat strained. However, where a discrepancy in the meaning of two language versions has been detected, the primary solution to the problem lies in the interpretation of the term in question.[125] Such interpretation, it is asserted, should be carried out in accordance with the Vienna Convention, taking into account the importance of the autonomy of the treaty as well as the legal predictability of the parties involved in the carriage contract.

Because the proposition that "contract for the carriage of goods by road" is limited to contracts for carriage by road only is in itself a proposition that the CMR convention is unclear in this respect and although the proposition that the article is unclear could be challenged, it triggers the need to interpret the scope of application clause of the convention. The CMR convention is authenticated in two language versions, French and English,[126] and it must be assumed that the drafters intended the two language versions to be identical. This is also the assumption under the Vienna Convention.[127] As the English and French versions are of equal status, the primary rule of interpretation of the Vienna Convention is article 33. Although the primary rule as regards multilingual treaties is that the different language versions are to be presumed to have the same meaning, where a difference in meaning is asserted to exist, that difference must be resolved. Where a treaty is authenticated in more than one language, the two versions are in fact of equal status. Therefore, the simple statement that the meaning of the English- and French-language versions differ in this respect does not mean that it is more correct than the English meaning. Even if the English version could

123 *Quantum Corporation Inc v Plane Trucking Ltd* [2002] 2 Lloyd's Rep 25 at 16. Heidbrink criticizes, by reference to the *Cambridge Advanced Learner's Dictionary*, translation of the word "for" as "permitting" as "somewhat forced" (J. Heidbrink, *Logistikavtalet* (2005) p. 52). Reading Mance LJ's opinion, it seems that he by no means holds that "for" is synonymous with "permitting", but that a contract which permits carriage by road and such carriage is eventually carried out should be considered a contract for the carriage of goods by road in accordance with CMR article 1.

124 It is noteworthy that the discussion on the significance of "for" is made in relation to what types of contract (e.g. clear contracts, contracts that allow for substitution etc.) is subject to the CMR convention, rather than whether carriage by road that is carried out under a multimodal contract of carriage, i.e. in addition to another mode of transport, is subject to the CMR convention.

125 Thus, although it may be asserted that a reading of article 1 of the CMR should pose no problem of interpretation, the mere proposition that there be more than one understanding thereof entails that interpretation must be carried out.

126 United Nations Treaty Collection, UN Treaty Series No 5742, v. 399 p. 189 (www.treaties.un.org).

127 Cf. article 33.3, which prescribes that "the terms of the treaty are presumed to have the same meaning in each authentic text".

be interpreted to mean the same thing as the French version this is not what is intended by the so-called reconciliation rule in the Vienna Convention.

The rule of interpretation of multilingual treaties, article 33 of the Vienna Convention, prescribes an order of interpretation which gives prominence to either the prevailing version or, if no language version prevails according to the treaty, the presumption of the identical meaning of the multiple versions. However, once article 33.3 is resorted to, a discrepancy between the terms of two versions has in fact been detected in a convention, and hence the value of the guidance given in the article may be questioned as the difficulty remains of asserting *which* same meaning the two versions are to be given. In relation to the CMR convention, the guidance given is thus that the French and English versions are to be presumed to have the same meaning, but where two meanings of the same term have been proposed, this guidance may seem difficult to follow. However, article 33.3 is not merely an assumption that allows an interpreter to refrain from consulting all authentic versions, but entails, according to the International Law Commission, an obligation for the interpreter to make "every effort … to find a common meaning for the texts before preferring one to another".[128] This seems to imply that it is only when non-negligible differences are disclosed that a need for interpretation and comparison is justified, as slight differences should be settled accordingly.[129] For this reason, as regards the CMR convention, the words "for" and *de* should be presumed to mean the same thing. That same meaning may be proposed to be a contract, which prescribes for the carriage of goods by road.

Where a difference in meaning is detected, which cannot be settled in accordance with article 33.3, interpretation is first to be carried out in accordance with the general rule of interpretation in article 31, and the supplementary rule in article 32. Only when such interpretation does not resolve the difference in meaning is the reconciliation rule in article 33.4 to be applied. The reconciliation rule entails that the interpreter has to make a choice between the two language versions and to apply the meaning found in the language version that better serves the object and purpose of the treaty.[130]

In the current case, it does seem that the two different meanings of the term "contract for the carriage of goods by road" proposed are not so much differences between the two language versions, but rather two possible readings of the term, independently of which language version is referred to. Interpretation according to the general and secondary rules will be discussed below. As regards the reconciliation rule of the Vienna Convention it is, as mentioned above, subsidiary

128 R. Gardiner, *Treaty Interpretation* (2015) p. 423 with reference to [1966] *Yearbook of the ILC*, vol. II, p. 225, para. 7.

129 Where such non-negligible discrepancies are detected, interpreting them is to be done according to the "general" rules of treaty interpretation in article 31, which include the understanding of treaty terms in accordance with their ordinary meaning and interpretation in conformity with the object and purpose of the treaty. However, this is only after the interpreter has found reconciliation of the two language versions impossible.

130 U. Linderfalk, "Tolkning genom sammanjämkning – Om Wienkonventionen om traktaträtten artikel 33(4), och traktattolkningens särskilda lära" (2012) 4 Tidskrift for Rettsvitenskap 458–490, at p. 481.

to general interpretation. It seems, however, suitable to touch upon the reconciliation rule at this point. The reconciliation rule requires the interpreter, when all other possibilities prescribed in article 33 are exhausted, to clarify the two (or more) differing meanings caused by the multiple original language versions and then simply choose the version that better serves the objective and purpose of the treaty.

The overarching object of uniform law is harmonization of legislation. The CMR convention is no exception to this rule.[131] However, as discussed previously, applying the aim of harmonization and uniformity as the object and purpose of a treaty with the intent of interpreting the treaty according to article 31.1 or article 33.4 of the Vienna Convention is rather unfruitful. For example, application of a uniform law treaty by analogy would certainly promote uniformity, but such an application is considered inconsistent with international law. The question then becomes what the object and purpose of the CMR convention is, in addition to the desire to harmonize the liability rules applicable to carriers by road. Considering the perceptibility of the rules, one purpose of the convention must be considered to balance the interests between the carrier and the shipper, the traditional view being that the shipper needs protection against the carrier who would otherwise impose unfair conditions on the shipper. Another purpose is purportedly the foreseeability for all parties vested in the harmonization as such, and the fact that the same rules apply to all transport within Europe as well as to the entire carriage. Both these purposes are seemingly best served by applying the English version of the first article of the treaty.[132]

4.3.1.3 Summary

In conclusion, it is held here that this linguistic argument in support of the non-applicability of the CMR convention to road carriage performed under a multimodal contract of carriage is based on a difference between the English and the French texts of the convention that is so insignificant that no problem of interpretation exists, and that certainly a common meaning of the two words is easily found as prescribed in the Vienna Convention article 33.3. Should a non-reconcilable discrepancy be found, interpretation should be carried out in accordance with the rules of treaty interpretation, which according to the Vienna Convention entails that the terms of a treaty are primarily to be interpreted according to the plain meaning of the words in their context.[133] The requirement of taking into account the context in which a treaty term is found should be understood as aiming to prevent an overly literal reading of the term.[134] Thus, besides the fact that the linguistic argument as presented above in itself appears an almost incomprehensibly theoretical grammatical exercise, which even without the rules

131 Cf. the preamble of the CMR convention (https://treaties.un.org/doc/Treaties/1961/07/19610702%2001-56%20AM/Ch_XI_B_11.pdf).

132 Cf. M. Hoeks, *Multimodal Transport Law* (2010) pp. 175–176.

133 Article 31.1.

134 R. Gardiner, *Treaty Interpretation* (2015) p. 197. The context in which a term is found is further primarily of importance if two or more possible ordinary meanings of a term are available.

of interpretation found in the Vienna Convention is somewhat far-fetched, the asserted reading of the term is not inconsistent with the international rules on treaty interpretation as recorded in the Vienna Convention. When, in addition, the word "every" is added to the picture ("shall apply to every contract for the carriage of goods by road"), the linguistic argument, as well as the purported need for interpretation of the sentence at all, appears somewhat strained.

4.3.1.4 The scope of application of the CMR convention and the *sui generis* theory

Interrelated to this discussion, or perhaps the other side of the same coin, is the discussion on the characterization of the multimodal transport contract as a contract *sui generis*.[135] If the multimodal transport contract is defined as a contract of its own sort, then, it is claimed, it does not constitute a contract for the carriage of goods by road, so that the CMR convention is not applicable to that type of contract. However, it is not entirely clear on what grounds the theory rests,[136] but it seems to have been a precondition for the drafting of the 1980 Multimodal Convention, which would otherwise have been in conflict with various unimodal conventions.[137] The *sui generis* theory may thus be based on the idea that the multimodal transport contract is simply something other than the unimodal transport contract or it may be based on the asserted idea that some unimodal liability conventions are not applicable to multimodal transport contracts. However, it seems that both arguments are based on each other and it is hard to see which is the chicken and which is the egg. If a multimodal transport contract is a contract *sui generis*, then it does not fit under the applicability of conventions such as the CMR and if the CMR convention is not applicable to road transport carried out under a multimodal contract, then the multimodal transport contract is a contract *sui generis*. It is clear that the *sui generis* theory is necessary for the possibility of fitting a multimodal transport convention, or any other legislation on multimodal transport, into the net of unimodal transport conventions, and so is the non-applicability of the unimodal transport conventions to the (unimodal) legs of transport carried out under a multimodal contract. It is asserted that the emergence of the theories relates to the development of multimodal liability regulations.

4.3.2 Other arguments for the non-applicability of the CMR convention to road transport under a multimodal contract

Besides the linguistic argument, the assertion that the CMR convention is not applicable to carriage by road performed under a multimodal transport contract is supported by other arguments. These arguments include the existence of certain undertakings

135 Cf. section 3.2.1.1 above.

136 D. Glass, *Freight Forwarding and Multimodal Transport Contracts* (2012) p. 336.

137 E. Selvig, "Multimodal transport: the 1980 U.N. Convention: papers of a one day seminar: Southampton University, Faculty of Law, 12th September 1980", at p. A17, para. 12.

made by the contracting states in the protocol of signatories. Another argument is the purported difficulty in applying the CMR convention to multimodal contracts due to other articles in the convention, which seem to presuppose a unimodal contract.

In evaluating these arguments, it is important to note that these circumstantial indications of the drafters' intentions should only be used as data for interpreting the convention where interpretation is necessary.[138] Thus it is the scope of application article of the convention in question that sets the scene. In a, perhaps imaginary, situation where the scope of application of a convention is crystal clear, other circumstances such as the fact that other articles of the convention do not fit well with the scope of application will not affect the scope of application – it will only entail that the convention is considered to be imperfectly drafted. Hence where the plain meaning of the term is clear, in a legal context, resort to other data for interpreting a certain term is not necessary. It is true that interpretation of a treaty includes consideration not only of the terms as such but also of the context in which the term is given and the object and purpose of the treaty.[139] It is further true that, according to the Vienna Convention, subsequent agreements and practice in application between the parties, as well as intended special meanings of terms, if such can be established, are to be taken into account as primary sources when interpreting a treaty. However, it must be borne in mind that treaties are entered into between sovereign states, and generally regulate the relationship between those states, and that accordingly the rules on interpretation of treaties are drafted with such treaties in mind. Conventions, often referred to as uniform law, that regulate the relationship between private parties, such as the conventions on carrier's liability for goods carried to the owner thereof, are drafted as legislation and therefore rules on interpretation of legislation may be more appropriate. However, it appears that the appropriate point of departure is the Vienna Convention, which seems to consider and give effect to the need for autonomous interpretation of uniform law as well as providing substantial rules of procedure for interpretation. That said, the interpreter must take into account the legal foreseeability legitimately expected by private subjects of uniform law.

In contrast with private agreements, where perhaps the intention of the parties prevails over the clear written text of the contract, this is not the case with legislation. Hence, where the reading of the convention is clear, the intention of

138 Although "interpretation" and "application" are often used as mutually exclusive terms (either the reader *applies* or, where the meaning is not clear, *interprets* the terms), and has been described as such (A.D. McNair, *The Law of Treaties* (1965) p. 365, fn. 1), it seems to be an artificial exercise to separate one from the other. For example, Gardiner holds that "Even 'when the meaning of the treaty is clear', this is the result of 'making out' that meaning", thus asserting that all reading includes interpretation (R. Gardiner, *Treaty Interpretation* (2015) p. 29). However, it must be said that there are degrees of interpretation; varying from reading a clear and unambiguous text to the inquiring into the meaning of an unclear and vague text. Thus, in the following "interpretation" will be used as depicting the "... secondary process which only comes into play when it is impossible to make sense of the plain terms of the treaty, or when they are susceptible of different meanings" (A.D. McNair, *ibid.*, at p. 365, fn. 1). For a discussion on the point of departure of the Vienna Convention in this respect, see section 4.2.2 above.

139 Article 31.1.

the drafters must often be disregarded in the protection of legal foreseeability.[140] Accordingly, it is primarily when the reading of the convention is ambiguous that the meaning thereof may be sought with resort to such arguments.[141]

Considering the wording of the first paragraph of article 31 of the Vienna Convention, which requires the interpreter to understand the terms of the treaty in accordance with the ordinary meaning of those terms as perceived in the legal, contextual (both as regards the written context in the form of preambles and additional agreements and actual context such as the sphere of business it sets out to regulate) and textual framework, the point where the applier is "allowed" to start interpreting the terms due to perceived ambiguity may be unclear. In other words, an ambiguity may be perceived due to incompatibility of the term with the rest of the treaty or due to statements in the written context, subsequent agreements or the *travaux préparatoires*. Thus, it is a "sneak peek" at the sources of interpretation that causes the ambiguity. It seems, however, somewhat strained to claim that the interpreter should disregard such indications and resort only to the reading of the term of the treaty in concluding whether a term is clear or not. Nevertheless, in the spirit of legal foreseeability it is perhaps sometimes necessary. In conclusion it is vital to endeavour to separate these circumstances when used as indications of an ambiguity from when they are used as sources of interpretation.

In the following sections the arguments put forward in support of interpretation of the CMR convention as not applicable to road transport carried out under a multimodal transport contract will be discussed and scrutinized through application of the rules of interpretation in the Vienna Convention. The question what constitutes a contract for the carriage of goods by e.g. road is not unique to carriage by road, but is intimately connected with the contractual approach to applicability. However, as mentioned, it is with reference to the CMR convention that most of the discussion has been carried out.

4.3.2.1 The intention to negotiate a separate convention on multimodal transport

In the Protocol of Signature of the CMR convention, the following statement can be found:

> On proceeding to sign the Convention on the Contract for the International Carriage of Goods by Road, the undersigned, being duly authorized, have agreed on the following statement and explanation:
> 1. [...]
> 2. *Ad article 1, paragraph 4*

140 T. Eckhoff, *Rettskildelære* (2001) pp. 73–74.

141 The point of departure of the Vienna Convention in respect of whether it presupposes the doctrine of clear meaning or not is discussed above. However, as a general rule it would seem that no applier of uniform law would consult the rules of interpretation in the Vienna Convention unless an ambiguity is detected. Interpretation according to that convention in the primary steps takes into account the context of the unclear term, including the text of the treaty, together with its preamble and annexes, as well as separate agreements between the parties in connection with the conclusion of the treaty; see article 31.1–31.2.

The undersigned undertake to negotiate conventions governing contracts for furniture removals and combined transport.

(original emphasis)

This agreement qualifies as context according to article 31.2 (a) of the Vienna Convention, in accordance with which the terms of the treaty are to be given their ordinary meaning. The statement has been claimed to indicate that the signatories intended to exclude road carriage under a multimodal contract from application of the convention.[142] An interesting feature of this agreement, which seems to have been disregarded by Koller, who refers to a citation by Haak rather than the original source, is that the agreement is made in relation to paragraph 4 of article 1, which regulates some explicit exemptions from applicability of the convention, of which combined transport is not one. It is hard to make any sense of this statement; it refers to the exemption of transport of postal items, funeral consignments and furniture removal from the sphere of application of the convention and obliges the signatories to negotiate a convention on combined transport. This could indicate that the signatories intended, although such transports were not exempted from the applicability of the convention, nevertheless to negotiate a separate convention, but it could also indicate, as has been advocated, that the drafters did not consider the convention applicable to such contracts.[143] It has also been argued that as the agreement refers to two types of transport, of which only one is explicitly exempted from the scope of application, the agreement indicates that the drafters intended the convention not to be applicable to multimodal transport in its entirety, which does not exclude applicability to a road leg of such transport.[144]

It has been held that article 31 of the Vienna Convention provides one single rule of interpretation, so that all paragraphs thereof are of equal status.[145] Hence, although ambiguous, the agreement in question is part of the context of the terms of the treaty, in light of which the ordinary meaning is to be settled and of the same standing as the object and purpose of the treaty.[146] Given the ambiguity thereof, it is, however, questionable what the agreement adds in the form of substantive information on the meaning of article 1 of the CMR convention. Further, when the agreement does not give any clear guidance on the interpretation of the unclear term, but merely provides circumstantial evidence on the intention of the

142 I. Koller, "Quantum Corporation Inc. v. Plane Trucking Limited und die Anwendbarkeit der CMR auf die Beförderung mit verschiedenartigen Transportmitteln" (2003) 2 TransportR 45–50, at p. 47; BGH 17 July 2008 (I ZR 181/05), at para. 23.

143 I. Koller, *ibid.*, at p. 47.

144 M. Hoeks, *Multimodal Transport Law* (2010) pp. 176–177.

145 M.E. Villiger, "The Rules of Interpretation: Misgivings, Misunderstandings, Miscarriage? The 'Crucible' Intended by the International Law Commission" in E. Cannizzaro (ed.), *The Law of Treaties Beyond the Vienna Convention* (2011) p. 114. See however Linderfalk who in his systematization of article 31 subordinates paragraph 2 under paragraph 1 in that he conditions the applicability of paragraph 2 (a) and (b) so that application of paragraph 1 leads to conflicting results (U. Linderfalk, *On the Interpretation of Treaties* (2007) pp. 154–155 (rules 7 and 8)).

146 Cf. article 31.2 (a). For a thorough analysis of the article, see *ibid.* ch. 5.

drafters, it rather belongs to the category of *travaux préparatoires*, which is only a secondary source of interpretative information.

It seems, in summary, that the only thing that can be held for certain is that the terms of article 1 of the CMR convention are to be interpreted to mean what is conveyed by the ordinary meaning thereof, as it appears in the context of i.e. that the signatories of the convention undertook to negotiate a separate convention on combined transport. It is important to keep in mind that the agreement in question forms part of the context, which contains other information, such as the arguments discussed in the following sections and the fact that article 1 contains a paragraph with explicit exceptions, of which multimodal transport is not one.

4.3.2.2 Arguments relating to the text of the convention

To the context in which an interpreted term of a treaty is to be given its ordinary meaning belongs the text of the treaty. The text includes the body of text of the treaty as well as e.g. maps, tables, diagrams, and so on that may be attached to a treaty.[147] Interpreting a term taking into account the textual context, i.e. the treaty or piece of legislation, may be referred to as systematic interpretation.[148] Such systematic interpretation may be based on the presumption of either a linguistic system or a logic system (or both). According to a linguistic system it is, put simply, presumed that the same words or terms are used in the same meaning, and that different words are used to signify different meanings, whilst, according to a logical system, the system is presumed to be free from logical contradictions.

The exhaustiveness of article 2

As an argument for the non-applicability of the CMR convention to multimodal contracts, it has further been held that since article 2 regulates a particular form of multimodal transport, this indicates that the only form of multimodal contract that the drafters intended the convention to be applicable to is the kind found in article 2 (mode-on-mode transport).[149] In relation to the Vienna Convention and its rules on interpretation of treaties, this argument involves the textual context and systematic interpretation based on the presumption that the treaty as a whole forms a logical system. In relation to the Vienna Convention, the argument could be formulated as, had the drafters of the convention presupposed application of the convention to multimodal transport, the introduction of article 2 would have been superfluous and illogical. As the convention is presupposed to make up a logical whole, article 1 must be considered to exclude multimodal transport.

This argument is perfectly logical and correct, as the CMR convention is not applicable to multimodal transport, with the exception of mode-on-mode transport as provided in article 2. The CMR convention is applicable to road transport; the question debated is whether it is applicable to road transport carried out under

147 U. Linderfalk, *On the Interpretation of Treaties* (2007) p. 103.

148 U. Linderfalk, *ibid.*, at p. 105.

149 F. Berlingieri, "Door-to-door Transport of Goods; can uniformity be achieved?" in *Liber Amicorum in Honour of Roger Roland* (2003) (pp. 37–55) at p. 42.

a multimodal contract. Put another way: whilst it is true that article 2 regulates one form (of many) of multimodal carriage, article 2 is not a scope of application provision in its pure form. Article 1 sets the frame for applicability as regards road transport. Article 2 on the other hand expands applicability to other modes of transport in the case of mode-on-mode transport. This is something completely different from the question whether the CMR convention is applicable to a road leg of a multimodal contract. It is not asserted that the CMR convention is to be applied to an entire multimodal contract of carriage; only to the road transport therein. Arguing that article 2 prevents the convention from being applicable to a road leg of a multimodal contract is, it is asserted here, equal to arguing that as the drafters did not extend the applicability of the CMR convention to multimodal contracts in general (i.e. the whole contract), the convention cannot be applicable to a part of such a contract that actually concerns road transport.[150]

Further, in cases where article 2 does not extend the CMR convention to transport by another mode because the goods are unloaded from the road vehicle, the result of arguing that the convention is not applicable to a road leg under a multimodal transport would be that a road transport including a sea or rail transport would only be subject to the CMR convention if the goods are not unloaded during the non-road leg of the transport. Where the goods are unloaded, no part of the transport will be subject to the convention.[151] This conclusion seems to be somewhat incompatible with the wording of article 2: "Where the vehicle containing the goods is carried over part of the journey by sea, rail, inland waterways or air, and [...] the goods are not unloaded from the vehicle, this Convention shall *nevertheless* apply to *the whole* of the carriage" (emphasis added). The wording seems undoubtedly to be based on the assumption that where the goods are unloaded the convention applies to *part of* the carriage, i.e. the road transport: despite the fact that the goods are actually

150 Hoeks claims that such an argument is contrary to the purpose of standardizing conditions under which carriage by road is undertaken and that whilst article 2 extends the applicability of the CMR, applying CMR to a road leg of a multimodal contract merely applies a road regime to road transport (M. Hoeks, *Multimodal Transport Law* (2010) pp. 179–180). On the same note, Lorenzon holds that article 2 of the CMR is not "multimodal in its nature" (F. Lorenzon, "Multimodal Transport Evolving: Freedom and Regulation Three Decades after the 1980 MTO Convention" in M. Clarke (ed.), *Maritime Law Evolving* (2013) 163–180, at p. 168).

151 In respect of a submission by Air France in the *Quantum* case, Mance LJ held:

> However, this submission would mean that a contract for carriage by road from Stockholm to Naples would be subject to CMR; that a contract for carriage from Stockholm to (say) Capri would also be subject to CMR, if the goods remained on their trailer for the short sea passage from Naples to Capri; but that no part of a contract for carriage by road from Stockholm to Naples and sea from Naples to Capri would be subject to CMR. Other, similar results can readily be envisaged, e.g. in respect of contracts for carriage from Spain to a Channel port in France or across the Channel into this country or from Eire to Marseilles (by roll-on, roll-off transport) with a possible final sea leg to Corsica. I do not think that either the drafters of CMR or participants in the international carriage of goods would regard it as sensible that rights and responsibilities for the long international trucking legs in such cases should depend upon whether a carrier by road does or does not undertake the final sea leg, or, if it does undertake it, upon whether or not it transports the goods on their trailer during it.
>
> (*Quantum Corporation Inc v Plane Trucking Ltd* [2002] 2 Lloyd's Rep 25, at para. 26)

carried by another mode than road transport, the convention applies, not only to the road transport, but to the whole carriage.

The existence of article 2 contributes to the interpretation of article 1 in as much as the textual context contains a regulation on multimodal transport and, assuming that the convention makes up a logical whole, this may influence the ordinary meaning of the terms of article 1. This logic dictates, according to some, that as article 2 regulates one form of multimodal transport expressly, other forms of multimodal transport are excluded from applicability and that if multimodal transport in general is covered by article 1, article 2 would be superfluous. The weakness of the argument is, it is asserted here, that applying the CMR convention to a road transport leg of a multimodal contract is not the same thing as applying the CMR convention to multimodal transport. Article 2 expands applicability to other modes of transport and its existence is perfectly logical even if the CMR convention is presumed to be applicable to road transports carried out under a multimodal contract. In fact, considering its wording ("shall nevertheless apply to the whole of the carriage"), its existence is then only logical.

Regardless of which is considered more logical, the existence of article 2 contributes to the textual context in which the terms of the treaty are to be given their ordinary meaning. It is a part of that textual context; and together with other circumstantial facts discussed it makes up the context.

The places of taking over and delivery by the road carrier

There are additional stipulations in the CMR convention that are claimed to be unsuitable and difficult to apply where the convention would apply to road transport under a multimodal contract and which, assuming that the convention makes up a logical whole, would have been drafted differently had the intention been that the convention was to apply to other contracts than purely unimodal road transport contracts. One such stipulation is the taking over of the goods and delivery of the same, of which at least one, according to article 1, must take place in a contracting state. When the taking over of the goods and the delivery thereof are understood to mean the taking over by a carrier from the initial consignor and delivery by a carrier to the final consignee, it has been claimed that application of the convention to a road leg of a larger transport is illogical, as the initial taking over and the final delivery may, in such a case, be completely unrelated to the road carriage, take place in states completely unrelated to the CMR convention and be done by a carrier who is not a road carrier.[152] The same arguments are relevant to other articles as well, such as article 17 (the liability of the carrier) and article 31 (place of bringing action). Applying the Vienna Convention, the arguments thus asserted can be translated into a proposal that it can be assumed that such application, i.e. to a road transport not taking place between contracting states, was not intended by the drafters, and only if the CMR convention is only

152 F. Berlingieri, "Door-to-door Transport of Goods; can uniformity be achieved?" in *Liber Amicorum in Honour of Roger Roland* (2003) pp. 37–55, at p. 40.

applied to purely unimodal contracts of carriage by road are the stipulations in question logical.

In opposition, it has been argued that if the taking over and delivery of the goods are understood as relating to the taking over for road carriage by the road carrier (which may be done from either the consignor or a previous carrier) and the delivery by the road carrier (to either the consignee or a subsequent carrier), application of the CMR convention to a road leg of a multimodal contract does not pose any problems in this respect.[153] In fact there is nothing in the CMR convention that contradicts that interpretation. The former reading of the taking over and delivery has been held to be too "literal" and instead the terms should be read in the full context of the CMR convention.[154] There are in fact examples of when the carrier is liable under the convention without ever "taking over" the goods from the consignor, such as in the case of sub-contracting. Further, the purpose of article 1 in this regard is merely a unilateral conflicts rule; what matters about "taking over" is that the carriage begins in one state and ends in another.[155]

In this respect it appears necessary to clarify the different contractual relationships very often present in multimodal transport. The multimodal contract, i.e. a contract that provides for carriage of goods by more than one mode (often "door-to-door"), is entered into between on the one hand a party who offers transport services, a contracting carrier, and, on the other hand, a party who is in need of transport services. The latter party may be the consignor (sender) or the consignee (receiver), depending on the underlying contract (such as a sales contract) between the consignor and the consignee.[156] With the exception for occasions when the contracting carrier disposes of more than one mode of transport, the contracting carrier will enter into contracts with sub-carriers for parts of the transport. In fact, the contracting carrier may enter into sub-contracts for all legs of the multimodal transport, e.g. due to lack of own capacity. These sub-contracts are likely to be unimodal, so that the carrier actually performing the carriage is likely to be liable under the "appropriate" rules, i.e. a performing road (sub-)carrier will be liable under the CMR convention (provided that the carriage is international etc.). The question of applicability of the CMR convention to road transports under a multimodal contract thus concerns only the relationship between the contracting carrier and the contractual opposite party.

With regard to modern transport patterns, the contracting carrier may never have the goods in its care. However, the performing carrier will obviously at some point have the goods in its care. The taking over of the goods may be

153 M. Hoeks, *Multimodal Transport Law* (2010) pp. 180–181.

154 M. Clarke, "A Multimodal Mix Up" (2002) JBL 210–217, at p. 215.

155 M. Clarke, "Intermodal Transport: CMR as Unimodal Plus?" available at www.juridicum.su.se, 2005.

156 In Swedish, the term sender (*avsändare*) is reserved for the party entering into the carriage contract with the carrier, whilst off-loader (*avlastare*) is used for the party delivering the goods to the carrier for carriage who then delivers the goods to the receiver (*mottagare*). The sender can thus be either off-loader or receiver. As far as understood, there is no equivalence in English as the consignor always equals the off-loader.

from the initial consignor or from a previous carrier, depending on at which point in the multimodal chain, the road transport takes place. The handing over of the goods may likewise take place in relation to the final consignee or to a subsequent carrier. In relation to the performing carrier, it is the contracting carrier who is the contractual opposite party, i.e. it is the carrier, denoted as contracting carrier in the multimodal transport contract who is the consignor.

Considering that the contractual relationship affected by the applicability or non-applicability of the CMR convention is hence one between a carrier who contracts for the entire multimodal transport and the transport customer (the consignor or the consignee), the goods are often never taken over by the contracting carrier but only by the performing road carrier in his place. Thus, wherever the taking over and/or delivery of the goods by the contracting carrier are understood to be is an artificial construction.

As mentioned above, "the place of taking over of the goods" as well as "the place designated for delivery" have by some been interpreted to mean the initial taking over of the goods by a carrier from the original consignor, e.g. the seller of the goods and the final delivery of the goods by a carrier to the final consignee, e.g. the buyer of the goods. Whilst nothing in article 1 proposes such an interpretation, it is perhaps a natural conclusion to draw for the interpreter with only the unimodal contract in mind.

The places indicated by article 1 designate geographical locations. As these geographical locations are the basis for the terrestrial scope of application of the CMR convention, they must logically be connected to the road transport. This is necessary both in order for the stipulation to make sense and in order for it to be legitimate; the contracting states to the CMR convention could hardly have intended the convention to be applicable to a road transport carried out between two non-contracting states based on the goods having been initially taken over, for transport by another mode, in a CMR contracting state. This cannot have been the intention behind the convention, and to the extent it would require a non-signatory state to apply the rules of the convention to a road transport unrelated to any contracting state, such application could hardly be expected.[157] Thus, the place of taking over the goods cannot be understood as anything else than the place of taking over of the goods by the road carrier for carriage by road. There is nothing to indicate that that taking over must be from the original consignor, and the term can therefore just as well be understood as denoting the taking over from another carrier. The same argument is applicable to the place of delivery in article 1.

157 As application of the CMR convention in this respect is based on the goods having been taken over by the carrier in a contracting state *or* delivered in a contracting state, the following example can illustrate the situation envisaged: goods are to be carried from Rotterdam to Lusaka in Zambia, via the port of Luanda in Angola. As the goods are taken over from the initial consignor in the Netherlands, a contracting state to the CMR convention, the convention would be applicable to international road transport between Angola and Zambia. This is obviously an absurd proposal, without any support, either in the convention itself or in legal writing.

The terms "place of taking over" and "place of delivery" are subsequently found in articles 17 and 31, which regulate the period of liability of the carrier and jurisdiction under the convention, respectively. It is generally accepted in international law, including under the Vienna Convention, that interpretation in relation to the textual context of the treaty presupposes that words or phrases used on multiple occasions in the text of a treaty should be assumed to bear a uniform meaning.[158] There is nothing that indicates that this main rule is not applicable to the terms in question as used in articles 1, 17 and 31.

To summarize, the terms "place of taking over" and "place of delivery" are found in articles 1, 17 and 31 of the CMR convention. As discussed above, it has been held that these terms prevent application of the CMR convention to road carriage under a multimodal transport contract. The reason presented is that such application could cause the convention to be applicable to road transport without any connection to a CMR contracting state when the initial taking over of the goods or final delivery of the same takes place in a contracting state, but this taking over or delivery is unrelated to the road transport. In opposition it has been held that in cases of the carriage being part of a larger, multimodal transport, the place of taking over should be understood as the taking over of the goods by the road carrier from either the initial consignor or from another carrier. In the same manner, place of delivery should be understood as the place where the road carrier delivers the goods, either to the final consignee or to a subsequent carrier. In this way application of the CMR convention remains related to its envisaged geographical scope. It is held here that this latter interpretation combines well with the systematic interpretation that follows from the Vienna Convention, article 31.1 and 31.2 (referring to the textual context of the convention interpreted). The former interpretation is, for the reasons accounted for above, unreasonable and impossible. However, the only alternative is not non-application of the CMR convention to road transport carried out under a multimodal contract. The alternative is thus instead to interpret the place of taking over as the place of taking over of the goods by the road carrier either from the initial consignor or from another carrier and the place of delivery should be understood as the place where the road carrier delivers the goods, either to the final consignee or to a subsequent carrier. All the legal consequences connected to the places of taking over and delivery found in article 1, 17 and 31 of the CMR convention conform to such an interpretation of the terms.

Accordingly, it is held here that it may seem natural to interpret the place of taking over as the taking over by the carrier from the initial consignor, and the delivery of the goods as the delivery to the final consignee, the consequence of which is the possible application of the CMR convention to road carriage unrelated to the contracting states. However, such an interpretation is only natural to an interpreter with the unimodal road carriage contract in mind. In contrast, the taking over by the road carrier must be considered separately from the taking

158 U. Linderfalk, *On the Interpretation of Treaties* (2007) p. 106, with references to Oppenheim, Haraszti and Bernhardt.

over from the initial consignor. Nothing in the convention indicates that the taking over must be from the initial consignor, or that the delivery of the goods must be to the final consignee. Understanding the places of taking over and delivery in the way advocated here leaves the convention constituting a systematic whole and without ambiguities.

THE DATE OF TAKING OVER THE GOODS AND THE DATE OF DELIVERY

Article 32 regulates the period of limitation in relation to claims against the carrier for loss of, or damage to, goods carried. In this article the taking over of the goods by the carrier and the delivery thereof reappear, as prerequisites relating to initiation of the period of limitation. Their presence in the current article has been pointed out in the discussion regarding applicability of the CMR convention to road transport under a multimodal contract of carriage and asserted as arguments by those opposing such application.[159] The period of limitation under the CMR convention is one year, starting from the time of delivery (in cases of partial loss), 60 days after the time of taking over (in the case of total loss) or three months after making the contract of carriage (in all other cases).[160] It has been argued that defining the delivery as delivery from the road carrier to a subsequent carrier, where the road carriage in which damage occurs (there may be several legs of road transport) is not the last leg of the multimodal transport, deprives the consignee of valuable time. The (final) consignee will not be able to inspect the goods and make any claims against the contracting carrier before (final) delivery of the goods is taken (unless the subsequent carrier reports any damage, in order to avoid any claims itself, which is not too farfetched if the damage is visible). This proposition is based on the presumption that the terms "taking over" and "delivery" are to be given the same meaning throughout the convention.[161] In accordance with what has been referenced above regarding systematic interpretation, this assumption is perfectly correct and fits well with interpretation in accordance with the Vienna Convention and constitutes autonomous interpretation of the CMR convention.

However, systematic interpretation has two sides to it and, whilst linguistic systematic interpretation focuses on the linguistic systematics in the text of the convention, logic systematic interpretation is based on the assumption that the treaty makes up a logical whole.[162] In using the context of a treaty to interpret its terms, both parts, linguistic and logical, should be fulfilled, but in the interpretation of a particular term it may not be necessary to invoke both. In the present case it is obviously the linguistic systematics of the treaty that is relevant and, in relation thereto, it is clearly of vital importance to distinguish the term, in this

159 I. Koller, "Quantum Corporation Inc. v. Plane Trucking Limited und die Anwendbarkeit der CMR auf die Beförderung mit verschiedenartigen Transportmitteln" (2003) 2 TransportR 45–50, at p. 47. See also M. Hoeks, *Multimodal Transport Law* (2010) p. 182.

160 The latter time limit is not of interest in the current discussion.

161 In opposition, Hoeks argues that the terms are to be given different meanings based on the fact that they refer to a place in space and a point in time respectively (M. Hoeks, *ibid.*, at p. 183).

162 U. Linderfalk, *On the Interpretation of Treaties* (2007) p. 105.

case a phrase, and its definition. Thus, words must be separated from phrases and when a word forms part of a phrase it does not necessarily bear the same meaning as when it is used as an independent word. When delivery is used in articles 1, 17 and 31 as well as in article 32 it is used as a part of a phrase, which is "place of delivery" in article 1, 17 and 31, but "date of delivery" in article 32. Just as the same words and phrases should be assumed to have the same meaning, different words and phrases are assumed to have different meanings.[163] Accordingly, it is not necessary to infer the same meaning to the two phrases. To the contrary, it is clear that they mean different things, in a linguistic sense. Whilst the former denotes the geographical place where delivery is taken, the latter denotes a point in time when delivery is made. Naturally, in a purely unimodal transport, these two features will coincide in as much that the goods will be at the place of delivery at the time of delivery. However, as in fact they are two distinct terms, nothing prevents them from being interpreted as denoting two separate features that do not have to coincide. Accordingly, the place of delivery would be interpreted as the place where the road carrier delivers the goods, be it the final consignee or a subsequent carrier, whilst the time of delivery is interpreted as the time when the final consignee takes delivery of the goods, and thus is able to inspect the goods.

On the other hand, the arguments submitted in order to prove the non-applicability of the CMR convention in those situations are of a very practical nature and refer perhaps more to the logical systematics of the convention. Thus, it is has been held that it would be to the detriment of the final consignee if the period of limitation starts running when the goods are delivered to a subsequent carrier.[164] This conclusion is based on the claim that place of delivery should denote the delivery by the road carrier to whomever takes delivery, the final consignee or a subsequent carrier, as well as on the presumption that the time of delivery and the place of delivery should be interpreted as compellingly coinciding. However, if it is accepted that the time of delivery and the place of delivery do not have to be coinciding, the effects in relation to the period of limitation do not have to be as detrimental as suggested.

Coming back to the structure of multimodal transport, if damage to goods occurs during carriage by road, the period of limitation of liability of the performing road carrier will always start at the time when the goods are delivered by the road carrier, i.e. to whomever that is; the final consignee or a subsequent carrier. Thus, where the final consignee is granted one year from the date when delivery is taken by the final consignee at the end of the multimodal transport, there may be a time gap that prevents the contracting carrier from recoursing the claim against the road carrier. In such a case, final liability will not be borne by the party responsible for the damage, but by the contracting carrier. It should also

163 A. Peczenik, *Vad är rätt? Om demokrati, rättssäkerhet, etik och juridisk argumentation* (1995) p. 332.

164 Hoeks argues that "it does seem rather unfair for the consignee to have to forfeit a part of the precious one-year period even before he takes delivery of the goods" (M. Hoeks, *Multimodal Transport Law* (2010) p. 182).

be stressed that, according to article 32.2 of the CMR convention, the period of limitation is interrupted by a simple written claim, i.e. the claimant does not have to start legal proceedings to interrupt the period of limitation. In that perspective, one year is not, it is asserted, a very short time.[165] If that period is shortened by a few days, weeks or a month does not, in that perspective, seem to be detrimental to the final consignee. It should also be emphasized that many jurisdictions allow the parties to extend the period of limitation, in accordance with section 3 of article 32.

To summarize, it is asserted that interpretation in accordance with the Vienna Convention supports the interpretation of "place of delivery" and "date of delivery" as denoting two diverse places in time and space, which do not necessarily have to coincide. Further, it is held here that interpreting the two terms as inevitably coinciding is not as detrimental to the final consignee as has been argued.[166] If "date of delivery" is interpreted to denote the time when the road carrier delivers the goods, and that date antedates the date when the final consignee takes delivery, the final consignee will indeed be deprived of parts of the one-year limitation period. It is, however, asserted that, put in perspective, a period of one year to inspect the goods and make a written claim is not an unreasonably short time, not even if the period is somewhat shortened. Such an interpretation also allows for the claim to be carried forward by the contractual carrier against the performing road carrier, which seems to be a correct localization of the cost, in the perspective of legal economic efficiency. It is also held here that it is preferable that the final consignee is deprived of some of the period of limitation, to the "place of delivery" being interpreted as necessarily denoting the delivery be the last carrier to the final consignee, considering that the CMR convention is a regional convention that should not, and indeed could not, be enforced where the road carriage does not start or end in a CMR contracting state.

4.3.2.3 Conclusions regarding the analysis of the proposed non-applicability of the CMR convention to carriage by road under a multimodal contract of carriage

The arguments brought forward in support of the proposition that the CMR convention is not applicable to road carriage under a multimodal contract of carriage, discussed above, relate to different rules of treaty interpretation. Whilst the "linguistic argument" found in the asserted difference in meaning between the French and English versions of the convention relate to article 33 of the Vienna Convention, the remaining arguments, relating to, on the one hand, the protocol

165 Cf. in this respect the period within which a buyer must make a claim in a sale of goods under the CISG (United Nations Convention on Contracts for the International Sale of Goods, Vienna, 1980) article 39, which states that the buyer must claim against the seller within a reasonable time after the disconformity of the goods has been discovered, which is likely to be shortly after the time of delivery as the buyer has an obligation to inspect the goods within such a short time as is practicable in the circumstances. Reasonable time varies but would likely not be considered one year other than in exceptional circumstances.

166 M. Hoeks, *Multimodal Transport Law* (2010) p. 185.

of signatories and, on the other hand, the remaining text of the CMR convention, relate to the primary rules of treaty interpretation found in article 31. It has been proposed above that in order to interpret the scope of applicability of the CMR convention, the interpretative data should be subsumed under the rules of treaty interpretation of the Vienna Convention and scrutinized in the order provided therein.[167]

Accordingly, although the prima facie reading of article 1 in English gives the seemingly clear result that the rules of the convention are to be applied to all contracts that provide for carriage of goods by road, without any other exceptions than what follows from the article itself (which does not include multimodal contracts), it has in fact been purported that the applicability of the convention is not as clear as it may first seem. The ambiguity of article 1 of the CMR convention that purportedly exists relates partly to the fact that the convention is drafted in two equally authentic languages, French and English. According to the Vienna Convention, the primary rule of the convention to consult, where a convention is drafted in more than one official language, is not article 31, but article 33. However, as it has been held that a comparison between the two versions, English and French, discloses a difference in meaning, this throws the interpreter right back to article 31, which needs to be pre-empted before the remaining rules of article 33 can be applied. The essence of article 33 in relation to the "linguistic argument" is that, should interpretation under the general rule of interpretation not clarify the ambiguity, the language version that best promotes the object and purpose of the CMR convention should be chosen over the other.

The arguments that relate to the context of the convention affects the interpretation to the extent that the ordinary meaning should be understood in its context (and in the light of its object and purpose).[168] These arguments were analysed above and the conclusions drawn were that neither the existence of a regulation of mode-on-mode transport in article 2, nor regulation of "taking over" and "delivery" in other articles, such as articles 17, 31 and 32, give any substantive guidance on how the term "every contract for the carriage of goods by road" is to be understood in its context. It was held that the existence of article 2, which regulates the extension of the CMR convention to other modes of transport, cannot be taken into account for either the non-applicability or the applicability of the CMR convention to road carriage under a multimodal contract. Further, the regulation of "taking over" and "delivery" in e.g. articles 17, 31 and 32 was held to support the non-applicability of the CMR convention to road carriage under a multimodal contract only if the interpreter has the unimodal contract in mind when interpreting the articles in question. If, on the other hand, the interpreter has the multimodal contract in mind, the articles seem to support the interpretation that the convention is applicable to road carriage under a multimodal contract. The protocol of signatories, lastly, becomes ambiguous when

167 Cf. section 1.2.1 above.
168 Cf. section 4.1.3.1 above.

read in conjunction with article 1.4, which states certain exemptions from the applicability of the convention.

The conclusion that the arguments brought forward in support of the non-applicability of the CMR convention to road transport under multimodal contracts of carriage are not sufficiently compelling does however not automatically mean that the convention *is* applicable to such carriage. The scope of application of the CMR convention will have to be interpreted afresh with the proper application of the rules of treaty interpretation, before any conclusions can be drawn.

4.3.3 The scope of applicability of the CMR convention

It was asserted initially in the current sub-chapter that the arguments brought forward in the discussion of the applicability of the CMR convention to carriage by road under a multimodal contract of carriage are often of a "pick-and-mix" character. Although, a court admittedly would be unlikely to carefully apply the rules of treaty interpretation rule-by-rule, it is not without importance that the interpretation of the terms of a treaty is carried out in such manner, at least in legal theory. Whilst the arguments presented in support of the non-applicability of the CMR convention to road carriage under a multimodal contract of carriage have been scrutinized above, the current section will be devoted to an attempt to settle the applicability of the CMR convention from a clean sheet, i.e. without regard to the arguments discussed above.

Accordingly, article 1 of the CMR convention will be scrutinized with the application of articles 31–33 of the Vienna Convention. As mentioned previously, being a bilingual treaty, interpretation should rightly start at article 33. Whilst articles 33.1–33.3 only guide the interpreter in settling which language version may prevail and do thus not give any substantive guidance in relation to actual interpretation, article 33.4 does. However, it is asserted here that a comparison between the two equally authentic language versions would detect no difference and that the starting point prescribed in article 33.3, that the language versions have the same meaning, is confirmed.[169]

The general rule of interpretation recorded in article 31, has been thoroughly discussed in section 4.2.2 above. Its application to article 1 of the CMR convention, and in particular the term "contract for the carriage of goods by road", which is the key in terms of pin-pointing the transactions that are subject to the convention, entails a quest for its ordinary meaning in its context and in light of the object and purpose of the treaty.

The ordinary meaning of the term "contract for the carriage of goods by road" is an agreement between two parties that relate to the transportation of cargo by means that move on roads. In the context of the further reading of article 1, the meaning of the term is further clarified. Thus, the agreement must be commercial, i.e. the performance of the transport must be in exchange for payment

169 M. Hoeks, *Multimodal Transport Law* (2010) p. 175.

of freight; the vehicle used must be a motor vehicle as defined in the Convention on Road Traffic; the transport must be border crossing; and by "goods" is meant any tangible item with the exception of postal items, furniture and funeral consignments.[170]

In relation to the question of whether the term "contract for the carriage of goods by road" includes or excludes contracts that provide for transport by other means of transport in addition to carriage by road, the context includes several data of interpretation. These data include the intention of the drafters to negotiate a separate convention on multimodal transport as expressed in the protocol of signature; the existence of article 2 that regulate multimodal transport and the fact that the rules of the convention are clearly adapted to unimodal transport and applying the rules to road transport under a multimodal contract of carriage entails several difficulties, such as how to settle the places of taking over and delivery as well as the dates of taking over and delivery. These data of interpretation have been analysed in the previous section, resulting in the conclusion that neither of them provides any substantial guidance on the interpretation of the term in question. It was held that whilst the stipulations relating to the place of taking over etc. in articles 1, 17 and 31 and relating to the date of taking over etc. in article 32 may indicate that the convention is primarily adapted to unimodal contracts of carriage, they definitely do not prevent such applicability. However, as interpretative data they seem to weigh in favour of the non-applicability of the CMR convention to carriage by road under a multimodal contract of carriage.

As far as the existence of the regulation of multimodal transport in article 2 of the CMR convention is concerned, this fact has been held to show that ro-ro transports are the only form of multimodal transports to which the convention apply. This statement is certainly true, but it was held above that applying the CMR convention to carriage by road under a multimodal contract of carriage is not applying the convention to multimodal transports; article 2 extends the convention to other forms of transport, which applying the CMR convention to carriage by road under a multimodal contract of carriage does not. As a data of interpretation of the term "contract for the carriage of goods by road", the existence of article 2 does not, it is held here, affect the interpretation at all.

The intention to negotiate a separate convention on multimodal transport as expressed in the protocol of signatories may prima facie appear as conclusive evidence of the intention of the drafters of the convention; there was no intention that the CMR convention was to be applied to such carriage, at least not in the long run. However, as discussed above, the protocol seems to show that the drafters did not expect the convention to be applied to road carriage under a multimodal carriage, at least not, it must be presumed, after a convention on multimodal transport was in place. However, whilst the undertaking to negotiate a separate convention on furniture removal is reflected by an exemption of

170 Exempted from the applicability of the convention are (1) carriage that is subject to any international postal convention, (2) carriage of funeral consignments and (3) furniture removal; cf. article 1.4.

such transports from the scope of the convention, transport under a multimodal contract is not.[171] As held above, the intention of the drafters as regards carriage under multimodal contracts of carriage is not clear, and the protocol of signatories does not add any clarity to the interpretation of the term "contract for the carriage of goods by road".

Further, as discussed in section 4.2.4 above, in interpreting uniform law the legal predictability must be considered and thus there seem to be good reasons to give less weight to the subjective intentions of the drafters of a convention, to the extent such intention deviates from the wording of the rules, than indicated by the rules of the Vienna Convention.[172] Thus, in uniform law, in contrast to the more traditional contractual treaty, no term should be interpreted against its clear meaning, even though it is established that another, special meaning was intended by the signatories. The interpretation of the scope of applicability should thus not be affected by the intention of the drafters only because this intention may be established (or is seemingly clear), but the rules of treaty interpretation should be applied in their internal order (with exception for articles 31.3 (a) and (b) and 31.4) and such intention may only be taken into account as part of the context or as *travaux préparatoires*, and then subject to the limitations provided for in the Vienna Convention.[173]

4.3.3.1 The context

In addition to the interpretative data presented above, which are usually used in support of the non-applicability of the CMR convention to road transport under multimodal contracts of carriage, the are other provisions in the treaty that may provide guidance as contextual interpretative data. One such provision is the term "every" that precede the term "contract for the carriage of goods by road" in article 1.[174] It is generally assumed that every term of a treaty bears a meaning, i.e. that no term is superfluous.[175] Accordingly, the term "every" has a purpose and alters the meaning of "contract for the carriage of goods by road", an alteration that is expansive rather than reductive. The ordinary meaning of "every" is the inclusion of all without exception.[176] Thus the term "every" entails that the term

---

171 M. Hoeks, *Multimodal Transport Law* (2010) pp. 176–177.

172 As discussed previously, articles 31.3 a) and b) as well as article 31.4 prescribes for the taking into account of the purely subjective intentions of the signatories (drafters), considerations that appear less appropriate in relation to uniform law treaties when these are applied between private parties. As far as *travaux préparatoires* are concerned these are, to the extent they fullfill the generally prescribed prerequisites of e.g. general availability (cf. section 1.2.5.4 above), they are generally not considered to give the interpreter the right to give a term a meaning that contradicts a clear term, and have their given place in the interpretation of uniform law. The justification therefore was developed in section 4.2.2 above.

173 Cf. sections 4.2.2.2 above.

174 "This Convention shall apply to every contract for the carriage of goods by road in vehicles for reward ...".

175 J. Hogg, "The International Court, Rules of Treaty Interpretation II" (1959–1960) 44 Minn L Rev 5–73, at p. 6 *ff.*

176 Obviously this may not lead the interpreter in any direction, as where the term "contract for the carriage of goods by road" is thought to be understood as unimodal contracts only, the term

"contract for the carriage of goods by road" includes more (contracts) than the term would have, had the term "every" not been there and the term "contract for the carriage of goods by road" should accordingly be interpreted widely, rather than narrowly.

Further, as mentioned above, article 1.4 stipulates the exclusion from the applicability of the convention of certain contracts of carriage, i.e. of postal items, for furniture removal and of funeral consignments.[177] Although these exemptions relate to the type of cargo carried rather than to the type of contract entered into, the fact that carriage under multimodal contracts of carriage is not included in the list of exemptions is an interpretative data that indicates the applicability of the convention to such contracts. Notable is that previous drafts of the convention included particular rules on furniture removal, rules that were excluded from the final draft as they were considered in need of more thorough discussion.[178] Instead the furniture removal was excluded and the parties undertook to negotiate a separate convention in relation thereto. In contrast, as regards multimodal transport, while the parties undertook to negotiate a separate convention, such transport was not explicitly excluded.

4.3.3.2 The object and purpose of the treaty

As discussed in section 4.2.2 above, the ordinary meaning of a term in its context should be understood in light of the object and purpose of the treaty. As further discussed, the object and purpose of a treaty is not the reasons of the state parties as these may be explained through the *travaux préparatoires*, but the very reason for the existence of the convention (its raison d'être).[179] The settlement of a treaty's object and purpose is interpretation in itself. Furthermore, there is generally no single object and purpose but rather objects and purposes of the treaty. In addition, certain articles of a treaty may have a particular object and purpose. Furthermore the object and purpose is always settled in relation to a particular interpretative issue; the interpreter is faced with two alternatives of interpretation and the question is which better conforms with the object and purpose of the treaty.[180] In practice, the object and purpose of the treaty as such, *in extenso*, may not have to be settled and in reality the question is rather which interpretative

"every" would entail that all unimodal contracts (for carriage by road) are included, without exception. However, the point is that the term "every" must be used as interpretative data before the interpreter interprets how the term "contract for the carriage of goods by road" is to be understood.

177 It may be held that the latter is exempted from the convention already as a funeral consignment could hardly be considered "goods", although the term "funeral consignments" is intended to cover also items accompanying the coffin (with mortal remains); see R. Loewe, "Commentary on the Convention of 19 May 1956 on the Contract for the International Carriage of Goods by Road (CMR)" (1976) 1 ETL 311–405, at p. 324.

178 R. Loewe, *ibid.*, at p. 324.

179 U. Linderfalk, *On the Interpretation of Treaties* (2007) p. 205. Linderfalk further holds that the object and purpose is the subjective rather than objective intention, i.e. it is the reasons for drafting the treaty according to the state parties that is relevant. However, it should be borne in mind that Linderfalk's approach solely focuses on "contractual" treaties rather than treaties of uniform law.

180 U. Linderfalk, *ibid.*, at p. 206.

alternative does not (or does to a lesser degree) serve the object and purpose of the treaty.[181]

Accordingly, as regards the applicability of the CMR convention the question of which interpretation of the scope of applicability serves the object and purpose of the convention better can also be put as a question of which interpretation serves the object and purpose to a lesser degree. Thus, the preamble holds the "standardizing the conditions governing the contract for the international carriage of goods by road" as an objective of the convention.[182] However, as appears from the discussion above and in section 4.2.2, settling the object and purpose of a treaty is not as simple as referring to the objective(s) as articulated in the preamble and, whilst the unification of rules in an international aspect is an inherent purpose of uniform law, other objects and purposes may also exist. In addition, it is sometimes held that a (subjective) reason for states to draft uniform rules in relation to road transport was to subject road carriers to certain regulation in order to even out its competitive advantage in relation to rail carriage (which was generally state owned).[183] Hence the mandatory applicability of the rules. Because of the dual imperative nature of the rules, i.e. the carrier may not grant the shipper more extensive rights than provided by the convention, no protective purpose seems to be embedded in the rules.[184] In relation to article 1 and the fact that the geographical scope of the convention is settled according to the contractual places of loading and discharge rather than the actual places thereof, one objective would appear to be the foreseeability of the parties. This objective could further be proposed to be embedded in the entire scope of application; foreseeability improves where the number of exempted contracts is kept to a minimum, hence the term "every contract". All these objectives – standardization/uniformity, foreseeability and non-circumvention (mandatory applicability) – are undoubtedly better fulfilled by an inclusive interpretation of the term "contract for the carriage of goods by road".

As far as supplementary means of interpretation are concerned, the preparatory works of the CMR convention have not been published and are, although accessible at the Library of the UN in Geneva, not available in the way that is generally required.[185] However, the conclusion above is confirmed, if not by the *travaux préparatoires*, by the author of the (unofficial) commentary to the convention published by UN in 1975, who holds that "If, in fact, another means of transport is subsequently used over part of the journey, CMR governs the carriage up to the

181 U. Linderfalk, *ibid.*, at p. 206.

182 Messent & Glass states the aim of the convention as standardization and uniformity (A. Messent and D. Glass, *CMR: Contracts for the International Carriage of Goods by Road* (2000) pp. 2 and 3). Likewise, Clarke holds the object to be the standardization as articulated in the preamble of the convention (M. Clarke, *International Carriage of Goods by Road: CMR* (2014) p. 8).

183 M. Clarke, *ibid.*, at p. 4.

184 In contrast, the Hague–Visby Rules are generally considered to have a protective purpose to the benefit of the shipper.

185 Cf. section 1.2.5.4 above.

transshipment between the road vehicle and the other means of transport, and this operation terminates the carriage by road."[186]

It thus seems that interpretation in accordance with article 31 of the Vienna Convention leads to a satisfactory result. However, for the sake of completeness, a discussion on the reconciliation rule in article 33.4 may be appropriate.

The reconciliation rule throws the interpreter right back into the "object and purpose" of the interpreted convention, albeit with a different purpose. Whilst interpretation in accordance with article 31.1 obliges the interpreter to give a term its ordinary meaning in light of the object and purpose of the treaty, reconciliation in accordance with article 33.4 obliges the interpreter, when the reading of the different language versions reflects different meanings, to choose the version that better serves the object and purpose of the treaty. True, article 31.1 may also require the interpreter to make a choice, but the choices available are only those that fit within the ordinary meaning of the terms.

4.3.4 The scope of applicability of the COTIF–CIM convention

The COTIF–CIM convention applies, according to its article 1 "to every contract of carriage of goods by rail for reward". Its wording in English is thus slightly different from the English wording of the CMR convention. However, the wording in French is identical to the wording of the mirroring terms of the CMR convention: *à tout contrat de transport ferroviaire de marchandises à titre onéreux.*[187] It is asserted here that no difference in meaning can be detected (cf. article 33.4 of the Vienna Convention) and that thus the main rule, i.e. that all authentic language versions shall be presumed to have the same meaning, prevails. In addition, should any difference in meaning exist, the French version shall, according to article 45 of the COTIF Convention, prevail.

Accordingly, interpretation of the scope of application of the COTIF–CIM convention is to be carried out in accordance with the general rules of interpretation in articles 31 and 32. As regards the ordinary meaning of the term "contract of carriage of goods by rail", the conclusion must mirror the conclusions made above in relation to the CMR convention, in particular as the French versions of the two conventions are identical. Accordingly, the term refers to an agreement between two parties where one party (the carrier) undertakes to carry goods by rail.[188] In addition, taking into account the following prerequisites of the article, the agreement must provide an obligation to pay freight for the transport. Lastly the carriage must be international. However, in contrast to the CMR convention

186 R. Loewe, "Commentary on the Convention of 19 May 1956 on the Contract for the International Carriage of Goods by Road (CMR)" in (1976) 1 ETL 311–405, at pp. 319–320.

187 The COTIF Convention is authenticated in three language versions: English, French and German. The relevant part in German reads: "jeden Vertrag über die entgeltliche Beförderung von Gütern auf der Schiene".

188 That the contract of carriage requires an undertaking to carry follows, not only from general transport law (cf. section 5.4.1 below) but also explicitly from article 6 §1 of the COTIF–CIM convention.

the carriage must take place between two member states. The formulation of the article indicates that whilst it is the place of delivery according to the contract that is relevant, it is the actual place of the taking over of the goods by the carrier that is relevant in relation to the place of departure.[189]

4.3.4.1 The context

As far as contextual interpretative data for the interpretation of the scope of application in relation to multimodal contracts of carriage are concerned, the following conclusions can be made. The terms "place of taking over" and "place of delivery" of the goods are verbatim to the terms in the CMR convention and thus the same conclusion is drawn. Thus, these terms do not provide any substantive guidance on the interpretation of the scope of application in relation to multimodal contracts of carriage. However, they do not contradict the applicability *ex proprio vigore* of the rules to carriage by rail under multimodal contracts. Also, article 20 §1 of the COTIF–CIM convention has the same wording as article 17 of the CMR convention,[190] so the same conclusions can be drawn. Likewise, the rules on the period of liability and the initiation of the period during which claims may be made, are similar.

The extension of the COTIF–CIM conventions to transports by other modes is more limited than article 2 of the CMR convention as it only applies to ancillary domestic transports and transfrontier carriage by sea or inland waterway where the particular line is registered with the OTIF. Article 1 §3 of the COTIF–CIM is worded slightly differently than article 2 of the CMR convention and states that under certain conditions "these Uniform Rules shall apply" rather than "this Convention shall nevertheless apply to the whole of the carriage". However, the same arguments are valid. Accordingly, neither the wording of article 1 §3, nor its mere existence, contradicts the applicability of the rules of the convention to rail transport under a multimodal contract of carriage.

4.3.4.2 The object and purpose of the treaty

As discussed, the terms of a treaty are to be understood not only in their ordinary meaning in their context, but also in light of the object and purpose of the treaty. The implication of the object and purpose of a treaty has been analyzed above.[191] Accordingly, the raison d'etre of the COTIF–CIM convention is the "eliminat[ion] of the obstacles which persist in the crossing of frontiers in international rail traffic"[192] rather than the mere harmonization of liability (and other)

189 Thus, the relevant part of the article reads: "when the place of taking over of the goods and the place designated for delivery are situated in two different Member States".

190 With the slight variation that "between the time when he takes over the goods" (CMR) has been substituted for "between the time of taking over of the goods" (COTIF–CIM), the latter being more neutral. This modernization does not seem to entail any difference in substance.

191 Cf. section 4.2.2.1 above.

192 Preamble of the 1999 Vilnius protocol. It should be pointed out that although the first railway treaty was drafted in 1890, the 1980 COTIF Convention is considered to be a new convention, rather than an amended version (SOU 2014:26 p. 43). The 1999 protocol is an amendment to the 1980 convention (*ibid.* p. 44).

rules. As mentioned previously, the rationale behind the original convention was focused on the railways rather than on the consingors.[193] The crossing of borders was complicated; there existed technical as well as legal obstacles. The considerable state interest that (still) exists in rail carriage, as well as in carriage by air, is a combination of the ownership interest in the carriers and the interest in controlling the use of the infrastructure (railway and air space respectively).[194] Therefore, whilst the road and sea carriage conventions "serve" the market with uniform rules, there is a considerable degree of cooperation in the conventions governing transport by air and rail.[195] Another purpose of the convention, before the 1999 amendment, was to prevent the misuse of the monopoly position enjoyed by railway carriers, a situation that has now changed.[196]

Accordingly, with the object and purpose of the COTIF–CIM convention to facilitate the crossing of frontiers in the carriage of goods by rail, as well as the continuation of the transport after the border crossing, it is obvious that the interpretation of the scope of application, that the rules of the convention apply to carriage by rail under a multimodal contract of carriage, must be preferred.

As regards supplementary means of interpretation, the *travaux préparatoires* may be used to confirm the interpretation settled for above.[197] During the deliberations leading up to the 1999 amendments, there seems to have been no discussion regarding the issue of the network system. Considerations relating to the possible conflict with other conventions due to the extension of the COTIF–CIM convention to other modes of transport, i.e. situations where the COTIF–CIM convention is applicable to carriage by other modes, were made.[198] A general observation is that, at the time, the network system seems to have been generally applied, and the discussion of the scope of application of the CMR convention in relation to multimodal transport had not yet taken off.[199] The discussion that seems to have taken place relating to the co-existence of the COTIF–CIM convention with other unimodal conventions focused on the principal object of the contract of carriage, i.e. the overall consideration theory. Thus it is held in the report that in settling the respective scope of application of the COTIF–CIM convention and the CMR convention, it should be considered whether the contract is for carriage by rail or carriage by road.[200] It should be further noticed that the initial proposal, that the COTIF–CIM convention would apply also to transfrontier supplementary carriage by road, was amended to the current application to

193 Cf. section 2.2.5 above.

194 S. Johansson, *An Introduction to Transport Law* (2014) p. 51.

195 In relation to air carriage, the use of national air space by foreign air carriers is regulated in the Convention on International Civil Aviation, signed in Chicago 7 December 1944.

196 Thus the obligation to carry imposed on railway carriers, which was removed by the 1999 protocol; see the Consolidated Explanatory Report, OTIF General Assembly AG 12/13 Add. 5 30.09.2015.

197 The deliberations of the 8th Revision Conference have been summarized by the OTIF secretariat in several explanatory reports, available att www.otif.org.

198 Consolidated Explanatory Report, General Assembly AG 12/13 Add. 530.09.2015.

199 Cf. sections 3.4 above and 4.4 below.

200 Consolidated Explanatory Report, General Assembly AG 12/13 Add. 530.09.2015, p. 12*f.*

domestic supplementary carriage by road. The discussion, as accounted for in the report, does not indicate that in the case of supplementary carriage by road that is trans-frontier the COTIF–CIM convention would not apply to the carriage by rail. Further, the very reason for the amendment to domestic road carriage only is the very risk of conflict with the CMR convention, a risk that would not be as imminent had the assembly not considered the CMR convention (as well as the COTIF–CIM convention) applicable to carriage under multimodal contracts of carriage.[201] In summary, it is asserted here that the *travaux préparatoires*, although not comprehensive on the issue, confirms the interpretation of the scope of application of the COTIF–CIM convention that it applies to carriage by rail under multimodal contracts of carriage.

4.3.5 Conclusions

It is generally not without difficulty that the threads of history are to be untangled in order to give an account of previous legal discussions and to draw conclusions therefrom. That said, some careful attempts will be made.

Accordingly, it seems that at the emergence of multimodal contracts, which diverged from previous customs to contract separately for each leg of a transport, the network system was applied without much hesitation. Even so, the need for a unified multimodal regime was perceived (as early as the 1930s, at which point, however, it was considered a theoretical issue without many practical implications[202]) and in the early 1970s the work was initiated on the UN Convention on International Multimodal Transport of Goods.[203] In connection therewith the issue of a possible conflict between the draft convention and existing unimodal conventions must have been raised, the answer to which was the proposition that the conventions regulating the carrier's liability on a unimodal level, primarily the CMR convention, did not apply to the unimodal legs of a multimodal contract.[204] With the non-entry into force of the said convention, the discussion seems to have somewhat abated, as is reflected by the quite unanimous European case law applying the CMR convention to international road stretches that form part of a larger, multimodal carriage contract.[205]

Coinciding with German attempts to draw up national legislation governing multimodal, as well as unimodal, transports, German scholars raised their voices

201 Consolidated Explanatory Report, General Assembly AG 12/13 Add. 530.09.2015, p. 13.

202 The Economic and Commercial Implications of the entry into force of the Hamburg Rules and the Multimodal Transport Convention, Report by the UNCTAD Secretariat, 1991 (http://unctad.org/en/Docs/tdbc4315rev1_en.pdf) p. 22.

203 For a summary of the history of the Multimodal Convention, see The Economic and Commercial Implications of the Entry into Force of the Hamburg Rules and the Multimodal Transport Convention: report by the UNCTAD secretariat TD/B/C.4/315/Rev.1 (1991) pp. 39–51.

204 E. Selvig, "Multimodal transport: the 1980 U.N. Convention: papers of a one day seminar: Southampton University, Faculty of Law, 12th September 1980", at p. A3, para. 2.

205 For a summary of some oft-cited German, Dutch and French cases predating 2008, see *Quantum Corporation Inc v Plane Trucking Ltd* [2002] EWCA Civ 350.

claiming that, for the reasons discussed above, the CMR convention cannot be applicable to carriage by road performed under a multimodal contract.[206] Such interpretation seems to have been in line with the eventually effected German national legislation.[207] In 2008 the German Federal Supreme Court, the BGH, followed German doctrine in holding that the CMR convention was not autonomously applicable to road transport carried out under a multimodal contract.[208]

It is of absolute necessity that uniform law is applied and interpreted uniformly in order for the harmonization sought to be realized.[209] Thus, the German position, if the expression is allowed, is troublesome in terms of the interruption to what, at the time, appeared to be consensual European case law it has caused. This alone does not mean that the position is wrong. Uniformity is not the sole consideration in applying and interpreting uniform law; correctness of interpretation and application are clearly important factors and a delicate problem is posed before the national court weighing what it believes to be a correct interpretation against uniformity, which would follow from adherence to foreign precedent.[210]

Interpreting the scope of application of the CMR convention has indeed proven to be difficult. Various interpretation data are mixed to the point where it is sometimes hard to distinguish the chicken from the egg. Further, "pure" interpretation is often mixed with pragmatic arguments regarding the necessity to apply the CMR convention to all road transport, even if carried out under a multimodal contract, due to lack of regulation of the multimodal transport contract.[211]

It is something of a mantra within the field of legal interpretation, be it interpretation of legislation or contracts, that interpretation is an art. Theories of interpretation have accordingly been described as a painter's palette, a smorgasbord

206 In 1996, Rolf Herber summarized the German BHG's standpoint entailing e.g. that the network principle was applicable to localized damage (R. Herber, "Zur Berücksichtigung des Tailstreckenrechts bei multimodalen Transportvertrag" in *Festschrift für Henning Piper* (1996), cited by L. Andersen Roost, *Multimodale Transporter* (2012) pp. 208–209). In 1992 an expert group was appointed, which in 1996 published its report with a proposal for new German transport legislation. New legislation eventually entered into force in 1998. However, discussions had arisen already following a decision by the BGH in 1987 (BGH 24 June 1987, ZR 127/85).

207 For an account of German national legislation, see L. Andersen Roost, *Multimodale Transporter* (2012) pp. 216–242.

208 German Federal Supreme Court BGH 17 July 2008, I ZR 181/05.

209 F. Berlingieri, "Uniform interpretation of international conventions" (2004) LMCLQ 153–157, at p. 154 and M. Gebauer, "Uniform Law, General Principles and Autonomous Interpretation" (2000) 4 Rev Dr unif 683–705, at p. 684. Hobhouse, on the other hand, holds that the uniformity sought through the implementation of uniform law is illusionary and the uniform law is more likely to cause disuniformity than uniformity (J. Hobhouse, "International conventions and commercial law: the pursuit of uniformity" (1990) 106 LQR 530–535, at p. 532).

210 Sturley, however, points out that the court is more likely to be weighing a correct interpretation that fits into the national legal system against another correct interpretation, which does not fit so good into the national legal system, but will contribute to international uniformity (M. Sturley, "International Uniform Laws in National Courts: The Influence of Domestic Law in Conflicts of Interpretation" (1986–1987) 27 Va J Int'l L 729).

211 Clarke argues that the real question is not whether or not the CMR was originally intended to apply to multimodal contracts, but whether or not it should do so. As the object and purpose of the convention is to standardize the conditions of international carriage of goods by road, and as no multimodal convention has entered into force, his conclusion is that it should (M. Clarke, "A Multimodal Mix Up" (2002) JBL 210–217, at p. 216, citing in part Gebauer [2000] ULR 683, p. 693).

of choices for the interpreter to justify a particular interpretation. It would seem that it is this latter feature that catches the essence of interpretation; there are no rules to follow but the interpreter must trust to skills gained in order to practice the art of interpretation. The lack of rules complicates scrutiny of interpretation. Objective interpretation may be a fiction and theories of interpretation may in fact be used as post-justification of the interpreter's intuitive decision. In relation to international conventions, this conclusion is somewhat modified by the rules of interpretation, which are indeed rules, found in the Vienna Convention.

Above, the arguments brought forward in support of the non-applicability of the CMR convention to carriage by road under multimodal contracts have been scrutinized under the rules of treaty interpretation. The conclusions that could be drawn from that review was that neither of these contextual arguments was conclusive in providing support for the non-applicability of the convention to the discussed contracts. Although the Protocol of Signature to the CMR convention, in which the contracting parties undertook to negotiate a separate convention for combined carriage, seems to show that the drafters of the CMR did not intend the convention to apply to multimodal contracts of carriage in the long run, for the reasons discussed no conclusions can be drawn as to the actual applicability of the convention based on this undertaking. In conclusion, it is asserted here that the arguments thus brought forward do not provide support for the conclusion that the CMR convention is not applicable to carriage by road under a multimodal contract.

Subsequently, a "fresh" analysis of the scope of applicability of the CMR convention was made. The general conclusion of that analysis must be held to be that the CMR convention applies to contracts of carriage by road and that there is no support to exclude certain contracts for carriage of goods by road from the scope of application of the CMR convention, in particular considering the object and purpose of the convention. In addition, an analysis of the scope of application of the COTIF–CIM convention was made. Taking into account the ordinary meaning of the terms of article 1, its meaning in context and with regard to the object and purpose of the convention, it was concluded that the convention applies to carriage by rail under multimodal contracts of carriage. It was also held above that the interpretation made is confirmed by the *travaux préparatoires*.

Further, on a more pragmatic note, it must be concluded that the interpreter of uniform law should perhaps look towards the horizon. Although it may be concluded that interpretation in accordance with the rules of the Vienna Convention to a large extent satisfies the rationale of autonomous interpretation, it does not cater for the dynamic evolution that uniform law is subject to. As Clarke holds: "uniform law is not to be frozen in time … it must be interpreted and developed dynamically".[212] Therefore, arguments relating to the need for the CMR convention to adapt to changing conditions may be significant although not relevant according to the Vienna Convention. As long ago as 1956 the need

212 M. Clarke, *ibid*, at p. 216,.

for a uniform system for multimodal carriage was recognized. However, despite serious attempts, no international regime governing multimodal carriage has yet been realized. Hence, today, we are left with the choice of either applying the convention to such contracts, or recognizing freedom of contract of the parties. Faced with this option, it seems unlikely that the drafters of the CMR convention would have chosen the latter; whilst they predicted the advent of multimodal transport and, whilst recognizing the need to regulate the carriage of goods by road by mandatory rules, the same drafters would not have been prepared to apply the CMR convention to carriage of goods by road when carried out under a multimodal contract. As unlikely as that would seem, today we can only resort to speculation in that regard. However, when it comes to the future of the convention, the question that should be put forward is "do we want the CMR convention to be applicable to international road carriage performed under a multimodal contract?". Although the mandatory applicability as such may be questioned,[213] considering the unmotivated difference between international unimodal carriage by road and international multimodal carriage by road, where the first would be regulated by mandatory rules and the second subject to complete freedom of contract (when the actual carrier might not even know under what sort of overriding contract he is performing the road transport), the answer should perhaps be "yes". Obviously, these observations have no independent effect on the interpretation of article 1 of the CMR convention, but it cannot be completely disregarded from that in practice similar arguments are not infrequently used by courts.

4.4 The scope of application of the Montreal Convention

At first glance, the Montreal Convention appears to be applicable to carriage by air rather than to contracts for air carriage.[214] Although the existence of a contract of, or agreement for, carriage seems to be presupposed, for example in articles 1.2, 9 and 18.4, a contract of carriage is not a formal prerequisite according to the literal reading of the scope of application article of the convention. In contemporary writing, the existence of a contract for carriage of goods has, however, been claimed to be a compulsory prerequisite for application of the Montreal Convention.[215] It may seem a rare occurrence that carriage by air is performed without prior agreement, particularly in light of the requirement in the Montreal Convention that carriage is performed against reward. However in relation to multimodal transport, the issue is not without relevance.[216] Additionally, because

213 F. Lorenzon, "Multimodal Transport Evolving: Freedom and Regulation Three Decades after the 1980 MTO Convention" in M. Clarke (ed.), *Maritime Law Evolving* (2013), pp. 163–180, at p. 167.

214 The Montreal Convention is applicable to carriage of passengers and luggage as well as carriage of goods by air. However, the carriage of passengers and luggage is disregarded in the following.

215 E. Giemulla, *Montreal Convention (Commentary)* article 1–3 and 1–18 (2006).

216 It may be asserted that a carriage of goods by aircraft for reward will seldom, if ever, take place without prior agreement and that, because of the second sentence in article 1.1, which prescribes applicability of the convention to gratuitous carriage by airlines, the situation may be even rarer. However, as will be discussed below, the question of the subject of applicability is of interest in

of modern practices, there may be frequent situations where contracts of carriage are not entered into prior to initiation of the carriage by air (as defined in article 18.3) and which are in fact never formally entered into, but rather entered into through the parties' actions.[217] Further, it has been asserted that the Montreal Convention applies only to unimodal contracts of carriage of goods by air.[218] The issue is however not extensively discussed, but will be subject to analysis in section 4.4.2 below.

4.4.1 A contract of carriage – a prerequisite?

Article 1.1 of the Montreal Convention states: "This Convention applies to all international carriage of ...cargo by aircraft for reward. It applies equally to gratuitous carriage by aircraft performed by an air transport undertaking."

The various prerequisites that have to be fulfilled in order for the convention to be applicable have been discussed above and, at this point, it is the subject of the scope of the convention that will be discussed. Accordingly, discussion will focus on whether the Montreal Convention lays down any requirements as regards the existence of a contract of carriage or if it simply applies to the actual carriage of goods by aircraft.

4.4.1.1 The ordinary meaning

As a starting point, the reading of article 1.1 suggests that the convention applies to the actual carriage of goods by aircraft: "this convention applies to ... *carriage*...". Further, the tempus used to denote the mode of transport, "*performed* by aircraft" can be contrasted with the tempus used in the CMR convention, "contract *for* the carriage". Whilst the former indicates that carriage has already been performed, the latter refers to a carriage, which is to take place in the future. This difference is natural if there in fact is a difference in the respective scope of application of the Montreal Convention on the one hand and the CMR convention on the other hand. A contract precedes performance and contains the carrier's promise to perform the carriage so agreed, at the time indicated in the contract, which, however, is always a later time than the time of entering into the contract. Where a set of rules applies to actual carriage, the rules are not, at least in theory, applicable until performance of the carriage has been initiated. This indicates that the Montreal Convention is not applicable to the contract of carriage by air, but to actual performance by that mode of transport.

relation to multimodal contracts of carriage. Further, the issue is interesting in relation to substitution of modes of transport, and in particular to undefined contracts of carriage.

217 Grönfors refers to such agreements as agreements entered into through direct contract forming legal facts (*direkt avtalsgrundande rättsfaktum*) (K. Grönfors, *Avtalslagen* (1995) p. 65).

218 P. Vestergaard Pedersen, *Transportret* (2008) p. 1014 and L. Andersen Roost, *Multimodale Transporter* (2010) p. 171. See further section 4.4.2 below.

However, whilst the objective meaning of the terms above may seem quite straightforward, the context may indicate otherwise.[219] Several articles of the convention refer to the contract of carriage and it may therefore be, and has been claimed, that a contract of carriage is in fact a prerequisite for application.[220] Although this conclusion is frequently advocated, the basis for the conclusion is often little discussed, and sometimes even not discussed at all.[221] The interpretation in question is thus often just stated as a fact. Where the grounds for such interpretation are actually discussed, the reason put forward is that the text of the convention clearly implies that the drafters had the contract of carriage by air in mind, considering the frequent reference to the contract of carriage as well as to the parties traditionally involved in a carriage contract, such as the carrier, consignor and consignee. Moreover, references are made to the *travaux préparatoires* in support of the said interpretation.[222]

4.4.1.2 The context

The General Rule of treaty interpretation, found in the Vienna Convention article 31, obliges the interpreter to give the terms of the treaty their ordinary meaning. However, in doing so the interpreter must take account of the context of the treaty, as well as the object and purpose thereof, and give the terms their ordinary meaning in context. The context has been discussed above and here it suffices to state that, for the purpose of interpreting article 1 of the Montreal Convention, the context includes the remaining articles of the convention. The question is accordingly whether the context of the Montreal Convention, primarily the remaining articles thereof, entails that the ordinary meaning of the terms of article 1.1 differs from the ordinary meaning as it appears from a plain reading. Several articles in the Montreal Convention refer to the contract of

---

219 Cf. The Rules of Interpretation according to the Vienna Convention, articles 31–33.

220 It may (rightfully) be questioned to what degree this question is of other than theoretical interest; carriage of goods by aircraft for reward will seldom, if ever, take place without prior agreement. However, as will be discussed below, the question of the subject of applicability is of interest in relation to multimodal contracts of carriage and if the Montreal Convention applies to *de facto* performance of carriage by air, the applicability of the convention to air carriage under a multimodal contract is indisputable. Further, the issue is interesting in relation to substitution of modes of transport, and in particular where such substitution is not consented to. Of more theoretical interest is perhaps *negotiorium gestio*, services provided without prior agreement, which, at least in continental European and Scandinavian law, may entitle the "gestor" to remuneration (T. Håstad, *Tjänster utan uppdrag* (1973)). Accordingly, a carrier who finds misplaced cargo and transports it to its correct destination most likely has a right to remuneration for doing so and thus the prerequisites for applicability of the Montreal Convention may be fulfilled. Because of the second sentence, which prescribes applicability of the convention to gratuitous carriage by airlines, the situation may be even rarer. However, it should be noted that *negotiorium gestio* does not include services that the provider intended to perform gratuitously.

221 P. Mendes de Leon, *Isabella Diederiks-Verschoor's An Introduction to Air Law* (2012) p. 135; M. Hoeks, *Multimodal Transport Law* (2010) p. 226; E. Giemulla, *Montreal Convention* Suppl. 6 (January 2010), article 1, p. 3 and P. Vestergaard Pedersen, *Transportrett* (2008) p. 1012. See also *American Block v Compagnie Nationale Air France* (1967) 386 F 2d 323.

222 M. Hoeks, *ibid.*, at p. 226.

carriage, such as articles 1.2, 9, 25–27, 33, 36 and 39. In the following sections, the implication of articles 1.2, 9 and 39 on the interpretation of article 1.1 will be discussed.

ARTICLE 1.2

Article 1.2 is part of the scope of application article of the Montreal Convention and contains a reference to the agreement between the parties.[223] It has even been held that this article explicitly demands the existence of a contract of carriage by air.[224] It is submitted here, however, that article 1.2 relates to the definition of "international carriage" and hence does not contain the stipulation thus proposed. Accordingly, article 1.2 states:

> For the purposes of this Convention, the expression "international carriage" means any carriage in which, according to the agreement between the parties, the place of departure and the place of destination, whether or not there be a break in the carriage or a transshipment, are situated either within the territories of two States Parties, or ....

The purpose of the article is to define the geographical scope of the convention. Thus, it is only carriage by air that starts in one contracting state and ends in another, which, with some additions later in the article, is subject to the rules of the convention. However, it is not the actual places of departure and destination that determine the applicability of the convention, but the places that were agreed between the parties. Hence, the contracting consignor, to use the previously defined term, will be able to settle the applicable rules based on the agreed places of departure and delivery. Any other order would place the contracting consignee in the hands of the carrier, and, for example, the so often practised substitution of air carriage for road carriage would potentially affect application of the rules.[225]

It is submitted here that the reference to the "agreement between the parties" in article 1.2 merely defines the places that form the basis for the geographical scope of the Montreal Convention. Its purpose is to settle what places of

223 Giemulla seems to draw a distinction between agreements and contracts to the effect that agreements are informal and contracts formalised in writing. As the previous "contract" in the Warsaw Convention was substituted for "agreement" in the Hague Protocol, the expression in the Montreal Convention entails that "the agreement need not form part of a contract of carriage" (E. Giemulla, *Montreal Convention* Suppl. 6 (January 2010), article 1, p. 6). This conclusion seems odd to a civil law jurist but may make sense to a common law jurist (the author himself seems to have one foot in each system: www.giemulla.com).

224 Koning holds that there are five cumulative requirements in article 1: (1) a contract of carriage (which, she admits, is not expressly clear, but follows from paragraphs 3 and 4 of article 1); (2) for international transport; (3) of persons, luggage or goods; (4) performed by aircraft; (5) for reward (or gratuitously under the conditions so settled). Thus, she holds that the contract of carriage must be for air transport (I. Koning, *Aansprakelijkheid in het luchtvervoer* (2008) pp. 60–61). Also, Giemulla seems to hold that the existence of a contract of carriage by air, rather than just a contract of carriage, is necessary, although the two terms appear to be used somewhat incautiously: see para. 29 of article 1 (E. Giemulla, *ibid.*, article 1, p. 18).

225 Also, unforeseeable events such as hijacking would affect applicability of the convention to a particular transport, as suggested by Clarke (M. Clarke, *Contract of carriage by air* (2010) p. 42).

departure and destination are relevant for application of the convention. It thus establishes that it is not the actual places where the goods are picked up and delivered by the air carrier that are important, but the places so agreed between the parties.[226] Accordingly, article 1.2, it is submitted, provides no support for the interpretation of article 1.1 that a contract of carriage is mandatorily required for application of the convention.

Article 9

Article 9 of the Montreal Convention, which regulates the effects of non-compliance with the documentary requirements of the articles preceding article 9, states:

> Non-compliance with the provisions of Articles 4 to 8 shall not affect the existence or the validity of the contract of carriage, which shall, nonetheless, be subject to the rules of this Convention including those relating to limitation of liability.

This article mentions not just the agreement between the parties, but also the actual contract of carriage. It relates to the consequences of the carrier's obligation to issue an air waybill, together with a few formal requirements of the waybill. Without this particular rule, the carrier could hold a vital key to the very existence of a contract of carriage; were unilateral action by the carrier of non-compliance with mandatory rules to render the entire contract invalid, the carrier could e.g. prevent legal consequences due to breach of contract by not issuing an air waybill. In addition, however, the article contains an interesting, and, considering article 1.1, perhaps curious, statement, indicating that the contract of carriage is subject to the convention rather than the actual performance of carriage by air: "[the contract of carriage] shall, nonetheless, be subject to the rules of this Convention".

As discussed previously, it is commonly assumed that a convention makes up a logical whole, and that therefore the norms expressed in the convention should be interpreted systematically and with avoidance of logical contradictions.[227] Thus, in interpreting a convention, the interpreter should avoid any interpretation that entails contradictions between different parts of the treaty.[228] If article 1.1 is interpreted to indicate that the Montreal Convention is applicable to performance rather than contracts of carriage, the question introduces itself whether this leads to a logical contradiction with article 9. It seems rather clear that the drafters of the Montreal Convention envisaged a contract of carriage to form the basis of carriage by aircraft. Such a starting point is, as concluded above, rather logical considering that carriage without prior agreement ought to be a rare occurrence. Nevertheless, the drafters have chosen to express the scope of application by referring to performance rather than a carriage contract. Conversely, presupposing the existence of a contract of carriage, mention of such a contract throughout

226 M. Clarke, *ibid.*, at p. 42.
227 U. Linderfalk, *On the Interpretation of Treaties* (2007) pp. 105–106.
228 U. Linderfalk, *ibid.*, at p. 107.

the convention is natural. For example, article 27 states that the carrier may waive any defence available under the convention and that the parties may conclude any condition in their contract as long as such condition does not conflict with the convention. This stipulation does not, in itself, demand the existence of a contract. In fact, it shows that the articles of the convention are not necessarily entirely compatible, and that the convention does not make up an altogether logical whole.[229] Accordingly, it is submitted that there is no contradiction between applicability to performance by air and mention of a contract of carriage in other parts of the convention.

Article 9 would thus not be logically contradictory to application of the convention to performance by air, not requiring the existence of a contract of carriage. However, article 9 *in fine* does indeed seem to indicate that it is in fact the contract of carriage that is the subject of the mandatory rules of the regime.

In addition to the rules on carrier's liability, the Montreal Convention contains a considerable number of rules on air waybills and other documentation as well as rules on the duties of the parties, which are found in its Chapter II. These rules impose obligations on the parties and do not in themselves depend upon the existence of a contract of carriage. They may however not be departed from by contract, at least not to the detriment of the contracting consignor. The rules are accordingly mandatory so that non-compliance therewith would generally entail some effect, such as invalidity of the underlying contract of carriage. Assuming that the Montreal Convention does not apply primarily to the contract of carriage but to performance of carriage by air, the non-compliance with the rules in the convention cannot render the contract of carriage invalid because the contract does not fall within the sphere of the convention. If the rules of the convention apply to performance of carriage by aircraft, the underlying contract, although presumed to exist, remains unaffected because the contract is not subject to the rules, and thus falls outside its competence. The statement in article 9 confirms this conclusion as it explicitly states that the contract of carriage is not affected by non-compliance with the rules in articles 4–8. In this interpretation, the rule in article 9 seems logically compatible with article 1.1.

True, article 9 clearly states that the contract of carriage is *nonetheless* subject to the rules of the convention. Thus, article 9 may support the interpretation of article 1.1 that the Montreal Convention is applicable to contracts of carriage. At the same time, it should be borne in mind that the wording of article 1.1 ought to weigh more heavily since that article, contrary to article 9, explicitly concerns

229 Article 27 states:

> Nothing contained in this Convention shall prevent the carrier from refusing to enter into any contract of carriage, from waiving any defences available under the Convention, or from laying down conditions which do not conflict with the provisions of this Convention.

which is not entirely compatible with either interpretation of the scope of application of the convention. Thus, the stipulation of the carrier's freedom to contract (or to refuse to do so) concerns dealings between the carrier and the contracting consignor before the convention applies to such dealings, independently of whether the convention applies to the contract of carriage or to the actual performance of carriage by air.

the scope of application. Besides, it must be remembered that interpretation in accordance with article 31.1 of the Vienna Convention must never establish a meaning of a term that is contrary to its objective meaning.[230]

CHAPTER V

Chapter V of the Montreal Convention regulates carriage carried out by a carrier (actual carrier) other than the contracting carrier. A point of interest in this respect is the term "contracting carrier" as well as article 1.4, which provides that: "This Convention applies also to carriage as set out in Chapter V, subject to the terms contained therein." Notably, the word "also" indicates that the type of carriage regulated in Chapter V is not covered by the previous paragraphs of article 1. Assuming that the Montreal Convention applies to actual performance by aircraft, the stipulation in article 1.4 appears somewhat redundant. Under such a presumption, the Montreal Convention applies to any actual carriage by aircraft as long as the contract provides that the carriage starts in one contracting state and ends in another. Where the contract of carriage thus provides for international carriage, purely national legs of the carriage are also subject to the rules of the convention. However, as Chapter V provides certain rules applicable not only to the contracting carrier, but also to the actual carrier, Chapter V would still enlarge the scope of application of the convention. Where sub-carriers are involved there are two layers of contracts; one between the contracting consignor and the contracting carrier and one between the contracting carrier and the sub-carrier. Assuming that the sub-carriage is domestic, the sub-carrier's liability towards the contracting carrier under the sub-carriage contract would not be subject to the Montreal Convention, save for Chapter V. Chapter V thus provides for back-to-back liability for the contracting carrier, as well as entitling the cargo interests to claim from the actual carrier directly.[231] As article 1 explicitly defines the scope of application of the convention, paragraph 4 serves a purpose. Accordingly, article 1.4, as well as the word "also", seems to be compatible with the interpretation of the Montreal Convention as applicable to actual carriage by air.

If, on the other hand, it is assumed that the Montreal Convention does require a contract of carriage for its applicability,[232] it has been held that such an interpretation is in fact contradicted by article 1.4.[233] The argument made is thus that article 1.4 is redundant where the convention is to apply to contracts of carriage rather than to performance. However, to the contrary the stipulation seems quite logical under such a presumption. Where the convention is considered applicable to the contract of carriage, the convention is only applicable to contracts that are international in the sense prescribed in article 1.2. Thus, sub-carriage contracts may fall entirely outside the scope of the Montreal Convention. Accordingly,

230 U. Linderfalk, *On the Interpretation of Treaties* (2007) p. 102.

231 I. Koning, *Aansprakelijkheid in het luchtvervoer* (2008) pp. 70–71.

232 It should be noted that the Montreal Convention refers only to "contract of carriage" and never to "contract of carriage by air".

233 I. Koning, *ibid.*, at p. 61.

article 39 et seq. hold that where the contract between the contracting consignor and the contracting carrier is international, all sub-carriage carried out under that contract is subject to the rules of the convention.[234] Therefore, inclusion of article 1.4 is, if not necessary, at least clarifying where the convention is also considered applicable to contracts of carriage.

In conclusion, therefore, article 1.4 seems to serve a purpose irrespective of which interpretation of article 1.1 it is contrasted with. Chapter V of the convention enlarges the scope of application of the convention to actual carriers where sub-carriage performed by that carrier would not otherwise have been subject to the convention, e.g. because of its non-conformity with article 1.2. As article 1 regulates the scope of application of the convention, a reference to the provisions of Chapter V in that article is in order. In fact, it promotes the uniformity and logic of the convention.

4.4.1.3 Performance or contract – conclusions

The ordinary meaning of the terms of article 1.1 of the Montreal Convention, "carriage of … cargo performed by aircraft", denotes that the convention is applicable to actual carriage rather than to the contract of carriage. Reading the remaining articles of the convention, the interpreter may, however, be somewhat confused. Thus, e.g. article 9 seems to indicate that the convention is in fact applicable to the contract of carriage rather than actual performance of carriage by air.

The context of a treaty is, according to the Vienna Convention, a means of interpreting ambiguous terms of a treaty. Thus, theoretically, where the objective meaning of a term is clear, using the context for interpretation thereof is superfluous. However, where the context confuses the interpreter it seems difficult to maintain that the term in question is unambiguous; the interpretational data affect perception of the term as clear or unclear (perhaps this could be termed the "sneak-peek problem").[235] The question is accordingly how the context may influence the primary understanding of the terms. No single rule of a convention can exist in a vacuum, which is confirmed by the Vienna Convention under which the ordinary meaning of a term in its context prevails rather than the ordinary meaning. Even if it has been held that interpretation and application are diverse, and that interpretation "is a secondary process which only comes into play when it is impossible to make sense of the plain terms of the treaty",[236] it seems somewhat artificial to make such a distinction. Likewise, it seems artificial to apply the terms of an article of a treaty, which

234 I. Koning, *ibid.* at pp. 70–71.

235 Cf. the discussion of the doctrine of clear meaning above. It is noted here that writers do not generally consider the "sneak-peak-problem". For example, Linderfalk in his conclusion of 44 rules of interpretation, holds that where the ordinary meaning of a term is clear, the provision should be understood in line therewith (rule 1) and that it is only when such interpretation leads to conflicting results that the context of the treaty is to be considered (rule 2) (U. Linderfalk, *On the Interpretation of Treaties* (2007) p. 387).

236 A.D. McNair, *Law of Treaties* (1961) p. 365, fn. 1.

is clear in itself, but where the context indicates that clarity is compromised, in accordance with the prima facie clear meaning. Thus the International Court of Justice, the ICJ, has held that the ordinary meaning of terms must make sense in their context in order for the court to settle for the interpretation suggested by the ordinary meaning.[237] This seems to be a reasonable approach and, thus, although "terms" clearly refers to the very words of a particular article of a convention, rather than to the entire convention,[238] these terms cannot be read separately from their context.[239] The "sneak-peek" is hence an obligation rather than a problem and the understanding and interpretation of the terms of a treaty must consider the entire convention.[240] However, it is always the ordinary meaning of the terms that is the starting point and no interpretation may neglect the text. Accordingly, no interpretation that does not emerge from the text can be accepted.[241]

The textual context of the Montreal Convention, i.e. the remaining articles of the convention, clearly indicates that the drafters presupposed the underlying existence of a contract of carriage. This is not in itself an indication that they envisaged the contract of carriage to be a mandatory prerequisite for applicability. It is submitted that article 9 is the strongest argument to the effect that the convention in fact applies to contracts for carriage of goods by air, rather than to performance thereof. Article 9 must, however, be considered subordinate to article 1 as far as defining the scope of application is concerned. Therefore, it is not an argument strong enough to change the ordinary meaning of article 1, which is application to performance of carriage by air, which does not *per se* require the existence of a contract of carriage.

4.4.2 Unimodal or multimodal transport

During the UNCITRAL working group meetings that eventually led to adoption of the Rotterdam Rules, the relationship of the new convention with existing transport conventions was discussed quite extensively. Various views were expressed regarding the possible risk of conflict between the Rotterdam Rules and the existing conventions. In the background study by the Secretariat, discussion on the applicability of the CMR convention to multimodal contracts

---

237 Gardiner summarizes the opinion of the ICJ as:

the ordinary meaning is the starting point of an interpretation; but only if it is confirmed by investigating the context and object and purpose, and if on examining all other relevant matters ... no contra-diction is found, the ordinary meaning is determinative.

(R. Gardiner, *Treaty Interpretation* (2015) p. 185).

238 R. Gardiner, *ibid.*, at p. 164.

239 A conclusion that supports the proposal that the Vienna Convention do not presuppose the doctrine of clear meaning but rather applies to interpretation in the sense of understanding; no ambiguity needs to have been detected before the rules of articles 31–33 are applied.

240 R. Gardiner, *ibid.*, at p. 181.

241 R. Gardiner, *ibid.*, at p. 165, citing H. Berglin; "Treaty interpretation and the impact of contractual choice of forum clauses on the jurisdiction of international tribunals: the Iranian forum clause decisions of the Iran–United States Claims Tribunal" (1985) 21(1) Tex Int LJ 39–65.

of carriage was briefly mentioned.[242] Thus the problem related to the scope of application of the CMR convention being "contracts for the carriage of goods by road" was mentioned. As for the perceived risk of conflict between the Rotterdam Rules and the Montreal Convention, the same discussion was not reiterated, which would indicate that problems of collision between the two conventions were not perceived. However, if the Montreal Convention is considered applicable to the *de facto* performance of carriage by air, a risk of conflict with the Rotterdam Rules is imminent.

Further, article 38.1 of the Montreal Convention contains an explicit rule regarding multimodal carriage:

> In the case of combined carriage performed partly by air and partly by any other mode of carriage, the provisions of this Convention shall, subject to paragraph 4 of Article 18, apply only to the carriage by air, provided that the carriage by air falls within the terms of Article 1.

There should accordingly be no doubt that the Montreal Convention, as a starting point, applies to air carriage, which is part of a multimodal carriage.[243] The wording of article 38.1 seems to presuppose applicability of the convention to air carriage, independently of any pre- or onward carriage by other modes; "this convention shall … apply *only* to the carriage by air". Thus, the rule does not prescribe such applicability but merely confirms what already follows from the convention, supposedly from article 1. In addition, article 38.1 holds that the convention is not applicable to any other mode of transport. Considering the wording of article 1.1, article 38.1 seems to state the obvious: if the convention is applicable to carriage performed by air, it is accordingly not applicable to carriage performed by any other mode of transport.

Assuming that the Montreal Convention requires the existence of a contract for the carriage of goods by air for its application, then the scope of application of the convention ought to be subject to the same discussion regarding its application to carriage by air under a multimodal contract as is the CMR convention. Assuming further that the Montreal Convention was accordingly to apply only to unimodal contracts of carriage by air, article 38.1 would be impossible to apply, as carriage would in that case never fall under article 1 if it were subject to a multimodal contract of carriage. It could be argued that the perceived requirement under the Montreal Convention of a contract of carriage does not necessarily entail the same problems of interpretation as the CMR convention since the two conventions are two separate international instruments and their

242 A/CN.9/WG.III/WP.29 – Transport Law: preparation of a draft instrument on the carriage of goods [by sea] – general remarks on the sphere of application of the draft instrument, accessible from the UNCITRAL website: www.uncitral.org/uncitral/en/commission/working_groups/3Transport.html.

243 However, as regards the CMR convention, it is not the multimodal carriage, but the multimodal contract, that is the problem; road carriage that is subject to a unimodal contract but part of a multimodal transport, i.e. the multimodal transport is not subject to one contract, is undoubtedly subject to the CMR convention.

wordings are not identical. However, as it has been claimed that the Montreal Convention requires for its application (1) transport of goods by aircraft, (2) under a contract of carriage by aircraft and (3) that the place of departure and place of destination according to that contract are in two contracting states, it would seem somewhat arbitrary to advocate the applicability of the Montreal Convention to carriage under a multimodal contract whilst holding the CMR convention non-applicable.[244]

On the other hand, the circumstances in which the perceived requirement of a contract of carriage is based, such as those in article 1.2 and article 9, only mention a contract of carriage, rather than a contract for carriage of goods by air. Thus, it may be argued that the convention only requires a contract of carriage for its application, irrespective of what mode of transport it provides for. This would mean that carriage by air subject to a multimodal contract is governed by the convention, as well as carriage by air under an unspecified contract of carriage. However, it is difficult to see what motives the drafters of the Montreal Convention could have had for such an awkward construction, especially since in fact the result will be the same as if the convention is considered to be applicable to performance of carriage by air, with a non-mandatory presumption of the existence of an underlying contract of carriage by air.

Assuming that the Montreal Convention is applicable to carriage of goods performed by air, it must be assumed that article 38.1 refers to multimodal transport in the legal sense, i.e. carriage by more than one mode subject to one single contract. Thus, the rule seems to hold that although there is one single contract of carriage, it is only the carriage by air that is subject to the convention. As mentioned above, this is not entirely compatible with the presumption of the convention as a logical whole. On the contrary, article 38.1 would seem to be a tautology, merely repeating what already follows from article 1.1.[245] However, the only interpretation of article 38.1 that makes it non-redundant is that the Montreal Convention applies prima facie to contracts of carriage in its undefined sense, but that where such a contract includes carriage by other modes in addition to carriage by air, article 38.1 narrows the application of the convention to the part of the contract performed by air only.

Several arguments can be made against such an interpretation. First of all: article 1.1 clearly limits the scope of application of the convention to carriage by

244 Cf. Vestergaard Pedersen who suggests that the CMR convention is not applicable to road transport under a multimodal contract (p. 984). He then asserts that the Montreal Convention requires a contract of carriage by air (p. 1012). Interestingly he then holds that the Montreal Convention is applicable to performance by aircraft being part of a multimodal transport to the extent it is subject to a contract for carriage by air (p. 1013). By the latter statement, either Vestergaard Pedersen means that the air carriage may be part of a multimodal transport, but not subject to a multimodal contract, or he is inconsistent in his reasoning (P. Vestergaard Pedersen, *Transportrett* (2008)).

245 As discussed in section 4.2.2 above, according to the rules of interpretation, the assumption can be made that the drafters of a treaty have not expressed themselves so that one rule becomes a legal tautology, i.e. every rule has an independent purpose and meaning and if a rule is interpreted to merely repeat a previous rule, such interpretation is inaccurate (U. Linderfalk, *On the Interpretation of Treaties* (2007) pp. 117–124).

aircraft. The inclusion of a mandatory prerequisite of the existence of a contract of carriage may be discussed, but although the rest of the convention refers to *contracts of carriage* rather than to *contracts for carriage by air*, an interpretation that extends the scope of application of the convention to any contract of carriage is no doubt, it is asserted here, stretching the tool of interpretation a bit too far. A second objection to be made against the thus proposed interpretation is that the scope of application is regulated by article 1 and the limitation of the scope, which the suggested interpretation of article 38 entails, ought to be included in article 1. Besides given that article 1 is headed "Scope of application", it would be not only an unconventional way of regulating the scope of application, but, considering the special features of uniform law discussed above it would undermine the legal foreseeability of the parties, i.e. the carrier and the consignor, whose actions will be subject to the mandatory rules of the convention.

Further, assuming that the Montreal Convention is applicable to contracts of carriage by air, article 38 would be difficult, if not impossible, to apply. The article would then provide that where carriage by air is performed under a multimodal contract, as multimodal transport under separate unimodal contracts would not have to be regulated separately (cf. above), the convention applies only to the carriage by air. So far, so good. However, the subsequent requirement that the carriage by air must fall under the provisions of article 1 complicates the equation; no multimodal contract would, it could be proposed with support from the legal theories discussed in section 4.3.1, qualify as a contract for the carriage of goods by air.

One last possibility remains: if the Montreal Convention is to be considered applicable to contracts for the carriage by air, if a contract of carriage is interpreted to include air carriage performed under a multimodal contract of carriage, then to a certain extent article 38 would provide clarifying information not necessarily immediately clear from article 1. Although it could be considered clear already from article 1.1 that it applies only to carriage by air, even when the underlying contract is a multimodal contract, article 38 is at least not a legal tautology in this respect. Further, the air carriage would qualify under article 1 as required by article 38.

The only reservations to such an interpretation are the CMR convention on the one hand, and regulation of carriage under multimodal contracts on the other. As thoroughly discussed in section 4.3 above, it is sometimes held that the term "contract for the carriage of goods by road" found in the CMR convention excludes any carriage by road not performed under unimodal road carriage contracts. The arguments therefore are to some extent unique to the CMR convention, such as the French version of the text and the undertaking found in the protocol of signatories. The difference in interpretation would nevertheless be disturbing. It could be asserted that the CMR, although a UN convention, is mainly a European matter whilst the Montreal Convention has global adherence and that interpretation of a regional convention should perhaps not be allowed to affect interpretation of a global convention. It could further be asserted that the interpretation that the Montreal Convention for its application requires the existence of a contract of carriage does not mean that the scope of application of that convention mirrors the scope of application of the CMR convention. In fact, this is a major difficulty with concluding that the Montreal Convention requires for its application a contract of carriage; as the prerequisite is only implied there is no term prescribing the application of the convention to contracts of carriage that can be compared with the scope of application of e.g. the CMR convention. There is a major benefit in endeavouring uniform interpretation of transport law as a whole.[246] Thus, interpretation of the individual conventions that entail disharmony within the collective of various unimodal conventions ought to be avoided.

Coming back to the Rotterdam Rules, the drafters of the "maritime-plus" convention have certainly presupposed the applicability of the Montreal Convention to carriage by air even when that carriage is performed under a contract that provides for multiple modes of transport, cf. article 82 of the Rotterdam Rules. The same position is supported by others.[247] It must accordingly be concluded that, even though there may be doubts as to the scope of applicability of the Montreal Convention, there can be no doubt that, based on article 38, it applies to carriage by air regardless of the type of contract such transport is carried out under.

Further, the following reflections can be made. In relation to the type of carriage contracts that have been referred to as undefined contracts of carriage and incorrectly defined contracts of carriage, the distinction between contract of carriage and contract of carriage by air is important. As article 38 refers to combined carriage rather than to contracts for combined carriage, the Montreal Convention would apply to carriage by air performed in relation to contracts that may not be multimodal at the outset, but are carried out by more than one mode of transport under the invocation of a right of substitution. However, this conclusion only holds to the extent that the convention applies to contracts of carriage (in general) rather than to contracts of carriage by air (assuming that the convention requires a contract of carriage for its applicability at all). Further, contracts that provide for transport by another mode, which is substituted for carriage by air, would be subject to the convention under the same assumption. As discussed above, the proposition that for its application the Montreal Convention requires not only a contract of carriage but that such contract must provide for carriage by air, does not seem to be well founded, but rather contradicted by the interpretation of the treaty. It is hence concluded here that the Montreal Convention applies to carriage by air performed in relation to undefined as well as incorrectly defined contracts of carriage, irrespective of whether the treaty is concluded to be applicable to actual performance of carriage by air or only when such carriage is subject to a contract of carriage.

4.4.3 Conclusions

It is quite clear that the Montreal Convention is based on a presumption that carriage performed by air is subject to an agreement, a contract of carriage.

246 Swedish Supreme Court NJA 2016 s. 563 para. 27.
247 M. Sturley *et al.*, *The Rotterdam Rules* (2010) p. 72.

This presumption is clear throughout the convention and quite natural. It seems unlikely, or at least uncommon, that carriage by air is performed without a preceding agreement. Further, to the extent carriage does takes place in the absence of a contract of carriage, it may not be subject to the rules of the convention anyway as, without a contract of carriage, the carrier may not be entitled to payment of freight, the latter being a prerequisite for the application of the Montreal Convention. However, in relation to multimodal carriage, transport by air may be carried without previous (express) agreement. The question is thus not without practical interest.

There is an overwhelming consensus that for its application the Montreal Convention demands the existence of a contract of carriage. Thus, Koning holds the contract of carriage as one of four cumulative prerequisites for application; Hoeks concludes that the general opinion is that the convention requires a contract of carriage; Dempsey and Milde hold, in relation to passengers, that crew members' presence on board is subject to a labour contract and not to a contract for international carriage, and seems thus to consider a contract of carriage necessary for application of the convention.[248] Again, Andersen Roost concludes, after some discussion, that the Montreal Convention requires a contract of carriage for its application,[249] as does Vestergaard Pedersen.[250] Giemulla holds that paragraph 1 read in conjunction with paragraph 2 "appears to impose the requirement of a contract of carriage".[251] Several authors do not consider the question in particular, but point to the presumption of a contract of carriage that seems to be obvious in the convention, although without making the distinction between prerequisite and presumption.[252]

Without opposing the arguments put forward in support of an interpretation to the effect that the Montreal Convention requires a contract of carriage for its application, which is mainly the frequent appearance of the contract of carriage in the remaining articles of the convention, there seems to be reason to question the ascension of a presumption to a prerequisite. The Montreal Convention expressly applies to carriage performed by aircraft. The prerequisites that clearly appear from the scope of application rule are: (1) carriage of cargo (etc.) performed by aircraft; (2) the carriage must be international; and (3) the carriage

248 P. Dempsey and M. Milde, *International Air Carrier Liability; The Montreal Convention of 1999* (2005) p. 67.

249 L. Andersen Roost, *Multimodale Transporter* (2012) pp. 163–165.

250 P. Vestergaard Pedersen, *Transportret* (2008) p. 1012. Ulfbeck and Taiger Ivø conclude that, according to Danish precedence, a requirement of a contract of carriage seems to be imposed, although their view appears to be that such a requirement does not find support in the text of the convention (V. Ulfbeck and S. Taiger Ivø, "Optioner og ansvar i transportaftaler" (2008) 4 Erhvervsjuridisk Tidskrift 331–343, at p. 332).

251 E. Giemulla, *Montreal Convention (Commentary)* Suppl. 6 (January 2010), article 1, p. 18.

252 In relation to article 1.2, Clarke considers the contract of carriage as the denominator for the international character of the transport, rather than as a prerequisite for application of the convention (M. Clarke, *Contracts for Carriage by Air* (2010) p. 42). Heidbrink holds that a contract of carriage is necessary; however, this statement seems to be made in relation to the practical necessity (no transport will ever take place for reward without a previous contract) rather than as a legal requirement (J. Heidbrink, *Logistikavtalet* (2005) p. 47).

must be for reward (or gratuitous if performed by an air transport undertaking). These requirements appear from article 1.1. The subsequent paragraphs define the internationality criteria (para. 2); clarify the status of successive carriage (para. 3) and extend application of the convention to actual carriers (para. 4). The scope of application rule contains no explicit requirement of a contract of carriage. However, the terms of article 1 must be interpreted in their context and indeed the rest of the convention frequently refers to the contract of carriage. The impact of the textual context on the interpretation of article 1 does not seem to be too great. Although the very reference to the contract of carriage may affect the ordinary meaning of the terms of article 1, these references are at the same time independent of the scope of application.

The presumption of a contract of carriage is, in the textual context of the Montreal Convention, indeed an implication that could affect the interpretation of article 1. However, in order to interpret the scope of application to target the contract of carriage rather than performance of carriage by air would be to give the term an entirely different meaning than its wording suggests. It is a rather unanimous stand-point within the legal field of treaty interpretation that no interpretation of treaties may depart from the ordinary meaning of the term interpreted. Thus, an interpretation to the effect that the Montreal Convention applies to contracts of carriage rather than to actual performance seems to be contrary to international law.

Against this conclusion it may be held that it has not been suggested that the Montreal Convention should be interpreted contrary to its wording. However, it is difficult to see how considering the contract of carriage to be a prerequisite for application of the convention would not amount to an interpretation contrary to the wording of article 1.1. Indeed, it is often held that such interpretation follows from paragraph 2 of the very same article 1. However, it has been shown above that article 1.2 merely refers to the agreement between the parties, as opposed to actual carriage, in order to define international carriage. It is suggested here that it does not follow from article 1 that for its application the convention requires a contract of carriage. It is admitted that the subsequent articles of the convention suggest that the drafters presumed the existence of a contract of carriage. This does not, however, necessarily entail that the convention should be considered applicable to contracts rather than to actual performance. To the contrary, it seems entirely plausible to consider the convention applicable to actual carriage by air, with the existing presumption of the actual existence of a contract of carriage. Under such an interpretation it is not necessary to consider the contract of carriage a prerequisite for application, but it is merely assumed to exist.

The conclusion thus drawn here is that it seems to be unquestionable that, based on article 38.1, the Montreal Convention applies to air carriage regardless of whether such carriage is part of a multimodal transport. However, the existence of the same article 38.1 does also complicate the interpretation of the scope of application of the convention. Thus, as discussed above, the interpretation that provides the best explanation for inclusion of article 38.1 in the convention seems to be that the Montreal Convention is applicable to contracts for carriage by aircraft, but that such contracts may be part of a multimodal contract of carriage, i.e. the opposite to what is often advocated regarding the CMR convention.

The inclusion of article 38.1 is harder to justify where the Montreal Convention is considered to be applicable to actual carriage by air. As concluded above, however, such interpretation has strong support, and it would therefore appear that article 38.1 is merely a restatement or clarification of what already follows from article 1. An interpretation to the effect that the Montreal Convention is applicable to actual carriage by air makes article 38.1 somewhat redundant, but it is held here that such interpretation is the better choice between two less perfect interpretations.[253]

4.5 The scope of application of the Hague–Visby Rules

The sphere of applicability of the Hague–Visby Rules is not explicitly clear, but has to be concluded from several articles of the convention. Whilst the geographical scope of the convention appears from article X, article II provides that the carrier is subject to the rules of the convention in relation to "every contract of carriage of goods by sea". However, the definition of the contract of carriage in article I (b) limits the scope of application to contracts of carriage under which a bill of lading (or similar document of title) is to be issued (see further below). This has led to the sometimes proposed interpretation that the rules apply to bills of lading.[254] Because there is a difference between applicability to contracts that prescribe for the issuance of a bill of lading and applicability to a bill of lading so issued, the interpretation of the scope of applicability of the Hague–Visby Rules will be further explored.[255]

4.5.1 Contract of carriage of goods by sea

Article II provides the material scope of applicability of the Hague–Visby Rules. Thus, the convention subjects *carriers* to the responsibilities and liabilities set out in the convention.[256] However, article II provides that the liability imposed on the carrier under the rules is germane "under every contract of carriage of goods by sea". Thus, the carrier is liable for carriage of goods but only in so far as, and

253 I read an article regarding interpretation of conventions in which the author held that perhaps it is not always possible to assume that the convention makes up a perfectly logical whole, but that sometimes it is just a matter of imperfect drafting. Although I have spent (too) much time trying to relocate that article, I have not succeeded; a problem that may be familiar to some.

254 P. Vestergaard Pedersen, *Transportret* (2008) p. 465.

255 The Hague–Visby Rules are generally incorporated into national legislation, such as the English COGSA, the Scandinavian Maritime Codes etc. Accordingly, the literature relating to the rules generally relate to the national legislation rather than to the rules as such, with the effect that such literature tends to be rather "national". Due to linguistic limitations, the literature referred to in the current section thus relates primarily to English and Scandinavian conditions.

256 "Carrier" is defined in article 1 (a) as the contracting carrier.

to the extent that, the carriage is subject to a contract of carriage. This suggests accordingly that the Hague–Visby Rules apply to contracts of carriage.[257]

The term "*under* every contract" seems to indicate that the contract of carriage sets the outer limits for the carrier's liability. For example, article II holds the carrier liable for the loading of the goods, but only in so far as the contract provides that the carrier is to perform the loading.[258]

The "contract of carriage" is further defined in article I (b) and is thus qualified to the extent that only contracts of carriage that are covered by a bill of lading, or similar document of title, are considered contracts of carriage under the rules.[259] There is an obvious non-conformity between the scope of applicability in article II to contracts of carriage (of goods) by sea and the definition in article I (b) of contracts of carriage. Rather than defining the term "contract of carriage by sea", the definition of the contract of carriage is made subject to the bill of lading being for maritime transport. The interrelationship between article II and article I (b) is not uncomplicated; however some of the confusion is likely due to the division between contracts of carriage and bills of lading, which was not as articulated in the 1920s.

Further, article III.3 contains an obligation resting on the carrier to issue a bill of lading to the shipper, if the shipper so requests.[260] The obligation thus prescribed entails a somewhat logical inconsistency if the convention is held to apply to bills of lading rather than to the contract of carriage. If the applicability of the rules of the convention presupposes the existence of a bill of lading, the obligation prescribed in article III is somewhat redundant.[261] Thus, the interpretation in question is not in coherence with the general rules of interpretation of treaties.[262] Accordingly, it must be presumed that this obligation only applies if the carrier has undertaken to issue a bill of lading. As will be discussed below, the convention applies to contracts of carriage covered by a bill of lading, i.e. a contract that prescribes (or allows) for the issuance of a bill of lading.[263] Thus, if the contract of carriage is not covered by a bill of lading, the rules of the

257 F. Sejersted, *Haagreglene* (1976) p. 32.

258 G. Treitel and F. Reynolds, *Carver on Bills of Lading* (2011) p. 657.

259 Article 1(b). In the current context, it is only the first part of the article that will be discussed. The latter part ("including a bill of lading ... between a carrier and a holder of the same") relates only to bills of lading issued in relation to a charter party. In fact the very last part ("from the moment ... between a carrier and a holder of the same") was added at the Brussels Conference in 1922 to make it clear that if a bill of lading is issued in relation to carriage under a charter party, the terms of the bill of lading do not replace the terms of the charter party as between the parties to the same (The Brussels Conference Proces-Verbaux, 24 October 1922, reproduced in M. Sturley (ed.), *The Legislative History of the Carriage by Sea Act and the Travaux Preparatoires of the Hague Rules*, vol. I (1990) p. 349 *ff.* at pp. 350–351). See also R. Temperley, *Carriage of Goods by Sea Act 1924* (1932) p. 16.

260 Article III.3 reads: "After receiving the goods into his charge the carrier or the master or agent of the carrier shall, on demand of the shipper, issue to the shipper a bill of lading showing among other things: ...".

261 Cf. *Anticosti Shipping Co v Viateur St-Amand* [1959] 1 Lloyd's Rep 352, at p. 354.

262 U. Linderfalk, *On the Interpretation of Treaties* (2007) p. 108.

263 *The Swedish Maritime Code* defines the applicability of the Hague–Visby Rules as "maritime carriage of goods between two states when a bill of lading is to be issued" (SFS 1994:1009, ch. 13 article 1). Likewise the preparatory works state regarding the applicability of the Hague–Visby Rules:

convention are not applicable to the carriage, and accordingly the shipper cannot invoke the right embedded in article III.3.[264] However, in relation to the Hague Rules, at a time when other transport documents were not as common, the prevailing opinion seems to have been that the rules obliged the carrier to issue a bill of lading, at least at the request of the shipper.[265] It was considered that, without this requirement, the rules would be too easily circumvented, and their mandatory application undermined. The interpretation thus advocated would entail that all contracts of (international) carriage of goods by sea would be subject to the Hague–Visby Rules, at least to the extent that the shipper so wished, and that the carrier would be obliged to issue a bill of lading.[266] Considering the decreasing use of bills of lading and the increasing use of alternative transport documents, this interpretation of the rules appears obsolete.

4.5.2 Covered by a bill of lading

Article II thus clearly requires a contract of carriage for applicability of the convention to the carrier's actions. The contract of carriage is further defined in article I (b) and is thus qualified to the extent that only contracts of carriage covered by a bill of lading are considered a contract of carriage under the rules. Although it seems to be widely accepted that the implication of article I (b) is that the convention applies to contracts of carriage that provide for the issuance of a bill of lading, irrespective of whether such document is actually issued,[267] the term "*covered* by a bill of lading" may appear to confuse this conclusion.

"It is thus a matter of maritime transport of goods between two states when a bill of lading is to be issued" (my translation) (Prop. 2013/14:243 p. 52).

264 As far as can be ascertained, Smeele is in opposition to this (F. Smeele, *Passieve legitimatie uit cognossement* (1998) p. 92). The statement is however made in relation to a discussion on the term "similar document of title".

265 F. Sejersted, *Haagreglerne* (1976) p. 99*ff.*, with references to the Swedish *travaux préparatoires*.

266 Such interpretation is contradicted by the discussion of the applicability of the rules of the Hague–Visby Rules to contracts of carriage that are not evidenced by a bill of lading, see M. Clarke, *International Carriage of Goods by Road: CMR* (2009) pp. 43–46. However, in the meaning of article III.3 thus proposed, the shipper would always have the right of requesting a bill of lading; so the discussion of whether the hypothetical contract provides for the issuance of a bill of lading would be superfluous. See also the discussion whether the Hague–Visby Rules can be invoked as:

> the manner in which the liability of the carrier by the other means of transport would have been determined if a contract for the carriage the goods alone had been made by the sender with the carrier by the other means of transport

because, it is claimed, contracts of short sea carriage seldom involve the issuance of a bill of lading (cf. A. Messent and D. Glass, *CMR: Contracts for the International Carriage of Goods by Road* (2000) pp. 56–59 and J. Thenuis, "The Liability of a Carrier by Road in Roll on-Roll of Traffic" in J. Thenuis (ed.), *International Carriage of Goods by Road (CMR)* (1987) p. 251.

267 G. Treitel and F. Reynolds, *Carver on Bills of Lading* (2011) p. 648, R. Aikens *et al.*, *Bills of Lading* (2016) p. 308, P. Todd, *Principles of the Carriage of Goods by Sea* (2016) p. 330, M. Dockray, *Cases and Materials on Carriage of Goods by Sea* (2004) p. 160, B. Eder *et al.*, *Scrutton on Charterparties and Bills of Lading* (2015) p. 10, R. Temperley, *Carriage of Goods by Sea Act 1924* (1932) p. 11, M. Özdel, *Bills of Lading Incorporating Charter Parties* (2015) p. 21.

A bill of lading is a document with several functions issued by the carrier; it is a receipt for the handing over to the carrier of the goods to be carried, it is a document of title, thus representing the goods; and it evidences the contract of carriage.[268] All types of transport document fill the first and third functions, but it is the second function, the function of the bill of lading as a document of title, that distinguishes it from other types of transport document, such as a (sea) waybill.[269]

It is generally held that a bill of lading is not in itself the contract of carriage, but evidence thereof.[270] Although a bill of lading often contains the agreement, or at least the carrier's general conditions of carriage, the bill of lading is normally issued after the goods have been loaded, or at least after the goods have been left in the care of the carrier (cf. its function as a receipt for the carrier's taking custody of the goods).[271] Logically, a contract of carriage must therefore chronologically precede issuance of the transport document.[272] However, in practice the transport agreement is often made as a "booking", which the parties may not perceive as entering into a contract. Such booking is however likely to be subject to the carrier's general conditions of carriage, so in fact a contract may very well be entered into through the booking and a contract can be said to have been entered into through the contracting consignor's real actions.[273]

In this perspective it may be hard to consider the contract as "covered" by a bill of lading. The ordinary meaning, in the current context, of the term "covered" is something that is enclosed in something else. This would seem to reflect the general practice that the bill of lading evidences the contract of carriage, i.e. the terms of the contract are enclosed in the transport document. This interpretation is adopted in English precedence; in *Pyrene Company Ltd v Scindia Steam Navigation Co Ltd* it was held that "In my judgment, whenever a contract of carriage is concluded and it is contemplated that a bill of lading will in due course be issued in respect of it, that contract is from its creation "covered" by a bill of lading."[274]

268 P. Vestergaard Pedersen, *Transportret* (2008) p. 271*ff*., T. Falkanger *et al*., *Sjørett* (2016) pp. 277–278, V. Haxthow, *Sjølovene* (2001) p. 106, O. Bokareva, *Multimodal Transportation under the Rotterdam Rules* (2015) p. 75, A. Møllmann, *Delivery of Goods under Bills of Lading* (2017) p. 10.

269 M. Clarke, *International Carriage of Goods by Road: CMR* (2014) p. 45.

270 F. Sejersted, *Haagreglerne* (1976) p. 32; R. de Wit, *Multimodal Transport* (1995) p. 252; H. Giermann, *The Evidentiary Value of Bills of lading and Estoppel* (2004) p. 10; A. Burrows, *English Private Law* (2013) p. 716 and P. Todd, *Principles of the Carriage of Goods by Sea* (2016) p. 250. See also the observation presented by the Norwegian delegation at the Brussels meeting in 1923, where it stresses that the convention must, in order to be clear, avoid using contract of carriage and bill of lading as synonyms (M. Sturley (ed.), *The Legislative History of the Carriage by Sea Act and the Travaux Preparatoires of the Hague Rules*, vol. I (1990) p. 419).

271 N. Gaskell *et al*., *Bills of Lading: Law and Contracts* (2000) p. 2.

272 C. Debattista, *The Sale of Goods Carried by Sea* (1998) p. 135, R. Temperley, *Carriage of Goods by Sea Act 1924* (1932) p. 10, Bills of Lading, Report by the UNCTAD secretariat TD/B/C.4/ISL/6 (1970) p. 10.

273 K. Grönfors, *Avtalslagen* (1995) pp. 64–65, F. Sanchez Calero, *El Contrato de Transporte Maritimo de Mercancias* (2000) p. 186.

274 *Pyrene Company Ltd v Scindia Steam Navigation Co Ltd* [1954] 1 Lloyd's Rep 321, at p. 329.

Further, the Norwegian as well as Swedish translations of the Hague–Visby Rules supports this interpretation.[275] Also, as mentioned, in the context of practical business, such interpretation corresponds to the customs of the trade.

That said, article X of the Hague–Visby Rules seems to indicate that the rules are in fact applicable to a bill of lading rather than to a contract of carriage. Article X gives the geographical scope of the Hague–Visby Rules.[276] As such it is secondary to the scope of application rule in article II.[277] However, according to its wording it seems to conflict with the ordinary meaning of article II, something which should be avoided in treaty interpretation.[278] Considering that, at the time of drafting the Hague Rules, the international carriage of goods by sea would very unlikely not be shipped under a bill of lading, the wording of the convention in general and article X in particular is perhaps not as contradictory as it may first seem. Hence, in interpreting the Hague–Visby Rules, the interpreter should bear in mind that for the drafters of the convention(s), the contract of carriage and the bill of lading were intimately connected, where one would not appear without the other.[279]

In relation to secondary sources of interpretation, the *travaux prépratoire* does not give much guidance. The particular wording of article 1(b) was changed from "'Contract of carriage' means a bill of lading" to the current writing at the October 1922 conference. The considerations for the change of wording are, however, not entirely clear. The former wording indicates that the drafters, as mentioned, did not seem to make a clear distinction between contracts of carriage and bills of lading. As mentioned above, the contract of carriage generally precedes the issue of a bill of lading and the only plausible interpretation of article 1(b) is that a contract of carriage only qualifies under the convention where it provides the shipper with the right to demand a bill of lading at the time the goods are handed over to the carrier.

---

275 The Norwegian translation of the term is "*en fraktavtale som inneholdes i ett konossement*", another translation of which would be "a contract of carriage that is included in a bill of lading" (cf. F. Sejersted, *Haagreglerne* (1976) p. 32). The Swedish translation is "*fraktavtal varom upprättats konossement*", i.e. a contract of carriage about which a bill of lading is issued (cf. C. Rune, "Haag-Visby-Reglerna" (1969) SvJT 12). Further, the Swedish Maritime Code defines the applicability of the Hague–Visby Rules as "maritime carriage of goods between two states when a bill of lading is to be issued" (SFS 1994:1009, ch. 13 article 1). Likewise the preparatory works state regarding the applicability of the Hague–Visby Rules: "It is thus a matter of maritime transport of goods between two states when a bill of lading is to be issued" (my translation) (Prop. 2013/14:243 p. 52).

276 Article X states: "The provisions of these Rules shall apply to every bill of lading relating to the carriage of goods between ports in two different States if ...."

277 In his dissertation, Clarke seems to regard article X as the only scope of application provision (M. Clarke, *Aspects of the Hague Rules* (1976) p. 8 *ff.*).

278 U. Linderfalk, *On the Interpretation of Treaties* (2007) p. 107.

279 For example, in the Report of the Maritime Law Committee on Bills of lading at the Hague Conference in 1921, it was held that "The law relating to carriage of goods by sea falls naturally under two heads, that relating to carriage under charter parties and that relating to carriage under bills of lading" (M. Sturley (ed.), *The Legislative History of the Carriage by Sea Act and the Travaux Preparatoires of the Hague Rules*, vol. I (1990) p. 93). See also Temperley who states that "the Rules seem to contemplate that there may be contracts for the carriage of goods ... which are not covered by a bill of lading or similar document of title" (R. Temperley, *Carriage of Goods by Sea Act 1924* (1932) p. 8).

Cumulating the scope of application *de facto* with the geographical scope of the convention, the following conclusion could be drawn. The Hague–Visby Rules apply to contracts that provide for carriage of goods by sea, where the port of loading is situated in a contracting state (or the bill of lading is issued in a contracting state) and the port of discharge is situated in a different state (not necessarily a contracting state), and under which contract the carrier is obliged to issue a bill of lading for the transport.

4.5.3 "In so far as such document relates to the carriage of goods by sea"

As concluded above, the scope of applicability of the Hague–Visby Rules refers to a contract of carriage covered by a bill of lading (or similar document of title). Whilst the interpretation of the term "covered" was analysed above, the term "in so far as such document relates to the carriage of goods by sea" is interesting in relation to multimodal transport contracts.

A bill of lading is not restricted to use in maritime transport, but could be issued for any type of transport, including multimodal transport. This could lead to the conclusion that the Hague–Visby Rules potentially could be applicable to an entire multimodal transport, as long as such transport is subject to a bill of lading. Such an interpretation would however have to be based on the (mis)understanding that the Hague–Visby Rules applies to the bill of lading rather than to the contract of carriage. Another plausible interpretation is that the rules apply per se to any contract of carriage, i.e. also contracts that provide for transport by other mode(s) in addition to sea transport, but that the term in question limits the applicability of the rules to the sea carriage.[280] The conclusion would then be that the Hague–Visby Rules apply to sea carriage under a multimodal contract of carriage as long as a bill of lading is, or is meant to be, issued. This latter interpretation seems to find some support in precedence as well as in the protocols from the negotiation of the convention.[281]

The ordinary meaning of the term "in so far as such document relates to the carriage of goods by sea" is fairly unambiguous and entails that the document of title should relate to sea carriage. However, it is not the actual wording of the term that may cause interpretative problems, but the effect thereof on the contract of carriage covered by a bill of lading. The question is thus, what is the implication of the term in question in relation to the contract of carriage?

Although article I of the Hague–Visby Rules defines e.g. the contract of carriage, it is article II that is the actual scope of applicability. As discussed above, article II relates the liability of the carrier under the convention to "every contract of carriage of goods by sea". Accordingly, the contract of carriage to which the convention applies is not only defined by the prerequisite that it has to be covered

280 J. Bredholt *et al.*, *Søloven* (2001) p. 264.

281 See e.g. *Mayhew Foods Ltd v Overseas Containers Ltd* [1984] 1 Lloyd's Rep 317 referenced below as well as the Hague Conference Report, 1 September 1921 (M. Sturley (ed.), *The Legislative History of the Carriage by Sea Act and the Travaux Preparatoires of the Hague Rules*, vol. I (1990) p. 93).

by a bill of lading, but also that it has to regard carriage by sea. Combining article II and article I (b), the convention applies to contracts of carriage by sea in relation to which a bill of lading is contemplated. However, under the assumption discussed previously that all terms of a treaty add a meaning to the treaty and thus no terms are redundant,[282] the term "in so far as such document relates to the carriage of goods by sea" ought to, in some way, alter that conclusion.

It is clear that the term "in so far as such document relates to the carriage of goods by sea" entails a specification of the bill of lading, and a common conclusion is that the term indicates that if the bill of lading concerns a multimodal transport, i.e. covers a door-to-door operation, the Hague–Visby Rules only apply to the sea transport.[283] Although this appears to be a correct interpretation, it is somewhat undermined by the fact that article II already limits the scope of applicability to contracts of carriage by sea. Although treaty interpretation operates from a starting point that a treaty makes up a logical whole and that, as mentioned, all terms of a treaty are included for a reason, the fact that the scope of applicability of the Hague–Visby Rules refers to contract of carriage by sea, and that the definition of the contract refers to the contract of carriage rather than the contract of carriage by sea and instead limits the bill of lading to sea carriage, is not entirely logical. To an interpreter with a unimodal state of mind, articles II and I (b) could be read to limit the scope of the convention to unimodal contracts of carriage by sea in relation to which a bill of lading for sea transport is issued, thus excluding multimodal contracts of carriage as well as multimodal bills of lading.

In fact, considering that the rules apply to contracts of carriage by sea, the applicability of the Hague–Visby Rules to sea carriage under multimodal contracts of carriage ought to be subject to the same objections as the applicability of the CMR convention.[284] Not surprisingly, propositions to this effect have been raised by German scholars.[285] However, the reason provided for the conclusion that the Hague–Visby Rules do not apply to sea carriage under a multimodal contract of carriage does not focus on the contract of carriage, but on the bill of lading.[286] Thus, it is asserted that a multimodal bill of lading does not "relate to the carriage by sea" as required for the applicability of the Hague–Visby Rules.

However, the term "in so far as such document relates to the carriage of goods by sea" could also, as mentioned, indicate that the rules apply to sea carriage even where the bill of lading also relates to other modes of transport, or to operations,

---

282 U. Linderfalk, *On the Interpretation of Treaties* (2007) p. 108.

283 G. Treitel and F. Reynolds, *Carver on Bills of Lading* (2011) p. 651; R. Aikens *et al.*, *Bills of Lading* (2016) p. 308.

284 In Denmark, where the non-applicability of the CMR convention to carriage by road under multimodal contracts of carriage is rather unanimously purported (U. Fabricius, *Lov om Fragtaftaler ved international vejtransport* (2005) p. 38; P. Vestergaard Pedersen, *Transportret* (2008) pp. 962–964), it has been held in relation to the Hague–Visby Rules that to the extent a contract of carriage includes transport by another mode, in addition to sea transport, the rules apply only to the sea transport (J. Bredholt *et al.*, *Søloven* (2001) p. 264).

285 M. Hoeks, *Multimodal Transport Law* (2010) pp. 319–320.

286 M. Hoeks, *Multimodal Transport Law* (2010) p. 319, with references to e.g. Ramming, Basedow and Herber (in German).

such as storage, to which the Hague–Visby Rules do not apply.[287] However, such interpretation would presuppose an interpretation of the term "contract of carriage by sea" to include carriage by sea under a multimodal contract of carriage.

The fact that the Hague–Visby Rules apply *ex proprio vigore* only to the actual carriage by sea, and not to any other operations possibly undertaken by the carrier, is further emphasized by article VII, which provides freedom of contract in relation to such operations.[288] Article VII is interesting as it in some way undermines the theory of non-redundance in relation to the Hague–Visby Rules. As the Rules clearly apply only to the time period between the loading and the discharge of the goods, article VII is materially redundant. It does, to some extent, add clarity and prevent uncertainty, but it is hard to see how an interpreter could come to any other conclusion regarding operations before loading or after discharge, even if article VII had not existed. Thus, to some extent it seems that the drafters of the Hague–Visby Rules preferred over-clarity to simplicity.

Assuming that this conclusion can be applied generally to the Hague–Visby Rules, article II and article I (b) are perhaps only clarifications of each other. Thus, the rules of the convention apply to contracts of carriage by sea, albeit only to the period between loading and discharge, according to which a bill of lading is to be issued and to the extent the bill of lading covers other transport or operations than the carriage by sea, the applicability of the rules is limited to the latter.

As regards secondary sources of interpretation, the *travaux préparatoires* supports the interpretation that "in so far as such document relates to the carriage of goods by sea" indicates that the rules apply to sea carriage even where the bill of lading also relates to other modes of transport to which the Hague–Visby Rules do not apply. It is clearly expressed by the drafters that the intention of the term is that the Rules would apply to sea carriage even where a through bill of lading is issued.[289]

4.5.4 Conclusions

In comparison with other conventions regulating the carrier's liability, the Hague–Visby Rules contain far fewer rules imposing obligations on the carrier

287 In *Mayhew Foods v Overseas Containers*, the English Queen's Bench Division applied the Hague–Visby Rules to a sea carriage which was subject to a multimodal contract of carriage. The judgment was based on the holding in *Pyrene v Scindia*, referred to above, in which it was held, *obiter*, that the rules apply to a contract or part of a contract, in so far as the latter relates to the carriage of goods by sea *(Mayhew Foods Ltd v Overseas Containers Ltd* [1984] 1 Lloyd's Rep 317, at p. 320). However, since the term "relates to carriage by sea" refers to the bill of lading rather than the contract of carriage, the English standpoint is somewhat unclear. In preparation for the Visby amendments, the UNCTAD secretariat in its report on bills of lading held that if the rules were to be extended to include port operations, the term in question would have to be amended (Bills of Lading, Report by the UNCTAD secretariat TD/B/C.4/ISL/6 (1970) p. 71).

288 Article VII.

289 The Hague Conference Report, 31 August 1921 pp. 75–76 (reproduced in M. Sturley (ed.), *The Legislative History of the Carriage by Sea Act and the Travaux Preparatoires of the Hague Rules*, vol. I (1990) pp. 181–182). In relation to the term, Sir Norman Hill expresses (at p. 77) that it would be better placed in article II, which provides the scope of applicability, an observation with which it is hard not to agree.

prior to initiation of the period of liability. In fact, it is only article III paragraph 1 that could be said to govern such obligations, and even that conclusion seems perhaps a bit strained. The scope of applicability and the period of liability are thus virtually identical. Therefore, it could be held that it is indifferent whether the convention applies to the contract of carriage or to the transport document.

That may be an accurate conclusion in practice but, in legal theory, it does not suffice to hold that the Hague–Visby Rules apply to either the contract of carriage or to the bill of lading. Based on the discussions above, it is held here that the convention applies to the contract of carriage. However, it only applies to such contracts of carriage subject to which the carrier is obliged to issue a bill of lading. Further the contract must provide for carriage by sea, where the port of loading and the port of discharge are situated in different states and at least the port of loading (or the place where the bill of lading is issued) is situated in a contracting state.

In relation to multimodal contracts of carriage, the applicability of the Hague–Visby Rules does not seem to have been much debated. It can be assumed that this is due to the general view that the convention is applicable to bills of lading. However, even based on the interpretation that the Hague–Visby Rules in fact apply to the contract of carriage, there ought not to be any problem applying the convention to carriage by sea performed under a multimodal contract. As noted above, the rules apply to contracts of carriage by sea. Contracts of carriage are defined in article I(b) as contracts of carriage covered by a bill of lading, in so far as such document relates to carriage of goods by sea. Accordingly, the rules apply to all contracts of carriage under which a bill of lading for sea carriage is issued. If the contract of carriage includes carriage by other modes than by sea, the Rules apply to the sea carriage. This interpretation is verified by the *travaux préparatoires*.

4.6 The scope of application of the Rotterdam Rules

The Rotterdam Rules as a comprehensive set of rules seem generally to be well considered. Although criticism may be directed against particular articles, or in general,[290] it is evident from the working group protocols that every article has been thoroughly discussed. In the end, for obvious reasons, many of the rules are nevertheless not entirely clear, presumably as a result of diplomatic compromises.

The working group protocols, the *travaux préparatoires* of the convention, are comprehensive and often clarifying.[291] Thus, where a term of the treaty is not entirely clear, the *travaux préparatoires* may likely provide an answer.

Therefore, the *travaux préparatoires* of the Rotterdam Rules take a dominant position in the writings on the rules since its adoption in 2008, and indeed even

290 See in particular W. Tetley, "Some general criticisms of the Rotterdam Rules" (2008) 14 JIML 625–628.

291 The *travaux préparatoires*, i.e. the working group documents, are available at www.uncitral.org.

before that.[292] In fact the preparatory works, consisting of the reports of the working group sessions and related documents, are often used as a primary source of interpretation. The reason therefor is undoubtedly the amplitude and easy access of the material, the close proximity of the negotiations (which ended in 2008) as well as the fact that many publications have been authored by working group delegates.[293] As the *travaux préparatoires* of the Rotterdam Rules provide answers to many questions of interpretation, recourse thereto is understandable, although perhaps not always justifiable. Even though the preparatory works of a treaty are often used as an integral part of the interpretation of that treaty, and such usage may find support as confirmation of the interpreted meaning of the term, where they are used to determine the meaning of that term, one of the prerequisites found in paragraph (a) and (b) of article 32 of the Vienna Convention should be satisfied before recourse is taken to the preparatory works. Accordingly, in the following any interpretation of the terms of the Rotterdam Rules will primarily be made in accordance with article 31 of the Vienna Convention, and resort to the *travaux préparatoires* will only be had on the premises provided in article 32 of the Vienna Convention.

4.6.1 General scope of application

The Rotterdam Rules are intended as a multimodal convention, although with "a pinch of sea salt".[294] Thus, as a starting point the convention subjects to its liability rules transports by any mode of transport, as long as the contract of carriage provides for international sea transport.

It has been suggested that the scope of application of the Rotterdam Rules is a combination of the contractual, documental and trade approaches.[295] Accordingly, the Rotterdam Rules apply to contracts of carriage, as defined in the convention, in liner-trade excluding carriage under charter parties.[296]

As a starting point, the Rotterdam Rules apply to contracts of carriage.[297] Although this scope of application is set out in article 5, it is the definition of the contract of carriage found in article 1.1 that really defines the scope of application of the convention. Thus, the contract of carriage is a contract between a carrier and a shipper, in which the carrier undertakes to carry goods in exchange for payment of freight.[298] The requirement that the carrier undertakes to carry goods

292 E.g. M. Sturley, "Solving the Scope-of-Application Puzzle: Contracts, Trades and Documents in the UNCITRAL Transport Law Project" (2005) 11 JIML 22–41.

293 E.g. M. Sturley *et al.*, *The Rotterdam Rules* (2010), in which all authors took part in the negotiations, and A. Von Ziegler *et al.* (eds), *The Rotterdam Rules 2008* (2010), in which publication the majority of the contributors were delegates in the UNCITRAL working group III.

294 M. Hoeks, "Multimodal carriage with a pinch of sea salt: door-to-door under the UNCITRAL draft instrument" (2008) 43(3) ETL 257–280.

295 M. Sturley *et al.*, *The Rotterdam Rules* (2010) p. 30.

296 M. Sturley *et al.*, *ibid.*, at p. 39*ff.*

297 Article 5. 1.

298 According to Thomas, such freight must be monetary, i.e. carriage of goods in exchange for services or goods does not qualify under the rules (R. Thomas, "The emergence and application of

in order to qualify as a carrier under the rules, underlines the focus of the convention on the contractual promise rather than actual performance of the transport.[299] The contract of carriage, as defined by the rules, does not have to be a unimodal contract, but may be multimodal as long as it *provides for* carriage by sea.[300] The contract of carriage must be international, in that the place of loading and the place of delivery must be situated in different states. However, carriage by sea must also be international, i.e. the port of loading and the port of discharge must be in different states.[301] Thus, under a multimodal contract of carriage, the port of loading and the port of discharge of the sea carriage must be situated in different states, as must the places of loading and delivery. The place of loading and the port of loading could be in the same state, as can the place of delivery and the port of discharge, but the place of loading and the place of delivery may never be in the same state for the contract to be subject to the Rotterdam Rules.[302]

4.6.2 "Provides for carriage by sea"

To some extent, the Rotterdam Rules are far more clarifying as regards the contract of carriage to which the convention applies than the other conventions considered here. Thus article 1.1 explicitly subjects all carriage by sea, even where carriage is part of a larger multimodal contract, to the rules. In addition, the convention prima facie subjects transport by other modes to its rules, where such transport is carried out under a multimodal contract that provides for carriage by sea. As elaborated in section 3.3, however, article 26 narrows the effect of article 1.1 to non-localized damage and article 82 further limits the scope of the article.

Of relevance in this respect is the provision that the contract must "provide for" carriage by sea. Previously in this chapter the implications of the term "contract for the carriage of goods by road" have been discussed, and in particular its implication as regards the type of carriage contract that is required for the CMR convention to be applicable. Although the Rotterdam Rules attempt to provide clarity to many questions of which the drafters were aware, such as the question of applicability of

---

the Rotterdam Rules" in R. Thomas (ed.), *The Carriage of Goods by Sea Under the Rotterdam Rules* (2010) p. 6 (para. 1.19)).

299 M. Sturley, "Scope of Application" in A. Von Ziegler *et al.* (eds), *The Rotterdam Rules 2008* (2010) p. 42.

300 Article 1.1.

301 Thomas questions whether, under a multimodal contract of carriage, the two prerequisites are really cumulative or if it suffices that the place of loading and the place of delivery are in different states. The author concludes that they are in fact cumulative (R. Thomas, *The Carriage of Goods by Sea Under the Rotterdam Rules* (2010) p. 8 (paras 1.29–1.36).

302 Hence it does not suffice that the sea carriage is international. Accordingly, in the event that goods are loaded in Kiruna in northern Sweden and carried by rail to the port of Narvik in northern Norway, from where they are carried by sea to the port of Göteborg, and therefrom carried by road to an inland destination in Sweden, the carriage will not be subject to the Rotterdam Rules. Likewise, a contract of carriage providing for sea carriage from Vancouver to Haines in Alaska with onward transport by road to Whitehorse, situated in Canada, would not be subject to the Rotterdam Rules as the place of loading and the place of discharge are situated in the same country.

unimodal conventions to multimodal contracts of carriage, some uncertainties still seem to remain. Thus, the Rotterdam Rules indeed leave no room for hesitation as regards application of the rules of the treaty where the contract of carriage provides for more than one mode of transport. However, as regards the status of contracts of carriage that either leaves the choice of transport mode open to the carrier (undefined contracts of carriage) or grants the carrier a right to substitute the mode of transport, which the carrier invokes (incorrectly defined contracts of carriage), the crucial point appears to be the term "provide for".

The term "provide for" is a key element for application of the Rotterdam Rules. As it is a requirement in article 5 that the carriage by sea is international, the entire contract of carriage is likely to be international if the sea carriage is international, i.e. the place of receipt and place of delivery are likely to be in different states if the port of loading and the port of discharge are in different states. Thus, a multimodal contract of carriage will frequently be subject to the rules in so far as it contains international sea transport. What, then, is required in order for a contract of carriage to "provide for" carriage by sea?

The ordinary meaning of the term "provide for" appears to indicate that the contract of carriage should stipulate carriage by sea.[303] Under such an interpretation, it is not sufficient that the transport is eventually carried out by sea. Given the context and the object and purpose of the convention, the meaning of the term should perhaps not be interpreted to that effect. In the general context of law, "provide for" is often used as a synonym for allowing for.[304] The difference between "stipulate" and "allow for" is quite distinct and whilst the former would be an entirely plausible interpretation, albeit strict, the latter would also encompass contracts of carriage that allow for carriage by sea regardless of by what mode the transport is eventually carried out, which is unquestionably too wide an interpretation.

The emergence, and increasing use, of open transport contracts, i.e. unclear contracts of carriage, is a factor affecting all regulation of carriers' liability, which would certainly have been clear to the drafters of the convention.[305] Thus, the general context of the modern shipping business may indicate that the provision should not be interpreted too narrowly.

In terms of the textual context of the treaty, the remaining articles of the convention do not seem to add much of relevance to the context. As far as the object and purpose of the convention is concerned, some guidance may be found in the convention's preambles. Being a UN organization, UNCITRAL Working Group III consisted of representatives from a large number of the world's nations and

303 A comparison between the English, French and Spanish, equally authentic, versions of the text does not seem to disclose any difference in meaning. The French text stipulates "*Le contrat prévoit* le transport par mer" and the Spanish version stipulates "*Dicho contrato deberá* prever el transporte marítimo de las mercancías".

304 The *Oxford Dictionary of English* (www.oxforddictionaries.com) explains "'Provide' as ... 2 [NO OBJECT] (provide for) Make adequate preparation for (a possible event): *new qualifications must provide for changes in technology [...]*2.2 (Of a law) enable or allow (something to be done): *the Bill provides for the setting of guaranteed service standards.*"

305 See e.g. Report of Working Group III (Transport Law) on the work of its twelfth session (A/CN.9/544, para. 62).

the final text of the convention was adopted by the UN General Assembly. In addition to the preamble drafted by the working group, the convention has a preamble relating to adoption of the convention by the General Assembly. As the vast majority of states that may come to ratify the convention are members of the UN, there seems to be no reason not to take the General Assembly preamble into account. Accordingly, the preambles contain a couple of statements of interest in ascertaining the ordinary meaning of the term in question. Thus, as far as multimodal carriage of goods is concerned, the preambles seem to indicate that the state parties envisaged the rules of the convention to provide a solution to the uncertainties that surround door-to-door transport as well as providing a tool adapted to the needs of modern carriage of goods.[306] The object and purpose of the treaty would accordingly indicate an extensive interpretation of the term "provide for", which does not exclude modern forms of carriage contracts that lack explicit agreements as regards the mode of transport.

In order to confirm the thus proposed interpretation, there seems to be reason therefore to take recourse to supplementary means of interpretation. As regards interpretation of the term "provide for", the *travaux préparatoires* of the Rotterdam Rules do shed some light. At the 12th session in 2003, concern was expressed that draft articles 1(a),[307] corresponding to what later became article 1.1, and 2,[308] corresponding to what later became article 5,

> might inappropriately exclude from the scope of the draft instrument those contracts that did not specify or imply that the carriage would be undertaken by sea but left it open whether part of the carriage would be undertaken by sea, or which part of the carriage would be carried out by sea.[309]

---

306 For example, the preamble drafted by the General Assembly contains the following statement: "*Concerned* that the current legal regime governing the international carriage of goods by sea lacks uniformity and fails to adequately take into account modern transport practices, including containerization, door-to-door transport contracts and the use of electronic transport documents" and the ordinary preamble holds:

> *Mindful* of the technological and commercial developments that have taken place since the adoption of those conventions and of the need to consolidate and modernize them, *Noting* that shippers and carriers do not have the benefit of a binding universal regime to support the operation of contracts of maritime carriage involving other modes of transport.

307 Reading:

> Contract of carriage means a contract under which a carrier against payment of freight undertakes to carry goods by sea from a place in one State to a place in another State and may include carriage by other [mode] [means] of carriage preceding or subsequent to the carriage by sea.

308 Reading:

> Subject to paragraph 3, this instrument applies to all contracts of carriage if (a) the place of receipt [or port of loading] specified either in the contract of carriage or in the contract particulars is located in a Contracting State, or (b) the place of delivery [or port of discharge] specified either in the contract of carriage or in the contract particulars is located in a Contracting State, or (c) [the actual place of delivery is one of the optional places of delivery specified either in the contract of carriage or in the contract particulars and is located in a Contracting State, or] (d) the contract of carriage provides that this instrument, or the law of any State giving effect to it, is to govern the contract.

309 Report of Working Group III (Transport Law) on the work of its twelfth session (A/CN. 9/544), para. 62.

Various suggestions seem to have been made in order to alleviate the concerns expressed. This appears to show that the drafters were in agreement that carriage performed by sea under e.g., undefined contracts, should be subject to the convention.[310] At the 15th session in 2005 the working group discussed whether the phrase "[a] contract that contains an option to carry the goods by sea shall be deemed to be a contract of carriage provided that the goods are actually carried by sea" should be included in the definition of the contract of carriage in article 1.[311] It seems to have been concluded by the working group that inserting the phrase would risk shifting the focus of application of the convention from the contract of carriage to performance. Further, it was proposed that a similar result could be achieved through "flexible interpretation".[312] In the end, no clarifications were included in the actual treaty text, not because the working group was not in favour of applying the convention to undefined and incorrectly defined contracts of carriage, but because further clarification was considered superfluous.[313]

In conclusion, it is held here that the *travaux préparatoires* confirm the meaning of the term "provide for" that appears from a general interpretation. Thus, in order to qualify under article 1.1 of the Rotterdam Rules, it is not required from a contract of carriage that it contains an explicit undertaking by the carrier to carry goods by sea, but it is sufficient that such carriage can be deduced as implicit in the agreement. On the other hand, performance alone does not qualify the contract as a contract of carriage under the rules.[314]

4.6.3 "In addition to"

Another question raised in relation to the definition of the contract of carriage under the Rotterdam Rules and the convention's multimodal application is the implication of the term "in addition to". Article 1.1 provides that the "contract shall provide for carriage by sea and may provide for carriage by other modes of transport in addition to the sea carriage". The prerequisite for application of the convention to other transport than carriage by sea is thus that the transport agreement provides for carriage by sea and in addition thereto for transport by other modes, such as road or rail. The question that arises is how transport by other modes than by sea is to relate to the carriage by sea. What is the implication of "in addition to"?

310 *Ibid.* paras 63–65.

311 Report of Working Group III (Transport Law) on the work of its fifteenth session (A/CN.9/576) para. 33.

312 *Ibid.* para. 33.

313 *Ibid.* para. 33. See also Sturley, who holds that "[w]hether a contractual undertaking provides for carriage by sea is a matter of contract interpretation. The contract may provide for sea carriage explicitly or implicitly." M. Sturley, "Scope-of-application in UNCITRAL Transport Law Project" (2005) 11 JIML 22–41, at p. 32.

314 Considering the apparent consensus within the working group that transport carried out by sea under a contract that allows for such carriage should also be subject to the rules (cf. M. Sturley, *ibid.*, at p. 32) the wording appears as not entirely adequate.

The Rotterdam Rules is first and foremost a maritime convention. It governs carriage by sea, whether this is preceded and/or succeeded by land transport or not. Even though it certainly, in some instances, governs other modes of transport, transport by sea is an absolute prerequisite. The ordinary meaning of the term "in addition to" is something that is added to the first. The first impression a reader may get is therefore that the transport by other modes than by sea must be supplementary to the carriage by sea, that is, that carriage by sea is to be the main mode of transport, supplemented by for example road transport from the port of discharge to the facility of the consignee. Such an interpretation would mean that only multimodal contracts of carriage where carriage by sea is the main mode of transport and transport by other modes are supplementary, i.e. of minor importance, in relation to the carriage by sea, are subject to the convention.

Being a UN convention, the Rotterdam Rules are drafted in six languages of equal status: English, French, Spanish, Arabic, Russian and Chinese. According to the Vienna Convention, treaties authenticated in different languages should be presumed to bear the same meaning.[315] An interpreter should therefore be allowed to read only one of the authenticated versions and rely on that version.[316] However, article 33.2 provides an assumption only, and the mere contention that the term in a different language version bears a different meaning obliges the interpreter to apply article 33.4, which holds that

> [e]xcept where a particular text prevails in accordance with paragraph 1, when a comparison of the authentic texts discloses a difference of meaning which the application of articles 31 and 32 does not remove, the meaning which best reconciles the texts, having regard to the object and purpose of the treaty, shall be adopted.[317]

On the other hand, where an ambiguity in the text of a treaty is revealed and that treaty is authenticated in another language than the one interpreted, it seems to be natural for an interpreter to resort to the other authenticated versions available for guidance on interpretation of the current term. In fact, a comparison between the authenticated versions may facilitate interpretation of an ambiguous term.[318]

Therefore, reading article 1, paragraph 1 in other authenticated languages than English could shed light on the meaning of the term in addition to the relation between carriage by sea and additional land (or air) transport. Accordingly, the French version of the term reads: "et peut prévoir, en outre, le transport par d'autres modes" and the Spanish version of the term reads: "podrá prever, además, su transporte por otros modos". The French version of the term "in addition to" is thus "en outre" and the Spanish version is "además". Both terms are rather translated by "also" than by "in addition to". Whilst "also" indicates that transport may be either solely by sea or by sea and another mode, without distinction,

315 Article 33.3 of the Vienna Convention.

316 U. Linderfalk, *On the Interpretation of Treaties* (2007) p. 356.

317 C.B. Kuner, "The Interpretation of Multilingual Treaties: Comparison of Texts Versus the Presumption of Similar Meaning" (1991) 40 ICLQ 953–964, at p. 955.

318 C.B. Kuner; *ibid.*, at p. 958.

"in addition to" indicates a dependence or inequality between the carriage by sea and the land transport. "In addition to" indicates that the transport by road (or air) must be carried out as a complement to the carriage by sea, i.e. constitute a non-principal part of the transport.

As the comparison between three of the authentic texts discloses a difference in meaning, the general rule of interpretation found in article 31 of the Vienna Convention, as well as the supplementary means found in article 32, are to be applied.[319] It is held here that the context and purpose of the Rotterdam Rules do not clarify the term; on the one hand the treaty has a clear multimodal ambition, which would indicate that contracts of carriage where the carriage by sea is of minor importance (as long as it is international) are also subject to the convention. On the other hand, the treaty is clearly a maritime convention, which is indicated by its title, by the fact that a sea carriage is a prerequisite, as well as by the fact that the sea carriage has to be international (as opposed to the entire transport having to be international), which would indicate that the rules only apply where the sea transport, in one way or another, dominates.[320]

Accordingly, recourse may, and must, be had to supplementary means of interpretation, and in the case of the Rotterdam Rules the preparatory work is close at hand.[321] Already at its first session in 2002 the Working Group agreed to request an extension of its mandate to consider applicability of the future convention to door-to-door transport where carriage by sea is complemented by one or more land transports.[322] The discussions carried out within Working Group III under the extended mandate were heterogeneous in that there was initial disagreement as to the port-to-port or door-to-door application of the convention. However, during the spring session in 2003, the delegations agreed that door-to-door application would best meet the needs of the trade.

The discussions regarding applicability of the convention to other transport than that carried out by sea thereafter focused on the issue of to what degree land and air transport were to be subject to the convention. The view seems initially to have been that the maritime part of a door-to-door transport should be the dominating mode of transport. Due to difficulties in determining what constitutes an ancillary transport, and due to the fact that road transport prior or subsequent

319 Cf. section 4.2.2. above and U. Linderfalk, *On the Interpretation of Treaties* (2007) p. 358.

320 Here, a parallel could be drawn with the tenor of the COTIF–CIM convention after the revision 1999, which regulates not only carriage by rail, but also transport by other modes that are carried out "as a supplement to transfrontier carriage by rail". In French the same article reads "*inclut, en complément au transport transfrontalier ferrovier, un transport*". The Swedish official translation reads: "*utöver gränsöverskridande järnvägstransport inbegriper*", but the *travaux préparatoires* (SOU 2004:92) indicates that the transport by another mode is to supplement (Sw: *komplettera*) the carriage by rail. The language used in the COTIF–CIM convention thus clearly implies that carriage by rail must be the principal mode of transport, and that other modes of transport are covered by the convention if such transport is carried out as a complement to the carriage by rail. However, it is not stated in what way such transport is to be supplementary, i.e. shorter in distance or otherwise.

321 Reports from Working Group III are published on the UNCITRAL website (www.uncitral.org) and easily accessible.

322 A/CN.9/510, at p. 11.

to carriage by sea may be of considerable distance, it was agreed during the spring session in 2003 that no attempt would be made to regulate the relationship between the maritime transport and other preceding or subsequent transport. Instead, the most practical way to regulate door-to-door transport would be to include all multimodal transports that include an international sea leg, independently of the relative duration of the carriage by sea, in the new convention.[323] The *travaux préparatoires* of the Rotterdam Rules thus indicate that the aim of the drafters was that the convention was to be applicable to all multimodal transport including international carriage by sea, as long as the place of loading and the place of delivery are not in the same state. Thus, it may be concluded that the drafters of the Rotterdam Rules intended that no distinction between carriage by sea and land/air should be made.[324]

Although there are indications in legal writing that application is to be restricted to multimodal transport where the sea leg is the dominating part of the transport,[325] it is concluded here that the Rotterdam Rules are to be applied to all multimodal transport that includes an international sea leg, and that no evaluation of the relationship between the sea carriage and transport by other modes should be made. The rules also apply where sea carriage is supplementary to other transport, as long as such sea carriage is international.

4.6.4 Conclusions

Despite the prerequisite of the inclusion of international sea transport in the contract of carriage, the Rotterdam Rules have the potential of becoming the multimodal regulation as far as intercontinental trade is concerned as such trade often includes a (dominating) sea transport.[326]

The Rotterdam Rules thus, prima facie, apply to the entire multimodal contract of carriage, i.e. carriage by any mode of transport, as long as the contract provides for international carriage by sea. Sea transport need not be the dominating

323 A/CN.9/526 at pp. 67 and 68.

324 D. Glass, "Meddling in the multimodal muddle? A network of conflict in the UNICITRAL Draft Convention on the Carriage of Goods [wholly or partly] [by sea]" (2006) LMCLQ 307–334, at p. 313.

325 In an article published in connection with the conference held at the signing ceremony in Rotterdam 2009, Berlingieri observes "the need for such carriage by other modes to be complementary to the carriage by sea". "Complementary" must be interpreted as subordinate in one way or the other, indicating that the relation between the different modes of transport does matter (F. Berlingieri, "Multimodal Aspects of the Rotterdam Rules", published at: www.rotterdamrules2009.com/cms/uploads/Def.%20tekst%20F.%20Berlingieri%2013%20OKT29.pdf, 2009). Van der Ziel notes that the convention, in addition to maritime transport, regulates "ancillary" transports by other modes, this too indicating subordination of the land (or air) transport (G. van der Ziel, "Multimodal Aspects of the Rotterdam Rules" in *CMI Yearbook 2009*, pp. 301–313). Both authors have participated as delegates for their respective countries – the Netherlands and Italy – during the UNCITRAL sessions, and obviously their opinions should be taken into account when interpreting the application issue. However, it is not clear from the articles on what these opinions are based.

326 This conclusion is drawn on a general level without regard to article 82, which may undermine the impact of the Rotterdam Rules at least as far as trade with Europe is concerned.

mode of transport: it only needs to begin in one state and end in another. Further, it is concluded that the rules do not contain a requirement that the carrier has explicitly undertaken to carry goods by sea: it is sufficient that such carriage is either implicit in the contract, or allowed for, and the transport is in fact carried out (wholly or partly) by sea. However, performance alone does not trigger applicability of the Rotterdam Rules.

4.7 Conclusion

It was held initially in the current chapter that, in relation to the primary research question ("To what extent can unimodal transport of goods conventions be applied to transport carried out under multimodal transport contracts?"), the scope of application of the conventions discussed plays a vital role. One of the propositions that supports the non-applicability of the CMR convention to transport by road under multimodal contracts of carriage is that the wording of the scope of application article is to be interpreted as to exclude such application.

As stated initially, part of the answer to the research question cited above is the scope of application of the unimodal conventions; it must be settled whether the articles of applicability prevents such application or not. Thus, the purpose of the current chapter has been to settle the scopes of application of the conventions discussed. Because treaty interpretation is subject to rules of international law, the rules of treaty interpretation must be fully understood before the terms in question can be interpreted. Therefore, the current chapter commenced with a discussion of the rules and theories of treaty interpretation, which was ended with the conclusion that, as a matter of international law, the interpretation of the terms of uniform law is subject to the Vienna Convention. The rules of treaty interpretation of the said convention appear to shelter for the same objectives that are enclosed in theories of *autonomous* interpretation of uniform law, The theories, albeit of merit, are however destined to remain theories unless supported by law.

Consequently, the rules of treaty interpretation of the Vienna Convention were methodically applied to the scope of application articles of the respective conventions. Through the analysis of the articles of applicability of the conventions that apply to contracts of carriage, i.e. the CMR convention, the COTIF–CIM convention, the Hague–Visby Rules and the Rotterdam Rules, it was concluded that the conventions themselves provide prerequisites that further define the contract of carriage by [road], although the actual contract of carriage is not defined, let alone the contract of carriage by [road]. The answer to the question of what constitutes a contract of carriage by [road], the answer to which is crucial for the subordinate research question:

> To what extent can contracts that provide for more than one mode of transport or are in fact carried out by more than one mode of transport be considered a contract for the carriage of goods by a particular mode of transport?

must accordingly be sought in a larger context. The most important conclusion to be drawn from the previous analysis is, however, that there is nothing in the scope of application articles of either convention that prevents the applicability to transport under multimodal contracts of carriage, to the extent such contract can be considered a contract of carriage by [road]. With this insight, the further interpretation of the term "contract of carriage by [road]" can be undertaken.

CHAPTER 5

The contractual approach to applicability and multimodal contracts

The analysis in the previous chapter resulted in the conclusion that the terms of the scopes of application of the unimodal conventions discussed do not *prevent* the application of the conventions to transport under multimodal contracts of carriage, at least not to the extent such contract can be considered a contract for the carriage of goods by [road]. This conclusion was based on an independent interpretation of the terms of the articles in question, an interpretation based on the rules of treaty interpretation of international law. However, although the starting point is an autonomous interpretation in accordance with rules 31–33 of the Vienna Convention, in order to interpret the term "contract of carriage by [road]", the treaty itself is not sufficient. Autonomous interpretation is thus insufficient, and the conclusion will be reached that the settlement of whether a certain contract can be considered a "contract of carriage by [road]" must be done in relation to national law of contracts. The second step of the analysis is thus construction and interpretation of the contract of carriage, which will have to be carried out in the particular case based on an actual contract. However, in order to illustrate the process, the contract of carriage will be analysed and categorized, after which these generalizatons will be subject to interpretation.

It is submitted that harmonization will not be undermined by this resort to national law, as it is assumed that the laws of contract of the states affected are fairly homogenous. This conclusion is based on an analysis of the Nordic and English law of contracts, two legal systems that are generally assumed to be heterogenous.

5.1 Introduction

Until a certain point in time, the network system appeared to have been somewhat taken for granted; as long as there is no uniform system, the unimodal conventions will have to be applied to the separate legs of a multimodal carriage.[1] However, with the influence of legal theories regarding the autonomous application of unimodal conventions to carriage under multimodal contracts the network system has become somewhat undermined.

The network system is based on unimodal conventions being applicable to carriage by the mode of transport regulated by the respective conventions although

1 Cf. section 3.2.2 above.

the carriage is subject to a multimodal contract.[2,3] Theoretically, this can be achieved either by extracting the unimodal fragments, legs, from the multimodal contract of carriage and consider a multimodal contract as a collection of unimodal contracts, or the multimodal transport contract can be regarded as a contract of carriage by each mode of transport without necessarily disassembling the multimodal contract into separate unimodal contracts. The latter proposition is based on the notion that a multimodal contract of carriage prescribes for carriage by two or more certain modes and that a multimodal contract of carriage is therefore a contract for the carriage of goods by each mode thus prescribed.

Undoubtedly, the network system does suffer from flaws that prevent the net from being seamless.[4] On the one hand, it is the multimodal aspects of the unimodal conventions that entail that the unimodal conventions overlap each other to some extent. Whilst this does not seem to have been an insurmountable problem, problems will arise when a contract is undefined as regards the mode of transport, or where there is an option for the carrier to substitute the agreed mode of transport. On the other hand, the network system does not provide a complete system due to the necessity for damage to be localized in order for any unimodal system to apply.

A critical question for application of the network system is whether the unimodal conventions are autonomously applicable at all to transport carried out under a multimodal contract. As regards the carriage by air convention, the Montreal Convention, it has been stated above that that convention is expressly applicable to air legs of a multimodal contract. However, in relation to undefined contracts of carriage or where the mode of transport has been substituted (what has above been labelled "incorrectly defined contracts of carriage") the application of the Montreal Convention is not without legal obstacles. As regards unimodal conventions that apply to *contracts* for the carriage of goods by the particular mode regulated by the respective convention (such as the CMR in relation to carriage by road, the COTIF–CIM in relation to carriage by rail and the Rotterdam Rules in relation to carriage by sea should the convention enter into force) the question whether a multimodal contract can be considered a contract for the carriage of goods by the mode regulated by the specific convention must be answered in the affirmative in order for the network system to be more than a theoretical approach.

2 Again, this statement relates to an international level; the gaps possibly created can be solved through national legislation, which, however, in the perspective of uniform law, seems to be unsatisfactory. See Røsæg who holds "the purpose of a Convention on harmonization of laws must be that the State Parties are not also free to promote alternative rules for the same subject area" (E. Røsæg, "Conflicts of Conventions in the Rotterdam Rules" (2009) 15 JIML 238–248, at p. 242).

3 This rather legalistic view was not the starting point for Grönfors in 1968. When discussing the network system, his focus is not on the actual applicability *ex proprio vigore* of the unimodal conventions, but rather on the problems that might emerge and the general suitability of the system (K. Grönfors, *Successiva Transporter* (1968) pp. 243–257).

4 Cf. section 3.2.2 above. Grönfors refers to it as the "primitive linkage system", which to his apprehension is inferior to a system of "overriding liability" on the part of the contracting carrier (K. Grönfors, *ibid.*, at p. 299).

Where applicability is based on the existence of a contract of carriage for a particular mode, application of the unimodal conventions to multimodal transport has been opposed on various grounds, which were thoroughly discussed above. However, it seems inevitable that the meaning of a contract for the carriage by any of the modes in question must be defined. In general, no legal definition of a contract is given in the conventions, and hence the formation and interpretation of these contracts is, as will be discussed below, left to national contract law. Whilst the contract of carriage is the very core of the prerequisite for application of the CMR convention, the COTIF–CIM convention and the Rotterdam Rules, it is not unessential under the Montreal Convention and the Hague–Visby Rules. Therefore, the contract of carriage is a key prerequisite in the law of carrier's liability in general, so that the contract of carriage must be defined and scrutinized.

Whilst it can be assumed that formation and interpretation of clear unimodal contracts does not cause much problem in relation to application of the said conventions, it is the question of their autonomous applicability to other forms of contracts of carriage that has caused debate. It is the propositions in relation to the CMR convention, holding that the convention is not applicable to carriage by road under a multimodal contract on the basis that a "contract for the carriage by road" should be interpreted as a "contract for the carriage by road, and road only", that is the peephole through which legal problems relating to applicability of the carriage conventions mentioned can be glimpsed. Issues like the status of undefined contracts of carriage, the consequence of performance in relation to contracts of carriage with an option to substitute mode of transport as well as the status of the multimodal contract of carriage are all dependent on defining the contract of carriage.

Indeed, in the Rotterdam Rules, for example, the contract for carriage of goods is defined,[5] but only as far as the modes of transport that the goods may be carried by in order for the rules to apply. Whilst such a definition would, in retrospect, have been very useful in the CMR convention, it does not give any guidance as to when a contract is to be deemed a contract for carriage by road, by rail or by sea or air.

Against the proposition that a contract that provides for e.g. carriage by sea and road is not a contract for carriage by road, the question has to be asked: what, then, is a contract for carriage by road? How is such a contract formed and defined?

5.2 The resort to national law for interpretation of treaties

International treaties are based on the assumption of the sovereignty of states and the autonomy of their rulers. This assumption is the rationale behind the restrictive interpretation of treaties, which traditionally has been the norm. The state is presumed to retain all rights that have not explicitly been waived. In

5 Rotterdam Rules, article 1.1.

relation to uniform law, accession by a state to a convention entails that the state waives its right to autonomy; the state is bound to reflect the uniform law in its national legislation and is thus not permitted to implement rules that contradict the rules of the uniform law. Accordingly, uniform law is usually considered not applicable *ex analogia*.[6] Uniform law is thus considered an exception from the normal rule of national autonomy, and where the uniform law does not claim applicability, national law remains in power. The issue is illustrated by the *Shell Chemicals* case from 1993, where the question was whether national law could be used to fill gaps in the CMR convention. As the CMR convention does not regulate the carrier's liability for delivery of the wrong goods to the consignee, which in the case caused the consignee substantial damage, the question was whether national law could be used to indemnify the consignee. The Commercial Court (the judgment was appealed but not in relation to applicability of the CMR convention) found that liability for damage not caused to the goods consigned for carriage was entirely outside the scope of the convention, and therefore subject to national law.[7]

5.2.1 The scope of conventions versus gaps

Uniform law is often held to be preemptive. To this effect, the English House of Lords held in 1997 that the predecessor to the Montreal Convention, the Warsaw Convention, was exclusive as to the liability of the carrier towards passengers carried, so that remedy could not be granted under national law where the convention provided none.[8]

The question is how this relates to the fact that national law is sometimes applied. As mentioned above, conventions of uniform law constitute an exception in relation to national law and thus what is not regulated by the rules of the convention ought to be regulated by national law. However, the preemptiveness applies to the entire scope of the convention.[9] There is accordingly a difference between non-regulation that falls within the scope of a convention and non-regulation that falls outside the scope.[10] Consequently, in order to define the line between a convention of uniform law and national law, the scope of the convention must be settled. In the English case referred to above, *Shell Chemicals*, the

6 This statement relates to the applicability of uniform law *ex proprio vigore*. A state may obviously extend the applicability of uniform law, which is sometimes done to the effect that uniform law which applies to international carriage by [road] is made applicable to domestic transports as well. However, such extention is a matter of national law, i.e. it is national law that is applied albeit the rules are identical to the rules of the uniform law. It is thus not a matter of application by analogy.

7 *Shell Chemicals UK Ltd v P. & O. Roadtanks Ltd* [1993] 1 Lloyd's Rep 114.

8 *Sidhu v British Airways* [1997] AC 430.

9 V. Ulfbeck, "Udtømmende konventionsregulering og fastlæggelsen af en konventions anvendelseområde" in *Festskrift till Lars Gorton* (2007) pp. 599–615, at p. 599.

10 As discussed in section 2.3.2 above, the Scandinavian maritime codes apply the Hamburg Rules to matters that fall outside the scope of the Hague–Visby Rules, e.g. the carrier's liability before loading and after unloading, which has been considered compatible with the international undertakings that follow from the ratification of the Hague–Visby Rules (J. Schelin, "Styckegodstransport enligt nya sjölagen – en replik" (1995) SvJT 865–874, at p. 866.

court held that the CMR convention related to the "liability of the carriers for loss of or damage or delay to the consigned goods"[11] and that other forms of damage thus lay outside the scope of the convention.

It is thus asserted here that there is a difference between the inside and the outside of the scope of a convention; within the scope the convention is preemptive, but outside the scope national law is applicable.[12] The effect of preemptiveness is that where a certain situation falls within the (material) scope of a convention, national law (or any other law) cannot be applied even if the situation is in fact not regulated in the convention.[13] In *Sidhu v British Airways* cited above, passengers sought a remedy against an airline for having been detained at a Kuwait airport for some weeks during the Iraqi invasion of the country in 1990. The House of Lords held that the situation was *per se* subject to the Warsaw Convention, and the fact that the convention provided no remedy for the kind of damage that the passengers claimed to have suffered entailed that the airline was not liable therefore. The judgment made clear the distinction between the scope of a convention and gaps therein.[14]

It has been asserted that the German courts have tended to view damage that is not regulated by the CMR convention as subject to liability under national law.[15] Thus, for example, the German Supreme Court, the BGH, held in 1979 that carriage of goods that was never completed (the goods were taken over, but the consignment never reached further than the carrier's trailer park due to the carrier's bankruptcy), was not governed by the CMR convention, and therefore the claim for damages due to "non-fulfilment" was to be settled according to national law.[16] This decision has been criticized for being incorrect on the grounds that the damage in question occurred during the period of the carrier's liability as defined in

11 *Shell Chemicals UK Ltd v P. & O. Roadtanks Ltd* [1993] 1 Lloyd's Rep 114, at p. 116.

12 Interestingly, the CISG, which is often held to provide for its own autonomous interpretation, actually refers the interpreter to national law in the case of (internal) gaps. Thus, article 7(2) of the convention requires the interpreter to primarily fill such gaps based on the general principles underlying the convention. However, it is expressly recognized that this may not always be possible and thus the interpreter is allowed to resort to the national law applicable. Accordingly, matters not expressly settled in the convention, but yet subject to the scope of the convention, i.e. what has been defined as gaps, may under certain conditions be filled by national law. It would thus seem unquestionable that matters not subject to the scope of the convention are to be regulated by national law.

13 S. Dempsey and S. Johansson, "Montreal v. Brussels: The Conflict of Laws on the Issue of Delay in International Air Carriage" (2010) 35(3) Air and Space Law 207–224, at p. 208. However, J. Wool and A. Jonovic do not seem to draw a sharp line between the two when holding that "Treaties are not comprehensive codes and do not occupy the whole field of their subject matter. There are significant points ... on which application of national law is required and helpful" (J. Wool and A. Jonovic: "The relationship between transnational commercial law treaties and national law – a framework as applied to the Cape Town Convention" (2013) 2 Cape Town Convention J 65 at p. 70).

14 Also referred to as external and internal gaps (C. Busch, "Identification of Gaps and Gap-Filling under the Common European Sales Law" in A. Colombi Ciacchi (ed.), *Contents and Effects of Contracts – Lessons to Learn from the Common European Sales Law* (2016) pp. 29–44, at pp. 31–32 and F. Enderlein, "Uniform Law and its Application by Judges and Arbitrators" in *International Uniform Law in Practice*, published by UNIDROIT (1988) 329–353, at p. 343).

15 M. Clarke, *International Carriage of Goods by Road: CMR* (2014) p. 14, 204*ff.*

16 BGH 9.2.79, referenced in (1980) 15 ETL 84 and discussed in M. Clarke, *ibid.* at pp. 211–212.

article 17.1 of the CMR – the goods were taken over but never delivered – and accordingly subject to the convention.[17]

Generally, uniform law sets out to govern a certain area of law. Thus, the rights and obligations of the road carrier in relation to carriage of goods under a contract of carriage by road are subject to the CMR convention and likewise the rights and obligations of a sea carrier in relation to goods carried under a contract of carriage that provides for the issuance of a bill of lading are subject to the Hague–Visby Rules. However, neither regulation is completely without what can be defined as "gaps". Accordingly, as mentioned previously, the CMR convention does not specify the carrier's obligations when the wrong goods are delivered, should such wrongful delivery cause other damage than damage related to delayed delivery of the right goods. Although it may be a conclusion near at hand that the drafters of the CMR convention did not envisage the particular problem, and thus the gap constitutes an oversight that has to be settled against other rules, this is, as will be clear from the following, generally regarded as an incorrect approach.

The conventions discussed regulate, first and foremost, the carrier's liability for goods carried. The background to the rules is the freedom of contract applied in the late nineteenth century, with contractual waiver of all and any liability on the part of the sea carrier as a result.[18] The Hague Rules were accordingly drafted against a presumption of non-liability and the liabilities set out in the rules must thus be regarded as exclusive. Even if the historical events behind the carriage by air, rail and road conventions are not identical, it is proposed here that the liabilities set out in these conventions must be considered against a presumption of the right to contract out of liability. Thus, "gaps" are not (to be considered as) oversights but as absence of mandatory liability.[19]

However, the relationship between uniform law and national law has two aspects and another question is resort to national law in order to interpret the terms of the treaty. Not all terms used in a treaty can, for obvious reasons, be defined in the treaty. It is generally considered that terms that have a legal implication are to be understood according to national law.[20] By legal implication in

17 M. Clarke, *ibid.*, at p. 208.

18 V. Ulfbeck, "Fortolkning af ansvarsfriskrivelser" in *Avtalslagen 90 år* (2005), pp. 481–498, at pp. 482–483.

19 In this relation; under English law the standpoint would be that where the contract provides no answer, the correct effect is that nothing is to happen:

> If the parties had intended something to happen, the instrument would have said so. Otherwise, the express provisions of the instrument are to continue to operate undisturbed. If the event has caused loss to one or other of the parties, the loss lies where it falls.
>
> (*Attorney General of Belize v Belize Telecom Ltd* [2009] UKPC 10)

20 Accordingly, Loewe holds that "the general problems of the law of contracts ... are therefore still governed by national law" (Commentary on the convention of 19 May 1956 on the contract for the international carriage of goods by road (CMR) (GE.75–30686), prepared by R. Loewe and published by the UN in 1975, p. 4). Fabricius holds that the CMR convention is not an exhaustive regulation and that therefore issues concerning e.g. the validity of contracts will remain governed by national law (U. Fabricius, *Lov om fragtaftler ved international vejtransport* (2005) p. 34). See also Norwegian *travaux préparatoires*, NOU 2012:10 p. 49. In the Swedish *travaux préparatoires* relating

this respect is intended legal figures, such as the term "contract", that only exist in relation to legal rules.[21] Unless the treaty in question provides rules on how a binding contract is entered into, a contract only exists as a legal figure if it fulfils the prerequisites of a binding contract in relation to the national law.[22] The rationale therefore seems to be the same as above: national law remains applicable in relation to everything that is not governed by uniform law.[23] However, as discussed above, interpretation of the terms of a treaty follows rules of international law. Thus, the question is whether resort to national law in order to interpret certain terms of a treaty can be justified. This will be the focus of the discussion below.

5.2.2 Autonomous interpretation and external context

As discussed in section 4.2.3 above, it is often held that uniform law is to be interpreted autonomously, the basic implication of which is that external sources are to influence uniform law as little as possible. Rather, the meaning of the terms used in uniform law is to be sought from within the treaty itself. It was further concluded in section 4.2.4 that the rules of interpretation recorded in the Vienna Convention to a large extent fulfil that ambition; in fact, there is no direct reference to external sources in the Vienna Convention. However, it was also proposed above that the context in the light of which the terms of a treaty are to be interpreted may include an external understanding of the terms. For example, the "ordinary meaning" of a term can only be drawn from external reference, i.e. the meaning of words cannot be sought from within the treaty, at least not as a starting point.

When the term "context" as it appears in the Vienna Convention is discussed, it is generally considered to refer primarily to the text of the treaty itself, its preamble and possible annexes, which is also the starting point of the convention itself.[24] The "text" of the treaty is used to ensure that interpretation of a particular term is in conformity with the idea of the treaty as a logical and consistent

to COTIF–CIM 1999 it is held that whilst the COTIF–CIM of 1980 governed the entering into the contract of carriage ("The contract of carriage shall come into existence as soon as the forwarding railway has accepted the goods for carriage together with the consignment note" (article 11 §1)) the new rules do not govern the formation of the contract of carriage, which is "regulated by national law" (SOU 2015:9 p. 83). Characterizing the changes to the COTIF–CIM 1999 is the approach of the rules to the CMR convention (SOU 2015:9 p. 80).

21 Another example of such a term is "damage". In its legal sense "damage" means such damage that is recoverable from e.g. a tortfeasor. What constitutes such damage is not always regulated in the convention, but will have to be determined though application of national law. In relation to the Montreal Convention, see Swedish Supreme Court NJA 2016 s. 900: "Just as little as the Montreal Convention contains a definition of what constitutes delay, does the convention provide any guidance regarding what kind of damage that entitles compensation" (my translation).

22 Which national law is a matter of the rules of private international law, and is outside the scope of this work.

23 N.B. the expressions "still" and "remains" above. This applies to issues not regulated in the convention and not to "gaps"; cf. section 5.2.1 above.

24 Vienna Convention, article 31:2.

whole.[25] To a certain extent, the "text" of the treaty, i.e. the treaty in its entirety, is interpretative data that lead to an autonomous interpretation. The "context" is further specified to include what could be defined as pre-contractual information as well as post-contractual agreements.[26] It seems to be the general opinion that the "context" is limited to the definition in article 31.[27] Under such an assumption the context is "internal", i.e. limited to the treaty itself and circumstances surrounding its conclusion and application.

The "ordinary meaning" of a term is considered primarily to refer to its everyday meaning, although it has been recognized that professional language is sometimes a more appropriate standard.[28] However, in fact, when professional terms are used, it would seem contrary to the principle of interpretation in good faith to understand the term according to its everyday meaning rather than its professional meaning and it has been held that such interpretation finds no support in the Vienna Convention.[29] Thus, the "ordinary meaning" of a term "in its context" would denounce the everyday or professional meaning of a term in the context, in a wide sense, of the treaty in which it is found. There is, however, a more profound complication when a term, which is to be understood in a professional meaning, is to be interpreted. Accordingly, whilst the "meaning" of a term may be sufficiently clear, the actual understanding thereof, in a professional sense, may not be undisputed. To such an interpretative problem, the context, as defined above, may not readily provide a solution.

Based on the previous discussion, it is asserted here that treaties of uniform law generally cannot be interpreted wholly autonomously.[30] Although the meaning of a certain term is unambiguous, the understanding thereof presupposes reference to sources other than those explicit in the Vienna Convention.[31] Accordingly, the "ordinary meaning" of a term "in its context" must include not only the normal understanding of the term in light of the context of the treaty in its entirety, but also the understanding of the term in its "external" context.

5.2.3 National law as context

Many of the terms in a treaty have not only an ordinary meaning that must be sought from outside the treaty itself, but a more profound meaning in a legal sense. Some terms have legal implications and without being given a legal meaning they are without much value.[32]

25 U. Linderfalk, *On the Interpretation of Treaties* (2007), ch. 4.

26 Vienna Convention, article 31:2–3.

27 U. Linderfalk, *On the Interpretation of Treaties* (2007) p. 126 (fn. 2).

28 U. Linderfalk, *ibid.*, at p. 67.

29 C. Lo, "Good Faith Use of Dictionary in the Search of Ordinary Meaning under the WTO Dispute Settlement Understanding" (2010) 1(2) Journal of International Dispute Settlement 431–445, at p. 443.

30 Cf. in particular sections 4.2.3 and 5.2.2.

31 "Rules depend on other rules for meaning …." (J. Merryman, "On the Convergence (and Divergence) of the Civil Law and the Common Law" (1981) 17 Stan J Int'l L 357 at p. 379).

32 A relevant example is the bill of lading. Whilst the Hague–Visby Rules contain prerequisites as regards what details should be included in a bill of lading, it does not provide the legal base for what constitutes a bill of lading as such. As discussed above, the prerequisite that differentiates the bill of

As discussed, interpreting legal terms against national definitions inevitably leads to a disharmonization of the uniform law. Such disharmonization can be avoided though autonomous interpretation, or by using other terms in drafting uniform law, which do not have a distinct national definition. To a certain extent, terms with a legal meaning may be defined in a treaty of uniform law itself.[33] Accordingly, "International Carriage" is defined in the Montreal Convention and the terms "carrier", "contract of carriage", "goods", "ship" and "carriage of goods" are defined in the Hague–Visby Rules.[34] In the CMR convention, the term "vehicle" is defined by reference to the Convention on Road Traffic.[35] The Rotterdam Rules contains a catalogue of definitions, amounting to 30 terms. In spite of this, there are terms with a legal implication that are not defined, one being "contract".[36] These terms are meaningless if not understood in relation to national law; legal figures that only exist if supported by a legal system (uniform or national).[37] Where not defined in the treaty, they cannot be interpreted autonomously. A relevant example is the bill of lading. Whilst the Hague–Visby Rules contain prerequisites as regards what details should be included in a bill of lading, it does not provide the legal base for what constitutes a bill of lading as such. As discussed above, the prerequisite that differentiates the bill of lading from other transport documents is its status as a negotiable document. However, in order for a document to be negotiable it has to comply with the laws of the jurisdiction in question that settles what constitutes a negotiable document. Another example is the contract of carriage, and, as mentioned above, it has been held in relation to the CMR convention that the contract, the formation, the validity and the interpretation thereof, remains an issue of national law.

Obviously, there are terms that are not legal figures in that respect, but legal terms that could be given any meaning. These terms can be interpreted wholly autonomously as, even though it would be rather complicated if a term in a treaty is given a completely different meaning than what would be expected,[38] they do

lading from other transport documents is its status as a negotiable document. However, in order for a document to be negotiable it has to comply with the laws of the jurisdiction in question that settles what constitutes a negotiable document.

33 A means of avoiding disharmonization advocated by K. Strandgaard in 1935 (K. Strandgaard, "Sørettens Internationalisering" (1935) 6 Nordisk Tidsskrift Int'l Ret 144–154, at p. 148).

34 See article 1.2 of the Montreal Convention and article 1 of the Hague–Visby Rules.

35 Article 1.2 of the CMR convention reads: "For the purpose of this Convention, 'vehicles' means motor vehicles, articulated vehicles, trailers and semi-trailers as defined in article 4 of the Convention on Road Traffic dated 19 September 1949."

36 By "defined" is not intended definitions such as that a contract is only considered a contract of carriage under a certain convention if it e.g. provides for the payment of freight, but a definition of the legal figure, i.e. what constitutes a legally binding contract.

37 Lestas holds that legal concepts generally gain their meaning as a result of national authoritative stipulations; the definition thereof depends on how the relevant concept is used in legal sources (G. Lestas, *A Theory of Interpretation of the European Convention on Human Rights* (2007) p. 48).

38 Which reminds of Lord Hoffmann's citation from *Through the Looking Glass* in *Investors v Bromwich*:

> Alice and Humpty-Dumpty were agreed that the word "glory" did not mean "a nice knock-down argument." Anyone with a dictionary could see that Humpty Dumpty's point was that "a nice knock-down argument" was what *he* meant by using the word "glory".
>
> (*Investors Compensation Scheme Ltd v West Bromwich Building Society* [1998] 1 WLR 896, at p. 914)

not need the support of legal rules in order to exist. Such interpretation would however be contrary to the "ordinary meaning" of the term and naturally not advocated by anyone. It is however obvious that, in interpreting a legal term, reference must be made to its external meaning; even if it is not given its distinct national meaning in a particular national system, the starting point must be its meaning in some national system.[39] As a starting point, it is thus asserted here that some terms, such as "contract", cannot be interpreted without reference to external sources. The question that draws attention is accordingly the relationship between interpretation of treaties and national law.

The conclusion was drawn above that treaties of uniform law constitute an exception to national law and that in areas of law to which a certain treaty does not apply, national law applies (which however does not mean that national law is to be applied as soon as uniform law does not provide a remedy). Thus, national law serves as the base on which uniform law is built. In relation to treaties of uniform law, the drafting thereof would be virtually impossible if it were not based on existing legal terms and concepts.[40] The material rules of uniform law, in whichever form they are made binding in a national legal system, are part of a legal context and constitute *lex specialis* in relation to general national law.[41]

As discussed above, the existing rules on interpretation of treaties do not entirely cater for the needs of uniform law in respect of interpreting legal terms and concepts. Although the "ordinary meaning" of a term may include the professional understanding of that term, it was suggested above that the professional understanding of a term may not be sufficient. For example, the professional understanding of the term "contract" could be "an agreement which is binding, i.e. the parties can enforce the agreement with the assistance of the legal system". However, in order to interpret the term in its capacity of a prerequisite for applicability of the treaty itself, this explanation may not suffice and thus other information regarding "contract" may be needed. In the conventions discussed, the term "contract" appears as part of the term "contract of carriage", which is further defined as regards the mode of transport. In order to understand the term "contract" as it thus appears, the interpreter may need to know e.g. how a contract is entered into, how the contents are settled, if it needs to be in any particular form or whether it may be oral. This information is not embedded in the ordinary meaning of the term, even if that ordinary meaning

39 It is asserted here that no lawyer is able to read a legal term without giving it, as a starting point, the legal meaning known to him or her. It would be uncritical to believe that a lawyer can interpret a legal term truly autonomously, i.e. from a blank page.

40 K. Strandgaard, "Sørettens Internationalisering" (1935) 6 Nordisk Tidsskrift Int'l Ret 144–154, at p. 148.

41 For example, although general law of damages would normally grant a party who has suffered damage full compensation for damage caused by the tortfeasor's negligence, the material rules of the Hague–Visby Rules only grants the party who has suffered damage a limited amount, and in some cases no damages although the carrier has been negligent (such as the case of negligent navigation). In relation to the limitation periods in international transport conventions, the Supreme Court of Sweden has held these to be *lex specialis* in relation to the general limitation period of 10 years (NJA 2016 s. 149, at p. 152). See also Swedish Supreme Court NJA 2014 s. 425, at p. 6.

is the professional understanding thereof. Rather, it must be sought from the underlying base of national law.[42]

It is proposed that the "context", as defined in article 31 of the Vienna Convention, does not actually admit reference to national law as part of the context of a treaty. The definition of the context is, perhaps with the exception of "the text of the treaty", focused on the subjective intention of the contracting parties. It is however held here that questions regarding interpretation of legal terms and concepts that appear in relation to uniform law treaties usually cannot be solved by reference to e.g. subsequent conduct or agreements concurrent with the treaty, or even a special meaning intended by the contracting parties. As discussed above, reference must be made to the underlying national law. It seems that the authorization of such reference is usually done through separating what is governed by the uniform law, and what is not; "general problems of the law of contracts … are therefore still governed by national law".[43] In some instances, the example given by Loewe is validity of contracts, it may be concluded that the treaty in question does not regulate the question at hand, so that resort is had to national law. However, when it comes to questions of interpreting the terms of a treaty, national law of contracts cannot be as easily separated from the uniform law. Accordingly, in order to interpret the term "contract of carriage by [road]", the interpreter must consider national law of contracts, but the reference to national law is not disconnected from application of the rules of the treaty. The reference to national law is instead part of the context in relation to which the terms of a treaty are understood. Although the context, as defined in the Vienna Convention, does not explicitly provide for the thus prescribed procedure, it is necessitated by the particularity of uniform law in relation to "ordinary" contract-like treaties.

On the other hand, resort to national law requires great precaution in order to prevent disharmonization. A warning example is the interpretation of the term "wilful misconduct" found in article 29 of the CMR convention. When interpreted by national courts, the term has come to have diverse implications in the various state parties, which has clearly disrupted harmonization and entailed a non-negligible amount of forum shopping.[44] Thus, with the assumption that no

42 To be clear: it is not advocated here that interpretation of legal terms in uniform law should simply be done by reference to the definition of the term in the national system where the interpretation takes place. As held above, such procedure will lead to disharmony and fragmentation as in the case of interpretation of the term "willful misconduct" in article 29 of the CMR convention; cf. below. What is held here is that interpretation by necessity starts from the understanding of the term in a particular national system, after which the term can be understood in relation to the objective of the treaty in question, i.e. autonomously.

43 Commentary on the convention of 19 May 1956 on the contract for the international carriage of goods by road (CMR) (GE.75–30686), prepared by R. Loewe and published by the UN in 1975, p. 4.

44 For this diverse application of article 29 the wording of the article itself is partly to blame; it refers to "default ... [which] according to the law of court or tribunal seised of the case, is considered as equivalent to wilful misconduct". Thus, some states, such as Austria and Germany, have expanded the article to comprise also gross negligence, whilst others allow only default with intent to qualify as wilful misconduct (M. Clarke, *International carriage of goods by road: CMR* (2014) p. 312*ff*.). Although the drafters of the CMR convention seem to bear most of the blame for this

legal terms of a treaty can be interpreted entirely without reference to the understanding of the term in national law, the question remains how to prevent disharmonization. On the one end of the scale, it is clear that the understanding of a legal term in a treaty must not simply equal the understanding thereof in the particular national system.[45] On the other end of the scale, an entirely autonomous understanding requires the definition of the term in the treaty.[46] For all the other cases along the scale, it would seem wise to consider the national definitions of a certain term from various state parties and consider the "ordinary meaning" of the term to be the "weighted" understanding thereof.[47] Thus, in order to preserve uniformity interpretation of legal terms and concepts should be made by reference to such common denominators of the law as can find support in the contracting states in general.[48]

5.2.4 Conclusions

In summary, in the interpretation of uniform law, reference to national law would seem to promote disharmonization rather than the harmonization that is the general goal of uniform law. Autonomous interpretation, on the other hand, preserves uniformity by referring the interpreter to seek the answer to interpretative questions from within the convention itself. Such interpretation is further promoted by application of the rules of treaty interpretation of the Vienna Convention. However, uniform law rests on the pre-existence of a system of law and it is intended to form part of the various systems of national law. It is not possible to draft uniform law without taking advantage of pre-existing law: a completely autonomous system is not possible.[49] It is asserted here that it is not desirable either as it would not only disrupt the legal system in which it is to act, but it would be completely impermeable and the actual purpose of the uniform law would be lost in a maze of definitions. Accordingly, entirely autonomous interpretation of uniform law is neither possible nor desirable, but resort must sometimes be had to national law.

When such reference to national law is made, justification in line with that the issue in question "remains subject to national law", seems to be made. The reference to national law is often, assumedly, so natural to many courts that the

---

disharmonization, it can still serve to illustrate the risks of involving national law in the interpretation of uniform law.

45 Although such interpretation, as discussed in section 4.2.2 above, has historically been the norm, in 1937 it was already seen as a problem (K. Strandgaard, "Sørettens Internationalisering" (1935) 6 Nordisk Tidsskrift Int'l Ret 144–154).

46 K. Strandgaard *ibid.*, at p. 148.

47 As far as the uniform law limited to European application is concerned reference to projects such as the DCFR (Draft Common Frame of Reference) facilitates the quest for the common denominator, but it should be remembered that such projects are of a soft-law character and in the case of interpretation of legal figures such as contracts, which as discussed demands the "support" of a legal system, such soft law may be inadequate.

48 It is recognized, however, that ultimately the conclusion and interpretation of a contract is a matter of national law. Thus, "common denominators" can never override the actual law of contracts.

49 J. Basedow, "The Renaissance of Uniform Law: European Contract Law and its Components" (1998) 18 Legal Stud 121, at p. 123.

relationship with the uniform law is not reflected upon.[50] Although accurate on the one hand, it does not reduce the confusion of the relationship between uniform law and national law. As elaborated, national law thus acts on two levels; one being outside the scope of uniform law, albeit on the same level; and the other one being the base level of general law, which form the necessary base of all *lex specialis*.

Those situations where understanding or interpreting a treaty of uniform law is not possible without reference to national law are characterized by use, in the treaty, of terms that are legal in their character and the legal implication of which cannot be found within the treaty of uniform law. It is asserted here that "contract of carriage by [road]" is such a legal term and that interpretation of that term is not possible without reference to national law of contracts.[51]

5.3 Categorizing transport contracts

The contractual approach, which was discussed in section 1.1.1, places the transport contract in focus. Although all conventions discussed in this work contain a definition or at least a qualification of the contract of carriage, the definition of the contract as such is not addressed but left to general legislation.

It is apparent that on many occasions the concept of the contract needs to be defined. When it comes to the application of unimodal conventions to unimodal contracts, the question how a contract for the carriage by [road] is to be defined is interesting, but perhaps rather theoretical and the answer does not differ from what constitutes a contract in general. However, some of the problems discussed in the following sections may still remain relevant in relation to unimodal contracts, such as the question of substitution of transport modes.

The multimodal contract places special focus on the transport contract as such in relation to the conventions that apply through the contractual approach. In order to apply the unimodal conventions to the separate legs of a multimodal transport in accordance with the network system, there must exist a *contract* for the transport of goods for each separate mode of transport. Even where a multimodal contract contains clear agreement on the mode of transport to be used for each leg, and the multimodal contract in question could thus be said to contain two or more unimodal agreements, the concept of the multimodal contract as a contract *sui generis* may prevent application of the unimodal conventions. In addition, there are various shapes of the transport contract that are multimodal in appearance, or at least not purely unimodal, that can be added to the picture. In order to discuss the applicability of the conventions that apply to contracts of

50 See e.g. the Swedish Supreme Court NJA 2009 N3, where legislation on unfair contracts terms is discussed in relation to a contract of carriage of passengers by rail and Southern Court of Appeal (HovR över Skåne och Blekinge) in T113–12, 2 May 2013, where the entering into a contract of carriage by way of proxy is discussed. Indeed, in relation to the latter case, the carriage of passengers by rail convention, the COTIF–CIV, would not be applicable until it has been established that a contract of carriage in fact has been entered into.

51 R. de Wit, *Multimodal Transport* (1995) p. 39.

carriage to multimodal contracts of carriage, the different types of contract of carriage that exist today will be inventoried.

Variations to the transport contract are many and in constant evolution. Not only has the transport contract evolved from the relatively straightforward unimodal contract to the multimodal contract. Modern door-to-door contracts are, it is often held, *in blanco* as far as the mode of transport to be used is concerned. It is thus often held that a transport buyer is only interested in the (timely) movement of its goods and therefore leaves the choice of route and transport mode to the professional judgement of the carrier. Further, contracts involving both transport as well as other services have emerged. These include not only storage of goods but repacking, mounting and similar services, to a degree where transport of the goods becomes subordinate to services performed.

Considering the many versions of the transport contract thus used, in order to draw any conclusions regarding the applicability of unimodal conventions in relation to this spectrum of transport contracts, it is necessary to distinguish between them.[52] Based on the mode of transport contracted for, three categories can be identified: the unimodal contract, the multimodal contract and the undefined contract, where the mode(s) of transport is to be decided by the carrier.[53] In addition, the transport contract which contains a right to substitute mode of transport stands out as an independent category, at least to the extent that the right of substitution is invoked by the carrier. This category is accordingly named "incorrectly defined contracts of carriage", as the mode agreed in the contract is not the mode by which the transport is later performed.

5.3.1 Unimodal contracts of carriage

Contracts of carriage of goods by a single mode of transport belong to the most basic form of transport agreement and are unquestionably subject to the respective conventions discussed in this chapter. Further, there seems to be unanimity that there are no form requirements and thus oral and other types of informal agreement qualify as contracts as far as the applicability of the regimes in question is concerned. In fact, it is asserted that a large amount of transport is not preceded by a formal contract in the sense of an antecedent agreement. Instead, a contract between the shipper and the carrier results in the issuing of a confirmation by the carrier. This confirmation will likely contain the carrier's general conditions along with the individual details of the transport, and is obviously at least proof of the contract entered into between the parties, but the shipper may very well describe the procedure as making a booking rather than entering into a transport contract. Hence, many transport contracts could be regarded as tacit agreements. Nevertheless, there seems to be no suggestion that these agreements

52 Transport service agreements will not be included in the discussion to follow and are thus not included in any category.

53 Although drafted independently, this distinction can be found elsewhere; see e.g. L. Andersen Roost; *Multimodale Transporter* (2012).

would not be subject to carriage conventions adhering to the contractual approach to applicability.

The unimodal contract of carriage is the core focus of these unimodal transport conventions and accordingly should pose no problems in relation to the conventions. However, some of the problems discussed below may also be relevant in relation to unimodal transport contracts. For example, if a carrier under a unimodal contract of carriage in accordance with the contract substitutes part of the transport for another mode, is the contract then a multimodal contract? The judgment by the Danish Supreme Court in 2008 (U.2008.1638H) mentioned above has been read so as to indicate that the position in Danish law is that invoking a substitution clause will not change the unimodal character of the contract.[54] However, as this conclusion entails that one liability regime will be applied to the entire contract, it must be based on the presumption that the regime governing the substituted for mode of transport can be avoided, thus that it does not apply mandatorily to performance or to a certain form of document. Where a convention or other legal regime bases its applicability on performance by a certain mode of transport, and that regime is mandatorily applicable, it is not possible to regard the contract as unimodal in the sense that it is subject to the regime applicable to the contracted for mode of transport only. The same result may follow where applicability is based on the existence of a certain form of document. Thus, it is precarious to make a general deduction to the effect that the contract should be governed in its entirety by the regime applicable to the mode of transport initially contracted for.

Another question relates to performance of undefined contracts; if a contract of carriage that does not specify the mode of transport to be used is carried out by a single mode, does that contract then constitute a contract for carriage by that single mode? Under German national law, the answer seems to be "yes" and hence an undefined contract will be considered a contract for transport by the mode by which it is carried out, as long as that mode is reasonably foreseeable.[55] In Sweden too, it has been asserted that performance of a contract of carriage is, or at least should be, relevant to conclusion of which liability rules to apply.[56]

A related question is the status of a contract for carriage by one single mode if that mode is in its entirety substituted for another mode of carriage. The contract as well as the transport is unimodal, but under which liability regime should the carrier's liability be settled? If the contracted for mode of transport is subject to a

54 Andersen Roost claims, with reference to the Danish Supreme Court HD 23 April 2008 (U.2008.1638H), that Danish law will not treat such a contract as a multimodal contract of carriage (L. Andersen Roost, *Multimodale Transporter* (2012) p. 58). However, as Ulfbeck and Taiger Ivø point out, it is likely that the case would have had a different outcome had the shipper been made aware of the likelihood that the option would be invoked (V. Ulfbeck and S. Taiger Ivø, "Optioner och ansvar i transportaftaler" (2008) 4 Erhvervsjuridisk Tidsskrift 331–343, at p. 337). Hence, the case should perhaps not be given such an undifferentiated interpretation.

55 L. Andersen Roost, *ibid.*, p. 68, with reference to Basedow, *Der Transportvertrag* (1987).

56 J. Ramberg, *The Law of Transport Operators* (2005) p. 25 and J. Ramberg, "Global Unification of Transport Law: A Hopeless Task?" (2008–2009) 27 Penn St Int'l L Rev 851 at p. 857.

liability regime that applies to contracts of carriage and the substituted for mode of transport is subject to a liability regime applicable to performance, and should the contract be considered not to be affected by the fact that performance is actually carried out by another mode of transport, as suggested above in relation to part-substitution, then a conflict between the two liability regimes arises.

These questions will be discussed further below and in relation to unimodal contracts of carriage it suffices to note that there are variations that complicate what prima facie appears as a clear-cut case.

5.3.2 Clear mode-to-mode multimodal contracts

The typical example of a multimodal contract is a contract of carriage that specifies transport as to be carried out by different modes of transport and between which places the goods are to be carried by such modes: for example, a contract for the carriage of a container of electronic devices to be carried from Bangalore in India to Mölndal in Sweden, which transport is to be carried out by rail between Bangalore and Chennai, by sea between Chennai and Göteborg and by road from Göteborg to Mölndal. The legal definition of multimodal contracts of carriage, which certainly corresponds with this notion, is often drawn from the l Multimodal Convention and is thus defined as "a contract whereby a multimodal transport operator undertakes, against freight, to perform or to procure the performance of international multimodal transport".[57] Multimodal transport is in turn defined as

> the carriage of goods by at least two different modes of transport on the basis of a multimodal transport contract from a place in one country at which the goods are taken in charge by the multimodal transport operator to a place designated for delivery situated in a different country.[58]

What constitutes a contract under which the carrier undertakes to carry the goods by at least two modes can obviously be discussed. It has been asserted that it suffices that the surrounding circumstances make it clear that the transport is intended to be carried out as multimodal transport.

Another question is the status of mode-on-mode carriage. Whilst the carriage of aircrafts or ships, laden with goods, by other modes of transport seems quite unrealistic, the carriage of trucks and railway cars by sea (ro-ro ferries) is common and the carriage of trucks by railway does exist. However, mode-on-mode transport is only explicitly regulated in the CMR convention.[59] Under article 2 of the CMR convention transport that involves carriage of a road vehicle and its

57 Article 1.3.

58 Article 1.1: This could obviously include unimodal contracts where transportation is eventually carried out by more than one mode under an option clause, as described above (cf. also M. Hoeks, *Multimodal Transport Law* (2010) pp. 62–64). The current division is made for the sake of clarity and should not be considered a position regarding the definition of the multimodal contract.

59 Article 1:3 of the COTIF–CIM convention regulates domestic carriage by road or inland waterway supplementary to transfrontier carriage by rail. Whilst the latter could include domestic crossing by ro-ro transport of a river, ro-ro ferry traffic in general is not referred to in the convention.

cargo by another mode of transport are, somewhat simplified, governed in their entirety by the convention. Such mode-on-mode transport appears to be most common in road carriage (ro-ro ferry traffic and rail carriage during which the road vehicle is carried by a rail car, e.g. through the English Channel tunnel), but also exists in rail carriage where the rail car is carried by ro-ro ferry.[60] The question is whether this mode-on-mode (or "piggy back") carriage should be classified as multimodal transport. During a ro-ro ferry transport of a road vehicle with cargo, the goods are in fact carried by sea and is, although to a minor degree considering the limited distance of a regular ferry crossing, subject to the particular risks of sea transport. On the other hand, the goods are still loaded onto the road vehicle, which in turn is carried on a ship. Whilst some writers hold that mode-on-mode transport is not to be classified as multimodal transport, based on the circumstance that no re-loading of the goods takes place,[61] others hold that it should indeed be classified as multimodal transport, as the transport is carried out by more than one mode.[62] In addition, in the debate regarding applicability of the CMR convention to road carriage under a multimodal transport contract article 2 of the CMR convention is frequently discussed without the multimodality of mode-on-mode transport being questioned.[63] The assumption on which article 2 of the CMR convention rests is clearly the former.[64] However, it is asserted here that mode-on-mode transports should be regarded as a form of multimodal transport and thus, where such transport is agreed or implicitly clear due to e.g. the agreed route, the transport agreement must be considered multimodal.[65]

Further, the impact of pick-up and delivery services may be discussed.[66] Where such transport, which is presumed to be of lesser importance in relation to the main transport, is performed in connection with an otherwise unimodal transport, the question is whether such services will change the character of "unimodal"

60 Mode-on-mode carriage of ships or aircraft seems somewhat unrealistic.

61 U. Fabricius, *Lov om Fragtaftaler ved international vejtransport (CMR)* (2005) p. 63. See also E. Selvig who concludes, regarding the Multimodal Convention, that article 30.4 of the convention, which refers to mode-on-mode contracts governed by article 2 of the CMR, "excludes certain types of contracts which some may consider to be multimodal contracts" indicating that the author himself does not regard them to be multimodal contracts (E. Selvig, "Multimodal transport: the 1980 U.N. Convention: papers of a one day seminar: Southampton University, Faculty of Law, 12th September 1980", at p. A3, para. 2).

62 L. Andersen Roost, *Multimodale Transporter* (2012) p. 57.

63 Clarke: "multimodal transport (or combined transport) can take more than one form and Article 2 is concerned with only one of them" (M. Clarke, "A Multimodal mix-up" (2002) JBL 210–217, at p. 212). See also K.F. Haak, "The harmonization of intermodal liability arrangements" (2005) ETL 11–51, at p. 24 and I. Koller, "Quantum Corporation Inc. v. Plane Trucking Limited und die Anwendbarkeit der CMR auf die Beförderung mit verschiedenartigen Transportmitteln" (2003) 2 TransportR 45–50, at p. 47.

64 Commentary on the convention of 19 May 1956 on the contract for the international carriage of goods by road (CMR) (GE.75-30686), prepared by R. Loewe and published by the UN in 1975, p. 17.

65 However, L. Andersen Roost seems to claim that a transport contract which contains a stipulation on piggy-back transport constitutes a contract for unimodal transport, although she holds that mode-on-mode transport is a form of multimodal transport (L. Andersen Roost, *ibid.*, at p. 57).

66 Grönfors discusses "accessory transport" and his definition of "successive carriage" refers to contracts where the main transport is carried out by multiple modes of transports, thus excluding supplementary carriage (K. Grönfors, *Successiva Transporter* (1968) pp. 97–100).

transport into multimodal transport. An example serves as illustration. A contract of carriage by air of certain cargo between Heathrow airport and JFK airport is entered into. In addition, the carrier undertakes to pick up the cargo from the shipper's premises north of London and deliver them to the consignor in New York City. Should this contract, presuming that air carriage and additional services are covered by the same contract, be considered unimodal or multimodal? In the Multimodal Convention, such pick-up and delivery services are exempted from the convention's application in that the character of an otherwise unimodal contract is not changed only because pick-up and delivery services are included in the carrier's undertaking.[67] Hence, under the definition of a multimodal contract given in the Multimodal Convention, contracts for transport by one main mode of transport, which also includes pick-up and/or delivery services by another mode, are not considered multimodal contracts. A mirroring approach is taken in the COTIF–CIM convention, which includes domestic pick-up and delivery services carried out by road or inland water way supplementary to international rail transport subject to one single contract of carriage, into its scope of applicability. Nothing is stated in the COTIF–CIM convention regarding the modal status of such a contract, but there is nothing to indicate that the contract is not to be regarded as multimodal. Nor does the Montreal Convention attempt to redefine the multimodal contract; it merely establishes a presumption of the point in time of any damage occurring in relation to carriage by air and ancillary pick up and/or delivery by another mode.[68] Where the damage can be localized to pick up or delivery, the Montreal Convention is not applicable, in contrast to the COTIF–CIM convention, which *applies* to such transport. The Montreal Convention seems thus to recognize the carriage by air contract that includes pick-up and/or delivery services as a multimodal contract, but it tries to avoid some of the difficulties that the network system would entail. In conclusion, pick-up and delivery services under the Montreal Convention and the COTIF–CIM convention can be compared to mode-on-mode transport under the CMR convention. In all three conventions ancillary and frequently occurring transport by other modes have been, in some way or another, subsumed under the respective convention, not changing the multimodal character of the contract, but attempting to avoid the problems connected with the network system and then mainly localization of damage to the actual mode during which it occurred.

67 E. Selvig, *ibid.*, at p. A3, para. 2. In article 1.1 of the Multimodal Convention multimodal transport is defined as the carriage of goods by at least two different modes of transport on the basis of a multimodal transport contract. Further, it is explicitly stated in the article that transports by one mode that however include operations of pick-up and delivery of goods shall not be considered as international multimodal transport. Some problems in application can be perceived as a multimodal contract is first defined as a contract prescribing transport by two modes, whereafter contracts for two (or three depending on whether the pick-up and delivery are performed by the same mode) modes of transport are excluded as far as they are subject to a unimodal contract. However, according to the definition given of the multimodal contract it seems impossible to carry out ancillary transport by any other mode under a unimodal contract, as that contract would then be a multimodal contract.

68 Montreal Convention, article 18.4.

A multimodal contract can be characterized either as a contract *sui generis* or as segmented carriage consisting of two or more unimodal transports. In the absence of a uniform system governing multimodal transport, the effect of the former is a state of freedom of contract as no international set of rules, mandatory or non-mandatory, regulates the carrier's liability. Contrasted with the current unimodal regulations, which are mandatory, this complete freedom of contract appears somewhat arbitrary and objectionable.[69] And even if freedom of contract may be acceptable, or even desirable, there are no compelling reasons why this should apply to multimodal carriers but not to unimodal carriers.[70]

However, as application of the network system is based on the autonomous application of the unimodal conventions, the question whether or not the unimodal conventions applicable to contracts of carriage by a certain mode of transport apply autonomously to contracts of a multimodal character is vital. In order for the network system to be applicable, there must be some form of justification, or logical explanation, of the applicability of the unimodal conventions to multimodal contracts of carriage. As far as conventions that apply to performance by a particular mode of transport are concerned, the application thereof to multimodal contracts reflects application to unimodal contracts of carriage. However, so far as the conventions that apply to contracts of carriage by a certain mode of transport are concerned, the multimodal contract of carriage must be rethought; the justification for applicability of the unimodal conventions in question must be that the multimodal contract is a contract of carriage for the carriage of goods by [road]. It appears that, generally, the multimodal contract is accordingly seen as several contracts; one for every mode anticipated by the parties, which thus entails that the unimodal conventions apply to the unimodal legs of the transport. However, the network system can also be justified by considering the contractually allowed for carriage by a particular mode effectuating a contract for the same mode. Thus, the multimodal contract of carriage is not regarded as several contracts of unimodal carriage, but as a contract that fulfils the prerequisite of being a contract of carriage by [road], where it prescribes such carriage.

As discussed previously in section 3.4, the issue whether the unimodal conventions that apply to contracts of carriage apply to carriage under multimodal contracts is heavily debated. The view that multimodal contracts are not subject to unimodal regimes has, as has been elaborated, given room for judgments such as the BGH 17 July 2008, the Danish Supreme Court of 23 April 2008 and the Dutch Supreme Court of 1 June 2012, the *Godafoss*.[71] Given these judgments and

69 J. Ramberg, *The Law of Transport Operators* (2005) p. 25.

70 Many reputable multimodal carriers no doubt have general conditions that mirror the core regulations of the current mandatory regimes; however it is the not-so-reputable carriers that could take advantage of the freedom of contract situation that the mandatory regulations seek to protect shippers from and there is no reason to assume that the multimodal field contains fewer such carriers than the unimodal fields, which is why the same reasons for protection of shippers assert themselves with equal strength.

71 German Federal Supreme Court BGH 17 July 2008, I ZR 181/05; Danish Supreme Court HD 23 April 2008 (U.2008.1638H) and Dutch Supreme Court, Hoge Raad, 1 June 2012, nr.10/05322.

the subsequent legal uncertainty, it is far from obvious that the network system applies *ex proprio vigore* to multimodal contracts of carriage. The only thing that is clear in this regard is that no party to a multimodal transport contract can presume the network system to be mandatorily applied without contractual reference thereto.

5.3.3 "Undefined" contracts of carriage

A contract may very well not specify by what mode of transport it is to be carried out.[72] A shipper may leave such choice to the professional judgment of the carrier and focus its main interest on price and time.[73] These undefined, or general, contracts of carriage are neither multimodal nor unimodal (but perhaps amodal) at the outset. The undefined contract of carriage needs to be specified in one way or another and it is perhaps not until carriage is actually performed that the mode or modes of transport are manifested.

However, where thus the mode of transport to be used has not been explicitly stated in the contract of carriage, the parties may nevertheless be considered to have agreed on the mode of transport. Although the written contract does not specify the mode of transport to be used, the parties can obviously have agreed separately on a certain mode of transport, but the choice may also be implicitly obvious, e.g. due to the route and/or the agreed price.[74] As will be discussed in further detail below, such a contract would under Scandinavian law be regarded as a contract for the carriage of goods by whichever mode was thus implicitly agreed; in both cases it is the common intention of the parties that the goods should be carried by the mode in question and, thus, such is their agreement.[75] Under English common law, it seems that implication of terms is surrounded by rules of strict scrutinization of the term suggested to be implied. Further, interpretation of contracts is to a larger extent subject to procedural rules that may prevent evidence of implied terms.[76]

---

72 Andersen Roost holds this type of contract to be a primarilty Scandinavian legal device (L. Andersen Roost, *Multimodale Transporter* (2012) p. 67). However, it is also discussed in other European literature (M. Hoeks, *Multimodal Transport Law* (2010) p. 85; W. Verheyen, "Fleximodal Contracts and the CMR: the Belgian approach" (2012) 18 (5) JIML 364–371; R. De Wit, *Multimodal Transport* (1995) p. 171 and D. Glass, "Meddling in the multimodal muddle" [2006] LMCQ 307, at p. 314). However, Glass asserts that the undefined contract of carriage is not as common as is often held (D. Glass, *ibid.*, at p. 314, fn. 53).

73 The existence of the undefined transport contract is often stated as an obvious fact, e.g. V. Ulfbeck and S. Taiger Ivø, "Optioner och ansvar i transportaftaler" (2008) 4 Erhvervsjuridisk Tidsskrift 331–343, at p. 331; J. Ramberg; *The Law of Transport Operators* (2005) p. 23 and M. Hoeks, *ibid.*, at p. 85. However, Glass suggests that this situation is mainly theoretical and that statistically shippers engaging freight forwarders do make their own decisions regarding mode of transport (D. Glass, *ibid.*, at p. 314, fn. 53). It is asserted here that the latter conclusion is a correct reflection of the "reality" and that it is mainly contracts for parcel services that are "undefined".

74 D. Glass, *ibid.*, at p. 314.

75 L. Andersen Roost; *ibid.*, pp. 63 and 66, which she holds also to be the case under German law.

76 See further sections 5.6 and 5.8.

Where, on the other hand, the choice of mode is entirely up to the carrier and nothing implies any contemplated mode of transport, the contract could perhaps be regarded as a transport contract separate from other types of transport contracts, a *sui generis* contract.[77] The question is what effect performance of the transport has on classification of the contract. Whilst it has been assumed that under Danish law this type of undefined contract is not subject to any mandatory regulation,[78] but to freedom of contract, and thus unaffected by the performance by the carrier, the situation under Swedish law is not thoroughly examined.[79] Under German national law the undefined contract of carriage will be subject to the liability regime applicable to the mode of transport by which it is performed.[80] Under English law, the *Quantum* case suggests that the CMR convention should be considered applicable to carriage by road under an undefined contract.[81] The judgment thus seems to imply, *e contrario*, that, under English law, an undefined contract of carriage is subject to the liability regime applicable to the mode by which it is carried out.

5.3.4 Incorrectly defined contracts of carriage

Most carriers today would probably, in the contract of carriage, reserve the right to substitute the agreed mode of transport for another. Common examples are "low flying aircrafts", i.e. trucks and trains that move air cargo from smaller airports to the larger hubs, where it is loaded onto planes for shipment to its final destination. Such substitution is thus not a breach of contract and the question is what happens to e.g. a contract for carriage of goods by air when the air transport is substituted for road carriage – does it become a carriage of goods by road contract? The contract is defined as a contract for carriage of goods by air in accordance with the parties' original intention. The contract, however, includes another intention by the parties: the carrier may substitute air transport for another mode. In utilizing the right to substitute the mode of transport, the carrier unilaterally changes the contract.

---

77 D. Glass, "Meddling in the multimodal muddle" [2006] LMCQ 307, at p. 314 and J. Ramberg, *The Law of Transport Operators* (2005) p. 25.

78 V. Ulfbeck and S. Taiger Ivø, "Optioner och ansvar i transportaftaler" (2008) 4 Erhvervsjuridisk Tidsskrift 331–343, at p. 337.

79 Although of the opinion that the undefined contract of carriage is a contract *sui generis*, Ramberg holds that there is room to argue that the carrier should be subject to a mandatory regime, which in that case would be the regime applicable to the mode of performance. However, he does not explain how this fits with the contractual approach to applicability under e.g. the CMR (J. Ramberg *ibid.*, at p. 25).

80 L. Andersen Roost, *ibid.* at pp. 67–68 with reference to German national legislation (BGB §315 and HGB § 407) and J. Basedow, *Der Transportvertrag* (1987) p. 58. Andersen Roost further holds that this entails that an undefined contract of carriage carried out by more than one mode of transport is regarded as a multimodal contract under German law.

81 The undefined contract is the situation described as variant (c); UK Court of Appeal, *Quantum Corporation Inc v Plane Trucking Ltd* [2002] 2 Lloyd's Rep 25. However, Andersen Roost draws the opposite conclusion from the judgment (L. Andersen Roost, *ibid.*, at p. 67), whilst de Wit holds that performance of an undefined contract does in fact affect which liability regime is applicable (R. de Wit, *Multimodal Transport* (1995) p. 171).

Some of the precedents accounted for above in section 3.4.1 actually concern this very situation. In the English *Quantum* case, mentioned in the previous section, an air carrier had substituted part of the contracted-for air carriage for road carriage.[82] The Court of Appeal considered that invocation of the right to substitute mode of transport by the carrier deprived the contract of the whole of its character of an air carriage contract, and applied the CMR convention to the road leg. In this case, it was undisputed that the parties had entered into similar agreements on previous occasions and that the carrier had substituted the same part of the carriage for road carriage on those occasions.

In the Danish judgment from 2008 the air carrier substituted part of the transport for carriage by road, which was allowed for under the contract.[83] The Danish Supreme Court considered that this did not change the character of the contract, which was expressly a contract for carriage by air[84] that the shipper had not had any reason to assume would be carried out otherwise.[85]

Additionally, a French court, the Commercial Court of Bobigny, has considered that an air carriage contract, under which part of the transport was substituted for carriage by road, does not lose its character of a carriage by air contract.[86] On the other hand, it seems that under German law a contract where a right of substitution is utilized so that transport is carried out by another mode of transport in addition to the agreed mode is regarded as a multimodal transport contract.[87] Hence performance of the contract by an additional mode of transport changes the character of the contract. In all three judgments, air carriage was partly substituted for road carriage. Thus, in fact, the contracts of carriage remained mainly for carriage by air, which under the overall consideration theory could justify application of air carriage liability to the entire transport.[88]

However, the contracted-for carriage may also be substituted in its entirety, or as to a major part, for another mode of transport. For example, where carriage

---

82 *Quantum Corporation Inc v Plane Trucking Ltd* [2002] 2 Lloyd's Rep 25.

83 Danish Supreme Court HD 23 April 2008 (U.2008.1638H).

84 Cf. a contract for carriage by air with a right for the carrier to substitute mode of transport, which could be considered a different thing from a contract for carriage by air without such a right.

85 The court seemingly opposed the unilateral right of the carrier to alter the agreed mode of transport and refused to allow that unilateral right to include alteration of the applicable liability regime, although the court held that the cargo interest should be allowed to choose between the two possible regimes.

86 Jugement du tribunal de commerce de Bobigny du 24 novembre 1995, Les Mutelles du Mans contre Transport Assistance Services (TAS), reported in (1996) 2643 Bulletin des Transports et la Logistique, 15 January, JURISPRUDENCE, cited by Ulfbeck and Taiger Ivø (V. Ulfbeck and S. Taiger Ivø, "Optioner och ansvar i transportaftaler" (2008) 4 Erhvervsjuridisk Tidsskrift 331–343, at p. 334.

87 L. Andersen Roost, *Multimodale Transporter* (2012) pp. 58–59 with reference to Brinkmann, *Der Luftfrachtersatzverkehr* (2009) p. 129 ff. Andersen Roost holds that under German law a unimodal contract containing an option for the carrier will make the contract a multimodal contract, but it must be assumed that it is only when the carrier utilizes that option that the character of the contract is changed.

88 M. Hoeks, *Multimodal Transport Law* (2010) pp. 71–73. Clarke has compared this theory to the proposition that a Bloody Mary is a non-alcoholic drink as it contains more tomato juice than vodka (M. Clarke, "A Multimodal Mix-up" (2002) JBL 210–217).

by road has been severely delayed the carrier may opt to carry the goods by air instead, perhaps in order to avoid severe penalty for delay under the contract of carriage. The question is whether the precedents referred to above would be applicable to such transport, or if they should be distinguished. Although the basic fact, i.e. that the contract has been entered into as a contract for carriage by one particular mode but the carrier has made use of an option to substitute the mode of transport incorporated into the contract, is the very same in both cases, in this case the contract does not retain its overall character as a contract for carriage by the mode agreed. On the other hand, the incorrectly defined contract of carriage is characterized by the fact the parties have not just agreed to carriage by the mode of transport expressly stated in the contract, but also to the right of the carrier to substitute that mode of transport for another. Therefore, perhaps it is appropriate that performance of the contract should govern which liability regime should apply.[89]

5.3.5 Two main categories

The four contract types outlined above are by no means clear-cut. The problems discussed may also be relevant to other categories than the one in relation to which they are mentioned. The legal issues raised in relation to applicability of unimodal conventions to multimodal transport contracts, undefined contracts and incorrectly defined contracts are entangled. However, in order to structure the legal issues in question, it seems to be possible to divide these types of contract into two groups or categories: clear contracts and unclear contracts.

Accordingly, *clear contracts* will refer to contracts that clearly state by which mode(s) a certain transport is to be carried out and between which places each mode is to be used. The contract may be ambiguous, so that it has to be construed, but only to a lesser degree.[90] If the contract is construed as a contract for another mode than the mode(s) that is clearly stated in the contract, such contract is referred to the category of unclear contracts, more particularly to "incorrectly defined contracts". Perhaps in fact clear contracts are best defined through the definition of unclear contracts: it includes all contracts that are not unclear.

The group of *unclear contracts* will refer to undefined contracts and incorrectly defined contracts accounted for above. Both categories comprise contracts that are transformable for one reason or another; undefined contracts must be supplemented either through constructing the parties' real intention or through

---

89 J. Ramberg; *The Law of Transport Operators* (2005) p. 25 and J. Ramberg, "Global Unification of Transport Law: A Hopeless Task?" (2008–2009) 27 Penn St Int'l L Rev 851, at p. 857. The question is discussed further in section 5.7 below.

90 If, for example, a contract specifies that a transport is to be carried out from a warehouse in the outskirts of Rotterdam to the port of Rotterdam where it is to be re-loaded onto a ship in order to be carried to Baltimore and the place of loading, the warehouse, is not situated by a railway station, the contract is easily construed to indicate that the transport between the warehouse and the port of Rotterdam is to be carried out by truck. The construction undertaken is very modest; it would seem that the parties have just omitted the specification by mistake.

actual performance of the transport. Incorrectly defined contracts allow for a substitution of transport mode and it is only when such substitution has taken place that the contract is incorrectly defined; before any substitution is done it is just a (clear) contract, which allows for substitution.[91]

These two categories are necessarily entangled and inseparable, but there are nevertheless benefits to the attempted separation into two categories, if not otherwise then at least for the sake of an overarching structure. As an example of the interrelation between the two categories, one may ask whether a contract that is unimodal but allows for substitution of transport mode, which is never invoked by the carrier, really can be categorized as a clear unimodal contract as it is not just a unimodal transport contract, but a unimodal transport contract with a substitution clause. In the following section the applicability of the unimodal conventions that apply to contracts of carriage to carriage under multimodal contracts will be analysed based on the two categories outlined.

5.4 The definition of the contract of carriage

The question what constitutes a contract for the carriage of goods by a certain mode of transport has two sides to it in relation to the application of unimodal conventions. First of all, it is a question of what is demanded from a contract in order to make it a contract for the carriage of goods by [road]. This question, which includes issues of whether the mode of transport must be explicit in the contract or whether it may be implied between the parties with regard to e.g. the freight cost, time for delivery and so on; and whether a contract called a contract for the carriage by road constitutes such a contract even if it includes provisions that are not entirely in accordance with the title of the contract, is a question that must be solved in accordance with the national law of contracts, as discussed above in section 5.2.

Secondly, it is a question whether a contract for the carriage of goods by more than one mode of transport constitutes a contract for the carriage of goods by e.g. road to the extent it is carried out by [road]. This question includes the issue whether a multimodal contract in which the modes of transport have been explicitly stated is to be considered as a contract for carriage by [road] to the extent such carriage has been agreed. Further, it includes the questions whether a contract for carriage by undefined modes of transport is considered a contract for the carriage of goods by [road] if it is carried out by [road] and whether a contract for carriage by [road], with an option for the carrier to substitute the mode of transport, is considered a contract for carriage by [rail] if it is carried out by [rail]. This latter question is a question of interpretation of the treaties, and, as such, although carried out by national courts, a matter of international law. Although

91 Contracts may be unclear for reasons other than that they are undefined or are subject to contractual substitution of transport mode. However, due to the rationale behind the current division between unclear and clear contracts, being two different models for analysis of the legal issues that arise, contracts that are ambiguous will have to be either referred to as clear contracts because the ambiguity is unproblematic and can easily be repaired, or as unclear contracts because they are so ambiguous that they are undefined contracts.

the two questions are intertwined and not easily separated, the latter issue will be discussed in relation to unclear contracts of carriage below, whilst the former will be discussed in relation to clear contracts of carriage in the following section.

However, before the modal character of the contract of carriage can be explored, the contract of carriage as such must be defined. Accordingly, in the following section the prerequisites relating to the contract of carriage in general transport law as well as in the conventions discussed will be explored.

5.4.1 Definitions in general transport law

The central characteristic of the contract of carriage is undoubtedly the carrier's undertaking to carry.[92] The undertaking to carry is usually regarded as an obligation of result, which can be contrasted with an obligation of performance.[93] Although the distinction is not always crystal clear, the main difference between the two is the focus on performance and result respectively: under an obligation of result, the result is the focus and who and how is of less importance, whilst under an obligation of performance the focus is on who performs, a classic example being the employment contract.

An undertaking to carry is usually mirrored by an undertaking to pay freight, and indeed this is an explicit prerequisite under the Montreal,[94] CMR, COTIF–CIM conventions as well as under the Rotterdam Rules. It can be discussed how far the undertaking to pay freight is a prerequisite for the definition of the contract of carriage, or if contracts for gratuitous carriage should also be classified as contracts of carriage.[95] As mentioned, several of the conventions governing carriage of goods are not applicable to gratuitous carriage.[96] This may, however, be explained by the mandatory application of these regulations; it would perhaps not be perceived as equitable if a carrier who undertakes to perform carriage without reward should be mandatorily subject to the liability rules of the conventions in question.

According to the Scandinavian maritime codes, freight is a non-mandatory prerequisite as far as contracts of carriage by sea are concerned; freight is thus to be paid unless otherwise agreed.[97] The freight obligation has been extensively

92 H. Hammarskjöld, *Om fraktavtalet och dess viktigaste rättsföljder* (1886) p. 3; K. Grönfors, *Fraktavtalet under etthundra år* (1986) p. 19; K. Grönfors, *Tolknig av fraktavtal* (1989) p. 57; R. de Wit, *Multimodal Transport* (1995) p. 19; A. Messent and D. Glass, *CMR: Contracts for the International Carriage of Goods by Road* (2000) p. 17; M. Hoeks, *Intermodal Transport Law* (2010) p. 45; L. Andersen Roost, *Multimodale Transporter* (2012) pp. 80 and 89 and M. Clarke, *International Carriage of Goods by Road: CMR* (2014) pp. 57 and 333.

93 M. Hoeks *ibid.*, at p. 45.

94 With the exception of free carriage carried out by a transport undertaking under article 1.1.

95 According to de Wit, in France and Belgium the payment of freight is a mandatory prerequisite for the existence of a contract of carriage, whilst in Germany and the Netherlands it is not (R. De Wit, *ibid.*, at p. 33).

96 See e.g. M. Clarke, *ibid.*, at p. 21, where Clarke holds that the definition of a contract of carriage under CMR requires the obligation to pay freight.

97 Article 13:10 (260) reads: "Unless otherwise agreed, the freight that corresponds to the current price at the time of the delivery of the goods for carriage is to be paid. The freight is to be paid upon taking over the goods." (my translation).

discussed, particularly the question of at what point in time freight is payable. It seems that, historically, freight was considered earned when the goods arrived at their destination and, accordingly, the obligation to pay freight occurred at that time and not before.[98] Later developments have entailed a right for the carrier to demand payment of freight upon taking over the goods for carriage; however, freight may have to be reimbursed by the carrier if the carriage, or parts thereof, is not completed.[99] Whilst payment of freight is an integral part of the contract of carriage, the promotion thereof to a prerequisite for the existence of a contract of carriage may be going too far for the simple reason that contracts for gratuitous carriage would not fall into any other contract category.[100] Accordingly, it is concluded here that contracts of carriage that do not entitle the carrier to freight should nonetheless be classified as contracts of carriage.[101] The starting point is, however, that a contract of carriage by default is a non-gratuitous contract and that a contract of carriage should only be deemed gratuitous if that is explicitly clear from the contract, i.e. the carrier may have the right to freight even where the freight is not clear from the contract. Gratuitous carriage is to a lesser degree covered by the mandatory regulations found in international conventions, i.e. the carrier is to a certain extent entitled to stipulate other conditions. As regards carriage by sea, the liability rules of the Hague–Visby Rules may under certain conditions be evaded based on article VI. Gratuitous carriage could be presumed to fulfill the criteria, but it is noteworthy that the contract of carriage need not provide for the issuance of a bill of lading in order for article VI to be applicable.[102]

Several of the conventions discussed thus require the contract to cover carriage against payment of freight, and it may be discussed whether this requirement must follow from the contract, explicitly or implicitly, or if a legal requirement to pay freight would suffice. Although the wording of the conventions, such as the CMR, seems to require payment of freight to be part of the parties' contractual agreement, it must be assumed that the intention of the provision is to exclude gratuitous carriage, and that accordingly it would not make any difference in terms of applicability of the convention if the right to require freight follows from law rather than from the contract of carriage.

---

98 H. Hammarskjöld, *Om fraktavtalet och dess viktigaste rättsföljder* (1886) p. 128; K. Grönfors, *Fraktavtalet under etthundra år* (1986) p. 120 and E. Selvig, "The Freight Risk" (1965) 7 Arkiv for Sjørett II–III3, 272, at p. 290 (re United Kingdom) and p. 299 (re Scandinavia).

99 K. Grönfors, *ibid.* at pp. 125–127.

100 As an illustration, a comparison could be made with a purchase agreement. In relation to a sales contract, an obligation to pay remuneration by the buyer is an absolute prerequisite for the contract category. However, contracts that do not contain such an obligation would fall into the contract category of gifts.

101 See, however, Selvig, who classifies the contract of carriage as a bilateral contract, thus presupposing a counterpromise by the shipper, i.e. an undertaking to pay freight (E. Selvig, *ibid.*, at p. 299).

102 The provision is rather interesting considering that the convention appears to apply only when a bill of lading is (to be) issued, but could also be regarded as support for the applicability of the convention to carriage by sea where no bill of lading is (to be) issued.

The carrier's undertaking to carry is complemented by several other undertakings, which are assumed to be included in the carrier's general obligations, and can be extracted from the liability rules of the applicable conventions. Accordingly, the carrier has an obligation not only to carry the goods and deliver them, but such delivery should be at the contracted place of delivery at the contracted time for delivery. In addition, the goods should be delivered in the same condition as they were received for carriage by the carrier and the carrier is obliged to deliver them to the consignee.[103]

The general characteristics of the contract of carriage may thus be concluded as a contract in which a carrier undertakes to carry goods, which undertaking entails duties such as a duty of care of the goods. Unless explicitly waived by the carrier, the contract of carriage entails a right for the carrier to receive freight for the carriage.

5.4.2 Definitions in the conventions themselves

As mentioned above, the conventions themselves give some, although not comprehensive, guidance. First of all, although a contract could, perhaps, be distinguished from an agreement to refer to something of a higher degree of certainty or form, such as a written agreement, there seems to be no reason to assume that in any of the transport conventions adhering to the contractual approach to applicability "contract" means anything else than a consensual agreement.[104] The contract as such is not defined in either the Rotterdam Rules or the CMR convention or the COTIF–CIM convention, but there appears to be no disagreement on the point that no formal requirements are imposed.[105]

In relation to carriage by sea, the Hague–Visby Rules do not define the contract of carriage, although the contract of carriage is qualified as having to relate to the carriage of goods and stipulate the issuance of a bill of lading relating to carriage by sea.[106] As regards the Rotterdam Rules, two preconditions are stipulated regarding the contract of carriage. First of all the carrier must undertake to carry goods from one place to another and, secondly, the carrier must require payment

103 E. Selvig, *ibid* p. 14. Andersen Roost divides the carrier's undertaking to carry into four sub-undertakings; the undertaking of transport, the undertaking of care, the undertaking of time and the undertaking of delivery, corresponding to the above-mentioned obligations that rest on the carrier (L. Andersen Roost, *Multimodale Transporter* (2012) pp. 89–93).

104 M. Hoeks, *Multimodal Transport Law* (2010) p. 45.

105 The Rotterdam Rules contains no explicit form requirements on the contract for carriage – the definition of the same concerns the contents of the contract. As article 3 states, seemingly exhaustively, instances when writing is required, and the contract of carriage is not one, then it can be assumed that the drafters did not intend the contract of carriage to require any form. As regards the CMR and the COTIF–CIM conventions, similarly, the conventions provide no guidance as to the issue of form. However, from case law the conclusion can be drawn that no form requirement has been identified; see M. Clarke, *International Carriage of Goods by Road: CMR* (2014) p. 59, with reference to Lg Bremen 6.5.65 (1966) ETL 691.

106 Article I. Cf. Section 4.5 above.

of freight in order to do so.[107] The undertaking to carry may include any modes of transport as long as maritime transport is one of them. Although the Rotterdam Rules leave out a definition of the *contract* as such, article 1.1 does provide a definition of the *contract of carriage*: a contract may not be deemed a contract of carriage (i.e. under the convention) unless the carrier undertakes to carry and in order to do so reserves the right of reward.

The CMR convention is construed somewhat differently, in such a way that it has been claimed that it does not contain any definition of the contract of carriage.[108] However, to the extent that the Rotterdam Rules and the COTIF–CIM convention can be said to contain such a definition, the CMR convention seems to do so too.[109] The CMR convention stipulates, although indirectly, that the contract must concern the carriage of goods by road in vehicles and that the carriage should entail a right for the carrier to demand payment of freight.[110] The CMR convention, however, does not explicitly require the contracting carrier to *undertake* to carry the goods, which has triggered the question whether the convention is applicable to freight-forwarding contracts.[111]

In line with its general resemblance to the CMR convention, the COTIF–CIM convention does not define the contract of carriage as such, either. Article 6.1 qualifies the contract of carriage by requiring that it contains an undertaking by the carrier to carry the goods and a right to request a reward for doing so.[112] Whilst under the Rotterdam Rules, if the carrier does not undertake to carry, the contract is simply not a contract of carriage, under the COTIF–CIM convention, if the carrier does not undertake to carry, the convention is not applicable to what could still be defined as a contract of carriage.[113]

107 Article 1.1.

108 M. Hoeks, *Multimodal Transport Law* (2010) p. 43.

109 Neither the Rotterdam Rules nor the COTIF–CIM convention really define a contract of carriage, as no definition of the contract as such is given (which the CMNI on the other hand does, see article 1 (1)).

110 However, Clarke holds that already the definition of a contract of carriage requires the obligation to pay freight (M. Clarke, *ibid.*, at p. 21). Although this definition of the contract of carriage makes the "for reward" prerequisite somewhat redundant, it prevents divergent interpretation of the scope of applicability of the convention.

111 Clarke holds that the CMR only applies to contracts where the carrier undertakes to carry the goods and thus exclude freight forwarding, which is instead governed by national law. His conclusion is not based on the wording of the CMR, but rather on the general definition of a carrier as a person that undertakes to carry goods (M. Clarke, *International Carriage of Goods by Road: CMR* (2014) p. 24). Other types of contract that concern carriage of goods, such as insurance contracts, would however not be subject to the convention due to their non-compliance with the prerequisite of "contracts for the carriage of goods".

112 Article 6.1 reads: "By the contract of carriage, the carrier shall undertake to carry the goods for reward to the place of destination and to deliver them there to the consignee." This can be compared with the definition of the contract of carriage in the Rotterdam Rules, which reads: "'Contract of carriage' means a contract in which a carrier, against the payment of freight, undertakes to carry goods from one place to another."

113 The difference may seem theoretical, but in relation to the definition of the contract of carriage, it means that the undertaking to carry is not a prerequisite for the existence of a contract of carriage (at least not in relation to the COTOF–CIM convention).

5.4.3 Conclusions

What can be extracted from the conventions themselves is contractual content, i.e. content that is necessary in order for the contract either to be classified as a contract of carriage (Rotterdam Rules) or for the conventions to be applicable to the contract of carriage (CMR and COTIF–CIM). The content thus extracted, the undertaking by the carrier to carry and the undertaking by the contracting consignor to pay freight, mirror the general idea of what the characteristics of a contract of carriage are.[114]

The conventions further mirror the duties of care etc. resting on the carrier in accordance with general transport law. Thus, the contract of carriage can be concluded to be non-controversial in terms of its characteristics in relation to other contracts.

The definition thus extracted does not, however, give any guidance on when a contract of carriage is a contract of carriage by a particular mode of transport. Whether a certain contract of carriage is one for carriage by [road], in the example above, is partly a matter of substance; the contract must somehow provide for such carriage. At the same time, from the perspective of the convention regulations, it is part of the scope of application definition. The contract of carriage by [road] is undefined and presupposed. From a unimodal perspective it is perhaps natural to see no need for a definition; it is conceivably later developments that have triggered such a need.

Defining the contract of carriage by [road] can be approached from two angles. One is the relationship between the undertaking to carry and the scope of application of the unimodal convention: if a general contract of carriage is distinguished partly by the carrier's undertaking to carry, then a contract for the carriage by [road] is perhaps distinguished by the carrier's undertaking to carry by [road]. On the other hand, the issue can be approached from a stricter law of contracts angle: at what point, and how, is a contract of carriage entered into and how are the contents thereof settled?

5.5 The (clear) contract of carriage of goods by [road]

The multimodal contract of carriage relates to the carriage of goods by more than one mode of transport. In relation to the law, rather than the business, of transportation the key factor is that a combination of transport modes is subject to one single contract of carriage.[115] The UN Convention on International Multimodal Transport of Goods is often taken as a starting point when defining the multimodal transport contract. The definition thus given requires that the carrier has

114 M. Hoeks, *Multimodal Transport Law* (2010) pp. 45–50, L. Andersen Roost, *Multimodale Transporter* (2012) p. 87 and E. Selvig, "The Freight Risk" in (1965) 7 Arkiv for Sjørett II-III2–3, 272, at p. 299.

115 E. Røsæg, "Conflicts of Conventions in the Rotterdam Rules" (2009) 15 JIML 238–248, at p. 239.

undertaken to carry goods by more than one mode, i.e. contracts that only allow the carrier to do so but lack an undertaking (i.e. in relation to the prerequisite of multiple modes of transport) by the carrier, would fall outside the scope of that convention.

The kind of contract of carriage captured by the scope of application of the Multimodal Convention is accordingly "clear contracts", explicitly outlining multimodal transport and its legs. Although transport contracts indeed have evolved and may not be thus clear, the clear multimodal transport contract is the point of departure in any discussion. As discussed previously in section 3.4, the encounter between unimodal regulations and multimodal contracts of carriage has initiated a discussion on the autonomous applicability of unimodal regulations to carriage under multimodal contracts. Accordingly, primarily in relation to the CMR convention, it has been argued that the convention is not applicable to road transport carried out under a multimodal transport contract. The arguments therefor relate in part to the wording of that convention, but of general interest to all unimodal carriage conventions is the argument that a multimodal contract of carriage that includes road carriage is not a contract for the carriage of goods by road, as required for the applicability of the CMR convention. The argument is thus that a contract for multiple modes of transport is *not* a contract for carriage by road, an argument that is captured in the *sui generis* theory and could be extended to other unimodal regulations as well.[116]

As discussed previously, the foundation of the *sui generis* theory is not entirely clear. However, the rationale behind categorization of contracts in general relates to the application of diverse sets of rules.[117] Thus, the need to avoid collision between the Multimodal Convention from 1980 and existing unimodal conventions is an obvious reason for the emergence of the theory. However, rather than pursuing this practical need as a reason for the theory, it seems to have been based on the applicability of the existing unimodal conventions. As discussed previously, the reasons put forward, in particular in relation to the CMR convention, are, on the one hand, a literal approach to interpreting the scope of application and, on the other hand, practical difficulties connected with the application of rules, so obviously adapted to unimodal contracts of carriage, to a leg of a multimodal contract of carriage where for example the carrier may never take over the goods from the shipper but from a preceding carrier. The core of the theory appears simply to be that the multimodal contract of carriage concerns transport by several modes of transport in contrast with unimodal contracts of carriage, to which the unimodal conventions apply.[118]

116 E. Selvig, "Multimodal transport: the 1980 U.N. Convention: papers of a one day seminar: Southampton University, Faculty of Law, 12th September 1980", at p. A17, para. 12.

117 Cf. section 3.2.1.1 above.

118 L. Andersen Roost, *Multimodale Transporter* (2012) p. 191. However, Andersen Roost does not agree with the *sui generis* theory but holds the multimodal contract of carriage to be a "new type of contract of carriage with particular needs for regulation" (at p. 192). The difference seems to be elusive.

Undeniably, the multimodal contract of carriage is a contract that has created new types of needs in relation to regulation of carriers' liability and a convention governing the multimodal contract as such would certainly solve many of the problems connected with the network system. However, even if the multimodal contract of carriage is considered a contract *sui generis*, unimodal regulations may be applicable to the legs of such a contract. The applicability of the unimodal conventions cannot be solved through settlement of the status of the multimodal contract. The applicability of these conventions can only be determined based on the conventions themselves. This means that the unimodal conventions may be applicable to transport carried out under a multimodal contract of carriage, in which case a multimodal convention or other regulation will make matters even more complicated.

Where a unimodal convention applies to a contract of carriage by a certain mode, the core of the issue of the convention's applicability to (clear) multimodal contracts of carriage is the definition of the contract of carriage, or rather the definition of the contract of carriage by [road]. What is required from the contracting consignee and the contracting carrier in order to consider their agreement to constitute a contract of carriage by [road]?

In relation to clear multimodal contracts of carriage, the definition of the contract of carriage is mainly relevant to the conventions that take the contractual approach to applicability. Where a convention applies to performance by a certain mode, there would be no doubt that the rules of that convention would apply to transport by the mode in question even where it is subject to a multimodal contract of carriage. As is clear from the discussion above, even the Montreal Convention, which applies to performance, does presuppose a contract of carriage, although, as asserted, it is not a prerequisite in the formal meaning. However, it has been concluded that that presumption does not concern a contract of carriage by air, but simply a contract of carriage. Further, the Montreal Convention (leading by example) explicitly applies to carriage of goods by air carried out as a part of a multimodal transport. Likewise, the even more recent Rotterdam Rules apply to contracts of carriage that provide for carriage by more than one mode of transport, as long as the contract includes international sea transport.

As regards the Hague–Visby Rules, there seems to have been no real discussion in legal writing regarding its application to sea transport subject to a multimodal contract of carriage. Even though the Hague–Visby Rules in fact apply to the contract of carriage of goods by sea, it is generally considered that it is the issuance of, or undertaking to issue, a bill of lading that is the triggering factor of mandatory application of the convention, which is likely to be the reason for the lack of discussion. It has been concluded above that the Hague–Visby Rules apply to contracts of carriage by sea under which a bill of lading is to be issued. Thus, in relation to multimodal contracts of carriage, the discussion of what constitutes a contract of carriage is definitely relevant. Further, in order for the rules to apply, the multimodal contract of carriage should contain an obligation for the carrier to issue a bill of lading. The Hague–Visby Rules requires that the bill of lading relates to carriage of goods by sea: however, there seems to be no reason to require the bill of lading to relate *only* to sea transport. Thus, a bill of lading issued for the entire multimodal transport should also fulfil the prerequisite, although the Hague–Visby Rules would govern only the sea carriage.[119]

In relation to the CMR convention, the definition of the contract of carriage is apparently relevant. It is the CMR convention, and the applicability thereof, that has been the centre of attention as regards the applicability of unimodal conventions to transports carried out under a multimodal contract of carriage, although the origin of the discussion on the multimodal contract of carriage as a contract *sui generis* is not related to the CMR convention in particular. The COTIF–CIM convention has not gained much attention in this respect, but for current purposes it is assumed that, due to the scope of application of the convention, the discussion on the contract of carriage is highly relevant in relation to that convention as well.

5.5.1 The contract (in essence)

The legal characteristics of the contract of carriage were outlined above. These characteristics define the contract of carriage compared with other types of contract and can be used in relation to the categorization of contracts. In defining the contract of carriage *by [road]* it is the contract as such that becomes the crucial element. Accordingly, approached from a law-of-contracts angle, the definition of the contract of carriage by [road] can be defined through interpreting the agreement between the parties.

The formation and interpretation of a carriage contract has been held above to be a matter of national law,[120] and the definition thereof may therefore vary depending on the national law being applied, and perhaps particularly depending on the relevant legal system. In fact, the contract as such must rest on the legal foundation of *a* legal system. As discussed above, the contract only exists in relation to legal rules; if a certain "contract" does not fulfil the prerequisites of the national system in question, it will not be recognized as a contract in its legal sense. However, in interpreting the rules contained in an international treaty uniformity is served if the interpreter aims, to the extent possible, at applying standards that are shared between the contracting states.[121] Thus, rather than applying distinctively national law, the interpreter should seek to find common denominators between relevant legal systems.[122] Nevertheless, in the end it is the national

119 K. Grönfors, *Successiva Transporter* (1968) p. 224*ff.* with reference to the preparatory works of the Swedish Maritime Code, NJA II 1936 s. 590.

120 Section 5.2 above.

121 This principle is reflected in CISG article 7(2); see further M. van Alstine, "Dynamic Treaty Interpretation" (1997–1998) 146 U Pa L Rev 687, at p. 735.

122 In search of common denominators of the laws of contract of the various European states, resort might be had to the C. von Bar and E. Clive (eds), *Principles, Definitions and Model Rules of*

rules, distinctive or shared with other contracting states, that settle the definition of a contract.[123]

Thus, the nature of a contract and the prerequisites for the formation of a binding agreement will be briefly discussed.[124] As mentioned in the introduction of this work, the main line of demarcation between the European states is often perceived to be between common law and civil law, perhaps in particular relating to the interpretation of contracts. Thus a brief comparison between the two systems seems unavoidable if any common denominators are to be found.[125] Accordingly, the following summary concerns civil law, mainly Nordic,[126] and English common law,[127] although without any aspirations as to completeness.[128] Further, the following discussion serves only as an illustration of

European Private Law, Draft Common Frame of Reference ("DCFR") (2009). However, it should be noted that albeit common principles have been extracted through extensive scholary research, the Model Rules are just that, model rules; *de lege ferenda* rather than *de lege lata*. As regards common law, reference may be had to the US Restatement (Second) of Contracts. However, in the current work the analysis is delimited to a European context, and in respect of the law of contracts, American law differs from English law (J. Cartwright, *Contract Law* (2016) p. 10*ff*).

123 Accordingly, international model rules, such as the Unidroit Principles of International Commercial Contracts (2010) or the Draft Common Frame of Reference, albeit the latter may serve as a source of information as regards common denominators, cannot be used in defining the contract.

124 Much thought has been put into theories regarding the point at which a binding agreement is formed and the basis therefore (see e.g. K. Grönfors, *Avtalsgrundande rättsfakta* (1993)). In his article "Avtals uppkomst – dags att se bortom avtalslagen" (2007) SvJT 673, J. Heidbrink summarizes the theories of Stang, Lehrberg and Grönfors and discusses the theories of will and trust, around which legal disagreement has circled since the Nordic common Contracts Act was enacted in 1915 (in Sweden). As regards Germany, see M. Pieck, "A Study of the Significant Aspects of German Contract Law" in *Annual Survey of International & Comparative Law* (1996), vol. 3:1, article 7, p. 116 and as regards France see P. Owsia, "The Notion and Function of Offer and Acceptance under French and English Law" (1992) 66 Tul L Rev 871, at p. 872). Although the discussion is indeed interesting, what is of relevance to the discussion at this point in the current work is the binding agreement as such rather than the mechanisms that make the agreement binding. However, to some extent the definition of a binding agreement cannot be referenced independently of theories on the mechanisms that bind the parties to an agreement.

125 The process of abstracting general principles inevitably separates the legal rules from its context, which in turn deprives the rule of any real meaning. In principle, a legal rule only has a meaning in its context, including the particular legal machinery within which it is effectuated (J. Merryman, "On the Convergence (and Divergence) of the Civil Law and the Common Law" (1981) 17 Stan J Int'l L 357, at pp. 378–379).

126 It should be noted in this respect that the Contracts Acts of Denmark, Norway, Sweden, Finland and Iceland are drafted in cooperation; cf. below. See also L. Sisula-Tulokas, "Nordic Hesitancy Regarding Part II of the CISG" (2012) 57 Scandinavian Stud L 293–295, at p. 293 ans J. Herre and L. Sisula-Tulokas, "CISG och de nordiska reservationerna" in *Festskrift till Lars Gorton* (2007) pp. 149–168. For linguistic reasons the references will be mainly to Danish, Norwegian and Swedish doctrine.

127 In common law systems the term common law is used for the body of law developed by the common courts, divergent from the law of equity, as well as from statutory law given by the parliament. However, here it will be used as a definition of a legal system where case law is the dominant source of law, such as in England and the USA, as opposed to civil law.

128 Cf. Eftestøl-Wilhelmsson who separates Nordic law from other European civil law, and thus divides the national systems of the European Union into "the common law legal family, the civil law legal family and the Nordic legal family" (E. Eftestøl-Wilhelmsson, *European Sustainable Carriage of Goods* (2016) p. 50).

how the interpretation of a supposed, generalized, contract of carriage could be carried out.

In both systems, a contract is the meeting of corresponding intentions of two parties, which is manifested either orally, in writing or through the actions of the parties.[129] This principle has been subsumed into the doctrine of offer and acceptance, which implies that where an offer is met by an identical acceptance a binding contract has been formed.[130] Under this doctrine the contract is really metaphysical, and the written contract is, in *theory*, but one means of evidencing the contents of the contract.

The doctrine of offer and acceptance is based on three prerequisites that are deemed necessary for a binding contract to be formed: the parties' intention to be bound, the communication of such intention and the perception of such communication by the other party.[131] A binding contract is presumed to be the result of the corresponding intention of the two parties, also expressed as the common intention of the parties. Step by step, an agreement is formed through communication by the offeror of an intention, or rather a wish, to enter into an agreement on certain terms, to the offeree. The offeree communicates an intention, or wish, to enter into an agreement on the terms proposed by the offeror as these were perceived by the offeree. The offeror is already bound by the offer at the time that it is communicated to the offeree and the offeree is bound by the acceptance.[132] The binding character of a contract follows from the general

129 G. Woxholt, *Avtaleinngåelse i og utenfor avtaleloven* (1995) p. 13.

130 K. Grönfors, *Avtalsgrundande rättsfakta* (1993) p. 17; R. Bradgate, "Formation of contracts" in A. Grubb (ed.), *The Law of Contract* (2007) pp. 233–595. In the Nordic countries, the doctrine of offer and acceptance is implemented in national legal systems through the similar versions of the Contracts Act (Sweden: Lag (1915:218) om avtal och andra rättshandlingar på förmögenhetsrättens område. Corresponding legislations in the other Nordic countries is; Finland: Lag om rättshandlingar på förmögenhetsrättens område (13.6.1929/228); Norway: Lov om avslutning av avtaler, om fuldmagt og om ugyldige viljeserlæringer (LOV-1918–05–31–4); Denmark: Lov of aftaler og andre retshandler på formerettens område (LBK nr 781 af 26/08/1996) and Iceland: Lög um samningsgerð, umboð og ógilda löggerninga nr. 7/1936). The doctrine implies not only that a binding agreement is formed upon acceptance by the offeree of an offer by the offeror, but also that the offeror is bound by his offer during a period, the length of which differs according to the situation, during which the offeree may consider the offer. Further, it is notably only the binding nature of offer and acceptance that is explicit from the Contracts Act, and the parties' mutual constraint to the agreement is but an implicit consequence. Under Nordic contract law the principle is not explicitly reproduced, but follows indirectly from the rules on formation of contracts and invalidity of contracts. For example, article 1 holds that an offer and an acceptance is binding on the emitter thereof, whilst article 33 provides for circumstances when contracts are not binding. However, the latter article, as well as the whole of Chapter 3 of the said code, in which article 33 is found, deals with legal acts (Sw. *rättshandlingar*) in general rather than contracts, legal acts being the unilateral act of one party (such as the remittance of an offer) rather than the agreement between two parties.

131 C. Ramberg and J. Ramberg, *Allmän avtalsrätt* (2016) p. 84.

132 Although the Contracts Act provides rules on the formation of contract, there is a general consensus that the Act does not provide exhaustive regulation thereof. Through the model of offer and acceptance, ideas of how legally binding contracts are entered into, are applied to everyday contracting. In Nordic contract law, contracts are formed constantly; the simplest agreement, such as a lunch date, in fact constitutes a contract and thus includes contractual obligations. Whilst the model is not so easily applied to negotiated contracts (see further below), it does provide a useful

principle of *pacta sunt servanda*,[133] but also, as far as the Nordic Contracts Acts are concerned, from the consequences that are stipulated regarding breach of contract.[134]

Accordingly, an agreement may be defined as an intention that is shared between two parties, which has been communicated through an offer and an acceptance.[135] Perhaps the outer border of the agreement, the agreement as such, can be defined as the intention by the respective party to be bound by an agreement, and the content of the agreement is the common intention between the parties. The agreement is in theory entirely subjective; it is the common subjective intention of the parties that constitute the contract.

However, although the starting point is the offer, the existence of an agreement is not entirely based on the offeror's subjective intention, both as regards the intention to be bound and the contents of the contract. Thus, if one party has communicated an offer, which is accepted by the other party, the offeror is bound by the agreement even if the offeror did not really intend, or wish, to enter into an agreement. The prerequisite of communication imposes a form, which, to the extent it is observed, entails the emergence of a binding agreement irrespective of the parties' *real* will or intention.[136] Further, as will be discussed below,

---

model to straightforward and so-called mass contracts, which are often entered into through an offer made by one party that is accepted by the other party. Due to its incompleteness, the model has been complemented by theories that strive to explain agreements that are not so easily subsumed under it. One example is the contract that is entered into through the parties' actions mentioned above, which appears to be common in carriage contracting (K. Grönfors, *Avtalsgrundande rättsfakta* (1993) p. 51). Although attempts have been made to apply the offer-and-acceptance model onto these types of contract (F. Schmidt *et al.*, *Huvudlinjer i svensk frakträtt* (1962) p. 44), others oppose the necessity to subsume all contracting under the model (K. Grönfors, *ibid.*, at p. 51; J. Heidbrink, "Avtals uppkomst – dags att se bortom avtalslagen" (2007) SvJT 673–708, at p. 706 and C. Ramberg, "En ny avtalslag" (2011) SvJT 32. See also G. Woxholt, *Avtaleinngåelse i og utenfor avtaleloven* (1995). A point of interest is the opposition to the generality of the offer-and-acceptance model, the implication of which is that a binding agreement may occur otherwise than according to the Contracts Act. The formation of a binding agreement must thus be based on something other than legislation, being, it is proposed, a general principle of law.

133 G. Woxholt, *Avtalerett* (2014) p. 23. The principle is not express in the current Nordic contract laws, although, at least as far as Norway is concerned, it used to be (J. Giertsen, *Avtaler* (2014) p. 8 with reference to King Christian V's Norwegian Law). Thus it seems that the binding force of the contract, which historically was expressed in (Norwegian) contract law, was so obvious in the early twentieth century that it was not perceived necessary to express it in the legislation drafted at the time. Johansson argues that the binding force of the contract comes from the voluntariness with which the contract is entered into (S. Johansson, "Något om avtalsfrihet, obligationsrätt och grundläggande fri- och rättigheter" (2013) 04/05 TfR 666–683, at p. 668).

134 K. Grönfors, *ibid.* at pp. 18 and 21. It is therefore perhaps more accurate to hold that an agreement, rather than being binding, entails certain consequences on the party that does not adhere to the terms thereof.

135 L-E Taxell, *Avtalsrättens normer* (1987) p. 85. However, the parties may demonstrate their intent by other means, such as through actual behaviour (G. Woxholt, *Avtaleinngåelse, ugyldighet og tolkning* (2001) pp. 83–92).

136 The Contracts Act does provide for some occasions where a party may evade the contract due to lack of real intention. However, these concern e.g. situations where that party has been forced or deceived into entering into the agreement; see the Swedish Contracts Act, articles 28–33.

communicative flaws may cause the contents of the contract to diverge from the subjective intention of the offeror. Thus, the contract as the metaphysical common intention of the parties is modified to the extent the communication of the intention would entail that the common intention is in fact not common, due to some form of misunderstanding.

The common intention of two parties to a common end (entering into an agreement) is thus the basis of formation of a contract. However, it is the communication of such intention that binds the communicator and thus the intention of one party would more accurately be defined as the intention as communicated, rather than the actual intention.[137] There is, however, a risk, which is inherent in all human communication, that a message is not perceived entirely as it was intended. Thus, either the offer as it was intended by the offeror (the theory of will) or the offer as it was perceived by the offeree (the theory of trust) must be decisive when the contents of the agreement are to be settled. This fundamental datum has for nearly one and a half centuries been subject to attempts at encapsulation into general theories of contract interpretation.[138] Although the theory of trust has been the dominating theory in Nordic legal writing, in reality the interpretation of contracts is based on a mix of both theories. Similarly, under English law, it is considered that the content of the offer must be considered not subjectively, as intended by the offeror, but objectively, as reasonably perceived by the offeree.[139]

In summary, legal theories relating to entering into a contract are shared between the civil law and the common law. Accordingly, a contract is the meeting of the intention by the respective parties to enter into a binding contract and the content thereof is the common intention between the parties. In general, no certain form is required. One model for the formation of a contract is the offer-and-acceptance model, which entails that a contract is formed when the offeror and offeree have exchanged an offer and an acceptance of corresponding content. The nature of the contract, as well as the binding force thereof, is rather laid down in a general principle of law, which only indirectly can be sifted out from (civil law) legislation. A contract is its contents and, as will be further explored below, the contents cannot always

137 It follows that, under the model of offer and acceptance, it is the offer made by the offeror that forms the basis of the contract.

138 Thus, the first theory to be enunciated was the theory of will (the theory was formulated in Germany during the latter part of the nineteenth century). Under this theory a declaration should be interpreted in accordance with the intention by the declaring party. Under a contract, this would normally be the offeror. Thus, the theory of will emphasizes the intention, or will, of the offeror and to a lesser degree considers the aspect of the addressee of the declaration, i.e. the offeree. The theory of trust, on the other hand, emphasizes the perception of the offer by the receiver, as long as such perception is reasonable. Thus, in interpreting a contract a reasonable perception by the offeree of the offer should be decisive. A third theory, the theory of declaration, gives precedence to the objective interpretation of the offer, regardless of the perception thereof by the offeror or the offeree (B. Lehrberg, *Avtalstolkning* (2014) pp. 26–28).

139 R. Bradgate, "Formation of contracts" in A. Grubb (ed.), *The Law of Contract* (2007), 233–595, at p. 235.

be settled without interpretation. However, a common starting point is the intention of each of the parties, as such intention has been communicated and perceived by the counterparty.

5.5.2 By [road]

The next question is how to settle whether a contract is a contract of carriage *by [road]*. As this is often done in retrospect – after a conflict has arisen – it is most likely obvious by what mode of transport the goods were carried. Therefore, it is in practice generally not a question of establishing whether a certain contract is a contract for road, rail, air or sea, but whether the contract that governed the transport can be considered a contract for the carriage of goods by the mode in question, which hence triggers application of the relevant international convention.

It has been held above that a contract is the common intention of two parties. Further, in order for a contract to constitute a contract of carriage such common intention must comprise an undertaking to carry (by one of the parties) and possibly other prerequisites, such as an undertaking to pay freight. As will be discussed later, the common intention may be explicit or implicit and may further be settled through contract construction and/or interpretation. Where the contract is a clear multimodal contract of carriage, the content of the contract (in relation to what modes to be used for the transport) is however not in dispute. The dispute instead relates to whether the contract of carriage may include other forms of transport and still be a contract of carriage by [road].

Contractually, the character of a contract of carriage, i.e. whether it concerns carriage by [road], is defined by the parties' common intention. Thus, it is held here, a contract of carriage by [road] is the meeting of the parties' intention to carry goods (and have goods carried) by that mode of transport. Accordingly, where the parties' intention is that carriage is to be performed partly by road, it is hard to see, from a contractual point of view, why that agreement is not a contract of carriage by road.[140] Where the prerequisite for applicability of certain rules is the existence of a contract of carriage by [road], it is asserted here that such a contract exists where the common intention of the parties to the contract of carriage includes the intention that the goods are to be carried by [road]. That the intention also includes that the goods are to be carried by other modes of transport in addition to [road] does not, contractually, change that conclusion.

This approach seems not to have been applied by the courts. In its older judgments, when the network system was applied, the German Supreme Court seems to have based such application on the hypothetical contract formula, i.e. it applied the convention that would have been applicable had the parties entered

140 As always in legal theory, a conclusion like this is theoretic, i.e. regard is not taken to issues related to the proving of the common intention or how the content of the contract is settled by a court. The latter question is however discussed in section 5.6 below.

into a separate contract for the particular leg of the multimodal transport.[141] The closest consideration can be found in the judgment by the Danish Supreme Court from 2008.[142] Although it eventually applied an overall characterization of the contract of carriage, the Danish Supreme Court considered the actual agreement between the parties. The court thus focused on the intention of the parties, primarily the contracting consignor, whose understanding was that the goods were to be carried by air, and only by air. However, the general conclusion is that courts have not considered the contract of carriage as the common intention of the parties, but have taken a much more formalistic view of the contract.[143]

The contract of carriage is a consensual agreement and, therefore, where the consensus is carriage by [road], the contract cannot be considered anything else but a contract of carriage by [road]. Needless to say, this conclusion is not affected by any formal label given to the contract of carriage; the substance of the contract of carriage is decided by the parties' actual common intention not on the label thereof.

5.5.3 Conclusions

The contract of carriage is characterized primarily by the carrier's undertaking to carry.[144] The contract is, in principle, a commercial contract, i.e. the presumption is that the carrier has a right to freight, although a contract for gratuitous carriage would still be categorized as a contract of carriage. Such contracts are, however, to a fairly large extent not subject to the mandatory rules of the conventions governing the carrier's liability.

A contract, or agreement, is formed through the coinciding intentions of two parties. Applied to carriage of goods, the contracting consignee's desire to have goods carried from one place to another is met by a carrier's undertaking to do so, and thus a contract is formed. The coinciding intentions will normally include other details than the actual carriage, such as freight, dates, type of goods and, perhaps, mode of transport. The contract will be categorized as a contract of carriage as it includes the carrier's undertaking to carry. Where the undertaking specifies by what, or which, mode(s) the transport is to be carried out, this contract particular is part of the parties' shared intention that forms the contract and, thus, from a contractual point of view, the contract must be regarded as a contract for carriage by that mode(s). Where the contract includes an undertaking by the carrier to carry by more than one mode of transport then, at least to the extent

141 Cf. section 3.4.1 above.

142 Danish Supreme Court, U.2008.1638H. Cf. section 3.4.1 above.

143 In a judgment from 16 June 2016, the Swedish Supreme Court analyses the contract of carriage. However, the question in dispute was whether the contract of carriage was clear on the fact that the cargo (potato ethanol for production of fine vodka) was particularely vulnerable to contamination by residues in the tank (NJA 2016 s. 563).

144 Note, in this respect, the Belgian Supreme Court's position that a transport contract is characterized by an initial consensus as to the mode of transport to be used (Cour de Cassation, 8 November 2004, C.03.0510.N); cf. section 3.4.1 above.

the parties have an explicit agreement to that effect, the contract for carriage provides for carriage by the modes in question. An undertaking to carry by [road] included in an undertaking to carry by other mode(s) in addition will not, from a contractual point of view, prevent the contract from being a contract of carriage by [road].

In all relevant conventions, the contractual aspects of the contract of carriage have been left to national law. Some criteria, such as the prerequisite that the carrier undertakes to carry goods and that the carriage is performed against payment of freight, are stipulated in these regulations, but the formation of contracts and determining to what extent a certain contract is deemed to contain e.g. an undertaking to carry, is not subject to the regulations in question. When determining whether a certain contract is a contract of carriage, or a contract of carriage by [road], as stipulated in the relevant conventions, reference should be had to the law of contracts, as intended. As has been shown above, the laws of contracts can be assumed to be fairly homogenous, which entails that uniformity will not be too compromised.

The conclusion drawn here is that where the common intention between two parties, which forms a contract of carriage, include an agreement as regards the mode(s) of transport, the contract of carriage is a contract of carriage for that mode(s) of transport. It may be asserted that a certain convention, such as the CMR, does not apply to carriage by [road] under a multimodal contract of carriage, but such a conclusion cannot be based on an interpretation of the term "contract of carriage by [road]". When interpreting the term "contract of carriage by [road]", reference should be had to the ordinary meaning of the term in its context, which in this case is the law of contracts. It is asserted here that it is simply not correct to contend that a contract of carriage which includes an undertaking to carry by [road], whether that undertaking also includes carriage by other modes or not, is not a contract of carriage by [road].

5.6 Unclear contracts

As defined in section 5.3, the category of unclear contracts refers, on the one hand, to contracts that are undefined, or open, so that the carrier is entitled to choose mode(s) of transport and, on the other hand, to contracts that are defined as regards the mode of transport, but where the carrier invokes a right to substitute mode of transport and the goods therefore are carried by another mode than initially intended.

As regards the applicability of unimodal conventions regulating the carrier's liability, unclear contracts cause problems due to this inherent lack of clarity. The contractual approach to applicability taken in many of the conventions presupposes some form of contractual agreement as regards the mode of transport; actual transport by a certain mode is not sufficient for applicability of these conventions. However, the mere fact that the written contract, or in general the booking note together with the carrier's general conditions of carriage, does not stipulate what mode of transport is to be used for a certain transport does not necessarily mean that the contract does not contain an understanding as to the mode of transport. The parties may very well have been in agreement regarding route and mode of transport. Further, factors such as price and time may clearly indicate that a certain mode of transport was anticipated. As regards incorrectly defined contracts, it is clear that when substitution of mode of transport is contractually allowed for, the rules relating to the originally agreed mode of transport are not to be applied. The question is instead whether the contract can be regarded as one for the mode eventually used to carry the goods, based on the wording of the contract of carriage.

The contracts discussed here are contracts that are not immediately clear as regards the mode of transport. The conventions governing the carrier's liability that are discussed apply to contracts of carriage by a certain mode of transport. In order to settle whether a certain contract is a contract of the kind that is required for the applicability of a certain convention, it seems appropriate to interpret the underlying agreement. As has been held above, the contract of carriage is formed through the coinciding intention of the contracting consignee and the carrier, and thus it must be considered whether the agreement in fact contains an understanding as to the mode of transport. If it does, it could accordingly be claimed to be subject to a certain convention that applies to contracts of carriage for the mode in question. From a law-of-contracts point of view, the actual contractual contents of an unclear contract must be established before the applicability thereto of the conventions in question can be settled. The actual contractual contents are settled through interpretation of the contract of carriage.

5.6.1 Interpretation of contracts

It has been concluded above that in civil law, as well as in common law, a contract is formed through the coinciding intentions of two (or more) parties. Thus, it follows that interpretation of contracts should seek to establish that common intention.[145] Certainly, where contract interpretation is brought into the picture, the common intention is in dispute and it has accordingly been pointed out that where the parties do not agree on the contents of a contract, theoretically no contract exists.[146] This would, however, be an extremely impractical conclusion, not to say devastating for the general interest of business. Therefore, a contract, the contents of which are disputed by the parties to it, will be considered valid and its contents interpreted and/or construed by the court faced with the task of resolving the dispute.[147] Thus, where two parties disagree on the contents of a contract, and

145 In Rt. 1993 s. 564 the Norwegian Supreme Court held that "The primary goal in all contract interpretation is to find out what the parties meant" (at p. 569) (my translation). However, Ramberg has dismissed this purported objective as "a fiction, a kind of technical white lie" (my translation) (J. Ramberg, "Avtalstolkningsmetoder" in *Festskrift till Gösta Walin* (2002) p. 511 citing Reu (fn. 20)).

146 C. Ramberg and J. Ramberg, *Allmän avtalsrätt* (2016) p. 145; A.P. Høgberg, "Tolkningsstiler vid kontraktstolkning" (2006) 41 Jussens Venner 61–108, at p. 71.

147 The "interpretation of contracts" has traditionally been separated from "implication of terms" (Sw: *utfyllnad*, which also includes the process of complementing a contract that does not regulate a

their intentions are in fact diverging, interpretation seeks to map the overlap of the parties' respective intention:

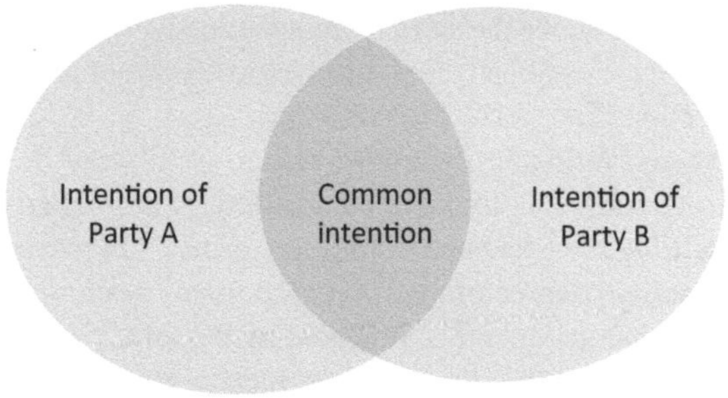

Interpretation of contracts relates to the essence of a contractual agreement, the common intention between the parties,[148] which in itself is intangible; the contract *is* the metaphysical agreement. The agreement may be evidenced in a written contract, but it always contains more facts than are evidenced in the contract, such as the parties' subjective understanding of the written text.[149] A contractual agreement is elusive rather than concrete, and the interpretation thereof contains an element of description; before the contract can be interpreted the interpreter must establish its contents. The two processes are, however, not strictly separated and will likely be entangled.

Common intention could be established either through a presumption that a written contract correctly reflects the parties' intention at the time of their entering into

certain issue with non-mandatory legislation filling such a gap) although a distinct line between them is hard, not to say impossible, to draw (cf. J. Samuelsson, *Tolkning och utfyllning* (2008) in particular ch. 11.3.4). The former connotes the procedure through which the *meaning* of a contract is to be established, and the latter connotes the additional procedure necessary to establish the full legal implication of a contract, which includes *adding* details to an agreement, which are not explicitly there (B. Lehrberg, *Avtalstolkning* (2006) pp. 16–17). For the current purposes, "interpretation" denotes all activities with the purpose of establishing the "correct" and "full" implications of a contract.

148 Samuelsson proposes that contract interpretation is the art of establishing the common intention between the parties and, just like interpretation of legislation, it concerns application of a method rather than application of rules. The intention captured in the agreement is subjective but yet objective; it is the comprehension of the communication by the receiver thereof, to the extent that can be considered legitimate, that forms the starting point for interpretation of a contract. Samuelsson gives an illustrative example in which a person agrees to buy something for a friend. If the friend claims the purchase not to be in accordance with the agreement, or "order", the discussion between the two friends will not likely focus on the intention of the friend who gives the order, but on the legitimacy of the execution of the order by the purchaser friend; "you said x, and for reasons y and z, it was legitimate for me to understand your order the way I did" (J. Samuelsson, *Tolkningslärans gåta* (2011) at p. 192).

149 Kramer argues that "communication is based upon a process of pragmatic interfence" and thus a communicative utterance is based on, and contains, a "background of social norms and [the communicator's] goals and principles". The lingusitic meaning, Kramer continues, is merely one element of the intended meaning and it is natural to any communicatee to infer the communicator's purpose and intention with the utterance. Thus any lingusitic meaning must be supplemented. It is this, Kramer concludes, which is the trend in (English) law of interpretation of contractual documents (A. Kramer, "Implication of Fact as an Instance of Contractual Interpretation" (2004) 63(2) CLJ 63 384–411, in particular pp. 385–387).

the agreement, or, through interpretation of data such as the parties' subsequent behaviour, the rightful expectations of one party based on the communication of the other. It will never be possible to establish the true intention of the parties: a court would then only practice the art of qualified guesswork. Therefore, interpretation of contracts seeks to establish the rightful expectations of the parties in relation to a common intention.[150]

In this context, the rationale for interpretation at all may be questioned. As mentioned, interpretation is both the understanding of ambiguous (explicit) contract terms and settling the existence of implicit terms.[151] In respect of the former, there is always a certain degree of interpretation in any reading or understanding of a text, although what in general is indicated by the term "interpretation of contracts" is the process of settling the "correct" meaning of a term between parties in disagreement. Accordingly, a court faced with the task of deciding which of the parties is "right" in respect of understanding a certain term of a contract, the court must undertake an exercise in interpretation, or else the court cannot fulfil its obligation. In respect of the latter, the fact that something is not explicit in a contract may just indicate that the parties did not intend to regulate the issue in question. Although this proposition can be challenged due to the fact that "doing nothing" does not solve the dispute at hand, it is proposed here that the implication is not a question of adding terms to the contract, but of making explicit terms that are implicit in the contract. Accordingly, to the extent a legal system recognizes that a contract is non-formal, implied terms are part of the contract and any proposition of such terms should be examined. It is quite possible to lay down that a written contract is the only evidence of the contract, and that thus no terms will be implied into the contract. However, such procedural rules elude the standing of the contract as a non-formal agreement, as only entirely oral agreements are accepted; once any part of an agreement has been written down, only the formal parts of the agreement are given the force of a legally binding contract.

Theories of contract interpretation are developed in an international setting and the similarities between (Western) national systems appear to be many. However, there is a line, if not sharp then at least defined, between common law and civil law.[152] The difference can, when analysed, be said to be largely procedural.[153] In

150 Even though reference is often made to "rules of interpretation", the interpretation of contracts is rather a method than a legal discipline subject to certain rules (J. Samuelsson, *Tolkningslärans gåta* (2011) ch. 8).

151 I intentionally refrain from using the expression "implying terms into a contract" as it seems to suggest that terms that do not actually exist are added to the contract. As I see it, implication of terms is a matter of making explicit terms that are an implicit, i.e. in respect of the intention of the parties, part of the contract.

152 Cf. Eftestøl-Wilhelmsson who separates Nordic law from other European civil law, and thus divides the national systems of the European Union into "the common law legal family, the civil law legal family and the Nordic legal family" (E. Eftestøl-Wilhelmsson, *European Sustainable Carriage of Goods* (2016) p. 50).

153 Whilst in Nordic law there is theoretically no limitation on the evidence allowed by a court in order to prove the contents of a contract, in English law interpretation is largely based on the written contents of the contract and the rules relating to admittance of evidence are much more formalistic; see below and A. Møllmann, *Certepartifortolkning* (2007) pp. 49 and 58.

the following, I make pretence neither of a complete analysis of interpretation of contracts nor of a comparative study of the interpretation of contracts under common law and under civil law. Instead, the purpose of the following is to give an indication of what data may be taken into account when considering whether a contract is one for carriage by [road].

5.6.1.1 The written contract

In English common law, the express terms of a contract, i.e. a written contract, are fundamental and cannot, as a starting point, be rebutted. In Nordic civil law, on the other hand, the express terms of contract are but one, although a very important, piece of evidence of the terms of the contract, which can be rebutted by proof to the contrary. Due to the existence of supplementary statutes that with predictability fill out any gaps in a contract, written contracts need to regulate only such obligations where the parties intend to diverge from the supplementary statutes.[154] In common law, however, contracts are sought to be complete, covering all terms, as filling out the contract is to a large extent at the discretion of the court.[155] Accordingly, whilst the common law interpreter of a contract is bound by the objective contents of an express contract, the civil law interpreter of a contract may consider pre-contractual representations, mistakes in declarations and implied terms of the contract, etc. Thus, the common law interpreter assumes that the intention of the parties is correctly reflected in the written contract, which is not necessarily the assumption of the civil law interpreter. Traditionally, therefore, common law interpretation of contracts has been considered fundamentally different from interpretation in civil law systems, where the common law approach has been regarded as inflexible and formal but, on the other hand, predictable to the parties.

In accordance with the principle of freedom of contract, and the freedom *to* contract, a contract, prima facie, defines its own normativity – any question of interpretation, or construction, is primarily to be found within the contract itself. It that respect, contract interpretation is autonomous.[156] However, interpretation

154 A common feature in civil law is the existence of non-mandatory legislation. Such non-mandatory legislation functions as a basis for the construction of contracts. Non-mandatory legislation often supplies a complete set of rules in relation to a specific form of contract, such as, for example, a sales contract. The parties may base their contract on legislation and only explicitly include such terms in their contract that diverge from the terms prescribed by legislation (to the extent that the legislation is non-mandatory). Often, however, the legislation will function as a gap-filler; the parties may not be particularly aware of the terms of the legislation, and thus never actually base their agreement thereon, but as their contract is not complete and contains gaps in a certain respect, the legislation will step in. This procedure should not, it is proposed here, be regarded as contract construction as such. The terms of the legislation apply with the force of law where the parties have not agreed otherwise, and are not enforced as implied or construed terms of the contract.

155 J. Cartwright, *Contract Law* (2016) pp. 216–217.

156 Samuelsson proposes that it is the individuality of the contract that distinguishes contract interpretation from other forms of interpretation, such as interpretation of legislation. He holds: "The norm that is to be interpreted and applied to settle the particular problem that exists in the individual case must be construed in relation to the circumstances *in the case at hand*" (J. Samuelsson, *Tolkningslärans gåta* (2011) p. 167 (my translation)). The contract, he states, has its own normativity, which is not legal, but still interpretation of contracts takes place within the legal sphere – the intention of the

of a contract cannot be done entirely autonomously, i.e. without reference to anything but the contract itself (in which case interpretation would be nothing but literal interpretation *in absurdum*). Thus, the interpreter must consider certain sources, or data, of interpretation.[157] Depending on the rules of admission of evidence applicable where the interpretation of a contract is carried out, there may be more or less limitation to these sources of interpretation.

Under English law, where a contract is in writing, the wording of a written contract has been known to be allotted decisive importance, which under the so-called "parol evidence rule" could not be rebutted by evidence of a diverging intent of the parties.[158] Where a written contract has been signed by both parties, such a contract is regarded as representing the intentions of the parties.[159] However, several other rules and exemptions undermine the severity of the parol evidence rule, to the extent that the validity of the parol evidence rule could be, and has been, questioned.[160] On the other hand, admission of evidence in relation to the actual content of a contract is to a large extent regulated and some evidence is considered inadmissible.[161]

---

parties is legal to the extent that the contract aims at a legally binding effect. However, this statement is adjusted by the existence of mandatory rules. These form part of the contract and, to the extent the contents of the contract contradicts those rules, adjust the contents thereof. This is particularly true in respect of contracts of carriage, where mandatory rules are the norm rather than the exception.

157 These sources of interpretation are sometime referred to as "rules of interpretation". However, with the exception of a few cannons of construction such as the minimum rule and the rule of *contra proferentem,* which are sometimes still referred to, these "rules" are, it is asserted here, in fact restatements of the sources of interpretation most frequently invoked.

158 Under English law an agreement does not have to be in writing in order to constitute a "contract". Where the contract is oral, the parties will have to prove the contents thereof.

159 From this rule there is no exception irrespective of whether the parties have read and understood the contents or not, although there are exceptions for e.g. fraud and misrepresentation (K. Lewison, *The Interpretation of Contracts* (2004) p. 47).

160 The parol evidence rule does seem to have been severely undermined from several exceptions, to the extent that its applicability can be questioned. Where previously the parol evidence rule, and other rules of the same kind such as the principle of estoppel, meant that interpretation of contracts was a non-issue, it has now found its way into the law of contracts discussion (J. Rosengren, "Engelsk avtalstolkning i ett svenskt perspektiv" (2010) 1 SvJT 2010 1–22, at p. 2, with reference to Atiyah, *Essays on Contract* (1988) p. 111). In *Investors Compensation Scheme Ltd v West Bromwich Building Society* [1997] CLC 1243, Lord Hoffmann emphasized that even where a word has a clear objective meaning, if it is clear that the parties intended another meaning, that meaning should be decisive for interpretation of the contract. This is evidently the opposite of the "parol evidence rule" and, although old habits die hard, the law seems to state that an interpreter should take into account all the background knowledge that has been available to the parties, which includes "absolutely anything" that affects the language used by the parties except for previous negotiations and subjective intent (S. Smith, *Atiyah's Introduction to the Law of Contract* (2005) p. 143).

161 As regards evidence relating to the negotiation and drafting of a contract, pre-contracts, representing a consensus between the parties may be admissible as evidence. However, drafts, not representing consensus, and evidence of the negotiations leading up to the final contract, are not admissible (K. Lewison, *The Interpretation of Contracts* (2004) pp. 58–59, referring to *National Bank of Australasia v Falkingham & Sons* [1902] AC 585 and *Prenn v Simmonds* [1971] 1 WLR 1381). The rationale has been held to be that negotiations and drafts do not represent any consensus between the parties and where a draft contains a different expression than the final contract, such drafts will not help the construction of the contractual words. As far as proof of negotiations is concerned, proving that one party considered particular wording to have a certain meaning does not mean that this is the interpretation commonly intended between the parties as the other party may have had a different conception of the meaning; ultimately interpretation of the language of the contract is for the court

Thus, in relation to actual interpretation of the terms of a written contract, the parol evidence rule would previously have meant that interpretation of a written contract would only be based on the objective meaning of the words.[162] No evidence proving the parties' (common) subjective meaning would have been admitted. However, this strict application of the parol evidence rule was eventually eased and, in 1997, the House of Lords summarized developments of the law of contract interpretation thus far in five principles, which considerably relax the strict approach to interpretation of written contracts found in the parol evidence rule.[163] In summary, the principles of the so-called Lord Hoffmann Restatement entail that interpretation of the wording of a contract has moved from strictly objective to subjective, although subjective is not to be understood as subjective in the sense that it is the meaning intended by the one party suggesting the wording, but the parties' common subjective intention. This means that where the parties have used the wrong word, this word is to be interpreted as meaning what the parties commonly intended it to mean, and not in accordance with its objective meaning.[164] Although an attempt has been made to relegate the parol evidence rule to history by the Lord Hoffmann Restatement, there is not complete consensus as to the legal justification

(K. Lewison, *ibid.* at pp. 58–59, referring to *The Rio Assu (No. 2)* [1999] 1 Lloyd's Rep 115 at 124, CA). On the other hand, where evidence contradicting a contract has not been admitted, a collateral contract has sometimes been found to exist (E. MacDonald, "Contents" in A. Grubb (ed.), *The Law of Contract* (2007) pp. 597–774, at pp. 607–647). A collateral contract consists of oral statements that limit or extend the written agreement and can thus alter the original contract in the same way as the contract could have been rebutted had it not been for the parol evidence rule. A commonly referred to example is *City & Westminster Properties Ltd v Mudd* [1959] CLJ 58 where a landlord had entered a new clause into a lease and orally promised the tenant not to impose it. The oral promise was found to be a collateral contract, which meant that the landlord could not impose the written clause in question on the tenant.

162 K. Lewison, *ibid.* at pp. 116–119.

163

> (1) Interpretation is the ascertainment of the meaning which the document would convey to a reasonable person having all the background knowledge which would reasonably have been available to the parties in the situation in which they were at the time of the contract. (2) Subject to the requirement that it should have been reasonably available to the parties and to the exception to be mentioned next, [the background] includes absolutely anything which would have affected the way in which the language of the document would have been understood by a reasonable man. (3) The law excludes from the admissible background the previous negotiations of the parties and their declarations of subjective intent. They are admissible only in an action for rectification. .... (4) The meaning which a document (or any other utterance) would convey to a reasonable man is not the same thing as the meaning of its words. The meaning of words is a matter of dictionaries and grammars; the meaning of the document is what the parties using those words against the relevant background would reasonably have been understood to mean. The background may not merely enable the reasonable man to choose between the possible meanings of words which are ambiguous but even (as occasionally happens in ordinary life) to conclude that the parties must, for whatever reason, have used the wrong words or syntax .... (5) The "rule" that words should be given their "natural and ordinary meaning" reflects the common sense proposition that we do not easily accept that people have made linguistic mistakes, particularly in formal documents. On the other hand, if one would nevertheless conclude from the background that something must have gone wrong with the language, the law does not require judges to attribute to the parties an intention which they plainly could not have had.
>
> (*Investors Compensation Scheme Ltd v West Bromwich Building Society* [1997] CLC 1243, at p. 1257)

These principles are sometimes referred to as The Lord Hoffmann Restatement.

164 Cf. rule 4 of the Restatement above.

of the restatement. Further, even though the five principles of the restatement are held to be based on a summary of developments in law up until 1997, later developments have been claimed to be characterized by consolidation rather than progress.[165] Thus, the parol evidence rule may not yet have been entirely defeated.[166]

Under Nordic civil law, the actual intent of the parties is generally given priority, even where contradicted by a written contract.[167] In fact, the parties' common intention displaces a written contract.[168] Nevertheless, where a written contract exists, any interpretation of the agreement will start with the wording of such written contract.[169] However, the interpreter is free to consider any submitted proof to suggest the existence of a common intention, which is either not clear from the contract or diverges from the contract. Interpretational data that are likely to affect interpretation include pre-contractual communication, prior agreements between the parties, circumstances such as the parties' behaviour at the time of entering into the contract, as well as afterwards, i.e. their behaviour in relation to fulfilment of the contract.[170] Thus, the intention of the parties is not merely drawn from the words uttered or written by that party, but from all circumstances, which have been relevant for perception of the offer by the opposite party.[171] The principal goal of any interpreter is to seek to establish that common intention and, in order to do so, the interpreter is bound neither by the written contract, if one exists, nor by other written documents, such as the offer and/or the acceptance.[172] The primary data of interpretation may be a written contract, but such a contract

165 G. McMeel, *The Construction of Contracts* (2011) p. vii.

166 M. Clarke; "Interpreting contracts – the price of perspective" (2000) 59 CLJ 18–20, at p. 19. Further, although *Investors v West Bromwich* and the Restatement has not been without impact in relation to English law, in an international perspective English law will likely be associated with the parol evidence rule for a long time.

167 J. Giertsen, *Avtaler* (2014) p. 117, K. Hauser, *Avtaletolkning* (1983) p. 378.

168 B. Lehrberg, *Avtalstolkning* (2003) p. 35 and A.P. Høgberg, "Tolkningsstiler vid kontrakatstolkning" 2006) 41 Jussens Venner 61–198, at p. 73.

169 C. Ramberg and J. Ramberg, *Allmän Avtalsrätt* (2016) p. 161.

170 J. Ramberg, Avtalstolkningsmetoder in *Festskrift till Gösta Walin* (2002) p. 504. In a Swedish Supreme Court judgment of 1991, the Supreme Court, HD, hence encapsulated the circumstances relevant to the interpretation of a contract as being: contract preliminaries; circumstances surrounding the negotiation of the contract; the wording of the contract; legal background (non-mandatory law, customs of the trade); the purpose of the contract and the context of the contract (C. Ramberg and J. Ramberg, *ibid.*, at p. 188).

171 O. Svensson, *Viljeförklaringen och dess innehåll* (1996) p. 43.

172 Generally, a written contract is an important, perhaps vital, source for interpretation (A. Adlercreutz and B. Mulder, *Avtalet: Lärobok I allmän avtalsrätt* (2013) p. 108 and B. Lehrberg, *ibid.*, at p. 34). Likewise, other written communication that may indicate the parties' intention may affect the interpretation of the contract. However, should the parties agree, or either party succeeds in proving, that the common intention differs from the terms of the written contract, the common intention prevails (B. Lehrberg, *ibid.* at pp. 33–34 and A.P. Høgberg, *ibid.*, at p. 73). The common intention *is* the contract. Therefore, as mentioned above, the parties, in accordance with the overall objective to establish the common intention of the parties, may disprove the clear meaning of the words of the contract (U. Bernitz, *Standardavtalsrätt* (2013) p. 83). In practice this means that where the parties in their contract have expressed X, but agree, or it can otherwise be established, that they both intended Y, the content of the contract is Y (C. Ramberg and J. Ramberg, *ibid.*, at p. 143; B. Lehrberg, *ibid.*, at p. 27 and U. Bernitz, *ibid.*, at p. 83). Normally, interpretation of a contract is only necessary where the parties disagree on the common intention and thus the interpreter needs to rely on other facts than the opinion of the parties.

may be complemented, or even displaced, by establishing a common intention, which has not been expressed in the written contract.[173] Accordingly, the palette of interpretation data available to the contract interpreter is rather ample; the interpreter may consider any data that contribute to the "rightful" understanding of the contract.

The discrepancy in contract interpretation that is often assumed to exist between civil law and common law seems accordingly to be not so significant. However, the discrepancy may be explainable as a procedural issue rather than an issue of contract interpretation, as the systems of admission of evidence are rather dissimilar. Thus, the tradition in common law states is to assume a rather formal position as to the admissibility of evidence. Whilst some evidence is admissible, other evidence is not, and the court should dismiss evidence that is inadmissible and dismissed evidence must be disregarded by the court. The parol evidence rule is a procedural rule on the admissibility of evidence in relation to contract interpretation.[174] The rule provides that where a written contract appears to be a complete document, it should be interpreted with disregard to external facts.[175] In other words, a contract provides for its own normativity, particularly where the contract is complete, which means that it is in no need of implication of terms with respect to a certain issue in dispute.[176] The rule has gradually been provided with exceptions, which have eventually come to excavate the rule.[177] Thus the rule came to prescribe conditions when evidence was admissible to demonstrate the intentions of the parties. One such condition was ambiguity of the contract.[178]

Although the procedural rule as regards admission of evidence is the virtual opposite in civil law systems such as the Nordic – there is no such thing as non-admissible evidence, although a court may dismiss evidence that is clearly unnecessary – the result may not be entirely different as the court will only consider evidence it finds relevant and of any value to the so-called "theme of evidence" (see further below).[179]

173 In addition to the data that the interpreter may thus consider in interpreting a contract, the interpreter is equipped with a few principles of interpretation. The value of such principles has been questioned (Grönfors, *Tolkning av fraktavtal* (1989) and J. Samulesson, *Tolkningslärans gåta* (2011)).

174 J. Hellner, "The parol evidence rule och tolkning av skriftliga avtal i svensk rätt" in *Festskrift till Bertil Bengtsson* (1993) p. 186. However, it has gradually become to be regarded more as a material rule (J. Rosengren, "Engelsk avtalstolkning i ett svenskt perspektiv" (2010) SvJT 1–22, at p. 6).

175 J. Hellner, *ibid*., at p. 188.

176 J. Samuelsson, *ibid*., at p. 170.

177 Although, already the primary prerequisite, its applicability to complete contracts has been claimed to have rendered the rule valueless (J. Rosengren, *ibid*., at p. 7, with reference to the Law Commission Report on the Parol Evidence Rule in 1986). Further, the parol evidence rule was even in 1959 held to be "no more than a self-evident tautology" (K.W. Wedderburn, "Collateral Contracts" [1959] CLJ 58–85, at p. 80).

178 These conditions were restated by Lord Hoffmann in the above-mentioned restatement of 1997; see *Investors v Bromwich* [1997] CLC 1243.

179 J. Hellner, "The parol evidence rule och tolkning av skriftliga avtal i svensk rätt" in *Festskrift till Bertil Bengtsson* (1993) p. 186. Rosengren holds that the parol evidence rule was in fact a tool, albeit somewhat blunt, to settle what evidence was relevant and what value to assign to it, in the same

5.6.1.2 The "common" intention

Since oral contracts are, as a matter of fact, subject to proof, and evidence as to their existence must obviously be admitted, the discussion on possible differences between common law and civil law systems has a natural focus on written contracts. Thus, the common law interpreter will commence any interpretation of a written contract with the terms of such contract. It has been held above that this will likewise be the natural starting point for a civil law interpreter. In respect of how the terms of the written contract are approached, the criterion of objectiveness, which is *per se* common, has been given slightly diverse substance.[180] The criterion according to the Lord Hoffmann Restatement is based on the common intention as that intention has been expressed in the contract and entails that interpretation of that expression should be settled in accordance with how that expression (the terms of the contract) would be perceived by a third party. That third party should admittedly have knowledge of the background of the contract, which includes "absolutely anything which would have affected the way in which the language of the document would have been understood".[181] However, in Nordic law, objectivity is limited to the intra-party relationship; it is the justified perception of a communication, such as the terms of a contract, by the opposite party that is the standard when interpreting a contract.[182] Accordingly, the ordinary meaning of a term should be decided based on how the term would be perceived by the recipient, as long as such understanding bears some objective justifiability. The understanding thereof is somewhat subjective, but the question whether the recipient was justified in that perception must be measured against an objective scale.[183] If the recipient understands the communication in a certain way based entirely on subjective conditions, such perception cannot be objectively justified; the effects of a certain communication must be foreseeable for the emitter. On the other hand, interpretation of a term

---

way as a civil law judge would do under the principles of free submission and valuation of proof (J. Rosengren, *ibid.*, at p. 8).

180 English law seems to a certain extent to believe that the civil law approach is subjective. This is not a correct observation, as a subjective approach would give the contract the contents intended by the offeror, i.e. the opposite of the *contra proferentem* rule; where a term of a contract is clear, subjective interpretation would be to ask for the content intended by the stipulator. As to English law in this respect see G. McMeel, "Prior negotiations and subsequent conduct – the next step forward for contractual interpretation?" (2003) 119 LQR 272–297, at p. 283 with reference to J. Steyn and p. 290 with reference to C.J. Posner.

181 *Investors v Bromwich* [1997] CLC 1243. This statement later clarified "absolutely anything" to entail anything which may be relevant for understanding by a third party: see *Bank of Credit and Commerce International SA v Ali* [2001] UKHL 8.

182 Commonly referred to as expression-oriented interpretation, see eg. A.P. Høgberg, "Tolkningsstiler ved kontraktstolkning" (2006) 41 Jussens Venner 61–108, at p. 70 and B. Lehrberg, *Avtalstolkning* (2003) p. 58.

183 Accordingly, the question is: would another recipient of the same communication have understood it in the same way? As an example, in the Danish case HD 23 April 2008 (U.2008.1638H) (cf. section 3.4.1 above), had the court considered the contract of carriage from a contractual point of view, a reasonable question would have been "was the contracting consignor justified in its perception that the goods would be carried by air during the entire carriage?" Considering the widespread use of "trucking", the answer may have been "no", depending on the contracting consignor's experience in transport contracting. In such a case, it is asserted here, the contract of carriage should have been considered a contract for carriage by air and road.

must be subjective in the sense that the context within which the contract is entered into affects the understanding of a term, i.e. the term must be understood according to its general meaning in its context.[184]

The Nordic and the English objectivity criteria may seem comparable and indeed the difference between a third party having all the relevant background information that the parties had at the time of entering into a contract and a party whose perception must not differ from how another person would have perceived the same communication may seem insubstantial. It is, however, asserted here, that the difference may prove to be decisive; the difference in fact is the starting point, or the presumption. Whilst in a Nordic setting the perception or understanding by the receiving party, the offeree, is accepted as long as there is nothing extraordinarily subjective in that perception, the English starting point is the perception of terms by an external party not having taken part in any negotiations. The presumption in the former criterion is that the receiver's perception is acceptable, and in the latter the starting point is truly objective: the perception by a third party, who will have access to the same information as the parties, but in fact not being a party. Despite the more admissive approach enunciated through the Lord Hoffmann Restatement, some bars to admissibility still remain.[185] Thus, no evidence relating to the parties' respective declarations or subjective intent will be allowed. From the objectivity criteria applied in Nordic civil law follows that, even if submitted, a judge would not be right in ascribing it any significance – the interpretation of a contract is not to be based on either party's subjective intent, unless that was communicated to the opposite party. It would seem that the same would follow from common law objectivity criteria.[186]

5.6.1.3 Contract preliminaries

Evidence of contract preliminaries is not admitted in English law. The rationale for not allowing such evidence has been justified partly by the assumption that

---

184 It was asserted above that the contract provides for its own normativity. However, the terms of a contract must be given a meaning that relates to an understanding outside the contract itself. Thus, although the contract is interpreted autonomously, it cannot be understood without reference to external knowledge, such as the ordinary meaning of the terms or the meaning of the terms in the legal or trade context. Normativity refers instead to the (legal) relationship between the parties to the contract. Any solution to an interpretative issue in an actual, practical case can only be found within the contract itself. Interpretative issue in this respect therefore does not mean the textual understanding of the terms, but rather the question of the treatment of a certain (actual) case under the contract. What necessitates interpretation is not a textual (or other) ambiguity as such, but an ambiguity caused by applying the contract to a particular issue (A.P. Høgberg, "Tolkningsstiler vid kontrakatstolkning" (2006) 41 Jussens Venner 61–198, at p. 66).

185 G. McMeel, *The Construction of Contracts* (2011) p. vii.

186 Against that background, the rule on inadmissibility would seem unnecessary to a civil law lawyer. However, the law of evidence is an integral part of common law, and it appears that declaring evidence as inadmissible appears more natural to a common law lawyer. The rationale behind the law of evidence seems to be, perhaps among other things, a belief that without it legal proceedings would be drowned by irrelevant evidence. In 1999, L.J. Staughton held that "It is hard to imagine a ruling more calculated to perpetuate the vast cost of commercial litigation" (cited by J. Rosengren, "Engelsk avtalstolkning i ett svenskt perspektiv" (2010) SvJT 1–22, at p. 8). It appears that this prophecy was not correct and that English litigants, just like civil law litigants, reduce the evidence submitted to such evidence as they believe to be relevant. See also G. McMeel, "Prior negotiations and subsequent conduct – the next step forward for contractual interpretation?" (2003) 119 LQR 272–297, at p. 289.

it would not be of much value, and partly by the objectivity criteria: a third party, such as a legal adviser, should be able to understand the contract without insight into the negotiations that preceded the contract and parties should be encouraged to properly express their intentions.[187] It has been held, however, that originally contract preliminaries were admissible to show the aim and object of a contract, but not in order to "add, vary or subtract" from the document, a nuance which was later lost and any evidence of contract preliminaries was considered inadmissible.[188] According to Nordic law of contracts, a party who realizes the subjective intention of the opposite party with which the first party does not agree is obliged to inform the other party of the apparent divergence in their respective intentions, since otherwise that party may be bound by the interpretation that corresponds to the other party's intention.[189] This rule obviously requires consideration of contract preliminaries. However, respecting the objectivity criteria, in either version, of evidence to show either party's subjective intention is superfluous. Thus, the objectivity criteria in interpreting contracts will to a large extent prevent consideration of such evidence, whether it is admitted or not; the means to a similar end is different. Lastly, in civil as well as in common law, a court may rectify a contract that does not correctly mirror the parties' common intention and to this extent common law admits evidence of contract preliminaries.[190]

5.6.1.4 Subsequent conduct

It may seem that the parties' subsequent behaviour in relation to fulfilment of a contract would be irrelevant in establishing the common intention at the time of entering into the contract. However, in fact it is telling in terms of how the parties actually did consider the scope of the contract, i.e. before a legal dispute arose.[191] Especially in long-lasting or consecutive agreements, a party's (or the parties') previous behaviour could influence interpretation, such as if a party has previously accepted certain behaviour, e.g. a particular way of contract performance, to which the opposite party has not objected.[192]

---

187 G. McMeel, *ibid.*, at p. 295, in which McMeel pleads for liberalization of English contract interpretation. However, considering Yihans article in 2014, it seems that McMeel's plead has yet to be hearkened to (G. Yihan, "A wrong turn in history: re-understanding the exclusionary rule against prior negotiations in contractual interpretation" (2014) 5 JBL 360–387).

188 G. Yihan, *ibid.*

189 Contracts Act § 6 (Sweden).

190 Whilst under common law this would be done under an action for rectification, under civil law a court would "simply" hold that the written contract does not correctly mirror the intention and establish the contents of the contract in accordance with the correct intention of the parties, i.e. there is no "rectification" of the contract. The former procedure seems natural against the background of the firm position of the written contract.

191 B. Lehrberg, *Avtalstolkning* (2006) p. 119.

192 Adlercreutz holds that subsequent behaviour by the parties does not constitute data for interpretation. However, it may have legal relevance as proof of what was the intention of the parties at the time of entering into the agreement (A. Adlercreutz and B. Mulder, *Avtalet: Lärobok I allmän avtalsrätt* (2013) p. 109).

As a main rule, such evidence of subsequent conduct is not admissible under English common law.[193] However, it will be allowed under the principle of "estoppel by convention". Estoppel by convention rests on the principle of the contract as the meeting of the parties' minds, i.e. their common intention. In order to show that the common intention deviates from the terms of the written contract, evidence of the parties' subsequent conduct will be admitted.

Under the rule of free admission of evidence practised in the Nordic legal systems, evidence of subsequent conduct is permitted. The evidential value thereof will, naturally, vary.[194] In submitting evidence to the court, a party is obliged, in respect of every piece of evidence submitted, to state the "theme of proof", i.e. the party must inform the court what is to be proven by the evidence submitted.[195] Subsequently, the court will have to evaluate the evidence submitted to it in respect of the theme stated.[196] As a general matter, there seem to be only a few purposes for submitting evidence of subsequent conduct: the themes of evidence available are limited. One reason could be to prove that one party has waived a certain right through the way performance under the contract was carried out.[197] Generally, however, one party's, in relation to the other party, beneficial application of the contract will not be deemed a general waiver in that respect.[198]

Another theme that might be proven through evidence of subsequent conduct is the very same as to which end English law would admit such evidence; that the parties' actual agreement differs from how it has been expressed in writing, which is shown by how the parties have performed their respective obligations.[199] In such a case, it would seem that an English court would also admit the evidence in question. In conclusion it is held that free admission of evidence will often not

193 G. McMeel, "Prior negotiations and subsequent conduct – the next step forward for contractual interpretation?" (2003) 119 LQR 272–297, at p. 293. In comparison with the parol evidence rule, this rule seems to have been less firm historically. The rule seems to have been firmly settled as law in the 1970s (G. McMeel, *The Construction of Contracts* (2011) pp. 220–221). Thus in 1982 Lord Denning held: "For many years I thought that when a meaning of a contract was uncertain you could look at the subsequent conduct of the parties to ascertain it. That seemed to me sensible enough. The parties themselves should know what they meant by their words better than anyone else" (*Amalgamated Investment & Properties Co Ltd v Texas Commerce International Bank Ltd* [1982] QB 84, 119).

194 Hauser points out that the relevance of an interpretative datum may differ depending on the theme of evidence and thus certain data may be relevant to one side, but not to the other (K. Huser, *Avtaletolkning* (1983) p. 469).

195 The system entails that, contrary to what seems to be the general fear in England, the courts are not drowned by evidence, which they have to dig through and appreciate the possible evidential value of. The system is in fact similar to the pre-trial procedure of discovery, although in the latter case the court is not involved. However, Hauser implies that the system allows counsel to be less particular in respect of what evidence is submitted, which would be desirable (K. Huser, *ibid.* at pp. 469–470).

196 P-O Ekelöf, *Rättegång IV* (2009) p. 170.

197 For example, if a party commences performance in respect of delivering a certain product, that party may be barred from claiming that the contract in fact related to another product, see e.g. NJA 1974 s. 345. Also, it is generally considered that, by paying the creditor, a debtor loses the right to dispute the existence of a debt or its extent where the full debt is paid.

198 B. Lehrberg, *Avtalstolkning* (2003) p. 111.

199 See Lord Denning in *Amalgamated Investment & Property Co Ltd v Texas Commerce International Bank Ltd* [1982] QB 84, at p. 119.

bring a different result than the detailed rules on admission found in English law: when scrutinized the two legal systems provide different routes to, if not the same at least neighbouring, ends.

5.6.1.5 Characterization of contracts under English law

The characterization of contracts under civil law has been discussed previously in section 3.2.1. As regards English law, characterization of contracts is interesting in relation to interpretation of contracts, as the need to characterize a contract may open for admission evidence that would normally be dismissed.

It seems clear that, under English law, characterization of a contract also rests on the substance of the contract rather than the label.[200] Thus, characterization of contracts will often involve a certain degree of interpretation, although it is often held that characterization of contracts is distinct from construction of contracts.[201] Due to the existence of statutory or other law conferring privileges or obligations upon certain categories of contract, characterization of contracts is deemed of vital interest, and the law therefore permits recourse to the "widest possible evidence".[202] Accordingly, in relation to a matter of the proper characterization of a contract, evidence of prior negotiations as well as subsequent conduct will be admitted.[203]

Characterization of contracts in this respect relates to determining whether statutory or other law is to be applied to the contract. Thus, it seems to be relevant in relation to carriage contracts and the applicability of mandatory conventions. Accordingly, in *Quantum*[204], subsequent conduct seems to have been considered in order to characterize the contract (which provided for air carriage but permitted the carrier to substitute mode of transport). The issue of characterization was not expressly considered, although it was held that "this evidence confirms Mr Rosen's statement that, unless some other option was chosen, the present contractual arrangement contemplated and provided for carriage by road".[205] Thus, the Court of Appeal places importance on prior dealings between the parties (performance of prior, identical, contracts) as well as negotiations that have taken place between the parties prior to signing the current contract.

---

200 G. McMeel, *The Construction of Contracts* (2011) pp. 18–19.

201 G. McMeel, *ibid.*, at p. 224.

202 G. McMeel, *ibid.*, at p. 224.

203 G. McMeel, *ibid.*, at p. 224. See also *A G Securities v Vaughan* [1990] 1 AC 417 in which the House of Lords held that "although the subsequent actions of the parties may not be [looked at] for the purpose of construing the agreements they may be looked at for the purposes of determining [the true character of the contract]." (p. 475*ff.*).

204 *Quantum Corporation Inc v Plane Trucking Ltd* [2002] EWCA Civ 350.

205 *Ibid* at para. 13. The question concerned a contract for carriage by air, which allowed the carrier to substitute mode of transport. The parties had on previous occasions contracted for the same carriage, on which occasions the carrier had substituted part of the transport for road carriage. According to the evidence submitted the consignee had requested the exchange of one sub-carrier for another road carrier due to the consignee's dissatisfaction with the current trucker (Plane Trucking). These pre-contractual discussions seem accordingly to have been considered by the court to render the current contract a contract for carriage by air and road, although the actual written contract did not stipulate anything to that effect more than the right for the carrier to so carry the goods.

On a general note, it seems to be requiring a great deal from courts to allow evidence to one certain end, but not to another, as it demands that the judge should disregard certain evidence, which has already come to the judge's attention, in settling a matter in relation to which the evidence in question would not be admitted.[206]

5.6.1.6 Implication of terms

Implication of terms is generally resorted to when a contract is incomplete (lack of contractual specification), and hence does not provide a solution to a certain issue that has arisen.[207] The line between interpretation of a contract and implication of terms therein may not be easy to draw, although seemingly straightforward. Under English law they are both subject to the same overriding principles of construction, such as the principle of objectivity.[208] Under civil law, both activities are covered by the umbrella of interpretation and, with the exception of implication of non-mandatory legislation, the difference between the two has not always been upheld.[209]

Implied terms are divided into three different types: terms implied in law; terms implied by custom; and terms implied by facts.[210] As regards terms implied in law, in a civil law system these will always be in the form of a statute. In a common law system, such "general default rules" may also be found at common law.[211] In addition, under Nordic civil law, terms may be implied into a contract based on the parties' previous conduct or commercial practice.[212]

What in English law is referred to as terms implied in fact relates to the intention of the parties, such as terms that, whether or not the parties had them in mind or would have expressed them if they had foreseen the difficulty, are implied by the court because of the court's view of fairness or policy or in consequence of rules of law.[213] Whilst under civil law any assertion of implied terms will be tried,

---

206 G. McMeel, "Prior negotiations and subsequent conduct – the next step forward for contractual interpretation?" (2003) 119 LQR 272–297, at p. 288.

207 G. McMeel, *The Construction of Contracts* (2011) p. 314.

208 G. McMeel, *ibid.*, at p. 315.

209 Samuelsson questions whether the rationale for the distinction, which was formulated in the spirit of legal realism, still exists (J. Samuelsson, *Tolkning och Utfyllning* (2008) pp. 241–242).

210 E. MacDonald, "Contents" in A. Grubb (ed.), *The Law of Contract* (2007) pp. 597–774, at p. 626. "Terms implied in law" signifies terms implied due to the certain nature of the contract; a certain rule has been laid down that is considered applicable to all contracts of a certain kind. Some terms are implied in a contract due to the customary background against which the parties have contracted. This can relate to a custom between the particular parties, such as inclusion of standard terms or a custom within the particular trade.

211 A relevant example is the seaworthiness condition that rests on a carrier by sea according to *Hong Kong Fir Shipping Co Ltd v Kawasaki Kisen Kaisha Ltd* [1962] 2 QB 28, CA.

212 In the case of sale of goods, commercial practice and the parties' previous conduct is expressly a part of the contract: Sale of Goods Act § 3.

213 As far as terms implied by the factual circumstances of the specific contract are concerned, these have been divided into three categories: (1) terms that the parties probably had in mind but did not trouble themselves to express; (2) terms that the parties, whether or not they had actually had them in mind, would probably have expressed if the question had been brought to their attention; and (3) terms that, whether or not the parties had them in mind or would have expressed them if they had foreseen the difficulty, are implied by the court because of the court's view of fairness or policy

under common law several conditions have been specified in case law as regards the term proposed to be implied.[214] Accordingly, common law requires that the term to be implied is "necessary", which is certified by passing a test such as the *officious bystander* test.[215] Subsequently the Privy Council has held that a decision to imply terms in fact should be based on one requisite only: "There is only one question: is that what the instrument, read as a whole against the relevant background, would reasonably be understood to mean?"[216] Implication of facts into a contract governed by English law seems to be subject to strict prudence and should, it has been asserted, only be used sparingly and cautiously and never to imply a term in conflict with the express terms of a contract.[217]

Terms implied in fact thus relate to the non-regulation of a certain issue by the parties in their contract. Considering that Nordic civil law contains a great deal of non-mandatory legislation that serves to fill such "gaps" in the parties' contract, and that courts may resort to the parties' previous conduct as well as commercial practice, the need for gap-filling based on individual implication is perhaps more limited than under English law. However, when the need arises,

---

or in consequence of rules of law. Whilst the third group primarily refers to terms that are implied in law or by statute, the two former refer to the intention, real or hypothetical, of the parties. In line with earlier refusal to imply terms into contracts, the current law is stated to include a hesitation to imply terms not expressly agreed upon. This is expressed as a presumption against implying terms, especially into written contracts (K. Lewison, *The Interpretation of Contracts* (2004) p. 157). Logically, the more detailed the written contract appears, the stronger the presumption against implying terms into it.

214 Thus, the term implied must (1) be reasonable and equitable; (2) be necessary to give business efficacy to the contract; (3) be so obvious that it goes without saying; (4) be capable of clear expression; and (5) not contradict any express term of the contract (*B.P. Refinery (Westernport) Pty Ltd v Shire of Hastings* (1978) 52 ALJR 20). It seems to be an open question whether these criteria are cumulative or not, although the view seems to be that they are cumulative (K. Lewison, *ibid.*, at p. 157 and *Shell UK Ltd v Lostock Garage Ltd* [1976] 1 WLR 1187).

215 The officious bystander test implies that the term must be so obvious to the parties that had an officious bystander suggested it to them, the reaction from them would have been "of course" (*Shirlaw v Southern Foundaries (1926) Ltd* [1939] 2 KB 206). It seems that this condition suffers from the weakness that the hypothetical answer by the parties is dependent on how the question to be hypothetically asked by the officious bystander is formulated by the court. Obviously, the question can be put in such a legally complicated way that the parties would reply "uh?" rather than "of course" (See K. Lewison, *ibid.*, at p. 166, with reference to *Spring v National Amalgamated Stevedores and Docker Society* [1956] 1 WLR 585). However, it points out the importance that the term proposed to be implied is obvious to both parties and thus in reality already a part of their agreement; cf. category (ii) posed by G. Williams as referred to above.

216 *Attorney General of Belize v Belize Telecom Ltd* [2009] UKPC 10, at para. 21. In para. 18 it is further held that:

> The instrument may not have expressly said so, but this is what it must mean. In such a case, it is said that the court implies a term as to what will happen if the event in question occurs. But the implication of the term is not an addition to the instrument. It only spells out what the instrument means.

Thus the test would seem to be whether the contractual document as a whole conveys the substance of a term, which is simply not expressed in that document. It was expressly held by the Privy Council that it was not the intention to add another test to the already existing tests, such as the business-efficiency test and the officious bystander test, but only to reformulate the common core of all these tests.

217 *Equitable Life Assurance Society v Hyman* [2002] 1 AC 408, at p. 459 (per Lord Heyn).

the problem faced by the courts is common; a contractual dispute referred to a court must be resolved. Thus, where the parties have not regulated the question in their contract, the court must resort to some other source. At common law the court may lay down a general rule applicable to all contracts of the same kind, a proceeding that seems to lie between implication of non-mandatory law and commercial practice in Nordic civil law.

It may be reasonable to ask whether an interpreter of a contract that lacks a solution to a certain issue that is under dispute between the parties can do anything but provide a solution to the dispute. If referred to a court, the court must after all provide the parties with a solution to the dispute. However, in *Belize Telecom*, Lord Hoffmann held that, in general, where the contract provides no answer, the correct effect is that nothing is to happen:

> If the parties had intended something to happen, the instrument would have said so. Otherwise, the express provisions of the instrument are to continue to operate undisturbed. If the event has caused loss to one or other of the parties, the loss lies where it falls.

The standpoint under English law is thus that, in most cases, the court should not imply terms into the contract, but the conflict will have to be solved based on the contract as it stands. There are, however, plenty of contractual relations where "nothing" is not an actual possibility: contractual disputes where "do nothing" does not solve the issue.[218] In a civil law system, there may be default statutory rules (such as those provided in the Swedish Sale of Goods Act), which may be resorted to by implication. Further, under Nordic law, the court may resort to previous conduct between the parties or customs within the trade. Under English law, however, in accordance with Lord Hoffmann's statement, the court would not seem to be allowed to imply terms into the contract. Perhaps it could be claimed that this is a matter of contractual interpretation and not of implication, i.e. other articles of the contract may indicate which of the parties is under the obligation in question. If so, the borderline between interpretation and implication would lie in that implication is carried out where "do nothing" is an actual option for the court. However, in fact it is a matter of adding terms to the contract. Further, such a conclusion does not seem to be in concordance with the general perception of what is meant by implication of terms, where expressions such as "ad hoc gap-fillers" can be encountered.[219]

As mentioned above, implication in fact and the procedural action of rectification may not always be easily distinguishable. They both concern the core

---

218 For example, if, under a sale of goods contract, the seller and buyer are located in different cities and the goods sold thus have to be transported from the seller to the buyer, but the contract does not regulate which of the parties is to arrange for transport. By "doing nothing" the seller may commit a breach of contract. The court faced with the dispute must hold either party responsible for arranging of transport; but to simply conclude that the contract does not provide an answer will not suffice.

219 G. McMeel, *The Construction of Contracts* (2011) p. 316 with reference to *Equitable Life Assurance Society v Hyman* [2002] 1 AC 408 at 459.

matter of the intention of the parties. The former concerns adjustment of a written contract in accordance with the common intention and the latter concerns adding terms that reflect what is assumed would have been the common intention – and therein lies the difference.[220] Due to what under English law is accordingly referred to as rectification, and which under Nordic civil law is merely interpretation, implication in fact appears to be approached from different angles. Thus, where a contract is silent as regards settlement of a certain issue, if there is any indication of how the parties would have resolved the issue in their contract, under Nordic civil law a court would approach the matter as interpretation; the written contract does not in full reflect the parties' contractual agreement and thus it can be corrected by way of interpretation.[221] Also in English law, implication and rectification are closely related and the best way to distinguish the two seems to be that whilst rectification concerns what the parties have actually agreed (but not put down in writing), implication concerns what the parties would have agreed (had they only thought of the issue).[222] In Nordic civil law, what is generally referred to as individual implication does not so much concern what the parties would have agreed but what is considered to be an appropriate solution based on e.g. the aim of the contract, the parties' overall interests or even general (public) interests.[223]

Implication of terms into a contract is a delicate matter, and it seems that a common feature in English common law and Nordic civil law is that interpretation is preferred over implication.[224] Thus, where the same result can be achieved through interpreting the existing terms of a contract, or through respecting terms that are considered to have been agreed between the parties but not expressed in their written contract (rectification), implication will not be carried out. This said, implication of statutory legislation, rules of common law, general principles of law, recognized commercial conduct and so on is less reluctantly done than implication of fact/individual implication.

Although sometimes proposed to be entirely different, the above review shows that, in essence, interpretation and construction of contracts under civil law and

---

220 G. McMeel, *ibid.*, at p. 340.

221 Lehrberg holds that "A precondition for implication is that the same result cannot be reached through interpretation" (my translation) B. Lehrberg, *Avtalstolkning* (2006) p. 191. See also K. Grönfors, *Tolkning av fraktavtal* (1989) p. 32.

222 G. McMeel, *ibid.*, at p. 340.

223 B. Lehrberg, *ibid.*, p. 19.

224 It has been held above that implication of facts and rectification are not easily distinguishable. It could obviously be questioned whether the distinction is necessary; after all implication has been held to constitute a sub-category of interpretation (G. McMeel, *ibid.*, p. 315). However, if interpretation is to be fenced by strict rules, i.e. prerequisites that must be fulfilled in order for certain interpretative measures to be "allowed", then the interpreter must be clear about which interpretative measure is applied. Otherwise, fulfillment of the prerequisite(s) cannot be verified. If the prerequisite(s) for application of rectification is "easier" to fulfill than the prerequisite(s) for implication, and the borderline between the two is unclear, then what should actually be classified as implication may be held to be rectification. However, if the *art* of interpretation is given the artistic freedom that will allow the interpreter, respecting overarching principles such as objectivity criteria (in the applicable version), to reach the most appropriate interpretation, then drawing the line between the two is less urgent.

under common law share their main features. There seems also to be a consensus that the significant difference that might once have existed has been attenuated and that English common law has approached civil law methods for contract interpretation.[225]

5.6.2 Interpretation of contracts in relation to uniform law

As discussed in Chapter 4, the conventions in question all relate to the contract of carriage. Although some qualifying prerequisites relating to the contract of carriage are found in the respective conventions, the general characterization thereof is not defined in any of the conventions. Thus, resort must be had to national law.

Characterization of the contract of carriage as such seems to be subject to international consensus. It is the transport undertaking, the promise to transport, that is the focus of the contract, whilst other duties also rest on the parties, e.g. the duty of care. Further, there seems to be a prerequisite that the contracting consignor undertakes to pay freight, or at least that such duty is explicitly waived. The contract of carriage is finally a non-formal agreement.

What constitutes a contract, i.e. at what point a binding contract is considered to have been entered into, must be considered left to national law. However, this does not appear to have been the cause either of any problems in practice or of any particular consideration in legal theory.

As regards the conventions that apply to contracts of carriage by [road] and their possible applicability to carriage under multimodal contracts of carriage, the contractual aspect seems to have been neglected. The question how to interpret the term "contract of carriage *by [road]*", which appears in several carriage of goods conventions, albeit with slight variations, has, on the other hand, caused problems in practice, as well as a great deal of consideration in legal theory. Being a treaty term, the term is to be understood in accordance with its ordinary meaning in the relevant context.[226] However, the problem facing the interpreter is not understanding the term *per se*, but settling the legal implications thereof: what is demanded from a contract of carriage in order to qualify as a contract of carriage of goods by [road] under a certain convention.

In this context it is often held that uniform law should be interpreted autonomously without resort to a nationally coloured understanding of legal terms for example. Accordingly, the term in question should not be interpreted based on national law of contracts. On the other hand, conventions governing the liability of carriers of goods do not purport to be totally comprehensive, i.e. the conventions are based on the existence of a legal context. In fact, all conventions discussed are to a certain extent based on existing legal concepts. As an example

225 J. Rosengren, "Engelsk avtalstolkning i ett svenskt perspektiv" (2010) 1 SvJT 1–22, at p. 18. See also Hellner, who, even before the Lord Hoffmann Restatement in 1997, concluded that the difference between English law "as it stands in the parol evidence rule" and Swedish law was mainly formal (J. Hellner, "The parol evidence rule och tolkning av skriftliga avtal i svensk rätt" in *Festskrift till Bertil Bengtsson* (1993)).

226 Vienna Convention on the Law of Treaties, articles 31–33 and section 4.2.2 above.

the Montreal Convention holds itself out to apply to carriage by aircraft, with only an implicit reference to the Chicago Convention, which regulates the definition of the term "aircraft";[227] the Hague–Visby Rules likewise does not provide a definition of the transport document, the bill of lading, which is required for its application. Similarly, it must be assumed that the contract of carriage required or presupposed under the conventions discussed has not been a matter of concern to the drafters.

Autonomous interpretation requires the interpreter to find a solution to an interpretative issue within the regulatory system itself.[228] However, this maxim can only apply within the area of law set out as regulated by the convention in question. As discussed in section 5.2 above, any convention, which is not entirely comprehensive, must rest on existing legal concepts.[229] Therefore, under the conventions governing carriers' liability, resort must be had to underlying legal concepts, such as that of the formation and interpretation of contracts.[230] That said, in the name of uniformity it seems appropriate to apply principles that are general, or at least shared by states within a certain sphere.[231] Accordingly, in the previous sections some conclusions have been drawn as regards common denominators between interpretation of contracts under English common law and under Nordic civil law and it is suggested here that it is appropriate to relate interpretation of the term "contract of carriage by [road]" to these findings.

---

227 The Convention on International Civil Aviation, done at Chicago 1944, annex 7, see E. Giemulla, *Montreal Convention (Commentary)* article 1–17 at 28 (2010).

228 van Alstine makes the comparison with a civil law state's civil code, which is comprehensive in its nature and under which resort may not be had to any other statute, but the filling of a gap must be done autonomously (M. van Alstine, "Dynamic Treaty Interpretation" (1997–1998) 146 U Pa L Rev 687). However, the reason for a civil code to be complete is because the various sections thereof cover "every" part of private law. A more accurate comparison with a uniform law convention would instead be a certain section of the civil code; the interpreter of the section governing sale of goods would obviously be allowed to refer to the section governing the formation of contracts to settle whether a binding sales contract has been entered into.

229 The concept of autonomous interpretation is clearly set out in article 7 of the CISG (United Nations Convention for the International Sale of Goods, done at Vienna 1980), which states:

> In the interpretation of this Convention, regard is to be had to its international character and to the need to promote uniformity in its application and the observance of good faith in international trade. (2) Questions concerning matters governed by this Convention which are not expressly settled in it are to be settled in conformity with the general principles on which it is based or, in the absence of such principles, in conformity with the law applicable by virtue of the rules of private international law.

Thus it is clear that it is non-settled questions that relate to matters governed by the CISG that are to be settled autonomously.

230 Which also, as mentioned previously, seems to have been the presumption of the drafters of the CMR; Commentary on the convention of 19 May 1956 on the contract for the international carriage of goods by road (CMR) (GE.75–30686), prepared by R. Loewe and published by the UN in 1975, p. 17.

231 In order to settle common principles, or common denominators, within a certain area of law, the interpreter cannot for obvious reasons compare the law of every state signatory to a certain convention (unless the signatories are very few). Therefore, the interpreter must select some jurisdictions, for example a selection of relevant jurisdictions with heterogeneous traditions or all jurisdictions within a limited geographical area.

5.6.3 Applying contract interpretation to unclear contracts of carriage

The question posed previously was "when is a contract of carriage a contract for carriage by [road]?" It was concluded that interpretation of the term *per se* is to be carried out in accordance with general principles of treaty interpretation and, in particular, the Vienna Convention. Thus, the term must be understood in its context, which includes both the textual context of the treaty itself as well as the actual context in which the treaty operates, such as the legal context. Where a treaty is not entirely comprehensive, and such comprehensive treaties ought to be fairly rare, the terms thereof rest on existing legal concepts such as, in this case, the formation and interpretation of contracts.

Accordingly, as the conventions scrutinized do not give much guidance as to understanding the term "contract for carriage by [road]", such existing legal concepts must be consulted as a part of the context. It has been suggested above that in order to conclude when a contract of carriage is a contract for carriage by [road], the law of formation of contracts must be consulted. Thus, as there is general consensus that the contract of carriage is a non-formal agreement, the key lies in the common intention of the parties. As regards a clear multimodal contract of carriage, therefore, there seem to be good reasons to conclude that where the contract of carriage provides for carriage by [road], i.e. that the common intention of the parties is that the goods are to be carried by road, the contract is in fact a contract for carriage by [road]. This conclusion is not changed by the fact that the contract also provides for carriage by other modes of transport.

Applying the above accounted for principles of contract interpretation, it is clear that where a contract of carriage stipulates that the goods are to be carried by [road], and this stipulation correctly reflects the intention of the parties, such contract cannot be classified as anything else but a contract of carriage by [road]. It seems further that both courts and scholars agree that if, under such a contract, the goods are not carried by [road] (such change of mode thus being a breach of contract by the carrier) this does not affect the character of the contract.[232]

However, as discussed above, there is a spectrum of carriage contracts not as clear as regards the mode of transport to be used for the transport in question. The two main categories are contracts of carriage where the mode of transport is undefined (and it is thus left to the carrier what mode is eventually used) and contracts of carriage where one mode of transport is agreed but another mode is actually used (without this switch constituting a breach of contract). As regards these types of contract of carriage, there is thus no explicit common intention regarding the mode of transport. This means that even if there clearly is a contract of carriage, the "by [road]" is not explicitly present. There may be reason, however, to ask whether this prerequisite may be implied in the contract or otherwise be asserted by way of interpretation of the contract. In the following,

232 Danish Supreme Court U 2008 1638H; Court of Appeal *Quantum Corp Inc v Plane Trucking Ltd* [2002] EWCA Civ 350; M. Hoeks, *Multimodal Transport Law* (2010) p. 83; V. Ulfbeck and S Taiger Ivø, "Optioner og ansvar i transportaftaler" (2008) 4 Erhvervsjuridisk tidskrift 331–343, at p. 333.

undefined contracts of carriage and incorrectly defined contracts of carriage will be discussed.

5.6.3.1 Undefined contracts of carriage

The contracts that in section 5.3 were referred to as undefined contracts of carriage were characterized by the feature that the mode of transport to be used by the carrier is not explicitly specified in the contract. On the contrary, these contracts state that the carrier is free to choose a suitable mode of transport. As a starting point, these contracts can therefore not be held to be contracts for the carriage of goods by [road]. However, there may be circumstances in relation to entering into a contract of carriage that could modify this prima facie conclusion. Accordingly, there may be an oral agreement between the parties in addition to the written contract of carriage concerning the mode of transport. In fact, it appears to be common practice that the actual agreement is oral and the written contract is in fact the carrier's general conditions, either provided at the time of "booking" the transport or on the back of the transport document. Further, the mode of transport may be evident from factors such as the route or price, or a combination of the two. There may also be previous practice between the same parties, i.e. the transport is preceded by previous transports between the same places at the same freight cost, all carried out by a certain mode. The question is whether such facts change the character of the contract. As discussed above, the answer may vary depending on the legal system within which the issue is to be settled. In Nordic civil law, these circumstances will definitely affect the interpretation of the contract of carriage.[233] Further, with the ongoing dilution of the parol evidence rule in England, there seems to be no question that such facts will not be entirely without impact on the interpretation of the contract of carriage.

As regards oral side agreements, the standing thereof is not as strong under English common law as in Nordic civil law. However, it was concluded above that the former is probably closer to the latter than traditionally has been the case. As mentioned, later developments have distanced English law from the parol evidence rule, under which, had it been strictly applied, any side agreement would have been completely disregarded (or, rather, any evidence as to proof of a side agreement would have been dismissed). In addition, under the procedure of rectification, the English courts may rectify a written contract so that it properly reflects the actual agreement. However, due to modern developments as regards English law of interpretation of contracts, what could previously only be achieved through the remedy of rectification has increasingly been solved by interpretation.[234] Although the range of evidence that is admitted in relation to interpretation is more restricted than in relation to rectification, the type of side agreements in question here would on a general level not seem to require evidence of prior negotiations, contract drafts, and so on (neither of which are even

233 Norwegian *travaux préparatoires*, NOU 2012:10 pp. 33–34.

234 G. McMeel, *The Construction of Contracts* (2011) p. 16. McMeel asserts that this development started in 1971 with *Prenn v Simmonds* [1971] 1 WLR 1381.

likely to exist), in order to be proven. Under Nordic civil law the side agreement would, on the other hand, certainly be recognized as a part of the contract, subject to the existence of evidence thereof.

Other facts, such as the agreed route and/or price, may indicate that a certain mode of transport was anticipated. Either the transport is to be carried out between two inland destinations without any railway connection, which indicates that the contract implicitly provides for carriage by road, or where a cargo of low-value, large-volume goods is to be carried from an American east coast destination to a port in Europe, the carriage contract implicitly provides for carriage by sea. It appears that under English common law, as well as under Nordic civil law, such implications may be considered when the contract is construed. Where details such as place of loading and place of discharge, freight payable, cargo characteristics, cargo value, and the like are clear from the written contract, the above concluded implications should also be clear to a third party; thus the principle of objectivity is respected.

In Belgium, the existence *per se* of implied terms relating to the mode of transport has been recognized by the courts of appeal.[235] However, the courts seem to require that such implied term are subject to the parties' consensus and thus terms have not been considered implied where data such as distance, route and the like indicate that a particular mode is to be used.[236] It has been suggested that the approach taken by the Belgian courts is the contractual approach and that the approach taken by the English court in the *Quantum* case[237] is the opposite thereof, i.e. an approach where the actual carriage decides which set of rules is to be applicable.[238] This, however, seems to be a misunderstanding of the judgment. The application of the CMR convention to the liability of the carrier for the damage that occurred during road transport was not based on actual performance and it was never questioned that the applicability of the CMR convention is based on the contractual approach: there has to be a contract for the carriage of goods by road.[239] The question that is extensively discussed in the judgment is what constitutes such a contract.[240] In the *Quantum* case, the court, spoken for by Mance

235 *NV De post v NV Gebroeders Lauwe David*, 2 September 2011, 2008/AR/1077, [2012] DAOR, 21, *NV DPD Belgium v P.J. Timmermans*, 31 October 2011, 2010/AR/875 and *TNT Express NV v Atlanta Europe NV e.a.*, 30 January 2012, 2010/AR/1670, [2012] NjW 510. These judgments rely on the Belgian Supreme Court case 8 November 2004 C.03.0510.N, referenced in section 3.4.1 above.

236 W. Verheyen, "Fleximodal Contracts and the CMR – the Belgian approach" [2012] 18(5) JIML 364–371.

237 *Quantum Corp Inc v Plane Trucking Ltd* [2002] EWCA Civ 350.

238 See J. Heidbrink, *Logistikavtalet* (2005) p. 53. Heidbrink uses the terms the "actual alternative" and the "contractual alternative", where the actual alternative defines an approach where the applicability of a unimodal convention is dependent on the existence of a (or any) contract of carriage and the applicable set of rules is pinpointed by the mode of carriage actually used, whilst the contractual alternative defines the applicable set of rules purely by the definition of the contract of carriage (at p. 48). Heidbrink has a distinctive contractual approach to the subject.

239 V. Ulfbeck and S. Taiger Ivø, "Optioner og ansvar i transportaftaler" (2008) 4 Erhvervsjuridisk tidskrift 331–343, at p. 332.

240 Perhaps the two approaches to the answer to this question could be expressed as "the letter of the contract approach" and "the content of the contract approach". Whilst the former is supported by

LJ, considered the contract of carriage from a contractual point of view and, rather than applying the set of rules generally applicable to the mode of transport by which the transport was actually carried out (which would be the opposite of the contractual approach), the court considered that a contract that allows for carriage by road *is* a contract for the carriage of goods by road where the carriage is wholly or partly in fact carried out by road. This is a purely contractual approach, although it considers the contract in its entirety, including the option vested with the carrier to carry by another mode than the mode primarily agreed. Thus, both the English Court of Appeal and the Belgian Supreme and Appellate Courts consider the contract of carriage in a wider perspective and accept that an agreement regarding the mode of transport may be implied in the contract. In the *Quantum* case, the terms implied consisted of previous conduct between the contracting parties: however, according to the judgment, carriage under an undefined contract would also classify as carriage by [road] if it was so carried out.[241] The Belgian courts, on the other hand, took a slightly stricter approach to the contract, even in the wider sense, and appear to have refused to imply mode of transport into the contract that is not supported by "hard" data such as transport documents.[242]

As mentioned above, there is general consensus that a carrier cannot change the applicable regime by changing the mode of transport without contractual support, i.e. if a change of mode amounts to a breach of contract by the carrier, the liability regime applicable to the mode of transport contractually agreed is applicable to the transport. However, where the contracts allows, or even obliges, the carrier to make a choice regarding mode of transport, it could be questioned why that choice should not be regarded as a part of the contract. Accordingly, where the parties have agreed that the carrier is to make the decision as to the appropriate mode of transport, the contract does in fact contain a common intention regarding the mode of transport: the parties have agreed that the mode of transport is to be decided by the carrier. At least in theory, all terms of a contract must be covered by the parties' common intention in order to form part of a binding

writers inclined to delimit the applicability of the CMR convention to contracts that explicitly provide for carriage by road, and for carriage by road only (e.g. I. Koller; "Quantum Corporation Inc v. Plane Trucking Limited und die Anwendbarkeit der CMR auf die Beföredrung nit verschiedenartigen Transportmitteln" (2003) TranspR 45–50; P. Vestergaard Pedersen, *Transportret* (2007) pp. 955–956. Fitzpatrick is not as clear as regards his personal view (P.G. Fitzpatrick, "Combined Transport and the CMR convention" (1968) JBL 311). However, he concludes (at p. 317) that the courts would probably not be prepared to look at the contract as performed rather than as made, as this would make the carriage itself "the nexus of application". The latter is supported by writers inclined to open the applicability of the CMR convention to all contracts of carriage that allow for carriage by road and where carriage is so performed (R. de Wit "Minimal Music: Multimodal Transport Including a Maritime Leg under the Rotterdam Rules" in R. Thomas (ed.) *The Carriage of Goods by Sea Under the Rotterdam Rules* (2010) pp. 91–111, at p. 109 and M. Clarke, "A multimodal mix-up" (2002) JBL 210–217).

241 *Quantum Corp Inc v Plane Trucking Ltd* [2002] EWCA Civ 350 at para. 16.

242 In summary, it seems that the courts on the one hand, sought proof of an implicit agreement in transport documents and similar and, on the other hand, considered whether the mode by which the goods carried was in fact the only possible alternative, in which case it appears that the court may have agreed to recognize an implied term (W. Verheyen, "Fleximodal Contracts and the CMR – the Belgian approach" [2012] 18 (5) JIML 364–371).

agreement.[243] Where an essential part of the contract of carriage, the mode of transport, is thus left to the carrier to decide, it could be argued that the contract actually contains an agreement regarding the mode of transport. The contract will provide for carriage by the mode of transport that the carrier later decides. The parties have agreed to let the carrier unilaterally fill a gap in the contract, and the mode of transport(s) chosen by the carrier therefore forms part of the contract. To make an analogy: if the parties in their contract of carriage had not agreed to the exact freight but made a provision that provided that the carrier was to decide the freight unilaterally after the transport had been carried out, it would not be correct to hold that the parties had omitted to regulate freight in their contract. Although the exact freight is not agreed, there is a provision that regulates freight and, subject to perhaps statutory regulation that disallows unfair contract terms (such as §36 of the Swedish Contracts Act), the freight thus decided by the carrier will have to be paid. Likewise, in an undefined contract of carriage, the common intention of the parties includes an agreement that the carrier is unilaterally to fill the gap regarding mode(s) of transport, which has intentionally been left out of the contract. Thus, it could be argued that the mode(s) of transport that the carrier eventually chooses is in fact part of the contract of carriage. From a contractual perspective, as long as the choice of mode of transport is contractually permitted, as opposed to a breach of contract, it is part of the contractual agreement.

On the other hand, contracts certainly exist that are truly undefined. In particular, this ought to be true regarding parcel services, which are not *per se* excluded from application of e.g. the CMR convention.[244] The customer of a parcel service will likely not pay any attention to by what/which mode(s) the parcel is carried, as long as it reaches the receiver within a reasonable time. In relation to such an indifferent customer there is certainly no common intention as regards the mode of transport.[245] The discussion is closely related to the question of the impact of performance, i.e. does performance affect the definition of an undefined contract of carriage, which is discussed in section 5.7 below. At this point it will only be mentioned that, for example under German national law, an undefined contract is

243 "In theory" as a party may very well be held to a contract signed by that party although he or she has in fact not taken note of the terms thereof and the terms therefore are actually not subject to that party's intention.

244 W. Verheyen, "The DPD-case: a case for a parcel-specific liability regime (2013) 48 ETL 3–12, at p. 4 with reference to *NV DPD Belgium v P.J. Timmermans* (2013) 82 ETL 82. It should be noted that postal services that are subject to an international postal convention are not subject to the CMR. Such an international postal convention refers to the Universal Postal Union (UPU). The member states of the UPU designate the postal services that are official in the sense that they are subject to the convention. Accordingly, the services provided e.g. by the Swedish Posten AB, the Norwegian Posten, the British Royal Mail, the French La Poste are subject to the postal convention, but not to e.g. the CMR. A point of interest in this regard is parcel services carried out by major parcel services, which are at the same time a national postal service provider such as DHL. Presumably, the parcel services provided by such operators are not subject to the CMR.

245 That said, parcel services are assumed to operate mainly by road and air, thus the mode(s) to be used are fairly predictable; a combination of air and road or road only. In e.g. intra-European parcel transports the choice between the two may not be obvious; transport between Paris and Rome could either be carried out by air and local road transport, or by road only, and would presumably depend on the carrier's business-related decisions.

considered to be defined through the choice made by the carrier, and the contract of carriage becomes subject to the liability rules relating to the mode of transport by which the transport is actually carried out.[246] Actual performance of an undefined contract of carriage will also have a decisive impact on defining the contract with the reasoning presented above: however, it will not be the actual causation, only the act by which the choice made by the carrier is manifested. It is, however, the actual choice, rather than performance, that completes an undefined contract of carriage.

In conclusion, it has been asserted here that the contents of a contract are subject to the contractual parties' common intention and thus, where a (written) contract does not explicitly specify the mode(s) of transport to be used to carry out transport, the contract may still provide therefor. Thus, the mode(s) of transport may be implied in the contract due to price, type of goods, route and/or locations. Further, where the common intention holds that either party is mandated to fill the contract with material content at a later stage, be it the settlement of the exact price, the choice of sub-carriers or the choice of suitable transport mode, that choice forms part of the contract once it is made. The choice made by the carrier in respect of the mode of transport is not in breach of contract, but contractually allowed for. Thus, by expressing the choice, orally, in writing or more commonly through actual carriage, the carrier fills a gap left in the contract with material content. Where a contract of carriage thus allows, or requires, the carrier to choose the appropriate mode of transport, once that choice is made the contract will be a contract of carriage for the mode thus chosen by the carrier.

5.6.3.2 Incorrectly defined contracts of carriage

It is generally assumed that contracts of carriage often contain an option for the carrier to substitute the mode(s) of transport agreed.[247] Thus, contracts that are clear as regards the mode of transport may change character due to the carrier's invoking a right to substitute the initially agreed mode of transport for another. The following discussion will concern how contractually allowed for substitution affects the contract of carriage.[248]

It has been asserted that such substitution does not change the "modal" character of the contract of carriage: a contract of carriage by [road] remains a contract for the carriage by [road] even if the goods are actually carried by another mode of transport.[249] This is also the conclusion drawn from the judgement of the

246 L. Andersen Roost, *Multimodale Transporter* (2012) p. 68, with reference to J. Basedow, *Der Transportvertrag* (1987) p. 58.

247 This assumption is confirmed by standard contracts used in the industry, see e.g. FIATA Multimodal Bill of Lading.

248 To clarify, the discussion concerns substitution that is contractually accepted; substitution that amounts to a breach of contract has been concluded above not to change the character of the contract of carriage.

249 L. Andersen Roost, *ibid.*, p. 75 and P. Vestergaard Pedersen, *Transportret* (2008) pp. 953–954.

Danish Supreme Court from 2008 (referenced in section 3.4.1 above).[250] In its judgment, the Supreme Court found that the substitution of air for road transport, although permitted under the contract, which was undisputedly a contract for carriage by air, did not change the character of the contract of carriage, which was considered a contract for carriage by air in its entirety, and thus not a breach of contract by the carrier.[251] The court did not analyse the transport contract in detail, but it seems that a vital fact for its conclusion was that no separate transport document was issued for the road transport.[252] Further, it seems to have been clear that the contracting consignor did not anticipate the substitution of carriage by air for road transport (which was done for a small part of the transport, during which the damage occurred).

The opposite view, that contractually permitted substitution does affect the modal character of the contract of carriage, has also been taken.[253] In the English Court of Appeal judgment in *Quantum* (referenced in section 3.4.2 above), the court found that the road segment of a transport, which under the transport contract was defined as an air transport, was governed by the CMR convention. Accordingly, invoking a right to substitute mode of transport by the carrier entailed that the contract was considered partly a contract for the carriage of goods by road.[254] However, it is clear that the Court of Appeal was influenced in its decision by the fact that the parties had anticipated that for part of the transport the carrier would invoke its option to substitute air transport for road transport.

Views on the implications of substitution of mode of transport are thus heterogeneous. The question is, as Ulfbeck/Taiger Ivø put it, whether the contract of carriage is to be characterized by the initially intended mode of transport, independently of what mode is eventually used, or if invoking by the carrier of an option to transport by a mode other than that initially agreed is to be regarded as a new agreement between the parties.[255] Whilst the former seems to countenance contracting for the mode of transport with most favourable liability rules, at least if the contract of carriage intended a written contract without regard to circumstances that imply a variation in the actual agreement, the latter will at least entail that the liability rules adapted to the actual mode of transport are applied. The theory seems, however, somewhat overly complicated.

250 V. Ulfbeck and S. Taiger Ivø, "Optioner og ansvar i transportaftaler" (2008) 4 Erhvervsjuridisk tidskrift 331–343, at p. 339.

251 Danish Supreme Court, U.2008.1638H.

252 V. Ulfbeck and S. Taiger Ivø, *ibid.*, at p. 339.

253 Regarding the overall characterization of contracts applied by the Danish Supreme Court, Clarke compares the theory to the assertion that a Bloody Mary is a non-alcoholic drink as it mainly consists of non-alcoholic tomato juice (M. Clarke, "A multimodal mix-up" (2002) JBL 210–217, at p. 211).

254 *Quantum Corp Inc v Plane Trucking Ltd* [2002] EWCA Civ 350. See also P. Laurijssen, "Quantum Corporation Inc. V. Plane Trucking Ltd. Revisited by German Supreme Court: considerations on the German Federal High Court's decision of 17 July 2008" (2009) 2 ETL 143–149.

255 V. Ulfbeck and S. Taiger Ivø, *ibid.*, at p. 333.

It appears to be generally accepted that, in interpretation of contracts, decisive importance is not placed on the heading of a contract; a "contract for the carriage of goods by air" is not a contract for air carriage if, despite its heading, the contract as such prescribes for carriage of goods by road. Thus, it is the contents of the agreement between the carrier and the contracting consignor that prevail. Accordingly, importance must be placed on the actual content of the contract of carriage. An alternative to the two possible ways to regard the contract of carriage that has been subject to substitution of transport mode presented by Ulfbeck/Taiger Ivø is to regard the existing contract as encompassing transport undertaken by other modes under an option for the carrier to do so. A "contract for carriage of goods by air" with an option to carry by road for part of the transport is not a contract for air carriage but a "contract for air carriage with an option". Thus, it is submitted, an invoked option adjusts the contract from an air carriage contract to an air and road carriage contract.[256] The common intention between the parties when entering into the contract is that the carrier may substitute part of the carriage for another mode, and thus the original contract encompasses the substitution of transport mode. As put by Latham LJ: "the concept of a contract for the carriage of goods by road embraces a contract providing for or permitting the carriage of goods by road on one leg, when such carriage actually takes place under such contract".[257]

That said, the standard clauses used by carriers in their general conditions of carriage, providing the carrier with an option to substitute the contracted for mode of transport, would appear not always to be an "active" part of the parties' common intention. Although the standard terms have become part of the contract of carriage, and thus on a conceptual level are part of the common intention, they are not an active part in that the contracting consignor may not be aware of the details thereof. Accordingly, it seems that the possible substitution of mode of transport may be more or less part of the agreement. A carrier who reserves the right to substitute modes of carriage by inserting an option clause in the contract of carriage does not commit a breach of contract if the goods are not carried by the presumed mode of transport. This is, however, not necessarily the same thing as substitution being contractual in the sense that it is agreed and/or anticipated between the parties. A contractual option clause must be regarded as a standard reservation made by most carriers and, in a particular case, the parties may not anticipate a change of modes. Where a contract for the carriage of goods by sea from Baltimore to Rotterdam is entered into, it would seem highly unlikely that a substitution of modes takes place – the only mode available is carriage by air, and for the freight charged for sea transport a carrier would hardly carry the goods by air. In such a contract of carriage, the option clause is probably considered by the parties to be merely a standard clause never to be invoked by the carrier. However, there are other situations where substitution of transport modes can be

256 This, however, does not necessarily mean that the CMR applies to the road leg; cf. the reasoning by the court in German Federal Supreme Court BGH 17 July 2008.

257 *Quantum Corp Inc v Plane Trucking Ltd* [2002] EWCA Civ 350, at p. 17.

anticipated in a particular case or at least so common as to be regarded a custom of the trade. Examples are the above-mentioned trucking services by airlines, the "low flying aircraft"; or substitution of rail transport for road transport due to limited rail capacity.

Where thus invoking by the carrier of the option clause can be expected, or at least ought to have been expected, by the shipper, the substitution is contractual in the sense that it is not only permitted but also anticipated, and therefore the carriage by air contract is in fact a carriage by air and road contract. This line of reasoning can to some extent explain the different outcomes in the Danish and the English judgments referred to above.[258] As analysed in detail in section 3.4.1, whilst the parties to the carriage contract in dispute in the *Quantum* case were considered by the court to have anticipated the use of road carriage between Paris and Dublin, the contracting consignor in the Danish case was considered by the court not to have been aware of the right to substitution reserved by the carrier in the contract of carriage, even less to have anticipated it. Accordingly, although this aspect was not discussed by either court, from a contractual point of view the former contract was in fact a contract for the carriage of goods partly by air and partly by road, and the latter contract was, as far as the common intention between the parties is concerned, in fact a contract for the carriage of goods by air only. Taking the contractual aspect into account, the different outcomes of the two judgments are thus, at least partly, explainable.

It is asserted here that an incorrectly defined contract of carriage must be individually analysed, before any conclusions regarding the characterization thereof can be drawn. However, on a general level it is submitted that an originally clear contract that includes an option to substitute mode of transport may, when interpreted, in fact be considered to provide for carriage by another mode, in addition or altogether, than the mode it prima facie appears to provide for. Such interpretation may, depending on the national context, take into account side agreements, previous negotiations, indications such as freight, route and so on, as well as subsequent conduct. Accordingly, what prima facie appears to be a contract for the carriage of goods by air may, when interpreted, in fact be considered a contract for the carriage of goods partly by air and partly by road, because, as in the *Quantum* case, the parties had previously entered into similar contracts under which the goods had repeatedly been carried by road between Paris and Dublin. On the other hand, the option to substitute the mode of transport may be considered to be a mere formality, with the actual agreement not containing any indication that the option is to be invoked, for example if cement is carried from the USA to Europe under a carriage of goods by sea contract. The only general conclusion that seems possible to draw regarding

258 Danish Supreme Court, U.2008.1638H and English Court of Appeal *Quantum Corp Inc v Plane Trucking Ltd* [2002] EWCA Civ 350. Other relevant cases are Rb Rotterdam 28 October 1999, S&S 2000, 35 (*Resolution Bay*), the Netherlands, Jugement du tribunal de commerce de Bobigny du 24 novembre 1995, *Les Mutelles du Mans v Transport Assistance Services*, France (referred to by V. Ulfbeck and S. Taiger Ivø, "Optioner og ansvar i transportaftaler" (2008) 4 Erhvervsjuridisk tidsskrift 331–343, at p. 334) and BGH 17 May 1989, Germany.

incorrectly defined contracts of carriage is that no universally applicable conclusions can be drawn. A general reflection is, however, that the problem is seldom approached from an interpretation of the transport contract angle, at least not explicitly.[259] It seems obvious that where the parties to a transport contract have prima facie agreed on a certain mode of transport and another one is used, the question that should be asked is: "is there a contract for carriage by the particular mode that was used to carry out the transport?" The answer to this question is not necessarily the same as to the question whether the substitution constitutes a breach of contract or not.

5.7 Performance as a contractual trigger

In Chapter 1 the different approaches to applicability taken in the different conventions regulating carriers' liability was discussed. In Chapter 4 it was concluded that these different approaches are not as different as they may first appear to be, but that there nonetheless is a difference between the purely contractual applicability found in the CMR convention and the COTIF–CIM convention and the performance-based applicability found in the Montreal Convention. Although the carriage by air convention is based on a presumption of the existence of a contract of carriage, it is performance of carriage of goods by aircraft that is the key to the convention's applicability. The contractual approach, on the other hand, places focus on the contract as such.

It has been concluded above that a contract of carriage has more dimensions to it than the words printed on the contract document (or perhaps only on the back of the transport document). In order to settle the parties' actual intentions, a contract of carriage must often be interpreted. Above it has been examined whether the parties' subsequent conduct may be used as interpretative data. The parties' subsequent conduct is truly an indicator of how the parties themselves have understood their agreement, as held by Lord Atkinson: "The parties themselves should know what they meant by their words better than anyone else."[260] However, the law as it stands under English common law is that subsequent conduct is not admissible as proof of the contents of a contract.[261] On the other hand, the exceptions to this rule are rather ample. For example, the exception for characterization of contracts could be applied to contracts where it can be assumed that a contract of carriage in its written form does not properly reflect the parties' intentions and the carrier can be assumed to attempt to evade otherwise applicable mandatory rules. Further, oral or partly oral contracts may be proved by subsequent conduct as well as through the remedy of estoppel by convention.[262] Thus, for all relevant purposes, it would seem that, whether the contract is undefined or incorrectly

259 See however David A. Glass, "Meddling in the multimodal muddle" [2006] LMCQ 307.

260 *Amalgamated Investment & Property Co Ltd v Texas Commerce International Bank Ltd* [1982] QB 84, 119.

261 G. McMeel, *The Construction of Contracts* (2011) p. 221.

262 For a detailed summary of the exceptions, see G. McMeel, *ibid.* at pp. 223–230.

defined, the actual performance of a contract of carriage, or other subsequent conduct, may be used to interpret the contract.

Thus, the mode of transport used by the carrier to carry out a contract of carriage may imply that a contract of carriage is in fact neither undefined nor incorrectly defined.[263] Through interpretation of a certain contract of carriage it may be concluded that the parties' common intention was that the goods were to be carried by [road]. The effect of performance is only in relation to the contract of carriage; it is not a question of introducing the modal (performance based) approach to applicability. Quite the opposite – where the rules of conventions such as the CMR apply to contracts of carriage, it must be established in relation to every contract that concerns carriage of goods, and which is not clear in respect of mode of transport, whether it concerns the carriage of goods by [road] and therefore is or is not subject to the rules of the convention.

The question how performance should be allowed to affect the decision on which rules are to be applied to a certain transport is often approached in a different way than proposed above.[264] Thus, the question has been asked whether performance of a transport could affect the qualification of a contract of carriage.[265] The question is asked in a way that entails that, if the answer to the question is "yes", performance would be allowed to change the contract retroactively and the convention in question would in fact be applicable to performance.[266] However, it is asserted here that, in relation to conventions that apply to contracts of carriage, performance is not the trigger *per se* of applicability of certain convention-based rules, but an aid to interpreting the contract of carriage.[267] This approach seems to have been taken in Germany where, according to its national law of transport, an undefined contract of carriage is considered concretized through the carrier's performance thereof and subsequently the contract is considered a contract for

263 Similarly, the transport document issued by the carrier would constitute such subsequent conduct that could influence the interpretation of the contract of carriage. The transport document is a unilaterally issued document (F. Sejersted, *Om Haagreglerne* (1976) p. 32) and thus objections may be raised; cf. below. However, to the extent the actually used mode of transport may be allowed to influence the characterization of the transport document, also the type of transport document issued (which is likely to correspond to the mode used for performance) could influence the interpretation. However, the issuance of e.g. a road bill of lading in relation to a multimodal contract does not render the entire carriage a road transport.

264 To Hoeks, however, it does not even seem to be an issue: "Whatever type of carriage is eventually chosen to perform the actual carriage determines which rules apply to the contract" (M. Hoeks, *Multimodal Transport Law* (2010) p. 86).

265 V. Ulfbeck and S. Taiger Ivø, "Optioner og ansvar i transportaftaler" (2008) 4 Erhvervsjuridisk tidskrift 331–343, at p. 335.

266 For example, Heidbrink divides possible applicability of unimodal conventions to undefined contracts of carriage into, on the one hand, the actual alternative and, on the other hand, the contractual alternative, indicating that the actual alternative in fact entails that the convention would be applicable to performance, whilst a strict approach where the convention would only be applicable to contracts where it is sufficiently clear that the goods are to be carried by the mode in question remains faithful to the contractual approach to applicability (J. Heidbrink, *Logistikavtalet* (2005) p. 48).

267 Ramberg holds that undefined contracts of carriage are, as a starting point, not subject to the unimodal transport conventions, but that it may be argued that they should, in order to avoid erosion of mandatory law, in which case the actual performance would trigger application of conventions such as the CMR (J. Ramberg, *The Law of Transport Operators* (2005) p. 25).

carriage of goods by the mode by which it was actually carried, as long as the chosen mode of transport is "reasonable".[268] Again, under Swedish national law relating to carriage of goods by road, it has been proposed that actual performance of a contract of carriage would subject the carrier to the national statute, as long as the mode of carriage is not entirely unexpected.[269] In Denmark, the Supreme Court judgment from 2008 discussed above, holds that invoking an option to substitute mode of transport does not change the character of the contract, but entitles the cargo interests to invoke the liability rules applicable to the mode of transport actually used, if preferable.[270] Ulfbeck/Taiger Ivø take a contractual approach *per se* to the issue, but complicate matters more than necessary. Accordingly, they suggest that invoking an option to substitute mode of transport could be regarded as establishing a new contract for the mode of transport that is actually used by the carrier.[271] Heidbrink, on the other hand, who in general has a profound contractual approach to issues relating to carriage of goods contracts, rejects the suggestion that performance of an undefined contract of carriage should be allowed to affect characterization of the contract, as an *ex post facto* assessment, which, he claims, is contrary to the fundamental values of contract law.[272] Perhaps the most obvious example of how the impact of performance is so closely linked to applicability of the various conventions rather than to interpretation of a contract of carriage is Andersen Roost, who states that the "*ex post facto* approach" to characterizing a contract of carriage is merely an *ex post* construction and that characterization of a contract should be based only on the contents of the contract.[273] As is hopefully sufficiently clear from the discussion above, it is held here that performance may serve as data of interpretation in settling the contents of a contract and that it is the very contents of the contract that should serve as the basis for determining the applicable rules. Thus,

268 Cf. L. Andersen Roost, *Multimodale Transporter* (2012) pp. 67–68.

269 Thus in the *travaux préparatoires* to the Act on Domestic Carriage by Road from 1974 (SFS 1974:610), it is asserted that the law is not only applicable where there is an express agreement regarding the mode of transport, but that if the carrier performs the carriage by a mode of transport "which the shipper did not have reason to expect", the law would not, at least not without hesitation, be applicable to the transport (Prop. 1973:33 p. 62). In Finland, the Governmental proposal relating to implementation of the CMR for international as well as domestic carriage by road, proposed that:

> Goods are often handed over for transport to a freight forwarder without an agreement regarding the mode of transport to be used between the parties. If carriage is actually carried out as road transport, the rules on e.g. the carrier's liability may be applicable.
>
> (My translation) (L. Sevón, *Förslag till lag angående avtal om godstransport på väg* (13/1974) p. 8)

See also J. Heidbrink, *Logistikavtalet* (2005) pp. 49–50. The Act on Domestic Carriage by Road mirrors the CMR.

270 Danish Supreme Court U.2008.1638H, at p. 1652. As pointed out by Ulfbeck and Taiger Ivø, the legal justification for this right to choose preferable liability rules is questionable considering the court's holding that the character of the contract does not change, i.e. the contract remains a contract for carriage by air, but the cargo interests would nevertheless be allowed to invoke the CMR, had they preferred (V. Ulfbeck and S. Taiger Ivø, "Optioner og ansvar i transportaftaler" (2008) 4 Erhvervsjuridisk tidskrift 331–343, at p. 340).

271 V. Ulfbeck and S. Taiger Ivø *ibid.* at pp. 333–334.

272 J. Heidbrink, *ibid.*, at p. 49.

273 L. Andersen Roost, *ibid.*, p. 69.

performance of a contract could influence categorization, even where the contents of the contract serve as the only basis for determining the character of the contract, as far as application of the conventions regulating carriers' liability is concerned.

It has been asserted that an approach that considers actual performance to an excessively large extent leaves power over liability with the carrier himself.[274] This proposition seems to have influenced the Danish courts.[275] However, in 1989, in another case concerning carriage of goods, the Danish Supreme Court ruled that a carrier was free to influence the applicable liability rules (CMR or the carrier's standard conditions) by discretionary electing of the type of container to be used for carriage, which choice would entail a choice between the CMR convention and the Hague–Visby Rules, under an option in the general transport agreement.[276] In this case it was hence not seen as a problem that the carrier was free to "choose" liability rules. Further, the "letter of the contract approach" also gives the carrier an unjustifiable power over his own liability: the carrier can contract for a preferable liability regime but can choose in which way to actually carry the goods. Alternatively, the carrier can contract for a certain mode of transport, carry the goods by another mode and thus cause his own standard conditions to be applicable instead of the liability regime envisaged by the shipper. The "letter of the contract approach" further entails that damages could be settled according to liability regimes not designed for the mode by which the goods were actually carried.

Accordingly, under the contractual approach, a set of rules is applicable to contracts of a certain kind, in the case of the CMR convention to contracts for the carriage of goods by road. In establishing whether a certain contract falls under the ambit of such a set of rules, it is the contract itself that holds the key. It is the contract in question that must be scrutinized in order to establish whether it is a contract for the carriage of goods by road or not. The core of the contract is the common intention of the parties to the contract. Where such common intention includes an option for the carrier to substitute the mode of transport envisaged by the parties, or freely choose the mode of transport altogether, the use of a certain mode of transport under such an option shapes the contract into a contract for

274 V. Ulfbeck and S. Taiger Ivø, "Optioner og ansvar i transportaftaler" (2008) 4 Erhvervsjuridisk tidskrift 331–343, at p. 335 (with reference to P. Vestergaard Pedersen, *Transportret* (2008)) and J. Heidbrink, *Logistikavtalet* (2005) p. 49). On the other hand, Hoeks holds that too much emphasis should not be placed on this freedom as in reality the carrier often does not have much of a choice; the route and the goods determine the mode of transport (M. Hoeks, *Multimodal Transport Law* (2010) pp. 86–87).

275 See the lower court's (Sø- og Handelsretten) judgment in U.2008.1638H at p. 1648.

276 U.1989.593H. The matter concerned the transport of TVs from Denmark to England. The carrier and the shipper had entered into a general agreement under which the carrier was free to supply a regular container or a box container at his discretion. The carriage was carried out by road, but during the sea traverse the box container would be re-loaded from the road vehicle whilst the regular container would be carried on the road vehicle, leaving the CMR applicable during the whole carriage pursuant to its article 2. In the former case the carrier's standard conditions were applicable to the damage in question, which occurred during storage in the Danish port. None of the road legs were then international as the sea traverse took place between Denmark and England.

the carriage of goods by the mode of transport in question. This conclusion is no more controversial than considering a ship building contract for the construction of two vessels with an option for a third vessel to be a contract for building three vessels, should the option be invoked.[277]

As regards the undefined contract of carriage, where the contracting consignor leaves the choice of mode, route, and so on entirely to the carrier,[278] it is, with reference to the discussion above, asserted that *truly* undefined contracts of carriage ought to be rare.[279] To professional contracting consignors, i.e. entities that frequently ship goods, the mode of transport that will eventually be selected by the carrier is often foreseeable and by way of interpretation the contract could be established to contain a regulation. To this conclusion there is however one major exception, that is, the contract for parcel services. Parcels as goods are sent on other premises than other types of goods, and the service resembles a postal service more than regular transportation of goods. It has been held that the existing unimodal conventions do not properly fit parcel services, e.g. as the liability limits of the liability conventions are almost absurd in relation to the low-weight, high-value goods often shipped by parcel services.[280] However, this is an issue not solved through discussion on applicability of the unimodal conventions but, it has been asserted, through separation of these services under special legislation.[281] As parcel service carriers seem to impose the network system through their standard terms, and thus strive to invoke unimodal liability regulations, it seems further that the discussion regarding the effect of actual performance on undefined contracts of carriage will in practice not entail much by way of useful conclusions.[282] If performance is allowed to affect characterization, the outcome will be an imposition of the network system, which the parcel carriers seem to achieve already through their general conditions. On the other hand, these conditions could also be applicable if performance is not allowed to affect an undefined contract of carriage, as the contract would, arguably, be subject to freedom of contract.

In conclusion, it is asserted here that generally, actual performance may affect the establishment of which, if any, mandatory rules apply to a contract of

277 In line with the reasoning in U.2008.1638H, the contract would still be a contract for the construction of two vessels.

278 See W. Verheyen, "Freight Integration: what is the way forward?" (2014) 49 ETL 31–42, at p. 31. However, as pointed out, an undefined contract of carriage is in fact not multimodal before the choice of modes of transport has been made by the carrier, and it is thus clear that the goods are to be carried by at least two modes of transport (M. Hoeks, *Multimodal Transport Law* (2010) p. 86 and D. Glass, "Meddling in the Multimodal Muddle?" [2006] LMCLQ 307, at p. 314).

279 Thus "truly undefined contracts of carriage" implies undefined contracts of carriage, which cannot by interpretation be concluded to include an agreement regarding the mode of transport.

280 W. Verheyen, "The DPD-case: a case for a parcel-specific liability regime?" (2013) 48 ETL 3–12.

281 W. Verheyen, *ibid*.

282 *NV DPD Belgium / Peter-Jan Timmerman*, Hof van Beroep te Antwerpen, 31 October 2011 (2013) 48 ETL 82. Some parcel services do not explicitly impose the network system, but set their default liability limit at a level corresponding to conventions such as the Hague–Visby Rules or the CMR convention.

carriage. This assertion is based on the fact that performance is one, of many, data that affect interpretation of a contract of carriage. A contract, which is prima facie undefined or incorrectly defined may, when all circumstances are considered, be found to implicitly provide for carriage by [road]. It is, to be clear, as a datum for interpretation that performance of a contract of carriage may affect characterization of the contract. Performance is not a requisite that, as such, affect application of the unimodal conventions unless the convention applies to performance rather than to contracts of carriage. Accordingly, there may be truly undefined contracts of carriage on which performance has no impact because interpretation of the contract will not reveal any implied presumptions as regards the mode of transport. Although purportedly uncommon,[283] performance would not affect the characterization thereof.

5.8 Conclusion

The purpose of the current chapter has been to interpret the term "contract of carriage by [road]" on a conceptual level. It was concluded in the previous chapter that the applicability of the unimodal conventions that are subject to analysis, to a large, albeit varying, extent is dependent on the "contract of carriage by [road]". Thus, in order to answer the primary research question posed initially, it was further concluded that this very term, which apparently causes problems in relation to interpretation of the scope of application, must be interpreted.

It was initially in the current chapter concluded that the conventions of uniform law, regulating the carrier's liability for goods carried, regulate a certain area of law but leave other areas of law to national law (or other uniform law regimes). The uniform law regulations are nevertheless founded on the existence of legal terms and concepts and, to a varying degree, the terms of the treaties include legal terms that are not defined in the treaty. Accordingly, to the extent a certain legal term is not defined in the treaty, it must be understood based on the underlying national law.

Accordingly, the contract of carriage by [road] was analysed against national law of contracts. As it was held that uniform law is best preserved uniform if interpretation is by reference to common denominators of national laws, a brief survey of, and comparison between, the English common law and the Nordic civil law was made. Further, as the multimodal contract of carriage comes in more shapes than the clear multimodal shape, the analysis was based on a categorization of the multimodal contract into clear contracts and unclear contracts, the latter including what were labelled undefined contracts of carriage and incorrectly defined contracts of carriage. The result of the analysis was, in broad terms, that the modal character of a contract of carriage depends on several factors, such as the actual agreement, implied terms, and so on and that a multimodal contract of carriage may very well be considered a contract of carriage by [road] in the individual case.

283 D. Glass, "Meddling in the Multimodal Muddle?" [2006] LMCLQ 307, at p. 314.

In conclusion, the prerequisite for applicability of conventions adhering to the contractual approach to applicability of a contract of carriage by [road] may very well be fulfilled where the contract of carriage provides for more than one mode of transport. The terms of the treaty must be interpreted against the national law of contracts and it is clear that the national laws analysed in the current chapter recognize that a contract is more than the actual written contract. The question whether a certain contract of carriage provides for carriage by [road] must thus be settled in relation to the individual contract, taking into account the intent of the parties in a wider sense than is provided by the written words of the contract. It is certainly clear that in considering the legal concept of the "contract", a clear multimodal contract of carriage that includes carriage by [road] constitutes a contract of carriage by [road] as required by e.g. the CMR convention. The fact that the contract of carriage also provides for carriage by other mode(s) does not affect this conclusion.

CHAPTER 6

General conclusions

6.1 Status quo

With the exception of the Rotterdam Rules, and possibly the Montreal Convention, the conventions discussed in this work were drafted with the unimodal contract of carriage in mind. The emergence of the multimodal contract of carriage, i.e. a contract that provides for carriage by more than one mode of transport, has, however, altered the reality, which the conventions are to regulate.

As the unimodal conventions apply to carriage by a certain mode of transport, the applicability of these unimodal conventions in relation to carriage under multimodal contracts has been questioned, at least in respect of the conventions that apply to contracts of carriage by a particular mode.[1] Whilst the primary argument relates to the circumstance that a multimodal contract of carriage includes (an) other mode(s) of transport in addition to the mode regulated by the convention in question, the discussion frequently also concerns the general unsuitability of the unimodal conventions in relation to transport that is part of a larger multimodal transport.[2] However, as has been asserted above, the mere fact that applying e.g. the CMR convention to road transport carried out under a multimodal contract of carriage is not unproblematic, does not mean that the convention is not applicable.[3] The scope of application of the conventions discussed follows from the terms of the conventions themselves and, where applicability is ambiguous, the terms need to be interpreted.[4]

Nevertheless, the current legal discussion is, although divided, in favour of the non-applicability of the conventions that apply to contracts of carriage by a particular mode, to multimodal contracts of carriage.[5] The arguments that have been put forward in relation to the question whether a contract of carriage may include other modes of carriage in addition to [road] transport, or if the contract must be a unimodal contract in order to be subject to the respective conventions, were scrutinized in section 3.4, where it was concluded that these arguments were not entirely convincing. Further, in section 4.3 it was concluded that when scrutinized against the rules of interpretation found in the Vienna Convention, these arguments do not entirely support the interpretation thus suggested.

1 Cf. section 3.4 where precedents and doctrine is discussed.

2 Cf. section 4.3 where the arguments brought forward are scrutinized.

3 Cf. sections 4.3.3 and 4.3.4 with conclusions regarding the applicability of the CMR convention and the COTIF CIM convention.

4 Cf. section 4.2.

5 Cf. section 3.4.3.

In addition to the arguments put forward in relation to the actual convention, support for the viewpoint that conventions, such as the CMR convention, are not applicable to carriage under multimodal contracts is found in the developments of legal precedent in Europe.[6] The applicability of the conventions in question is always subject to the jurisdiction of national courts, and to the extent it is possible to refer to European precedent it is based on judgments by national courts, not formally obliged to consider judgments by other national courts. A critical review of the cited precedents shows, however, that the judgments in question are not as distinct regarding the question of applicability of the unimodal conventions as would be desirable.

The starting point of the analysis in the current work has hence been that the legal discussion regarding the scope of applicability of the unimodal conventions adhering to the contractual approach to applicability is not sufficiently thorough. The scope of applicability of a convention should, if perceived to be ambiguous, be settled by interpretation of the terms of the convention. The arguments put forward should further be systemized in accordance with the rules governing such interpretation, rather than being brought forward in a random manner. The scope of applicability of each of these conventions is focused on the existence of a "contract of carriage of goods by [road]" and it is this very term that must be interpreted under articles 31–33 of the Vienna Convention.[7] Consequently the proper interpretation of the term is in accordance with the ordinary meaning in its context and in the light of the object and purpose of the treaty, and with support of the supplementary means of interpretation prescribed in the Vienna Convention.[8]

6.2 A theory of the applicability of unimodal conventions to multimodal transports

The legal arguments that have been asserted to disprove applicability of the unimodal conventions that adhere to the contractual approach to applicability, primarily the CMR convention, are of different hierarchy. Whilst the argument that a multimodal contract of carriage is not a contract for the carriage by [road] relates to actual interpretation of the scope of applicability provision, other arguments, including the proposed difficulties in application of the terms of the convention caused by certain provisions or the undertaking by the signatory states in the protocol of signature to negotiate a multimodal convention, are not independent facts, but part of the textual context of the treaty that may be used to settle the ordinary meaning of a term. Accordingly, it is the term "contract of carriage by [road]" that is central and the understanding thereof the key to applicability of the conventions in question.

6 Cf. section 3.4.1.
7 Cf. section 5.1.
8 Described in section 4.2.2.

Although the conventions do contain some prerequisites as regards the contract of carriage, these only concern certain provisions that must be contained in the contract, such as in the case of the Hague–Visby Rules that the carrier is obliged to issue a bill of lading, and do not concern the issue of what a contract for the carriage of goods by [road] actually *is*.[9] Rather, like all uniform law, the conventions regulating the carrier's liability for goods carried are based on the existence of a legal system. Not all legal terms and concepts are defined in the uniform law itself.[10] Understanding the legal terms contained in a uniform law treaty cannot, it is asserted here, be completely autonomous, but must draw on external sources. It was concluded in section 5.2 that outside the scope of applicability of a uniform law treaty, national law remains applicable. Accordingly, it has been asserted, in relation to the CMR convention, that national law of contracts is applicable to questions relating to the contract of carriage. To the extent that the uniform law does not regulate the formation and interpretation of the contract of carriage, it can thus be established that national law governs the issue. However, it is asserted here that with respect to interpretation of the term "contract of carriage by [road]", in relation to the scope of applicability of a certain convention, resort to national law forms part of the context in relation to which the ordinary meaning of the term is to be settled. It is accordingly not so much a question of applying national law, but using it as interpretative data.[11] On the other hand, to the extent a certain contract can be considered a contract of carriage by [road] according to national law, a convention applicable to such contracts is applicable to the contract in question.[12]

The interpretation of a particular contract, and the settlement of whether it may be considered a contract of carriage by [road], must be done individually in each case. However, some general conclusions may be drawn based on general types of contracts of carriage. As the contract of carriage is not a homogenous type of contract, for the sake of systematization the different types of contracts of carriage are, in the current work, divided into four sub-categories, namely clear contracts (unimodal and multimodal respectively), undefined contracts and incorrectly defined contracts of carriage.[13] With the exception of the clear unimodal contract of carriage, all sub-categories will conceivably involve problems of applying the conventions discussed. Thus the clear multimodal contract of carriage certainly does involve such problems, and the undefined and incorrectly defined contracts may likewise involve problems relating to application, to the extent these are eventually performed by more than one mode of transport.[14] It

9 Cf. section 5.4.2.

10 Cf. section 5.2.4.

11 Cf. section 5.2.3.

12 Provided, of course, that other prerequisites, relating to the contract of carriage or otherwise, are fulfilled.

13 Cf. section 5.3.

14 In this respect it should first of all be noted that it is only transports that are carried out by more than one mode of transport under one single contract of carriage, which, in a legal sense, is considered multimodal. Thus, transport can be multimodal *per se*, but where each leg of the transport is subject

could be discussed whether the latter types of contract are in fact multimodal but, against the background of the impact of performance above, it is asserted here that they often are. Accordingly, to the extent that *undefined and incorrectly defined contracts* are carried out by more than one mode of transport and this was reasonably clear to the contracting consignor at the time of entering into the contract of carriage, the contract should be interpreted as constituting a multimodal contract of carriage. Thus, the multimodal contract itself is heterogeneous.

In relation to transport law, it was concluded that the *contract of carriage* is a non-formal agreement, the most essential part of which is an undertaking by the carrier to carry goods.[15] Although neither an undertaking to pay freight nor settlement of the mode(s) of transport to be used are imperative prerequisites for the contract of carriage *per se*,[16] in relation to applicability of the conventions discussed the contract of carriage must contain an obligation of payment of freight by the contracting consignor as well as a designation of what mode(s) is/are to be used for carriage.[17] As regards the mode of transport to be used for the carriage, it was concluded that this prerequisite would be fulfilled as long as the contract of carriage *as interpreted* prescribes for such carriage.[18]

The national law of contracts to be used for the interpretation of the contract of carriage obviously depends on the circumstances in the particular case. However, in order to draw some general conclusions, the law of contracts of England and the Nordic states respectively have been used as an illustration. With the purpose of extracting possible common denominators, a comparison between the two systems was drawn above.[19] Accordingly, it was concluded that interpretation of contracts under Nordic civil law and English common law share some common features and, although English common law still retains some of its hesitation towards allowing facts such as contract preliminaries, contract drafts and the parties' subsequent conduct to affect interpretation of a contract, the conclusion was drawn that determining whether a contract of carriage is one for carriage by [road] may draw on interpretative data such as those mentioned and that not only contracts that expressly provide for a certain mode of transport can be deemed to constitute contracts for such carriage. Thus, circumstances such as the character of the goods carried in combination with the route agreed and the freight charged may indicate that the parties presumed a certain mode of transport to be used and thus the contract would be deemed a contract for carriage by that mode. It is accordingly asserted that the term "contract of carriage by [road]" should be interpreted as including all contracts where it can be settled that the parties agreed, explicitly or implicitly, to carry goods by [road] and that, in executing

---

to a separate, unimodal, contract of carriage it is not subject to any discussion as regards the applicability of conventions such as the CMR.

15 Cf. section 5.4.1.

16 It was concluded that an undertaking to pay freight is contractually a presumed part of the contract, i.e. the carrier has a right to claim freight unless the parties have agreed otherwise.

17 Cf. section 5.4.2.

18 Cf. section 5.8.

19 Cf. section 5.6.1.

such interpretation, data other than the actual written contract may be taken into consideration.

The term "contract of carriage by [road]" is accordingly, it is asserted here, the crucial prerequisite as regards applicability of the conventions in question. The interpretation proposed above focuses on the contract itself. Whether the contract is to be regarded as a contract of carriage by [road] should be settled in accordance with the law of contracts. Thus, the contract should, where it includes a common agreement to the effect that goods are to be carried by [road], be regarded as a contract of carriage by [road]. According to principles of contractual law, there is no ground for the proposition that a contract of carriage for [road] and another mode of transport is not a contract of carriage by [road]. Where the contract is not explicit as regards the mode(s) of transport it should be interpreted and, to the extent the contract according to the national law applied is interpreted to include an agreement for the carriage by [road], it falls within the scope of the relevant convention. In this respect it has been stressed that national law that is particular and unique to a particular state should be avoided and instead principles of contract law that are, or at least can be presumed to be, common to the contracting states should be applied in order to avoid de-harmonization of uniform law.

6.3 Do the terms of the unimodal conventions prevent applicability to multimodal contracts of carriage?

However, other prerequisites of applicability may cause problems. These prerequisites have been analysed in Chapter 4 above, in particular in relation to the CMR convention. It was concluded that, in general, terms such as the "place of taking over of the goods", as prescribed in article 1 of the CMR convention, which could be understood as the place of taking over by the carrier from a previous carrier just as well as from the consignor, are not as clear-cut as proposed by some writers. As advocated, it is the "contract of carriage by [road]" that is the key element of the scope of application and, accordingly, the place of taking over, which refers to the geographical scope of applicability, is not a decisive term in respects other than in relation to the spatial applicability of the convention.[20] Thus, even if "the place of taking over of the goods" was to be understood as indicating the place of taking over of the goods from the consignor, which, as asserted, could be by the carrier of another mode of transport with the result that the CMR convention would be (theoretically) applicable to road transport between third party states (i.e. non-signatories to the CMR convention), this merely forms a contextual data of interpretation in relation to the term "contract of carriage by [road]".

It is clear that, according to the Vienna Convention, the textual context of the treaty in its entirety is to be taken into account in interpreting the terms of a treaty.[21] The ordinary meaning is the "very fleeting starting point", which "is

20 Cf. section 4.3.2.
21 Cf. section 4.2.2.

immediately and intimately linked with the context".[22] Accordingly, the ordinary meaning of a term must be supported by the context, i.e. primarily the text of the treaty, including its preamble and annexes, in order to be settled as the "correct" meaning. Thus, to the extent other articles of the treaty appear to contradict a certain interpretation, that interpretation may have to be reconsidered. In relation to the CMR convention it has been asserted in legal discussion that, as mentioned, the "place of taking over of the goods" and the "place designated for delivery" in article 1; the (asserted) exhaustiveness of article 2, the date of taking over the goods and the date of delivery thereof in article 32 as well as the undertaking in the protocol of signatures to negotiate a multimodal transport convention, all show that the CMR convention is not intended, and is clearly unfit, to be applied to carriage by road under a multimodal contract of carriage. These articles, as well as the protocol of signatures, are clearly part of the textual context of the CMR convention, and thus may affect understanding of "contract of carriage by road". In section 4.3.2 these contextual arguments have been thoroughly discussed and interpreted through application of the Vienna Convention, with the conclusion that the textual context of the CMR convention does not contradict interpreting "contract of carriage by road" to include carriage by road under a multimodal contract of carriage.

Although the discussion regarding applicability of the COTIF–CIM convention to carriage by rail under a multimodal contract of carriage is relatively absent, the same argumentation as in relation to the CMR convention would be relevant due to the similarity of the scope of applicability of each of the two conventions.[23]

As regards carriage by air and sea, it was concluded that whilst the Montreal Convention presupposes the existence of a contract of carriage, it is not a formal prerequisite for applicability of the convention and the convention is hence in essence applicable to actual performance of carriage by air.[24] It is also clear from the Montreal Convention that it applies to carriage by air under a multimodal contract of carriage. Further, in relation to the Hague–Visby Rules, although it is often assumed that it applies to bills of lading, in fact it applies to contracts of carriage by sea under which the carrier is obliged to issue a bill of lading.[25] Also this undertaking is a matter that could be subject to findings through interpretation of the contract of carriage. Thus, implicit agreements, prior conduct, and so on may establish an obligation for the carrier to issue a bill of lading, thus subjecting the contract to the Hague–Visby Rules. Although a bill of lading by definition is a consignment note, it is very often the only written documentation of the contract of carriage. Formally, however, the bill of lading is not a contract of carriage but only evidence thereof.[26]

22 R. Gardiner, *Treaty Interpretation* (2015) p. 181.

23 Cf. section 4.3.

24 Cf. section 4.4.

25 Cf. section 4.5.

26 It has also been discussed whether the Hague–Visby Rules applies when the bill of lading is "multimodal", i.e. a through bill of lading is issued; cf. section 4.5.3 (*in fine*).

The conclusion was thus drawn in Chapter 4 that the terms of the unimodal conventions do not as such prevent applicability of the conventions to unimodal legs of a multimodal contract of carriage. Rather, the conventions apply to carriage by the designated mode of transport, under the precondition that the carriage is subject to a contract of carriage, which sufficiently clearly provides for such carriage.

It has however also been asserted that, in particular, the land carriage conventions and possibly the Hague–Visby Rules, on a more general level, are not intended to be applied to carriage under multimodal contracts of carriage.[27] Clearly, the conventions governing the carrier's liability for goods carried that are discussed and analysed in the current work all date from different periods, although the common denominator is that they all at least descend from conventions drafted in a setting very dissimilar to transportation as it appears today. In fact, the first convention governing railway liability was drafted in the late nineteenth century, the Hague Rules were adopted in 1924 and the first carriage by air convention was adopted in 1929. In this perspective the CMR convention, adopted in 1956, appears quite "young". It is however the only convention that has not been updated since its first adoption. These circumstances entail that the rules of the respective conventions are adapted to a reality quite different from that of today. As mentioned initially, at the time of drafting the original conventions, transport was generally carried out on a unimodal basis and the rules drafted reflect such procedures. To some extent, the more recent updates of the conventions discussed relate to the issue of multimodal contracts of carriage. The conclusion could therefore be drawn that questions such as the applicability of the conventions to multimodal transport was not an issue at the time of their drafting and the fact that for example the CMR does not relate to the issue could mean that it was a non-issue at the time. Another example is the prerequisite in the Hague–Visby Rules that the contract of carriage provides for issuance of a bill of lading. At the time of drafting the Hague Rules, carriage of goods (as opposed to carriage under charter parties) by sea was under a bill of lading and the fact that the rules are drafted the way they are perhaps only reflects commercial practice at the time, rather than excluding carriage by sea under other forms of transport documents from applicability of the convention.

Because assumptions about the reality to which a drafted regulation, uniform law or national legislation, is to apply will inevitably eventually be incorrect, due to the fact that reality changes in unforeseeable ways, the regulation will sooner or later be inadequate, at least if it is to be interpreted in accordance with its meaning at the time of enactment.[28] Unfortunately, conventions, and in particular conventions of uniform law, are not easily adapted to such new reality.[29] Rather,

27 Cf. section 4.3.2.

28 M. van Alstine, "Dynamic *Treaty Interpretation*" (1997–1998) 146 U Pa L Rev 687, at pp. 702–703, 715; W. Eskridge, *Dynamic Statutory Interpretation* (1994) pp. 50–55.

29 An example near at hand is carriage by sea. After the Hague Rules were adopted in 1924, no attempt at modernizing has been entirely successful. Whilst the Visby amendments to the original Hague Rules have been adopted by almost 90 states, just 25 states have ratified the Visby amendments.

it is the interpretative understanding of the regulation that must change with changing times.[30] It has thus been held that interpreting and applying uniform law must not be "rigidly anchored to the specific expectations of the original designers" and that "interpreters must play an active role in filling substantive gaps and ameliorating the rigidity in an international commercial law convention".[31] Although these statements primarily refer to the understanding of general terms such as "good faith" and "reasonableness", which accordingly should reflect the times during which they are interpreted rather than the understanding of the terms by the drafters, it is also relevant in relation to interpretation of the material rules of uniform law. Because if uniform law is not adapted to changes in the relevant field of commerce, changes in society and technical development, uniform law will soon be outdated. Thus, dynamic interpretation takes into account the present societal, political and legal context.[32] In relation to uniform law, dynamic interpretation will promote uniformity by preventing the regulations from becoming obsolete.[33]

It is asserted here that the understanding of rules drafted in a different setting must take into account that setting. Through an understanding of the legal, commercial etc. context at the time of drafting a uniform law convention, the interpreter can understand the rationale behind the terms of the treaty and adjust the interpretation of such terms to subsequent changes in technology, commercial practice and legal context.[34] An overly literal understanding is, it is asserted here, counter-productive and entails that the conventions become obsolete. On the other hand, treaties of uniform law must be subject to special considerations, such as the foreseeability of the law by the parties subject to it, and, although it would serve the continuous existence of uniform law treaties, any dynamic interpretation thereof should take such considerations into account. Thus, by understanding commercial practice in 1956, an interpreter of the CMR convention can understand the rationale behind the drafting of the article of applicability of the convention. Understanding and interpretation of the terms should be allowed to

Even less successful have been later attempts to draft entirely new regulations, such as the Hamburg Rules and the Rotterdam Rules.

30 A metaphor, which is particularly illustrative of the discussion regarding transport regulations, has been advanced by Aleinikoff in relation to national legislation in the USA:

> Congress builds a ship and charts its initial course, but the ship's ports-of-call, safe harbours and ultimate destination may be a product of the ship's captain, the weather, and other factors not identified at the time the ship sets sail.
>
> (A. Aleinikoff, "Updating Statutory Interpretation" (1988) 87 Mich L Rev 20, at p. 21)

31 M. van Alstine, *ibid.*, at p. 776.

32 W. Eskridge, "Dynamic Statutory Interpretation" (1987) 135 U Pa L Rev 1479, at p. 1479.

33 van Alstine holds that formal amendments to uniform law are often prevented by legal and practical obstacles and thus "only an active judicial interpretation of a convention can 'keep this ship afloat', because there is little hope 'that [legislative]' rescue will arrive" (M. van Alstine, *ibid.*, at p. 777).

34 The same considerations must obviously also be made when using the drafting history of these conventions, the *travaux préparatoires*, as a source for interpretation; the historical aspect must be taken into account in order to avoid a static interpretation of the treaty.

evolve rather than remain static. Taking into account the changes in commercial practice (containerization and practice of multimodal transport contracts) as well as the legal context (no multimodal liability convention has yet entered into force and later conventions take multimodality into account) and applying the aims of the drafters (uniformity in the law of the carrier's liability and the mandatory application thereof), interpretation of the particular terms of a treaty should allow for application of the convention to carriage of goods by road carried out under a multimodal contract of carriage.

The applicability of the Montreal Convention and the Hague–Visby Rules to the air and sea legs, respectively, of a multimodal contract of carriage is rarely questioned. As regards the Montreal Convention, article 38 provides explicitly, or at least *e contrario*, that the convention is applicable to air carriage under a multimodal contract of carriage.[35] Further, even if the Montreal Convention was considered applicable to contracts of carriage, rather than to actual performance, it was noted in section 4.4.1 above that article 1 only suggests that there be a contract of carriage and not a mode specific contract. Therefore, such contract of carriage could be a contract for carriage by air, but it could also be a multimodal contract of carriage. As regards the Hague–Visby Rules, they apply to contracts of carriage covered by a bill of lading, in so far as the bill of lading relates to carriage of goods by sea. Accordingly, it was concluded, the rules apply to all contracts of carriage under which a bill of lading for sea carriage is to be issued. It was further concluded that the rules apply only to carriage by sea, and not to the entire multimodal transport, as the period from loading of the goods onto a ship until the time they are discharged.

The Rotterdam Rules, lastly, apply to contracts of carriage where an undertaking to carry goods at least partly by sea can be extracted. According to the convention's scope of application, it applies where a contract of carriage provides for carriage by sea, which may be supplemented by carriage by other modes (in which case the convention prima facie applies to the entire carriage, i.e. also to carriage by other modes than by sea). "Provides for" was concluded to entail that it is sufficient that carriage by sea can be deduced as implicit in the agreement, but performance alone does not qualify the contract as a contract of carriage under the rules. It was further concluded that the drafters intended the convention to be applicable to carriage by sea carried out under a contract of carriage, which does not explicitly oblige the carrier to carry by sea, but merely allows the carrier to do so.

In light of the above, the conclusion is drawn that the context of the conventions in question, and in particular the CMR convention, does not prevent

35 Article 38.1 of the Montreal Convention provides:

> In the case of combined carriage performed partly by air and partly by any other mode of carriage, the provisions of this Convention shall, subject to paragraph 4 of Article 18, apply only to the carriage by air, provided that the carriage by air falls within the terms of Article 1.

Cf. also section 3.3.1.

application thereof to carriage by [road] under multimodal contracts as long as the multimodal contract of carriage, under the law of contracts applicable, can be considered to constitute carriage by [road].

6.4 Briefly on the consequences of the non-applicability of the network system

Considering the structure of the existing unimodal conventions, the network system inevitably entails certain legal issues, such as non-regulation of non-localized damage, possible overlaps in applicability and difficulties in the application thereof due to the unimodal drafting style of the conventions. These legal issues have been thoroughly discussed.[36] The conclusion is that the network system is by no means either "seamless" or the perfect solution.

For reasons that have been elaborated, all conventions discussed are mandatorily applicable within their respective scopes of applicability.[37] Within the applicable limits of liability, actual as well as monetary, carriers are thus subject to non-negotiable liability.[38]

The *sui generis* theory presented above asserts that conventions regulating unimodal contracts of carriage are not applicable to carriage under multimodal contracts.[39] The result of this is the absence of any rules regulating the liability of contracting carriers that undertake transport under a multimodal contract of carriage. Rather, the parties would be free to set their own contractual terms. However, this freedom of contract is not only a freedom, but also an obligation. The *sui generis* theory entails not only that no mandatory rules are applicable, but that, on an international level and also in many national systems, no rules apply. In the absence of non-mandatory rules, the parties thus must draft contracts that are "complete" in the sense that no conditions can be left to non-mandatory legislation. This either places great responsibility on the parties, or forces one party to accept the conditions imposed by the other party, in a stronger position. The latter situation is the very situation sought to be avoided through the existing unimodal conventions.

It may be asserted that there is no longer a general leverage on the part of carriers, but that contracting consignors may very well have a stronger position to enforce their own conditions. Accordingly, there is no "weaker interest" that needs to be protected by mandatory rules and thus freedom of contract is in fact desirable. Whether this assumption is accurate or not, it is asserted here that such considerations may be taken into account in the drafting of new, or revised,

36 Cf. sections 3.2.2 and 3.3.2.

37 Cf. section 2.2.

38 With the exception of the CMR convention, carriers may undertake more extensive liability than enforced through the respective rules.

39 Cf. section 3.2.1.1.

legislation or uniform law.[40] However, interpretation of the scope of application of unimodal conventions should not be influenced by the interpreter's possible conviction as to the redundancy of mandatory rules. Further, the imbalance between unimodal contracts of carriage being subject to mandatory rules and multimodal contracts of carriage being subject to freedom of contract appears unjustifiable.

6.5 The research questions revisited

The aim of the current work has been to analyse the applicability of existing transport of goods conventions to multimodal transport contracts. Accordingly, the primary research question was initially held to be: *to what extent can unimodal transport of goods conventions be applied to transport carried out under a multimodal transport contract?*

Further, as the applicability of the conventions subject to analysis are all, to some extent, dependent on the existence of a contract of carriage for the particular mode governed by the convention in question, the subordinate research question was thus held to be: *to what extent can contracts that provide for more than one mode of transport or are in fact carried out by more than one mode of transport be considered a contract for the carriage of goods by a particular mode of transport?*

Although it is apparent at this point that the two research questions can only with difficulty be separated, but are rather two sides of the same coin, the subordinate research question is the focus of Chapter 5. The theory presented, recapitulated above, entails that the answer to the secondary research question is, in short, to the extent such a contract can be considered a contract for carriage by the particular mode of transport under national law of contracts, taking into account the rules of contract interpretation and, in particular, terms implied in the contract.

Consequently, the answer to the primary research question is, in short, "to the extent the contract of carriage, as interpreted under national law of contracts, can be considered a contract for the carriage of goods by [road]".

Given the conclusions above, the deduction must be that there are legal preconditions to applying the network system, i.e. to consider the unimodal conventions discussed autonomously applicable to the relevant legs of a multimodal contract of carriage. This conclusion is based on the scope of applicability of the conventions and, as far as concerns the conventions applying the contractual approach to applicability, an interpretation of the term "contract of carriage of goods by [road]" in accordance with the rules of treaty interpretation.

40 It may be noted that the "new" Rotterdam Rules are to apply mandatorily to contracts that fall within its scope of applicability. Thus, the need for mandatory rules was obviously perceived as necessary by UNCITRAL Working Group III.

BIBLIOGRAPHY

Literature

Adlercreutz, Axel and Mulder, Bernard, *Avtal: Lärobok i allmän avtalsrätt*, 2013 (13th edn, Norstedts)

Aikens, Richard, Lord, Richard and Bools, Michael, *Bills of Lading*, 2016 (2nd edn, Informa Law from Routledge)

Aleinikoff, Alexander T., "Updating statutory interpretation" (1988) 87 Mich L Rev 20

Alstine van, Michael, "Dynamic treaty interpretation" (1998) 146 U Pa L Rev 687 (687–793) (1998)

Andersen Roost, Lissi, *Multimodale Transporter*, 2012 (Diss.) (Jurist- og Økonomforbundets Forlag)

Blume, Peter, *Juridisk Metodelære*, 2004 (Jurist- og Økonomforbundets Forlag)

Basedow, Jürgen, "The renaissance of uniform law: European contract law and its components" (1998) 18 Legal Stud 121

Bengtsson, Bertil, "Prejudikat eller lagstiftningsreformer?" in H.C. Bugge et al (eds) *Lov, Liv og Lære – Festskrift till Inge Lorange Backer*, 2016 (Universitetsforlaget) 33–48

Bergelin, Håkan, "Treaty interpretation and the impact of contractual choice of forum clauses on the jurisdiction of international tribunals: the Iranian forum clause decisions of the Iran-United States Claims Tribunal" (1985) 21 Tex Int LJ 39–65

Berlingieri, Francesco, "A comparative analysis of the Hague–Visby Rules, the Hamburg Rules and the Rotterdam Rules", www.uncitral.org/pdf/english/workinggroups/wg_3/Berlingieri_paper_comparing_RR_Hamb_HVR.pdf

Berlingieri, Francesco, "Multimodal aspects of the Rotterdam Rules", www.rotterdamrules2009.com/cms/uploads/Def.%20tekst%20F.%20Berlingieri%2013%20OKT29.pdf

Berlingieri, Francesco, "Door-to-Door Transport of Goods: can uniformity be achieved?" in *Liber Amicorum in Honour of Roger Roland*, 2003 (Larcier) 37–55

Berlingieri, Francesco, "Uniform interpretation of international conventions" (2004) LMCLQ 153–157

Berlingieri, Francesco, "Implementation of Maritime Conventions: a review of the methods used" (2013) 4 LMCLQ 443–475

Bernitz, Ulf, *Standardavtalsrätt*, 2013 (8th edn, Norstedts)

Boe, Erik, *Rettskildelære under debatt*, 2012 (Universitetsforlaget)

Bokareva, Olena, *Multimodal Transportation under the Rotterdam Rules: Legal Implications for European Carriage of Goods and the Quest for Uniformity*, 2015 (Diss.) (Faculty of Law, Lund University, Sweden) (not officially published)

Bradgate, Robert, "Formation of contracts" in A. Grubb (ed.), *The Law of Contract*, 2007 (3rd edn, LexisNexis Butterworths) 233–595

Bredholt, Jørgen, Martens, Jesper and Philip, Allan, *Søloven med kommentar*, 2001 (3rd edn, Jurist- og Økonomforbundets Forlag)

Busch, Christoph, "Identification of gaps and gap-filling under the common European sales law – a model for uniform law instruments?" in Colombi Ciacchi, Aurelia (ed.), *Contents and Effects of Contracts – Lessons to Learn from the Common European Sales Law*, 2016 (Springer) 29–44

Bugden, Paul and Lamont-Black, Simone, *Goods in Transit*, 2013 (3rd edn, Sweet & Maxwell)

Burrows, Andrew, *English Private Law*, 2013 (3rd edn, Oxford University Press)

Bylander, Erik, "Avgöranden utan plenum i Högsta domstolen" (2011/12) 3 JT 503–512

Bäckdén, Paula, "The land carrier's liability – strict with exemptions or presumed?" (2011) XLVI (5) ETL 503–511

Cartwright, John, *Contract Law*, 2016 (3rd edn, Hart)

Clarke, Malcolm, *Aspects of the Hague Rules* (Diss.), 1976 (Martinus Nijhoff)

Clarke, Malcolm, "A multimodal mix-up" (2002) JBL 210–217

Clarke, Malcolm, "Intermodal Transport: CMR as Unimodal Plus", www.juridicum.su.se), 2005

Clarke, Malcolm, "The Convention on the Contract for the International Carriage of Goods by Road 1956: willful misconduct – and again" (2008) 2 JBL 184–190

Clarke, Malcolm, *Contracts for Carriage by Air*, 2010 (2nd edn, Lloyds)

Clarke, Malcolm, *International Carriage of Goods by Road: CMR*, 2014 (6th edn, Informa Law from Routledge)

Clarke, Malcolm and Yates, David, *Contracts of Carriage by Land and Air*, 2004 (Lloyds)

CMI (Comité Maritime International), *The Travaux Préparatoires of the Hague Rules and of the Hague–Visby Rules*, 1997 (Antwerp)

CMI Singapore Planning Committee, "Door-to-door transport", *CMI Yearbook 2000* 118–121

Crema, Luigi, "Disappearance and new sightings of restrictive interpretation(s)" (2010) 21 EJIL 681–700

Damme, Isabelle van, *Treaty Interpretation by the WTO Appellate Body*, 2009 (Oxford University Press)

Dascal, Marcelo and Wróblewski, Jerzy, "Transparency and doubt: understanding and interpretation in pragmatics and law" 1988) 7 Law and Philosophy 203–224

Debattista, Charles, *The Sale of Goods Carried by Sea*, 1998 (2nd edn, Butterworths)

Dempsey, Paul and Johansson, Svante O., "Montreal v. Brussels: the conflict of laws on the issue of delay in international air carriage" (2010) 35(3) Air and Space Law 207–224

Dempsey, Paul and Milde, Michael, *International Air Carrier Liability; The Montreal Convention of 1999*, 2005 (Centre for Research in Air and Space Law)

Derlén, Mattias and Lindholm, Johan, "Judiciell activism eller prejudikatbildning? En empirisk granskning av Högsta domstolen" (2016) SvJT 143–158

Diamond, Anthony, "The Rotterdam Rules" [2009] LMCLQ 445–536

Diedrich, Frank, "Maintaining uniformity in international uniform law via autonomous interpretation: software contracts and the CISG" (1996) 8 Pace Int'l L Rev 303–338

Dockray, Martin, *Cases and Materials on the Carriage of Goods by Sea*, 2004 (2nd edn, Cavendish Publishing)

Dor, Stephane, *Bill of Lading Clauses & the International Convention of Brussels*, 1924 (Hague Rules), 1969 (2nd edn, Witherby & Co Ltd)
Driscoll, William and Larsen, Paul B., "The Convention on International Multimodal Transport of Goods" (1982–1983) 57 Tulane Law Review 193–281
Eckhoff, Thorsten, *Rettskildelære*, 2001 (5th edn, Jan Helgesen Universitetsforlaget)
Eder, Bernard et al, *Scrutton on Charterparties and Bills of Lading*, 2015 (23rd edn, Sweet & Maxwell)
Eftestøl-Wilhelmsson, Ellen, *European Sustainable Carriage of Goods*, 2016 (Routledge)
Ekelöf, Per-Olof, *Är den juridiska doktrinen en teknik eller en vetenskap*, 1951 (Gleerup)
Ekelöf, Per-Olof, *Rättegång IV*, 2009 (7th edn, Norstedts, Institutet för rättsvetenskaplig forskning 38)
Enderlein, Fritz, "Uniform Law and its Application by Judges and Arbitrator", *International Uniform Law in Practice, UNIDROIT*, 1988 (Oceana Publications Inc) 329–353
Entchev, Ivo, "A response-dependent theory of precedent" (2011) 30 Law and Philosophy 273–290
Eskridge, William, "Dynamic statutory interpretation" (1987) 135 U Pa L Rev 1479
Eskridge, William, *Dynamic Statutory Interpretation*, 1994 (Harvard University Press)
Fabricius, Ulla, *Lov om Fragtaftaler ved international vejtransport (CMR)*, 2005 (3rd edn, Jurist- og Økonomforbundets Forlag)
Falkanger, Thor, and Bull, Hans Jacob, *Sjørett*, 2016 (8th edn, Sjørettsfondet Akademisk)
Falkanger, Thor, Bull, Hans Jacob and Brautaset, Lasse, *Scandinavian Maritime Law*, 2008, 2011 (2nd and 3rd edns, Universitetsförlaget)
Fitzpatrick, P.G., "Combined transport and the CMR convention" (1968) JBL 311–319
Frändberg, Åke, "Statutory interpretation against the background of a general typology of interpretation" in D. Prawitz (ed.), *Meaning and Interpretation*, 2002 (Almqvist&Wiksell) 231–251
Frändberg, Åke, *Rättsordningens idé*, 2005 (Iustus, Skrifter från Juridiska Fakulteten i Uppsala 96)
Gardiner, Richard K., "Treaty interpretation in the English courts since *Fothergill v Monarch Airlines*" (1980) 44(3) ICLQ 620–628
Gardiner, Richard K., *Treaty Interpretation*, 2015 (2nd edn, Oxford University Press)
Gaskell, Nicholas, Asariotis, Regina and Baatz, Yvonne, *Bills of Lading: Law and Contracts*, 2000 (Informa Law)
Gebauer, Martin, "Uniform Law, General Principles and Autonomous Interpretation" (2000–2004) Rev dr. unif 683–705
Giemulla, Elmar et al, *Montreal Convention (Commentary) Annotated*, continuous (Kluwer)
Giermann, Heiko, *The Evidentiary Value of Bills of Lading and Estoppel*, 2004 (LIT Verlag)
Giertsen, Johan, *Avtaler*, 2014 (3rd edn, Universitetsforlaget)
Glass, David, "Article 2 of the CMR convention – a reappraisal" (2000) JBL 2000 562–586
Glass, David, "Meddling in the multimodal muddle?" (2006) LMCLQ 307–334
Graver, Hans Petter, "Høyesterett og rettsutviklingen – førti år etter" in H.C. Bugge et al (eds), *Lov, Liv og Lære – Festskrift till Inge Lorange Backer*, 2016 (Universitetsfolaget) 242–254
Grönfors, Kurt, "Om Konventionstolkning" (1957) SvJT 16–21

Grönfors, Kurt, *Successiva Transporter*, 1968 (Institutet för rättsvetenskaplig forskning no 50)
Grönfors, Kurt, *Fraktavtalet under etthundra år*, 1986 (Jure, Skrifter utgivna av Sjörättsföreningen i Göteborg 66)
Grönfors, Kurt, "Fraktavtalet och den allmänna avtalsrätten" (1988) SvJT 181–202
Grönfors, Kurt, *Tolkning av fraktavtal*, 1989 (Jure, Skrifter utgivna av Sjörättsföreningen i Göteborg 67)
Grönfors, Kurt, *Avtalsgrundande rättsfakta*, 1993 (Nerenius & Santerus)
Grönfors, Kurt, *Avtalslagen*, 1995 (3rd edn, Fritzes) (later editions ed. by other authors)
Grönfors, Kurt, "Styckegodstransport enligt nya sjölagen" (1995) SvJT 323–338
Gorton, Lars, *The Concept of the Common Carrier in Anglo-American Law*, 1971 (Skrifter utgivna av Sjörättsföreningen i Göteborg, no 43 [Scandinavian University Books])
Haak, Krijn F., *The Liability of the Carrier under the CMR*, 1986 (Diss. in translation) (Stichting Vervoeradres)
Haak, Krijn F., "Ro-Ro Transport under CMR, Art 2: the Dutch Solution" (2005) LMCLQ 308
Haak, Krijn F., "The harmonization of intermodal liability arrangements" (2005) ETL 2005 11–51
Haak, Krijn F. and Hoeks, Marian, "Intermodal transport under unimodal arrangements" (2003) 5 TransportR 89–102
Haenni, Joseph, "Carriage by rail" in R. Rodière (ed.), *International Encyclopedia of Comparative Law*, vol. XII, *Law of Transport*, 1972 (Librairie Dalloz)
Hambro, C.F., *Den private sjörätten*, 1881 (2nd edn, P.A. Norstedt & Söner)
Hammarskjöld, Hjalmar, *Om fraktavtalet och dess viktigaste rättsföljder*, 1886 (Diss.) (Almqvist & Wiksell)
Hancock, Christopher, "Multimodal transport and the new UN Convention on the carriage of goods" (2008) JIML 484–495
Hancock, Christopher, "Multimodal transport under the Convention" in R. Thomas (ed.), *A New Convention for the Carriage of Goods by Sea – The Rotterdam Rules*, 2009 (Witney) 34–51
Haxthow, Viktor, *Sjølovene*, 2001 (26th edn, J. Holvik, Universitetsforlaget)
Heidbrink, Jacob, *Logistikavtalet*, 2005 (Diss.) (Iustus)
Heidemann, Maren, *Methodology of Uniform Contract Law*, 2007 (Diss.) (Springer)
Heidemann, Maren, "The autonomous interpretation method in international law with particular reference to the proposed European Sales Law II" (2013) 94 Amicus Curiae 28–36
Hellner, Jan, "*The parol evidence rule* och tolkning av skriftliga avtal i svensk rätt" in *Festskrift till Bertil Bengtsson*, 1993 (Nerenius & Santérus) 185–205
Hellner, Jan et al., *Speciell avtalsrätt II Kontraktsrätt 1:a häftet*, 2016 (6th edn, Wolters Kluwer Sverige)
Herber, Rolf, "The European legal experience with multimodalism" (1989–1990) 64 Tul L Rev 611
Herre, Johnny and Sisula Tulokas, Lena, "CISG och de nordiska reservationerna" in *Festskrift till Lars Gorton*, 2007 (Juristforlaget) 149–168
Hobhouse, John, "International conventions and commercial law: the pursuit of uniformity" (1990) 106 LQR 1990 530–535
Hoeks, Marian, "Multimodal carriage with a pinch of sea salt: door-to-door under the UNCITRAL draft instrument" (2008) 43(3) ETL 257–280
Hoeks, Marian, *Multimodal Transport Law*, 2010 (Diss.) (Wolters Kluwer)

Hogg, James F, "The International Court, Rules of Treaty Interpretation II" (1959–1960) 44 Minn L Rev 5–73

Honka, Hannu, "UNCITRALs konventionsutkast om transport av gods" (2005) 4–5 Tillämpningsregler, Tidsskrift utgiven av Juridiska föreningen i Finland 530–540

Honka, Hannu, "General provisions" in A. von Zielger et al (eds), *The Rotterdam Rules 2008*, 2010 (Kluwer Law International) 27–38

Horty, John F., "Rules and reasons in the theory of precedent" (2011) 17 Legal Theory 1–33

Huser, Kristian, *Avtaletolkning*, 1983 (Diss.) (Universitetsforlaget)

Håstad, Torgny, "Rättstillämpning i strid med lag" in B. Flodgren et al (eds), *Vänbok till Axel Adlercreutz*, 2007 (Juristförlaget I Lund) 167–180

Høgberg, Alf-Petter, "Tolkningsstiler vid kontraktstolkning" (2006) 41 Jussens Venner 61–198

Jantzen, Johs., *Godsbefordring til sjøs*, 1952 (2nd edn, Fabritius & Sønners Forlag)

Johansson, Svante O., "Något om avtalsfrihet, obligationsrätt och grundläggande fri- och rättigheter" (2013) 04/05 TfR 666–683

Johansson, Svante O., *An Outline of Transport Law*, 2014 (2nd edn, Jure)

Jonas, David and Saunders, Thomas, "The object and purpose of a treaty: three interpretative methods" (2010) 43 Vand J Transnat'l L 565–609

Karan, Hakan, *The Carrier's Liability under International Maritime Conventions*, 2004 (Diss.) (Edwin Mellen Press)

Koller, Ingo, "Quantum Corporation Inc v. Plane Trucking Limited und die Anwendbarkeit der CMR auf die Beföredrung nit verschiedenartigen Transportmitteln" (2003) TranspR 45–50

Koning, Ingrid, *Aansprakelijkheid in het luchtvervoer*, 2008 (Diss.) (Paris Legal Publishers)

Kramer, Adam, "Implication of fact as an instance of contractual interpretation" [2004] CLJ 63(2) 384–411

Kristoffersson, Eleonor, "Att använda prejudikat och annan rättspraxis i rättstillämpningen" (2011) 10 SvSkT 835–849

Kuner, Christopher B., "The interpretation of multilingual treaties: comparison of texts versus the presumption of similar meaning" (1991) 40 ICLQ 953–964

Laurijssen, Peter, "Quantum Corporation Inc. v. Plane Trucking Ltd. revisited by German Supreme Court: considerations on the German Federal High Court's decision of 17 July 2008" (2009) 44(2) 143–149

Lehrberg, Bengt, *Avtalstolkning*, 2014 (6th edn, IUSTÉ)

Lestas, George, "The truth in autonomous concepts: how to interpret the ECHR" (2004) 15(2) EJIL 279–305

Lestas, George, *A Theory of Interpretation of the European Convention on Human Rights*, 2007 (Diss.) (Oxford University Press)

Lewison, Kim, *The Interpretation of Contracts*, 2004 (3rd edn, Sweet & Maxwell) (5th edn, 2011)

Linderfalk, Ulf, "On the meaning of the 'object and purpose' criterion, in the context of the Vienna Convention on the Law of Treaties, Article 19" (2003) 72 Nordic J Int'l L 429

Linderfalk, Ulf, *On the Interpretation of Treaties*, 2007 (Springer)

Linderfalk, Ulf, "Tolkning genom sammanjämkning – Om Wienkonventionen om traktaträtten artikel 33(4), och traktattolkningens särskilda lära" (2012) 4 TfR 458–490

Linderfalk, Ulf, "Is treaty interpretation an art or science? International law and rational descision making" (2015) 26(1) EJIL 169–189

Lo, Chang-Fa, "Good faith use of dictionary in the search of ordinary meaning under the WTO dispute settlement understanding" (2010) 1(2) JIDS 431–445

Loewe, R, *Commentary on the Convention of 19 May 1956 on the Contract for the International Carriage of Goods by Road (CMR), UN*, 1975 (GE.75–30686)

Lorenzon, Filippo, "Liability of the carrier for loss, damage or delay" in Y. Baatz et al, *The Rotterdam Rules: A Practical Annotation*, 2009 (Informa Law from Routledge) 45–71.

Lorenzon, Filippo, "Multimodal transport evolving: freedom and regulation three decades after the 1980 MTO Convention" in M. Clarke (ed.), *Maritime Law Evolving*, 2013 (Hart Publishing) 163–180.

Lowe, Vaughan, *International Law*, 2007 (Oxford University Press)

Macdonald, Elizabeth, "Contents" in A. Grubb (ed.) *The Law of Contract*, 2007 (3rd edn, LexisNexis Butterworths) 597–774

Mankabady, Samir, "Some legal aspects of the carriage of goods by container" (1974) 23 Int'l & Comp LQ 317–338

Mankabady, Samir, "The Multimodal Transport of Goods Convention: a challenge to unimodal transport conventions" (1983) 32 Int'l & Comp LQ 120–140

Margetson, Nicholas J., *The System of Liability of Articles III and IV of the Hague (Visby) Rules*, 2008 (Diss.) (Paris Legal Publishers)

McMeel, Gerard, "Prior negotiations and subsequent conduct – the next step forward for contractual interpretation?" (2003) 119 LQR 272–297

McMeel, Gerard, "Language and the law revisited: an intellectual history of contractual interpretation" (2005) 34 Comm L World Rev 256

McMeel, Gerard, *The Construction of Contracts*, 2011 (2nd edn, Oxford University press)

McMeel, Gerard and Grigoleit, Hans C., "Interpretation of contract, the common European sales law in context" in G. Dannemann and S. Vogenauer (eds), *The Common European Sales Law in Context: Interactions with English and German Law*, 2013 (Oxford University Press), 341–372

McNair, Aron D., *Law of Treaties,* 1961 (Clarendon Press)

Meij de, Pelle, "Interpretatie van verdragen van uniform (vervoer) recht" (1998) ETL 607–647

Mendes de Leon, Pablo and Diederiks-Verschoor, Isabella, *An Introduction to Air Law*, 2012 (9th edn, Wolters Kluwer)

Merryman, John H., "On the convergence (and divergence) of the civil law and the common law" (1981) 17 Stan J Int'l L 357–388

Messent, Andrew and Glass, David, *CMR: Contracts for the International Carriage of Goods by Road*, 2000 (3rd edn, Lloyds)

Mestad, Ola, *Om force majeure og risikofordelning i kontrakt*, 1991 (Diss.) (Universitetsforlaget)

Milde, Michael, "Liability in international carriage by air: the new Montreal Convention" (1999) 4 Unif L Rev 835–860

Møllmann, Anders, *Certepartifortolkning – i nordisk og engelsk ret*, 2007 (Diss.) (Jurist- og Økonomforbundets Forlag)

Møllmann, Anders, *Delivery of Goods under Bills of Lading*, 2017 (Routledge)

Nicolosi, Salvatore Fabio, "Disconnecting humanitarian law from EU subsidiary protection: a hypothesis of defragmentation of international law" (2016) 29 Leiden Journal of International Law 463–483

Nikaki, Theodora, "The obligations of the carrier to provide seaworthy ships and exercise care" in R. Thomas (ed.), *A New Convention for the Carriage of Goods by Sea – The Rotterdam Rules*, 2009 (Witney) 89–110

Olsen, Lena, "Rättsvetenskapliga perspektiv" (2004) SvJT 105–145

Østenstad, Bjørn H., "Sårstelldommen (Rt. 2010 s. 612) – prejudikat for kva?" (2014) 53(8) Lov og Rett 484–501

Owsia, Parviz, "The notion and function of offer and acceptance under French and English law" (1992) 66 Tul L Rev 871–918

Özdel, Melis, *Bills of Lading Incorporating Charter Parties*, 2015 (Diss.) (Hart Publishing)

Påhlsson, Robert, "Skatterättspraxis i utveckling principer för rättsfallsanalys" (2011) 3 Skattenytt 115

Palmer Olsen, Henrik, "International courts and the doctrinal channels of legal diplomacy" (2015) 6 (3–4) Transnational Legal Theory, 661–680

Peczenik, Aleksander, *Juridikens metodproblem*, 1980 (Gebers)

Peczenik, Aleksander, *Vad är rätt? Om demokrati, rättssäkerhet, etik och juridisk argumentation*, 1995 (Fritzes, Institutet för rättsvetenskaplig forskning 156)

Peczenik, Aleksander, *Juridikens teori och metod*, 1995 (Fritzes)

Pieck, Manfred, "A study of the significant aspects of German contract law" (1996) 3 Ann Surv Int'l & Comp L 111

Ramberg, Christina, "Makten över avtalsrätten" in B. Flodgren et al (eds), *Vänbok till Axel Adlercreutz*, 2007 (Juristförlaget i Lund) 419–427

Ramberg, Christina, "En ny avtalslag" (2011) SvJT 32–45

Ramberg, Christina and Ramberg, Jan, *Allmän avtalsrätt*, 2016 (10th edn, Wolters Kluwer Sverige)

Ramberg, Jan, "The law of carriage of goods – attempts at harmonization" (1973) 17 Scandinavian Stud L 211

Ramberg, Jan, "Deviation from the legal regime of the CMR (Art. 2)" in J. Theunis (ed.), *International Carriage of Goods by Road (CMR)*, 1987 (Lloyd's of London Press) 19–30

Ramberg, Jan, "Is multimodal transport a contract *sui generis* also within the field of EU competition?" in H-J. Bull and H. Stemshaug (eds), *EC Shipping Policy – The 17th Nordic Maritime Law Conference 2–4 September 1996*, 1997 (Juridisk Forlag) 163–168

Ramberg, Jan, "Avtalstolkningsmetoder" in *Festskrift till Gösta Walin*, 2002 (Norstedts Juridik) 499–511

Ramberg, Jan, *The Law of Transport Operators*, 2005 (Norstedts, Institutet för rättsvetenskaplig forskning 186)

Ramberg, Jan, "Global unification of transport law: a hopeless task?" (2008–2009) 27 Penn St Int'l L Rev 851–857

Ramberg, Jan and Herre, Johnny, *Internationella Köplagen (CISG)*, 2009 (3rd edn, Norstedts)

Rasmussen, Uffe L., "Additional provisions relating to particular stages of carriage" in A. von Zielger et al (eds), *The Rotterdam Rules 2008*, 2010 (Kluwer Law International) 133–149

Rosengren, Jonas, "Engelsk avtalstolkning i ett svenskt perspektiv" (2010) 1 SvJT 1–22

Rousseau, Pierre, *Histoire des transportes*, 1961 (Fayard)

Roth, M. and Happ, R., "Interpretation of uniform law instruments according to principles of international law" (1997) 2 Unif L Rev 700–710

Rune, Christer, "Haag-Visby-Reglerna" (1969) SvJT 12
Ruud, Morten and Ulfstein, Geir, *Innføring i Folkerett*, 2011 (4th edn, Universitetsforlaget)
Røsæg, Erik, "The network principle – an eligible solution or a necessary evil?" in J. Schelin (ed.), *Future Logistics and Transport Law*, 2005 (Jure) 71–78
Røsæg, Erik, "Conflicts of Conventions in the Rotterdam Rules" (2009) 15 JIML 238–248
Samuelsson, Joel, *Tolkning och Utfyllning*, 2008 (Diss.) (Iustus, Skrifter från Juridiska fakulteten i Uppsala 112)
Samuelsson, Joel, *Tolkningslärans gåta*, 2011 (Iustus, Skrifter från Juridiska fakulteten i Uppsala 117)
Sanchez Calero, Fernando, *El Contrato de Transporte Maritimo de Mercancias*, 2000 (Aranzadi Editorial)
Sandgren, Claes, "Är rättsdogmatiken dogmatisk?" (2005) 118 (4–5) TfR 648–656
Schelin, Johan, "Styckegodstransport enligt nya sjölagen – en replik" (1995) SvJT 865–874
Schelin, Johan, "Methods of interpreting the CMR convention" [2002] TranspR 382–385
Schelin, Johan, *Lastskadeansvaret*, 2015 (Poseidon Förlag AB)
Schmid, Andreas, "Austria: carriage of goods: rail and road (case comment)" (1995) 3(10) Int ILR G199–200
Schmidt, Folke et al, *Huvudlinjer i svensk frakträtt*, 1962 (2nd edn, Norstedts)
Sejersted, Fredrik, *Haagreglerne*, 1976 (3rd edn, Universitetsforlaget)
Selvig, Erling, *The Freight Risk*, 1965 (Arkiv for Sjørett 7, 1965–1978)
Selvig, Erling, *The Hamburg Rules, Marius no 31B*, 1978 (Scandinavian Institute of Maritime Law, Oslo)
Selvig, Erling, "Multimodal transport: the 1980 U.N. Convention: papers of a one day seminar: Southampton University, Faculty of Law, 12th September 1980"
Sevón, Leif, *Förslag till lag angående avtal om godstransport på väg*, 1974 (Helsingfors: Lagstiftningsavdelningen vid Justititeministeriet)
Sisula Tulokas, Lena, "Om konventionstolkning – att äta kakan och ha den kvar" (1987) Marius 132
Sisula Tulokas, Lena, "Nordic hesitancy regarding Part II of the CISG" (2012) 57 Scandinavian Studies in Law 293–295
Smeele, Frank, *Passieve legitimatie uit cognossement*, 1998 (Diss.) (Kluwer-Deventer)
Smith, Stephen, *Atiyah's Introduction to the Law of Contract*, 2006 (6th edn, Clarendon Press)
Spanjaart, Michiel, "GODAFOSS: the applicability of the CMR within multimodal contracts of carriage" (2012) 7 TranspR 278–282
Strandgaard, Knud, "Sørettens Internationalisering" (1935) 6 Nordisk Tidsskrift i Internationel Ret 144–154.
Sturley, Michael, "International uniform laws in national courts: the influence of domestic law in conflicts of interpretation" (1986–1987) 27 Va J Int L 729–802
Sturley, Michael (ed.), *The Legislative History of the Carriage by Sea Act and the Travaux Préparatoires of the Hague Rules*, vols I–III (1990) (Fred B. Rothman & Co)
Sturley, Michael, "The history of the COGSA and the Hague Rules (1991) 22 J Mar L & Com 1–57

Sturley, Michael, "Solving the scope-of-application puzzle: contracts, trades and documents in the UNCITRAL Transport Law Project" (2005) 11 JIML 22–41

Sturley, Michael, "Scope of Application" in A. von Zielger et al (eds), *The Rotterdam Rules 2008*, 2010 (Kluwer law International) 39–50

Sturley, Michael et al., *The Rotterdam Rules*, 2010 (Thomson Reuters)

Sundberg, Jacob, "Avtalstyper och typavtal" (1961) SvJT 11–30

Svensson, Ola, *Viljeförklaringen och dess innehåll*, 1996 (Diss.) (Nerenius & Santerus)

Sørensen, Max, "The modification of collective treaties without the consent of all the contracting parties" (1938) 9 Act Sc JG (1938) 150–173

Taxell, Lars-Erik, *Avtalsrättens normer*, 1987 (Åbo Akademis förlag)

Temperley, Robert, *Carriage of Goods by Sea Act 1924*, 1932 (3rd edn, Stevens and Sons Ltd, London)

Tetley, William, *Marine Cargo Claims*, 2008 (4th edn, Éditions Yvon Blais)

Tetley, William, "Some general criticisms of the Rotterdam Rules" (2008) 14 JIML 496–511

Theunis, Jan, "The liability of a carrier by road in roll on-roll of traffic" in J. Thenuis (ed.), *International Carriage of Goods by Road (CMR)*, 1987 (Lloyd's of London) 235–257

Thomas, Rhidian D., "An appraisal of the liability regime established under the new UN Convention" (2008) 14 JIML 496–511

Tiberg, Hugo and Schelin, Johan, *On Maritime and Transport Law*, 2016 (Skrifter utgivna av Axel Ax:son Johnsons institute för sjörätt och annan transporträtt, no 26)

Tjernberg, Mats, *Regeringsrättens strikta lagtolkning,* 2013 (Skattenytt) 14

Todd, Paul, *Principles of the Carriage of Goods by Sea*, 2016 (Routledge)

Treitel, Guenter and Reynolds, F.M.B, *Carver on Bills of Lading*, 2011 (3rd edn, Sweet & Maxwell)

Twiss, Sir T. (ed.), *The Black Book of Admiralty*, 1871 (Longman & Co., London)

Ulfbeck, Vibe, *Fortolkning af ansvarsfriskrivelser, Avtalslagen 90 år*, 2005 (Norstedts Juridik) 481–498

Ulfbeck, Vibe, "Udtømmende konventionsregulering og fastlæggelsen af en konventions anvendelseområde" in *Festskrift till Lars Gorton*, 2007 (Juristförlaget) 599–615

Ulfbeck, Vibe and Taiger Ivø, Stinne, "Optioner og ansvar i transportaftaler" (2008) 4 Erhvervsjuridisk tidskrift 331–343

UNCTAD Secretariat, *Bills of Lading*, 1970 (Geneva)

UNCTAD, United Nations Conference on a Convention on International Multimodal Transport, vol. II – Draft convention on international multimodal transport as at the closure of the first part of the session of the Conference and Reports of the Conference, TD/MT/CONF/17/add.1, 1981 (Geneva)

UNCTAD Secretariat, The economic and commercial implications of the entry into force of the Hamburg Rules and the Multimodal Transport Convention, 1991 (New York)

Verheyen, Wouter, "The DPD-case: a case for a parcel-specific liability regime?" (2013) 48 ETL 3–12

Verheyen, Wouter, "Freight integration: what is the way forward?" (2014) 49 ETL 31–42

Verheyen, Wouter, "Fleximodal contracts and the CMR: the Belgian approach" (2012) 18(5) JIML 364–371

Vestergaard Pedersen, Per, *Transportret*, 2008 (Thomson)

Villiger, Mark E., "The rules of interpretation: misgivings, misunderstandings, miscarriage? The 'crucible' intended by the International Law Commission" in E. Cannizzaro (ed.), *The Law of Treaties Beyond the Vienna Convention*, 2011 (Oxford University Press) 105–122

Vis, Wilhelm C., *International Unification of Private Law: The Multilateral Approach, Remarks, Proceedings of the Annual Meeting* 1986, vol. 80 (American Society of International Law), 233–243.

Waibel, Michael, "Demystifying the art of interpretation" (2011) 22(2) EJIL 571–588

Waldock, Humphrey, "Third report on the law of treaties", *Yearbook of the ILC*, vol. II, 1964 (ILC) 5–66

Wedderburn, K.W., "Collateral contracts" [1959] CLJ 58–85

Wilson, John F., *Carriage of Goods by Sea*, 2010 (7th edn, Pearson Education)

Wit de, Ralph, *Multimodal Transport*, 1995 (Lloyd's Transport Law Library)

Wit de, Ralph, "Minimal music: multimodal transport including a maritime leg under the Rotterdam Rules" in R. Thomas (ed.), *The Carriage of Goods by Sea Under the Rotterdam Rules*, 2010 (Lloyd's List) 91–111

Wool, Jeffrey and Jonovic, Andrej, "The relationship between transnational commercial law treaties and national law – a framework as applied to the Cape Town Convention" (2013) 2 Cape Town Conv J 65–129

Woxholt, Geir, *Avtalerett*, 2014 (9th edn, Gyldendal akademisk)

Woxholt, Geir, *Avtaleinngåelse, ugyldighet og tolkning*, 2001 (4th edn, Gyldendal Akademisk)

Yihan, Goh, "A wrong turn in history: re-understanding the exclusionary rule against prior negotiations in contractual interpretation" (2014) 5 JBL 360–387

Ziel van der, Gertjan, "Multimodal aspects of the Rotterdam Rules", *CMI Yearbook*, 2009 (CMI) 301–313

Zimmermann, Reinhard, *The Law of Obligations: Roman Foundations of the Civilian Tradition*, 1996 (Clarendon Press)

Zweigert, Konrad and Kropholler, Jan, *Sources of International Uniform Law 1: Private and Commercial Law*, 1971 (Sijthoff)

Travaux préparatoires

Sweden

SOU 2015:9
SOU 2014:26
Prop. 2013/14:243
Prop. 1993/94:195
Prop. 1973:33
NJA II 1936 s. 590

Norway

NOU 2012:10
NOU 1972:11

UNICITRAL

Working Group III, 2002–2008, Transport Law (available at: www.uncitral.org)

Precedents

Belgium

Supreme Court

TNT v Mitsui Marine and Sony, 8 November 2004, C030510N, [2004] Arr Cass, 1767; [2006] ETL, 228

Court of Appeal

NV DPD Belgium/Peter-Jan Timmerman, Court of Appeal Antwerpen, 31 October 2011, ETL 2013:48 p. 82
NV De Post v NV Gebroeders Lauwe David, Court of Appeal Brussels, 2 September 2011, 2008/AR/1077
Court of Appeal Antwerp, 15 March 1989, ETL 1989 p. 574

Denmark

Supreme Court

U.2008.1638H
U.1989.593H

Martime and Commercial Court

FED 2000.3023 SH

England

A G Securities v Vaughan [1990] 1 AC 417
Amalgamated Investment & Property Co Ltd v Texas Commerce International Bank Ltd [1982] QB 84 at 119
Anticosti Shipping Co v Viateur St-Amand [1959] 1 Lloyd's Rep 352
Attorney General of Belize v Belize Telecom Ltd [2009] UKPC 10
B.P. Refinery (Westernport) Pty Ltd v Shire of Hastings (1978) 52 ALJR 20
Bank of Credit and Commerce International SA v Ali [2001] UKHL 8
City & Westminster Properties Ltd v Mudd [1959] CLJ 58
Equitable Life Assurance Society v Hyman [2002] 1 AC 408
Fothergill v Monarch Airlines Ltd [1980] 2 All ER 696
Hong Kong Fir Shipping Co Ltd v Kawasaki Kisen Kaisha Ltd [1962] 2 QB 28, CA
Investors Compensation Scheme Ltd v West Bromwich Building Society [1998] 1 WLR 896
James Buchanan & Co Ltd v Babco Forwarding & Shipping (UK) Ltd [1976] WL 46847
Mayhew Foods Ltd v Overseas Containers Ltd [1984] 1 Lloyd's Rep 317
Pyrene Co. Ltd v Scindia Steam Navigation Co. Ltd [1954] 1 Lloyd's Rep 321
Quantum Corp Inc v Plane Trucking Ltd [2002] EWCA Civ 350
Shell Chemicals UK Ltd v P. & O. Roadtanks Ltd [1993] 1 Lloyd's Rep 114
Shell UK Ltd v Lostock Garage Ltd [1976] 1 WLR 1187
Shirlaw v Southern Foundaries (1926) Ltd [1939] 2 KB 206
Sidhu v British Airways plc [1997] 2 WLR 26
Silber v Islander Trucking [1985] 2 Lloyd's Rep 243
Thermo Engineers Ltd. V. Ferrymasters Ltd. [1981] 1 Lloyd's Rep 200

Germany

Federal Supreme Court

BGH 17 July 2008, ZR 181/05
BGH 17 May 1989, ZR 211/87
BGH 24 June 1987, ZR 127/85
BGH 2 September 1979 (1980) 15 ETL 84

The Netherlands

Supreme Court

Hoge Raad, 1 June 2012, nr.10/05322, the *Godafoss*

District Courts

Rechtbank Rotterdam, 28 October 1999, the *Resolution Bay*

Sweden

Supreme Court

NJA 2016 s. 900
NJA 2016 s. 563
NJA 2016 s. 149
NJA 2014 s. 425
NJA 2009 N3
NJA 1983 s. 3
NJA 1974 s. 345

Court of Appeal

Svea Court of Appeal, 18 January 2016, T9128–14
Southern Court of Appeal (HovR över Skåne och Blekinge), 2 May 2013, T113–12

USA

American Block v Compagnie Nationale Air France (1967) 386 F 2d 323
Weiss v El Al Israel Airlines (2006) 433 F Supp 2d 361
Wolgel v Mexicana Airlines (1987) 821 F 2d 442

INDEX